Turning Toward the Victim

Turning Toward the Victim

The Bible, Sacred Violence, and the End of Scapegoating in Quaker Perspective

Thomas Jay Gates

WIPF & STOCK · Eugene, Oregon

TURNING TOWARD THE VICTIM
The Bible, Sacred Violence, and the End of Scapegoating in Quaker Perspective

Copyright © 2025 Thomas Jay Gates. All rights reserved. Except for brief quotations in critical publications or reviews, no part of this book may be reproduced in any manner without prior written permission from the publisher. Write: Permissions, Wipf and Stock Publishers, 199 W. 8th Ave., Suite 3, Eugene, OR 97401.

Wipf & Stock
An Imprint of Wipf and Stock Publishers
199 W. 8th Ave., Suite 3
Eugene, OR 97401

www.wipfandstock.com

PAPERBACK ISBN: 979-8-3852-4605-2
HARDCOVER ISBN: 979-8-3852-4606-9
EBOOK ISBN: 979-8-3852-4607-6

VERSION NUMBER 06/06/25

Cover image: Fritz Eichenberg, "The Casting of the Lots," from Eichenberg, *Works of Mercy*, edited by Robert Ellsberg (Maryknoll NY: Orbis, 1992). © 2025 Estate of Fritz Eichenberg / Licensed by VAGA at Artists Rights Society (ARS), NY.

Emphasis added to Scripture quotations.

Unless otherwise noted, Scripture quotations are from the New Revised Standard Version, copyright © 1989 National Council of the Churches of Christ in the United States of America. Used by permission. All rights reserved worldwide.

Scripture quotations marked GNB are from the Good News Bible © 1992 American Bible Society. Used with permission.

Scripture quotations noted as GNV are from the Geneva Bible, 1599 ed. Published by Tolle Lege Press. All rights reserved.

Scripture quotations noted as JB are from the Jerusalem Bible, copyright © 1968 by Darton, Longman & Todd LTD and Doubleday and Co. Inc. All rights reserved.

Scripture quotations noted as KJV are from the King James or Authorized Version.

Scripture quotations marked NAB are from the New American Bible, revised edition, copyright © 2010 Confraternity of Christian Doctrine, Washington, DC, and are used by permission of the copyright owner. All rights reserved.

Scripture quotations marked NASB are from the (NASB®) New American Standard Bible®, copyright © 2020 by The Lockman Foundation. Used by permission. All rights reserved. lockman.org

Scripture quotations marked NEB are from the New English Bible, copyright © Cambridge University Press and Oxford University Press 1970. All rights reserved.

Scripture quotations marked NET are from the New English Translation Bible® (https://netbible.com), copyright ©1996, 2019, used with permission from Biblical Studies Press, LLC. All rights reserved.

Scripture quotations noted as NIV are from the Holy Bible, New International Version®, NIV®, copyright © 2011 by Biblica, Inc.™ Used by permission of Zondervan. All rights reserved worldwide. www.zondervan.com. The "NIV" and "New International Version" are trademarks registered in the United States Patent and Trademark Office by Biblica, Inc.™

Scripture quotations marked NJB are from the New Jerusalem Bible, copyright © 1985 by Darton, Longman & Todd Ltd and Doubleday, a division of Bantam Doubleday Dell Publishing Group, Inc. Used by permission. All rights reserved.

Scripture quotations marked REB are from the Revised English Bible, copyright © 1989 Oxford University Press and Cambridge University Press. Used by permission. All rights reserved.

Scripture quotations noted as Rheims are from the Rheims New Testament.

Scripture quotations noted as RSV are from the Revised Standard Version, copyright © 1971 National Council of the Churches of Christ in the United States of America. Used by permission. All rights reserved worldwide.

Dedicated to the memory of

Raymond Downing, MD
(1949–2020)

Ray was an author (*Biohealth, Death and Life in America, The Wedding Goes on Without Us, Global Health Means Listening*), fellow physician, soul mate, and a great encouragement to me in my early attempts at writing. It was on his bookshelf, in Lugulu, Kenya, in August 2000, that I first encountered René Girard's *Things Hidden Since the Foundation of the World*—a book Ray claimed to have not understood, but for me, the beginning of a twenty-five-year journey.

The idea that some lives matter less is the root
of all that is wrong with the world.

—Paul Farmer, MD (1959–2022)

Contents

Acknowledgments | xi
Prologue: Scapegoating, the Cross, and the Lynching Tree | xiii
Introduction: Conviction, Convincement,
 and Conversion in Quaker Context | 1

Part I: Conviction: Violence, the Bible, and the Human Condition | 11
1 Mimetic Theory in a Nutshell | 17
2 Three Murders | 28
3 A Murder Averted: Abraham's (Non-)Sacrifice of Isaac | 36
4 Joseph and His Brothers: Deconstructing Myth | 42
5 Job: A Failed Scapegoat | 49
6 The Suffering Servant | 57
7 Jonah: A Reluctant Prophet | 64
8 "The Spirit of the Lord Is Upon Me": How Jesus Read Scripture | 70
9 Casting Stones | 77
10 Casting Out Demons | 82
11 Crucifixion as Revelation | 88
12 The Gospel of—and for—the Disinherited | 96
13 Conviction in the Experience of Early Friends | 104
14 Conviction Today | 114

Excursus I: God in Process: The Slow Work of God | 125

Part II: Convincement | 133

15 The Road to Emmaus | 137
16 Paul on the Road to Damascus | 144
17 Convincement in the Experience of Early Friends | 152
18 Convincement Today | 164

Excursus II: New Light on Atonement | 172

Part III: Conversion of the Heart | 183

19 The Scandal of—and in—the Gospels | 187
20 The Transformation of Desire | 194
21 Discipleship as Imitation | 200
22 "In Christ": Paul's Gospel of Participation | 209
23 The Two Seeds and the Refiner's Fire | 221
24 The Way of the Cross | 228
25 The Lamb's War | 237
26 Truth in the Heart | 246
27 Scapegoats, Sacrifice, and Victims | 255
28 "Conversion of the Heart" for Friends Today | 266

Epilogue: An Easter Reckoning | 279
Bibliography | 293

Acknowledgments

MY SINCERE THANKS TO the many who have contributed in ways large and small to this project: to my Pendle Hill colleagues, Dorothy Henderson, Steve Chase, Frances Kreimer, and Benigno Sanchez-Eppler, for their close reading and helpful comments; to others who have read and commented on portions of the manuscript: Brian Drayton, Douglas Gwyn, Noah Merrill, Lloyd Lee Wilson, Adria DiCapua, Timothy Ashworth, Nancy Bieber, and Christoper Stearns; to Mary A. Crauderueff, curator of Quaker Collections at Haverford College, for her help in locating obscure seventeenth-century pamphlets; to the participants in the New Year's Retreat at Ben Lomond Quaker Center, December 2019; to the members of Lancaster Friends Meeting who participated in the 2019 Lenten Bible study; and most of all, to my wife and partner Elizabeth Gates, for her patience and quiet encouragement over these last three years.

Prologue
Scapegoating, the Cross, and the Lynching Tree

> The lynching tree *is* the cross in America.
>
> —JAMES H. CONE[1]

THIS INQUIRY BEGINS WITH a number and a question.

The number is 6,391. As numbers go, it is large, but not so large as to be beyond our comprehension. It would take a person about seven hours to count to 6,391. Since each number is a person, and each person has a name, it would take a bit longer, perhaps a couple of days, to read the names. That would be tedious but certainly a task that is well within the realm of human possibility.

We could have chosen a larger number: perhaps 7,000,000, which is the number of Jews who perished in the Nazi Holocaust; or 800,000, which is the estimated number of Rwandans killed in the genocide of 1994; or the uncounted millions who died in the Belgian Congo, starting at the end of the nineteenth century.[2] Those numbers seem nearly

---

1. Cone, *Cross and Lynching Tree*, 158. Emphasis added.

2. Hochschild, *King Leopold's Ghost*, 3, 233. Current estimates are that Belgian colonial rule in the Congo from 1880 to 1920 (roughly corresponding to America's "lynching era") directly resulted in five to ten million deaths—approximately one-half

incomprehensible, but 6,391 is at least within the realm of what we can conceive.

Six thousand three hundred ninety-one is the number of African Americans documented to have been killed by lynching, beginning with the end of slavery in 1865.[3] The "lynching era" in American history ended only in the 1950s, within the lifetime of some of us. But the legacy of the lynching era lives on, in our contemporary debates about police violence toward African Americans, mass incarceration, and the persistent racial inequities that plague American society.

This number, then, leads to a question: *What is it that led some of our American forbearers to brutally torture and kill others of our American forbearers—too often under the banner of "traditional values," and even religion?* The number cries out for an explanation, and a reckoning.

Isabel Wilkerson points us to a place to start. In *Caste: The Origins of Our Discontents*, she looks at three historical examples of discrimination and oppression: the Dalits (Untouchables) in India, the Jews in Nazi Germany, and African Americans during slavery and the subsequent Jim Crow era. She cites the Leviticus ritual of the scapegoat, where the sins of the community were ritually transferred to the "escape goat," which was then expelled into the wilderness. Wilkerson suggests that not just individuals but entire castes can play the role of scapegoat. "A scapegoat caste has become necessary for the collective well-being of the castes above it and the smooth functioning of the caste system."[4] She sees African Americans in the Jim Crow era as such a scapegoat caste, and victims of lynching as quite literally scapegoats.

A further clue comes from the African American theologian James Cone, who has written that "the cross and the lynching tree interpret each other."[5] He goes on to illustrate a point to which we will return, how the crucifixion "contaminates" the future persecution of all scapegoats:

---

of the population.

3. Equal Justice Initiative, *Lynching in America*, gives the number as 4084 deaths by lynching in twelve Southern states, from 1877 to 1950, and a further 307 deaths in eight states outside the South. A subsequent 2020 report, *Reconstruction in America*, concludes there were more than 2000 deaths by lynching between the end of the Civil War and the end of Reconstruction. These numbers should be considered minimums, since it is likely that some lynchings were never documented. In addition, the numbers do not include the hundreds of Mexicans and Mexican Americans lynched in the American Southwest over the same time period.

4. Wilkerson, *Caste*, 190–91. The story of Wilkerson writing her book is told in the recent movie directed by Ava DuVernay, *Origin*.

5. Cone, *Cross and Lynching Tree*, 161.

> The crucifixion of Jesus by the Romans in Jerusalem and the lynching of blacks by whites in the U.S. are so amazingly similar that one wonders what blocks the American Christian imagination from seeing the connection. . . . *Every time a white mob lynched a black person, they lynched Jesus.* The lynching tree *is* the cross in America.[6]

Womanist and process theologian Karen Baker-Fletcher makes much the same point: "African Americans connected lynching with crucifixion, because both the lynched and the crucified defy the claims of empires no matter how small or large the empire may be—a sharecropping town in the deep southern United States or an imperialistic nation." She cites the poem "Christ Recrucified" by Contee Cullen and a short story by W. E. B. Dubois (both from the 1920s) that both make the link between crucifixion and lynching explicit.[7]

Taking these clues from Wilkerson, Cone, and Baker-Fletcher, I propose to approach the question about lynching indirectly, by looking at the dynamics of scapegoating and what has been called *sacred violence*, particularly as it unfolds in the Bible. Sacred violence can be understood as violence that on some level appears to be sanctioned, approved, and even instigated by God. As we shall see, the unfolding biblical story exposes sacred violence to "subversion from within,"[8] where stories of scapegoating are common but told from the perspective of the innocent victim, which has the effect of undermining scapegoating. This long process culminates with the crucifixion of Jesus, but we can understand the significance of the crucifixion only by beginning with the Hebrew Scriptures that were so foundational to Jesus's own worldview. We will see that in the passion, crucifixion, and resurrection, the dynamics of scapegoating and sacred violence came to be decisively unmasked.

In this exploration, I will be relying heavily on the modern scholar who has done more than anyone else to explore the importance of this scapegoating dynamic, the French polymath and cultural critic René Girard (1923–2015), as well as some of his interpreters. Girard's seminal 1986 book *The Scapegoat* explores the crucial role of scapegoating in the

---

6. Cone, *Cross and Lynching Tree*, 31, 158. Emphasis on entire sentence in original; emphasis on single word added.

7. Baker-Fletcher, *Dancing with God*, 129. In her discussion she cites Cullen's 1922 poem "Christ Recrucified" and Dubois's 1920 short story "Jesus Christ in Texas" (128–34).

8. For Girard interpreter James Alison, the expression "subversion from within" is a recurring refrain; see Alison: *Raising Abel*, 32–33, 82, 96, 107, 124–25, 138, 140; *Joy of Being Wrong*, 44, 59, 121–22, 133, 161.

origin of sacred violence; in subsequent books he speaks of "lynching" and "lynchers" dozens of times to describe the human propensity to this kind of violence.[9] Girard's insight into the role of the scapegoat in sacred violence comes in part from his deep reading of the Bible, with the Gospel accounts in particular providing the interpretive key.

The word "lynching" of course does not appear in the Bible; it is a particularly American contribution to the English language—and has an unfortunate Quaker connection. Charles Lynch was a Virginia Quaker who, at the time of the American Revolution, became a justice of the peace in Bedford County (and was eventually disowned by his Quaker meeting for taking an oath of office). No longer a Quaker, Lynch became a militia officer, and in 1780 presided over summary trials at an unofficial court, authorizing harsh punishment of British loyalists, without cause. He subsequently lobbied the Virginia Assembly to retroactively legalize his actions. A *Lynch law* thus originally meant any ex post facto justification for extralegal actions. Although Lynch evidently was an enslaver, his extrajudicial actions seemed to be directed at British loyalists rather than African Americans. Only in the nineteenth century did *lynching* and *lynch law* come to describe mob actions directed against African Americans.[10]

This is not a book about lynching in this narrow sense. But it is a book about a certain type of human violence, of which both lynching and crucifixion are prime examples. Beginning with an attempt to reckon with lynching in American history, we are brought first to a consideration of scapegoating—and then to the archetypal example of scapegoating, Jesus's passion, crucifixion, and subsequent resurrection (however we might understand that). In a word, it brings us to Easter, or perhaps more accurately to "the Easter event" (passion/crucifixion/resurrection/post-resurrection appearances).

What has this to do with Quakers? In my fifty years of worshipping among mostly (but not entirely) liberal Friends, I have observed that contemporary Quakers are uncomfortable with Easter. In this, Quakers are perhaps not unlike others in the liberal Christian traditions, and so

---

9. Girard, *Job*. Interestingly, Cone acknowledges Girard as one of the very few white scholars who have recognized this link between the cross and the lynching tree (Cone, *Cross and Lynching Tree*, 171n4). See also Girard, *I See Satan Fall*, 64–70. Wilkerson does not refer to Girard's work.

10. See Wikipedia: "Lynching"; "Charles Lynch (Judge)." Baker-Fletcher makes the same point about the origin of "lynching" (but without the Quaker connection) (*Dancing with God*, 133).

what I have to say specifically about Quakers may also resonate within the wider tradition.

Unlike Christmas, when we are mainly at ease with the symbolism of the season, with Easter we seem at a loss, perhaps even a bit embarrassed, by the concrete details. We know the story—the passion, the empty tomb, the various Easter appearances of the risen Christ—but mostly we have rejected the standard interpretation of that story. That interpretation, known as the atonement, attempts to explain (not always very successfully) what Christians through the ages have experienced: that the life, death, and resurrection of Jesus of Nazareth have unique saving and transforming significance.

Early Friends shared this *experience* (though not the standard *interpretation*). For them, the presence of the Inward Christ transformed their lives and empowered them to free their lives from the deception, oppression, and violence of the wider society. Among other consequences, it led them to nonviolently resist the wider society's attempt to cast them in the role of scapegoat.

In light of our central Quaker convictions about nonviolence, what might contemporary Friends be able to learn from both the original Easter event, as well as from early Quaker experience of the Inward Christ and their frequent references to "bearing the Inward Cross"? This is not an easy or simple question, and for many readers may require a stretch into unfamiliar territory. The question cannot be answered outside the larger context of both the Hebrew and New Testament Scriptures. In particular, we will see that uncovering the perspective of the victim is crucial to the way the Bible came to unmask and subvert the role of sacred violence and the scapegoat mechanism. It is Girard's contention that *if we do not see this, we will have missed what is most important in the biblical narrative.*

My thesis in this book is that René Girard's insights into the dynamics of sacred violence (so-called mimetic theory, more fully explained in ch. 1), as well as the experience of early Friends, can be powerful tools in our quest to grasp these challenging truths. I seek to demonstrate that the significance of the Easter event has everything to do with the propensity of humans toward a specific type of violence—and how that might be overcome.

These are hardly peripheral issues. As I write this at the end of 2024, the world is witnessing "hot" wars, in Ukraine, Gaza, and Lebanon, as well as deadly (but largely forgotten) civil conflicts in Sudan, Ethiopia, Yemen, Haiti, Syria, and eastern Congo. Recent mass shootings in the US often have an imitative quality, characterized by escalating rivalry and vengeance. Alexei Navalny's death in a Siberian penal colony in early 2024 was a dramatic reminder that those in positions of power still make blatant use of scapegoats. And at the end of 2024, the United States reelected a president whose entire campaign revolved around finding scapegoats. The relevance of our subject is as close as the morning newspaper or, these days, the ever-present news feed in our pocket.

Girard asks, "Why is there so much violence in our midst? No question is more debated today. . . . Of all the threats presently looming over us, the most dreadful one, as we well realize, the only real threat, is ourselves."[11] If we agree that the various forms of violence—the unnecessary creating of victims—is *the* human problem, then our challenge is to find ways to overcome violence. Using *violence* to overcome *violence* has utterly failed; history decisively shows that violence only begets more violence. As we shall see, it is only through the perspective of the innocent victim that we have any chance of ending the spiral of reciprocal violence.

In the aftermath of the resurrection, Jesus's disciples "underwent a profound shift in their understanding" of both human nature and the nature of God, gaining what Girardian theologian James Alison succinctly calls "the intelligence of the victim." Simply put, the intelligence of the victim involves a new understanding of "the relationship between God and victims."[12] God is revealed as having nothing to do with human violence; this nonviolent God is revealed through victims, and is to be found on the side of victims.[13] Alison emphasizes the central importance of this intelligence of the victim:

> As it becomes possible to perceive humans as constitutionally violent [through the crucifixion], so it becomes possible to understand God as completely without violence. What allows the intelligence of the victim to be applied to human culture is the completely gratuitous self-giving of God that is anterior [prior] to it. . . . For it to be possible to understand God as love (1 John 4:7–11), it was necessary that the human victim be revealed. Only the revolution wrought by the intelligence of the victim made this understanding possible. That God is completely without violence, that God is love, was a discovery made possible only by the self-giving of Jesus to death, and therefore the discovery that our awareness of God had, up till then, been distorted

11. Girard, *One by Whom Scandal Comes*, 3.
12. Alison, *Knowing Jesus*, 34.
13. Alison, *Knowing Jesus*, 43; see all of ch. 2, "The Intelligence of the Victim," 33–58. Also, Alison, *Joy of Being Wrong*, 80–83, 95–102.

by our own complicity in violence, unrecognized and projected onto God. That distortion is undone. So the intelligence of the victim works two ways: revealing the human being, and revealing God, simultaneously . . . part of the same discovery.[14]

But understanding violence is only part of our task. At its best, our Quaker and Christian tradition has always pointed beyond our all-too-obvious faults, to a new and transformed way of living. This new reality has gone by a variety of names: eternal life, life more abundant, a new birth, salvation, liberation, redemption, the new covenant, life "in Christ," the new Jerusalem, the kingdom of God. The Easter event is not just about crucifixion but resurrection. Put another way, we are unlikely to overcome violence by focusing on overcoming violence; we will need a new vision, a higher calling that allows us to transcend our failings.

Here, too, the intelligence of the victim is central. Jesus possessed this intelligence during his earthly ministry, but time and again the gospel account indicates that the disciples could not understand. However, for the disciples, "with the resurrection comes the intelligence of the victim." This intelligence—this wisdom—is something given through the risen Christ, and it makes possible an entirely new basis for human belonging.

> What is offered is the possibility for humans to form a new society which does not need victims or exclusions in order for its sense of identity to be built up. . . . Membership in this new Israel involves a new way of relating to the victim. It involves the unlearning of all those patterns of behavior that depend on, or tend to produce, victims of whatever sort. Simultaneously, it involves learning how to relate to, side with, stand up for, those who are cast out, excluded and so on. It involves living for others in such a way that those doing so are always prepared to run the risk of expulsion and exclusion themselves rather than basing their security on expelling and excluding others. This is bearing witness to the truth which comes from the victim.[15]

Turning Toward the Victim: The Bible, Sacred Violence, and the End of Scapegoating in Quaker Perspective is part Bible study, part dialogue with early (and contemporary) Friends, and part primer on René Girard's anthropological insights. As I hope to show, these three perspectives inform one another in surprising and mutually reinforcing ways.

---

14. Alison, *Joy of Being Wrong*, 83.
15. Alison, *Knowing Jesus*, 72–73.

The victim to whom we first turn is Jesus, the crucified and risen one—but through the crucifixion's "contamination" of all subsequent scapegoats, we turn ultimately to *all* victims of scapegoating, to what Girard calls "the modern concern for victims."[16] As we will see, even in the wake of the biblical revelation, scapegoating has not ended, but its nature has fundamentally changed. The *end* of scapegoating here has a double sense, both as *cessation* or coming to an end, and end as *purpose* or *telos*.[17] The dynamics of scapegoating have changed, but the underlying telos remains the same: to bring order and stability to the status quo—but always at the expense of innocent victims.

---

16. Girard, *I See Satan Fall*, 166–68. Chapter 13, 161–69, is called "The Modern Concern for Victims." See below, ch 27.

17. Heim, "End of Scapegoating."

Introduction

Conviction, Convincement, and Conversion in Quaker Context

THE TASK I HAVE set before us in the prologue is vast; we will need a workable framework to help focus our exploration. In seeking to connect insights from biblical sources, early Friends, and Girard's anthropological understanding, it will be useful to employ the traditional Quaker terminology of conviction, convincement, and conversion as our overall framework. This can be confusing, since the three words have a similar etymology and overlapping meanings. Seventeenth-century Friends used each of these words in a distinctive and somewhat idiosyncratic way, which can lead to misunderstanding. Because of this potential confusion, let me first state the sense in which I am using these words, and then proceed to a more in-depth discussion.

Conviction is the state of being convicted—found guilty—either by God or one's conscience. This often involves a sense of one's personal shortcomings, but also includes a felt sense of complicity in social structures that were built on oppression, deceit, and coercion. Conviction is a kind of *revealing* of this underside of human society, and our personal involvement in it.

Convincement is the first step toward overcoming the alienation that is implied in the experience of conviction. It is the first glimpse of "the infinite ocean of light and love, which flowed over the ocean of darkness and death."[1] Convincement involves a kind of *surrender*, entailing "releasing our ego's grip on our lives and opening our hearts in trust to a power greater than ourselves."[2] Convincement for early Friends could be sudden and dramatic, or it could extend over weeks or months.

Conversion, as used by early Friends, was *not* an instantaneous experience of salvation, of the Holy Spirit coming into the heart, but rather a slow and gradual process of *turning* toward the Light, toward God. Conversion was the gradual reorientation of one's life, learning to discern leadings, learning to be faithful in the context of a covenant community. To distinguish this lifelong process from the more common sense of conversion as a sudden experience, I will refer to this as "conversion of the heart."

This framework of conviction, convincement, and conversion is not original to me; a case can be made that it succinctly expresses what has always been the essence of Quaker praxis or practice (in contrast to theory).[3] For the purpose of analysis, these three words can appear to describe a linear sequence, but in actual experience it is often an iterative process, repeated over and over again at successively deeper levels.

Moving now to a more extended explanation, we will start with convincement, the term most familiar to contemporary Friends.

It is common for Quakers today to describe themselves as a "convinced Friend." Convinced is here contrasted to birthright Friend, with the implication that one came to accept Friends beliefs as an adult. For many contemporary Friends, convincement has the connotation of having been intellectually persuaded by rational argument, and so it can seem a rather bland affair. Many now come to Friends at midlife or beyond, often because they find in Quakerism an endorsement of values they already hold, such as peace, social justice, a contemplative approach to life, or simply a discomfort with the trappings of other denominations. Convincement for many today is then not so much an experience of radical life transformation, but more the finding of a comfortable home. This is quite different from how seventeenth-century Friends understood and experienced convincement.

---

1. G. Fox, *Journal*, 19.

2. Merrill, "Invitation," para. 13. The framework of revealing, surrender, and turning as an alternative to conviction, convincement, and conversion, is his.

3. For Quaker praxis as conviction/convincement/conversion, see, e.g., Guiton, *Early Quakers*, 4–6; Tousley, "Sin, Convincement," 172–75 (she speaks of sanctification rather than conversion); Hoover, *Walking in the World*; L. Wilson, *Holy Surrender*, 12; L. Wilson, *Essays*, 37; L. Wilson, *Memoir*, 240.

The idea of Friends being convinced of Quakerism goes back to the very beginning. A word search for "convinced" in George Fox's *Journal* gives 186 results, with phrases like "convinced of the truth," "some were convinced," "many were convinced," or even "hundreds were convinced" typical.[4] By contrast, a word search for "conversion" yields not a single reference from Fox's *Journal*.

On the surface, this is odd. In the Christian tradition, "conversion" has long been the preferred way of describing the experience of coming to belief. The Bible does not give us much guidance here; both "convincement" and "conversion" are used sparingly in the KJV. By the seventeenth century (and for centuries before), "conversion" came to predominate, with the meaning some amalgamation of Jesus's call to repent (from the Greek *metanoia* [to turn around]), and Paul's dramatic experience on the road to Damascus (but see ch. 22 below, for how Paul's experience has been widely misinterpreted).

Why would Quakers choose instead to use "convincement" to describe this spiritual transformation? Although early Friends often adopted the language of Scripture, "convincement" does not appear in the KJV, and "convince" appears just seven times.[5] Sometimes "convince" has the connotation of "win over" (Acts 18:28).[6] At other times, "convince" has the connotation of "conviction" (Jas 2:9).[7] In what is perhaps the closest biblical parallel to early Friends use of "convincement," John 16:8 suggests that when the Holy Spirit comes, it will "convict" (NIV) or "convince"(RSV) the world "concerning sin and righteousness and judgment."[8]

One plausible reason that Friends chose to describe themselves as "convinced" is that overwhelmingly early Friends, including Fox, were already committed Christians before they became Quakers; they were not "new Christians." Indeed, many had passed through a "hyper-Puritan" stage, when they were not just Christians, but among the most earnest and zealous of all believers. It seems possible that early Friends spoke of convincement rather than conversion in a self-conscious effort to

---

4. See http://dqc.esr.earlham.edu.

5. See https://www.biblegateway.com.

6. In Acts 18:28, Apollo is said to have "mightily *convinced* the Jews ... shewing by the scriptures that Jesus was Christ" (KJV; the NRSV gives this as "powerfully refuted").

7. When "ye commit sin, and are *convinced* of the law as transgressors" (Jas 2:9 KJV).

8. However, the KJV renders the Greek here as "*reprove* the world of sin." I am grateful to Paul Anderson for pointing this out in a Zoom conversation on June 13, 2022.

differentiate themselves from their Puritan opponents. Calvinist and Puritan theology had come increasingly to emphasize the moment of conversion as the critical experience in one's salvation. Many early Friends would have experienced such conversion in their pre-Quaker lives—and ultimately found it insufficient.

Early Quakers may also have spoken of convincement to make a theological point. For Puritans then and Evangelicals now, conversion is believed to be the time when the Holy Spirit enters into the heart of a believer. By contrast, Quakers held that the Inward Light was universally present in all, and one needed only to be awakened to what was already present.[9]

As we seek to understand exactly what early Friends meant by convincement, it is important to recognize that the meaning of words has changed over the centuries. "Convincement" comes from the same Latin root as "conviction," and several Quaker historians have pointed out that in the seventeenth century, convincement could also have the meaning of conviction—to be pronounced or proved guilty.[10] Something of this double meaning survives in our modern usage of *conviction*, which can mean either one's deeply held values and beliefs or, alternatively, to be found guilty in court. In the seventeenth century, *convincement* likewise had this double meaning, and in the usage of early Friends could mean either to be found guilty or to change one's deeply held beliefs—sometimes with both meanings simultaneously. A biblical example of this changing meaning is John 8:46, where Jesus asks rhetorically, "Which of you *convinces* me of sin?" (KJV). This makes no sense in modern usage, so newer translations render the verse as "Which of you *convicts* me of sin" (NRSV) or "proves me guilty of sin" (NIV).

Reflecting this original double meaning, some have spoken of convincement as "a two-stage process."[11] The first stage was convincement in the negative sense of being found guilty—what we are calling conviction. Recall that in seventeenth-century England, there was a nearly unquestioned belief in universal human depravity, so sin in the abstract was not the issue. Rather, this first stage of conviction seems to have been a visceral experience by early Friends of their own personal complicity

---

9. Caldwell, *Inward Light*, 5.

10. For example, Punshon, *Reasons for Hope*, 74; P. Dandelion, *Introduction to Quakerism*, 23; Gwyn, *Apocalypse of the Word*, 133; Martin, *Our Life Is Love*, 62. To my knowledge, the first to make this point was Pickvance, "Conviction and Convincement."

11. Abbot et al., *A to Z*, "Convincement," 63.

in a system of deceit, oppression, and alienation from God that involved every aspect of society, including the established church. As Joseph Pickvance helpfully describes it, for early Friends the first step in convincement was to feel themselves "*convincingly convicted*" of sin.[12]

For our purposes, it seems best to name the first (negative) step in this two-step process as *conviction*, which is true to the original double meaning of convincement but less confusing to contemporary ears. Inevitably, conviction will bring up the question of sin, about which we will have more to say in subsequent chapters. But for now, suffice to say that this can be very difficult for contemporary Friends, living as we do in the wake of Enlightenment humanism. We do not necessarily share the prevailing assumption in mid-seventeenth-century England, that human nature is first and foremost fallen and sinful. With our more optimistic view of human nature, it can be difficult for us to appreciate the intensity of the conviction/convincement process that early Friends were describing and experiencing.

In some tension with contemporary Quakers, early Friends largely shared the Calvinist and Puritan view that God is both sovereign ("in charge," in today's parlance) and the source of all good. Humans, in their fallen state, were incapable of doing anything good without God's grace—including taking even the first steps toward their own salvation.[13] So when the first generation of Friends experienced the Inward Light leading them toward transformation ("salvation"), their Puritan presuppositions led them to conclude that these "promptings of love and truth in the heart" must be from God. Early Friends therefore insisted that the Light was divine and not human; put simplistically, *if it was good, it must*

---

12. Pickvance, "Conviction and Convincement," 10. Emphasis added.

13. To venture perhaps too far into the theological weeds: followed to its logical conclusion, this dual belief in God's sovereignty and human incapability led to the Calvinist belief in "double predestination," that God decided before time who would be saved and who would be damned, and this was beyond human choice or even influence. On this specific point, Friends decisively rejected Calvinist/Puritan belief in predestination. Friends position was more "Arminian" (after the Dutch Reformed theologian Jacobus Arminius, 1560–1609): God desires and offers salvation to all, but it is up to the individual to respond to this universal offer. In Quaker terms, the Light is in all, but it is an individual's free choice to accept or reject the Light. The Puritan criticism of the Quakers was that this made salvation ultimately up to the individual's will, which the Puritans saw as contrary to God's complete sovereignty. This was a lively debate in the mid-seventeenth century but will strike most Friends today as irrelevant to our concerns. It is also worth noting that most Evangelicals today reject strict Calvinist predestination and, through the influence of John Wesley in the eighteenth century, are Arminian in their beliefs about salvation.

be from God. This assurance that the Light represented nothing less than the inbreaking of God into their lives further contributed to the intensity of the convincement process.

Since the first half of the twentieth century, Friends have been critical of this earlier worldview as overly "dualistic,"[14] leaving contemporary Friends more open to quasi-humanistic interpretations of the Light. Absent the somewhat stark dualism of early Friends, Quakers today (though obviously with exceptions) are less likely to experience convincement with the same intensity as early Friends. As Elton Trueblood once observed, "*The Quakers have ceased to quake.*"[15]

In the framework here proposed, we will reserve *convincement* to describe the second half of the two-stage process: the experience of the Light that not only *convicts* us of sin but also *empowers* us to overcome it. In the New Testament, this transformation paradigmatically followed an encounter with the Risen Christ, or, in Paul's letters, with the Spirit. For early Friends, it was variously described as an encounter with the Light, the Inward Christ, the seed of God, or simply truth. It often followed months or even years of spiritual darkness, desolation, and intense disillusionment with the endless ecclesiastical and doctrinal disputes of the Puritans. When it came, it was often experienced as a sudden, positive, and unmerited breakthrough. As Fox says in describing his own pivotal experience, "and when I heard it [the inward voice] my heart did leap for joy."[16]

This leaves us with the third term, *conversion*. Even after convincement, early Friends often experienced a long period of inward conflict, as "two thirsts,"[17] "two spirits," or "two seeds"[18] struggled for preeminence, a process early Friends sometimes called "the refiner's fire" (Mal 3:2).[19] From the Quaker perspective, we can think of conversion not as a one-time event (as it was for Puritans), but as a lifelong process of learning

---

14. One could argue that early Friends worldview was dualistic in an ethical sense (good/evil), but not in a metaphysical sense (matter/spirit). See Trueblood, *Robert Barclay*, 18–19, 163. Also on early Friends, dualism, and Barclay: compare Rufus Jones's introduction to the first edition of Braithwaite, *Second Period of Quakerism* (1919), with Frederick Tolles's introduction to the second edition (1961), esp. xxxiin1.

15. Trueblood, *Robert Barclay*, 218. Emphasis in original.

16. G. Fox, *Journal*, 11.

17. G. Fox, *Journal*, 12.

18. Penington, *Works*, 2:441. Fox also spoke of two seeds; see also J. Whitehead, "Enmity Between Two Seeds." See below, ch 23.

19. See Martin, *Our Life Is Love*, 59–66, for a helpful discussion. See also ch. 23 below.

to discern and heed the true Spirit or seed, while overcoming the other. John Punshon writes, "Early Friends did not use the word 'conversion' as we use it today.... [They] were reluctant to use the word conversion in the conventional sense and preferred to apply it to the period of self-examination and amendment of life that followed a positive response to the convincement process itself."[20] The Catholic monastic tradition has sometimes referred to this lifelong process as "the conversion of manners"[21] or, more commonly today, "conversion of the heart." Early Friends typically talked of "living up to the measure of one's light," "bearing the daily cross," or even "perfection" (which often led to misunderstanding).

NEW LIGHT

I have great admiration for the insights and heroic witness of early Friends. I have been inspired by their stories and writings and by those contemporary Friends who have explored our historical roots in depth.[22] In many ways, I can only echo the words of the great American philosopher and psychologist William James, writing in 1902: "The Quaker religion which [George Fox] founded is something which is impossible to overpraise. In a day of shams, it was a religion of veracity rooted in spiritual inwardness, and a return to something more like the original gospel truth than men had ever known in England."[23]

But we don't live in the seventeenth century. Although there are some striking parallels between their time and ours,[24] we live in a very different world from early Friends. Consider all that we have experienced and come to understand between their time and ours (a very partial list, in rough chronological order): the rise of modern science, beginning with Galileo and Newton; the eighteenth-century European Enlightenment, with its boundless confidence in human reason; deism, skepticism, and atheism, followed by the evangelical response; the Industrial Revolution, with unprecedented material prosperity made possible by fossil fuels; Darwin and the theory of evolution; public health and modern medicine, with the

---

20. Punshon, *Reasons for Hope*, 63, 76.
21. L. Wilson, *Essays*, 37.
22. I have in mind here Hugh Barbour, Lewis Benson, Douglas Gwyn, Gerard Guiton, Lloyd Lee Wilson, John Punshon, Brian Drayton, Marcelle Martin, Rex Ambler, Rosemary Moore—and no doubt many others.
23. James, *Varieties of Religious Experience*, 25.
24. See, e.g., Gwyn, *Seekers Found*, ch. 1; Martin, *Our Life Is Love*.

doubling of life expectancy over the last 150 years; modern psychology and the discovery of the unconscious; modern physics, with the "weirdness" of relativity and quantum theories; cosmology, with our understanding that the universe started with a big bang, some thirteen billion years ago; and now mass communication, culminating in the internet. Human progress since the time of early Friends has been truly astounding.[25]

But this has hardly been a history of unalloyed progress. The underside of modernity has given rise to urban industrial squalor, environmental degradation, a legacy of colonial imperialism, two world wars, civil wars too numerous to count, the Holocaust and other genocides, pernicious and persistent racism, a nuclear arms race, postmodern anomie and alienation, runaway global capitalism, and now, global climate change and the threat of mass extinction. In the words of Friend Eden Grace, "We become aware of all that is not right, of how far we and our human community have fallen from God's intended goodness. . . . If you're not heartbroken by the injustice and suffering of this world, *you're not paying attention.*"[26]

Our queries ask, "Are you open to new light, from whatever source it may come? Do you approach new ideas with discernment?"[27] Given the profound changes in our world, perhaps it is an appropriate time to bring new light to the basic Quaker praxis of conviction, convincement, and conversion, to see whether they might still be relevant (as I believe they are).

Being "open to new light, from whatever source" is hardly a radical proposal. For most of our history, Quakers have been influenced by "new light" from outside our Society, from deism and Evangelicalism in the eighteenth century; to the holiness movement and the social gospel in the late nineteenth century; to more recent influences from depth psychology, feminism, various liberation theologies, and even nontheism.

The new light that most interests me has no single name but is sometimes referred to as "mimetic theory" or "mimetic anthropology" (to be explained in more detail in ch. 1). Most often it is referred to by the name of its originator and most prominent proponent, René Girard. One aim of this book is to show that Girard's insights can shed new light not only on the dynamics of scapegoating violence but also on each of the

---

25. For a somewhat one-sided celebration of that progress, see Pinker, *Enlightenment Now*.

26. Grace, *Good News to Oppressed*, 21. Emphasis added.

27. Britain Yearly Meeting, *Quaker Faith and Practice* 1.02.7.

elements of the Quaker praxis of conviction, convincement, and conversion, helping us to reclaim them for a new day. Girard's insights compete with others, but, as I hope to show, they have great explanatory power and important implications, and are therefore worthy of exploration.

Girard is not a theologian, so he starts not with theological abstractions but what he himself calls "anthropology." Because his work is rooted in an understanding of the cultural dynamics of violence, Girard would seem especially relevant to Friends ongoing work for peace and justice. In particular, Girard's exploration of the relation of violence to religion has been groundbreaking.

Girard also provides profound insights into the Bible, the subject of many of his almost thirty books. The Bible has always been "very precious to me," as it was to early Friends, and integrating the Bible with my Quaker beliefs has been a bit of a lifelong preoccupation.[28] In my decades of conversations with Friends, I have found that the single most common reason cited for their resistance to the Bible is "all that violence." But Girard shows that the struggle to overcome human violence—and to dissociate the Divine from all projections of human violence—is at the very heart of the biblical narrative. Girard sees the Bible as the story of one people's halting and largely unconscious effort to turn their attention away from *the guilt of the scapegoat* and toward *the innocence of the victim*, with momentous implications.

As stated in the prologue, this is part Bible study, part dialogue with Friends, and part primer on Girard's mimetic theory. My hope is that this three-way conversation will further illuminate the Quaker praxis of conviction, convincement, and conversion in a way that is relevant for Friends today. The remainder of the book is organized into three parts, each focused on further exploration of one of these three terms. For each of the three parts there is an introduction, followed by a number of chapters elucidating relevant biblical texts from a Girardian perspective, and ending with two chapters exploring the relevance of the word for early Friends and for Friends today.

---

28. G. Fox, *Journal*, 34. See Gates, *Opening the Scriptures*.

PART I

Conviction
Violence, the Bible, and the Human Condition

> What is violence doing in the Bible? It is telling us the truth, the truth about our human condition, about the fundamental dynamics that lead to human bloodshed, and most particularly, the truth about the integral connection between religion and violence.
>
> —Mark S. Heim[1]

If conviction is the first aspect of what we are calling the "Quaker praxis," then Friends will want to know: What is it that we are we supposed to be convicted of? If conviction was central to the experience of early Friends, we need to formulate a credible answer to that question.

Sin, of course, has been the traditional way of talking about "what we are convicted of." In its widest sense, we can think of *sin* as *whatever separates us from God*. We have seen that early Friends shared with their Puritan opponents the belief that sin was real (i.e., we are in fact separated from God), but they differed from the Puritans in their confidence that sin was not ultimate.[2] Sin is not our most important attribute, and

---

1. Heim, *Saved from Sacrifice*, 101.
2. Graves, *Preaching the Inward Light*, 61–66, is a good summary of early Friends views on sin and its overcoming.

the separation can be overcome—not by our own efforts but through the work of the Inward Light. Theologically, this meant that Friends rejected the doctrine of original sin[3] but without denying the practical reality of sin. Although not greatly concerned with the "notions" of abstract theology, early Friends knew the *experience* of separation from God—as well as its overcoming.

Doubtless there are many things that can separate us from God, but Girard and his collaborators have focused on the role of violence, and in particular the role of *sacred violence* that is rooted in the scapegoat mechanism, which we will explore in more detail in chapter 1. For now, we can simply say that Girard sees in the Bible the unfolding story of one people's struggle to overcome the human tendency toward violence. In effect, Girard has uncovered a universal propensity for humans to use one kind of violence, sacred violence (violence attributed to or sanctioned by the gods), to overcome other kinds of violence. In his view, all archaic cultures were built on this foundation of sacred violence—with implications that continue into the present.

This view of sin as violence finds support in the early chapters of Genesis. In the well-known story of the garden of Eden, Adam and Eve's disobedience results in "the fall" and their expulsion from the garden. But in the story of Adam and Eve in Gen 3, sin is never mentioned. The word itself appears first in chapter 4, when the Lord tells an angry Cain that "sin is lurking at your door; its desire is for you." Cain ignores the warning and subsequently murders his brother Abel. It is violence and murder that are first described as sin.

In the story of Noah and the great flood, the "sin of all humanity . . . is characterized with one single word: *violence*."[4] Genesis 6:11 states unequivocally, "Now the earth was corrupt in God's sight, and the earth was *filled with violence*." Numerous passages from the prophets Hosea, Micah, Isaiah, and Ezekiel make the same point: violence and the shedding of blood are the basic sins of humanity.[5] For example, Ezekiel denounces Jerusalem as "a city that sheds blood. . . . You have become guilty by the

---

3. The "doctrine of original sin" is attributed to Augustine of Hippo in the fifth century; it was central to the theology of sixteenth-century Reformer John Calvin, whose thought was in turn influential for the English Puritans. Note that Jewish theology, although certainly conversant with *sin*, contains no comparable doctrine of *original sin*.

4. Schwager, *Must There Be Scapegoats*, 48.

5. Schwager, *Must There Be Scapegoats*, 48–53.

blood you have shed . . . the princes of Israel . . . are bent on shedding blood" (Ezek 22:4,6).

Girard commentator Michael Hardin has written, "The problem of violence is *the* human problem, and it is also *the* problem of religion."[6] It is therefore hardly surprising that violence emerges as a major theme in the Hebrew Scriptures. Make no mistake about it: the Bible is a violent book. Raymund Schwager, an early colleague of Girard, has tallied over six hundred instances in the Hebrew Bible where a person, king, or nation attacks, kills, or destroys another person, king, or nation. And it is not just human violence: Schwager counts over a thousand texts that speak of *God's* anger, vengeance, judgment, or punishment. "The theme of God's bloody vengeance occurs in the Old Testament even more frequently than the problem of human violence. . . . The universality of avenging and condemning divine violence parallels the universality of human violence."[7]

Schwager points out that in the large majority of these actions, God's violence is mediated through human violence; i.e., God uses humans to inflict punishment on other humans—so we are still in the realm of human violence. "God vents his anger by delivering evildoers to other [violent] human beings."[8] Schwager summarizes his findings by stating unequivocally "that violence is the most central theme of the Old Testament."[9]

"All that violence" has become a major obstacle for contemporary Friends, and indeed for many thoughtful Christians, as they assess the role of the Bible in their faith. Quakers are a peace church; why should we attend to ancient Scriptures that seem to endorse violence and even genocide? Faced with texts so at odds with our values, there are several possible approaches.

First, we could reject the entire Bible as at best irrelevant and at worst a pernicious influence on our culture. We see violence and innocent victims in the text, and therefore we reject the text. This strategy is not unknown among contemporary Friends—but, I would argue, amounts to "throwing out the baby with the bathwater."

A second strategy is that of Marcion, who lived in the second century CE. Marcion maintained that the Hebrew Scriptures told the story of the violent and vengeful God of Israel who was responsible for the creation of

---

6. Hardin, *Mimetic Theory*, 21. Emphasis in original.
7. Schwager, *Must There Be Scapegoats*, 47, 55.
8. Schwager, *Must There Be Scapegoats*, 62.
9. Schwager, *Must There Be Scapegoats*, 66.

a world in which evil prevailed. This god was distinct from and lower than Jesus's Abba, and had nothing to do with Christianity. Marcion advocated a very truncated Christian canon, consisting of a version of Luke's Gospel and ten of Paul's letters—entirely omitting our Old Testament. His views were declared heretical, but we still find echoes of Marcion in some modern approaches that basically ignore the Hebrew Scriptures.

A third strategy is to gloss over the violence, to cherry-pick out "the good parts." We all do this to some extent; everyone reads the Bible selectively. The weekly lectionary readings in the liturgical churches tend not to highlight violent psalms, or stories of murder, rape, and vengeance, any of the "texts of terror" that Phyliss Trible has brought to our attention.[10] This approach is a constant temptation to most Bible readers—but if we simply ignore all that is distasteful or disturbing, we risk missing valuable insights about the dynamics of violence.

A fourth approach, still uncommon, is what is advocated here. Rather than glossing over human and divine violence, this strategy sees the human tendency to violence as central to any responsible reading of the Bible. The overall trajectory of the unfolding story is the Hebrew people's dawning and uneasy awakening to the human propensity to project human violence onto the gods and into the heavens, and their incipient rejection of scapegoating or sacred violence. This gradual awakening starts with a sensitivity toward innocent victims, progresses to prophetic doubts about a religion centered on sacrifice, and culminates with the "subversion from within" of sacred violence by Jesus's life and death. In a world where sacred violence and innocent victims still abound, we would do well to attend to this underlying biblical theme, and it is here where Girard's perspective is invaluable.

In regard to violence in the Bible, theologian Anthony Bartlett sums up this fourth strategy, what we might call the Girardian thesis:

> The very prevalence of violence in the Bible, alongside a progressive theme of nonviolence, suggests that this is the true problem that the text has been struggling with all along. It is out of the biblical reaction against oppression that a deeper, more truly radical revolution of compassion and forgiveness is born. What is really striking is to see an emergent questioning of the default of violence and an alternative possibility of genuinely nonviolent humanity.[11]

10. Trible, *Texts of Terror*.
11. Bartlett, *Signs of Change*, 15.

This fourth strategy echoes George Fox's reading of the Hebrew Scriptures. Fox of course did not share contemporary Friends disregard of the Bible, for he saw in it stories that revealed his own inward condition. For him, the value of the Hebrew Scriptures was to be found in the "types, figures, shadows" that pointed to the "substance," which is Christ.[12] From Fox's *Journal*:

> They could not know the spiritual meaning of Moses', the prophets', and John's words . . . unless they had the Spirit and light of Jesus; nor could they know the words of Christ and of his apostles without his Spirit. But as man comes through by the Spirit of God to *Christ who fulfills the types, figures, and shadows*, promises, and prophecies that were [about] him, and is led by the Holy Ghost *into the truth and substance* of the Scriptures, sitting down in him who is the author and end of them, then they are read and understood with profit and great delight.[13]

In contemporary language, we can think of characters and stories in the Hebrew Scriptures as being proto*types* that pre*figure* and fore*shadow* the reality of Christ, "the giving and forgiving victim." At least for Girard, and perhaps also for Fox, this foreshadowing is not a matter of knowing or foretelling the future with any degree of certainty, but more a vague and mostly unconscious groping toward an elusive truth that will ultimately be fully revealed, first in the Easter event and then (for Fox) in our experience of the Inward Christ. In other words, the violence so prevalent in the Hebrew Scriptures is to be read in light of the New Testament and ultimately in the Light of Christ, inwardly revealed.

Another way to understand this fourth perspective is to see that the Bible does not contain a single coherent or consistent revelation. Rather, as Brad Jersak points out, the "polyphony of voices" in Scripture "faithfully contrasts *two* revelations": a revelation about us, and a revelation about God.[14] The first revelation, concerning the fallen human condition, reveals our sin, which includes our death anxiety, the nature of mimetic desire and the scapegoat mechanism, and especially "our human propensity to demand retributive justice and sacralize retribution through sacrificial religion." The second revelation concerns God's desire to restore humanity to the image of God, through self-giving love. This second

---

12. Pickvance, *Reader's Companion*, 130.
13. G. Fox, *Journal*, 32. Emphasis added.
14. Jersak, *More Christlike Word*, 235, 236. Emphasis in original.

revelation "counters retribution with restoration, justice-as-punishment with justice-as-mercy, wrath with forgiveness, and death anxiety with resurrection life."[15]

With this understanding of the two contrasting revelations, it therefore becomes "nonnegotiable that we read particular texts in the context of the whole story"; in other words, that we not confuse the first revelation with the second.[16] Texts that depict God as characterized by wrath, vengeance, and retribution are revelations about humanity, not God.

Part 1 is an investigation of *conviction,* and this will be for many Friends the biggest challenge, since it inevitably brings up the whole question of *sin*. I will begin with a summary of Girard's mimetic theory (ch. 1), then move on to a close reading of several passages from both the Hebrew Bible and the Christian Gospels (chs. 2–12), passages that illustrate Girard's thesis of a gradually unfolding questioning and then rejection of scapegoating or sacred violence. Part 1 concludes with some extended reflections on the potential relevance of conviction and sin for both early and contemporary Friends (chs. 13 and 14).

A secondary goal here is to demonstrate that a careful reading of these biblical stories is the best way to grasp Girard's underlying insights. Although he did not come to his insights through biblical scholarship, Girard did find abundant confirmation for his insights in the Bible—and in many ways, reading the Scriptures with him is the best way to understand the relevance of mimetic theory. By necessity, this will be a highly selective compilation, chosen to illustrate rather than exhaust the evidence.

Following Girard and his interpreters, I will argue that there is one specific sin for which we all stand convicted: *scapegoating violence*. In Girard's understanding, scapegoating or sacred violence is the means by which a community achieves internal cohesion and unity, through collective violence toward an excluded individual or group, and so always at the expense of innocent victims. Girard's insights suggest a tangible way to think about sin and the experience of conviction, while at the same time providing an overarching framework from which to understand the unfolding story of the Bible.

---

15. Jersak, *More Christlike Word*, 198.
16. Jersak, *More Christlike Word*, 198.

1

Mimetic Theory in a Nutshell

> For over 50 years Girard has been asking three big questions: What draws societies together? What causes them to disintegrate? . . . And what is the contribution of religion to this?
>
> —MICHAEL KIRWAN[1]

BEFORE WE CAN DELVE into the biblical texts, it will be helpful to have at least a basic understanding of René Girard's *mimetic theory*. This has been described as a comprehensive "theory of culture," with major implications in the fields of anthropology, hominid evolution, sociology, psychology, religion, literary criticism, and (our main concern here) biblical interpretation. Scores of books have been written on the subject, so what follows is necessarily an oversimplification, meant to convey at least some sense of the breadth and explanatory power of mimetic theory.

Girard never claimed to be a theologian; when asked to characterize mimetic theory, his reply was simply "anthropology." More than once, he approvingly quotes Simone Weil, who said that "before presenting a 'theory of God,' a *theology*, the Gospels present a 'theory of man,' an

---

1. Michael Kirwan, in Girard, *Evolution and Conversion*, viii.

anthropology."[2] This chapter is thus about anthropology, and specifically an anthropological account of the emergence of archaic religion.[3]

René Girard's interests were wide ranging; his ideas do not fit easily into any academic specialty, which may account for his relative neglect within academia. In addition, early in his career, and largely because of his scholarly insights, he underwent a Christian conversion, which he always felt gave the academy a ready excuse to neglect his contributions. He has been called by one recent reviewer "perhaps the most underrated great thinker of the twentieth and early twenty-first centuries."[4]

Despite all this, Girard was elected to the American Academy of Arts and Sciences in 1979. In 2005 he became one of the forty "immortals" of the prestigious Académie Française, in recognition of a lifetime of literary and scientific achievement; at his induction he was described as "the Darwin of the human sciences."[5] Girard spent most of his academic career at Johns Hopkins (1957–68 and 1976–81), the State University of New York at Buffalo (1968–76), and Stanford (1981–95).

Girard was born in 1923 in Avignon, France, and his early education was in occupied Paris during World War II. He came to the US in 1947, to pursue a PhD in history at Indiana University. While a graduate student, he was asked to teach courses on French literature, and it was in the field of literary criticism that he made his first contribution. *Deceit, Desire, and the Novel* (1961 in French, 1965 in English) is an exploration of conflict among literary characters in some of the great nineteenth-century European novels, conflict that he saw as rooted in what he would later call mimetic desire and rivalry.

Girard next turned his attention to anthropology, with his groundbreaking *Violence and the Sacred* (1972, 1977), an investigation of myths and rituals from around the world, emphasizing the role of violence and sacrifice in the emergence of archaic religion. In *Things Hidden Since the Foundation of the World* (1978, 1987) he gives his first comprehensive account of mimetic theory, including his central thesis that the

---

2. Girard: *I See Satan Fall*, 44; *Evolution and Conversion*, 9. Emphasis in original.

3. Following Girard, I use the word "archaic" quite freely, as in "archaic religion" or "archaic culture." Archaic conveys not just old, but any culture prior to the emergence of legal institutions, when mimetic rivalries were dealt with largely on the basis of revenge and blood feuds. Archaic religion refers to those primitive religions based on ritual sacrifice, deeply rooted in the scapegoat mechanism, where the sacred is simultaneously benevolent and dangerous.

4. Bratton, Review of *Towards Reconciliation*, 370.

5. Michel Serres, quoted in Gifford, *Towards Reconciliation*, 102.

Judeo-Christian Scriptures provide the key to interpreting the anthropology of sacred violence. His other major works include *The Scapegoat* (1982); *Job, the Victim of his People* (1985); *A Theatre of Envy: William Shakespeare* (1990); *I See Satan Fall Like Lightening* (1999); *The One by Whom Scandal Comes* (2001); *Evolution and Conversion* (2004); and *Battling to the End* (2007).

A sympathetic reviewer once referred to Girard as "one of the last hedgehogs alive today," alluding to Isaiah Berlin's aphorism: "The fox knows many things, but the hedgehog knows only one big thing."[6] The reviewer continues by saying that Girard knew *two* "big things," which are closely related: *mimetic desire* and *the scapegoat mechanism*. His mimetic anthropology is built entirely on these two pillars.

Perhaps the best way to approach Girard's mimetic theory is through the lens of anthropology and human evolution. In Girard's view, humanity's fundamental characteristic is our enormous capacity for imitation. Toddlers learn language by imitating their parents' speech; older children learn play and social skills by imitating playmates; and adults learn survival skills by imitating more experienced members of the group. *Humans learn by imitating others.* "We don't learn to imitate; rather we learn by imitating."[7]

Fundamental to our understanding of human evolution is that our hominid ancestors, over the course of millions of years, traded genetic instinct for larger brains. With the loss of instinctive behaviors, hominids came to rely increasingly on behavior learned by imitation. Although the higher primates have some capacity to learn by imitation ("monkey see, monkey do"), this capacity is vastly increased in hominids, with their increased brain size.[8]

The observation that humans learn by imitation is by no means original to Girard—it goes back at least as far as Aristotle, who said that "man is the most mimetic of all animals."[9] Girard's key contribution is to see that among the many attributes that humans learn by imitation

---

6. Roberto Calasso, quoted by Antonello and Rocha, "Introduction," in Girard, *Evolution and Conversion*, 1.

7. Rabe, *Processing Mimetic Reality*, 74.

8. Long after Girard pointed to the importance of mimesis, neurologists in the 1990s discovered that the human brain contains so-called "mirror neurons" in the motor cortex, which fire in response to simply *observing* the actions of others. This gives a solid neuroanatomical basis for Girard's insights concerning the fundamental importance of mimesis. See Garrels, "Convergence."

9. Girard, *One by Whom Scandal Comes*, 6.

is *desire*. Human beings learn *what* to desire by imitating each other's desires: "We desire according to the desire of the other.... It is the social other, the social world which surrounds us, which moves us to desire, to want and to act."[10] Girard names this process *mimesis* (from the Greek, to imitate), rather than imitation, to distinguish it from mere mimicry and to convey that it is largely an unconscious process.[11]

If you doubt the reality of mimetic desire, ask any parent what happens when two toddlers are together in a room full of toys. Inevitably, they come into conflict, as both come to desire the one toy that the other desires.[12] The advertising industry is also intimately acquainted with the mimetic nature of desire; they sell products not by convincing you of the product's superior quality but by showing desirable people who desire that product, so you should desire it too. Simply put, we desire what others desire, *because the other desires it*.[13]

Girard contrasts this mimetic understanding of desire with what he calls "the romantic myth," the thoroughly modern notion of an "autonomous self" that spontaneously comes to desire an object (or in the case of romantic love, another person) solely on the basis of that object or person's innate desirability, without any influence from another.[14] James Alison lightheartedly calls this romantic myth the "blob and arrow" model of desire: the autonomous self is an ill-defined "blob" located somewhere deep within us, and from this blob we shoot forth arrows of desire, aimed at those objects that we desire. "The desire for the object comes from the 'I' which originates it, and thus the desire is authentically and truly 'mine.'"[15]

By contrast, Girard sees the self not as the isolated *authentic self* of modern understanding, but an *interdividual self* that is given to us by the "social other," from whom we learn *what* to desire.[16] We are not isolated individuals but instead live in a complex web of relationships that shapes our identity—and our desires.

The idea that desire is largely mimetic runs counter to the spirit of contemporary humanistic psychology—but the biblical world actually

10. Alison, *Jesus the Forgiving Victim*, 401.
11. Warren, *Compassion or Apocalypse*, 15–18.
12. Warren, *Compassion or Apocalypse*, 18.
13. Reeve, "Mechanisms of Internal Cohesion," 163.
14. Warren, *Compassion or Apocalypse*, 22–25.
15. Alison, *Jesus the Forgiving Victim*, 398.
16. Girard, *Things Hidden*, 283–416.

had a quite sophisticated understanding of mimetic desire, even if called by another name. In the Hebrew Scriptures, the second half of the Decalogue forbids the various ways one might harm one's neighbor: murder, adultery, stealing, lying. But the Tenth Commandment forbids us to *covet*. It begins by listing various possessions of your neighbor that you should not covet (house, wife, slave, field, ox, donkey), before finally recognizing that the problem is not the objects but *covetousness*: "Thou shall not covet . . . *anything* that belongs to your neighbor" (Exod 20:17; Deut 5:21). "To covet" is the Hebrew Bible's equivalent of mimetic desire.

The New Testament term for mimetic desire is "lust," which has a much broader meaning than our modern connotation of sexual desire. For example, Jas 4:1–2 (a text often quoted by early Friends in support of their peace testimony) reads: "From whence come wars and fightings among you? Do they not come from your *lusts* that war within you? Ye lust, and have not: [so] you kill" (KJV). The NIV translation makes the connection with mimetic desire even more explicit: "What causes fights and quarrels among you? Don't they come from your *desires* that battle within you? You *desire* but do not have, so you kill. You *covet* but you cannot get what you want, so you quarrel and fight."

What the Bible understands, and Girard emphasizes, is that *mimetic desire* can and does lead to *mimetic rivalry*. If I desire an object (or person) largely because I perceive someone else also desires it, we quickly become rivals for possession of that object or person. We *covet* and *lust* after what others have, which brings us into conflict. In modern societies, we often have ways of sublimating or otherwise disguising that rivalry, but archaic human groups lacked these moderating influences. Left to itself, mimetic desire will intensify and spread to others, almost like a contagion.

Girard posits that primitive groups would have been susceptible to periodic "mimetic crises," when mimetic rivalry (over food, mates, the best cave: whatever) consumed the group in runaway competition and rivalry, leading to a Hobbesian "all-against-all" state of chaos and anarchy—exactly the "wars and fightings among you" described in James. Having lost the lower animals' dominance/submission instinct, human groups are especially vulnerable to escalating and lethal violence within the group.[17]

---

17. Lower animals, including the great apes, often fight, but they have a strong dominance/submission instinct, which generally acts as a brake and prevents a "fight to the finish." (There are, however, well-documented instances of chimps in the wild killing other chimps, almost always lone individuals from another group.) Humans,

This potential for unchecked in-group conflict has profound evolutionary implications. For nearly all of human prehistory, humans lived exclusively in small bands of hunter-gatherers, with the upper limit on group size determined by the number of persons with whom an individual could develop a direct relationship.[18] It seems obvious that evolutionary success by our ancestors required some level of in-group cooperation, even altruism—the capacity to confer benefits on others in the group, even at some cost to oneself.[19] And yet, standard evolutionary theory holds that the fitness and reproductive success of the *individual* drives evolution, and so cannot easily account for the emergence of altruism.[20] This mismatch between the evolutionary interests of the individual (to survive and reproduce) and the interests of the group (to foster cooperation and group survival) has been called "the fundamental problem of social life."[21]

So, we have a conundrum: evolutionary success would require a high degree of group cohesion and altruism, but mimetic desire and rivalry constantly threatened to undermine social cohesion. We know that primitive Homo sapiens must have solved this problem, since, after two hundred thousand years of quiet existence, they burst out of Africa between fifty and a hundred thousand years ago and subsequently outcompeted (and perhaps exterminated) other Homo species, like the Neanderthals and Denisovans.[22] How did our ancestors solve this "fundamental problem of social life"?

---

having lost this instinct of submission, are thus prone to lethal violence in a way that other mammals are not. See Warren, *Compassion or Apocalypse*, 93–94.

18. It has been proposed that the upper limit of primate group size is limited by the relative size of the neocortex. By extrapolation from primate studies, that number in Homo sapiens is around 150, the so-called "Dunbar number," after anthropologist Robin Dunbar, who first proposed it in 1992. This concept is controversial within evolutionary anthropology; nevertheless, the larger point is not contested: primitive humans existed in relatively small groups, with some type of functional constraint or upper limit on group size. Girard's mimetic theory gives a plausible reason for that upper limit: mimetic rivalry. See Wikipedia, "Dunbar's Number."

19. Bowles, "Conflict: Altruism's Midwife."

20. Darwin was aware of this conundrum and proposed that evolution could also take place on the level of group selection, which could account for altruism. By the 1960s, this view was largely rejected by evolutionary biologists (more for ideological than empirical reasons). See David Wilson, *Darwin's Cathedral*, 5–12.

21. David Wilson, *Darwin's Cathedral*, 7. From a non-Girardian perspective, Wilson shows how archaic religion might have contributed to the solution of this fundamental evolutionary problem.

22. New Scientist, *Human Origins*, 63–119.

Girard's mimetic theory proposes a specific answer to this question. He posits that when a primitive group descends into mimetic crisis, an "all-against-all" state of anarchy and chaos, mimetic energy at some point could be transformed. It might start with a single individual pointing to another individual, with the preverbal equivalent of "it's all his (or her) fault." Others quickly imitate the accusative gesture, and in an instant, the *all-against-all* chaos is transformed into an *all-against-one* mob. In essence, the identified victim serves as a lightning rod, conducting the free-floating hostility of the group into a controlled channel. The single victim may be vulnerable because of some physical defect or marginalized status, but in the end, the choice of a victim is arbitrary. This is *the scapegoat mechanism* (sometimes called the *single victim* or *victimary* mechanism) for which Girard is best known.

Two things are worth emphasizing. First, the mob does not see its action as an unwarranted accusation against an innocent victim; that is a modern understanding. For the original scapegoating to be successful, the group must see the victim as truly guilty, usually of some unspeakable crime that fully deserves the punishment about to be unleashed. Second, the episode is truly transformative. Whereas before the group was consumed by an all-against-all fury, now the same group is unified against a single victim. When that victim is killed or expelled, there is no longer an enemy, and the community is reconciled.

The group has unconsciously stumbled onto a solution to "the fundamental problem of social life" and achieved a workable degree of group cohesion. The scapegoat mechanism has provided a real solution to a real problem—but at the expense of an innocent victim. Furthermore, if it was mimetic rivalry that caused the problem, it was also mimesis that provided the solution, by redirecting violence to a single "surrogate" victim.

To the primitive group, this would have seemed nothing short of miraculous. The mutilated body in their midst was the cause of their disorder but now is seen as the cause of their new-found unity. The victim is (falsely) blamed as the malevolent source of the destructive chaos but now is experienced as the benevolent source of reconciliation. Only a supernatural being can account for these extraordinary powers: "*The victim/culprit must be a god*—for who else could effect the saving reversal . . . from a negative to a positive valency?"[23] In sacrificing a scapegoat, the group has experienced the *sacred*—which derives from the same Latin root as "sacrifice."

23. Antonello and Gifford, *How We Became Human*, xxxv. Emphasis added.

For Girard, this explains why archaic gods invariably possess a mix of threatening and benevolent power. He does not see this "founding murder" as a single event but a "proto-event" that recurred countless times and in countless variations. Groups that stumbled onto this single-victim (or victimary) mechanism were able to achieve a degree of group cohesion that allowed them to survive and flourish. Groups that did not would have perished, due to their inability to solve the problem of intra-group violence.[24] In this way, "the founding murder" can be said to have given rise to *all* surviving cultures. Human beings, says Girard are not "self-domesticated," but *"it is religion, it is sacrifice, that domesticated [them]."*[25]

There is a further, disturbing implication of Girard's thesis: all human culture, and all archaic religion, is *founded on a lie*—the lie that the demonized and scapegoated victim was guilty of horrendous crimes, and thus responsible for the community's problems; and the lie that projects human violence onto the divinized victim, making gods rather than humans the source of our violence. This transmutation of the victim of human violence into a divine being is the primal act of idolatry, revealing a propensity that has bedeviled humans ever since.

Eventually, the unity of the group would have faded, and new challenges to group cohesion would have arisen. But if a group could somehow recapture the positive effects of the previous act of scapegoating, group cohesion might be restored. This, according to Girard, is the origin of ritual sacrifice, so ubiquitous in archaic and ancient cultures. Girard's *Violence and the Sacred* is a comprehensive survey of sacrificial rituals from across the broad range of anthropology and myth, in which he finds abundant confirmation for the origins of ritual sacrifice in a previous act of spontaneous scapegoating.

In addition to giving rise to sacrifice, the original act of spontaneous violence leads to two other pillars of archaic culture. *Prohibitions* or taboos strictly regulate those actions most likely to give rise to mimetic rivalries, commonly around violence, sex, and food. Thus, prohibitions seek to minimize the risk of mimetic crises arising in the first place. *Myths* are the stories that cultures tell to explain the origins of rituals and prohibitions—explaining but at the same time always disguising or obscuring their violent origins. We will look more closely at the role of myth in chapter 4.

---

24. Girard, *Evolution and Conversion*, 49.
25. Girard, *Evolution and Conversion*, 90. Emphasis in original.

Paul Gifford summarizes Girard's view of the connection between violence, the sacred, and the emergence of culture:

> The sacred, in other words, is generated by violence misrepresented, misinterpreted, mythically hypostasized. Myth itself . . . is a falsified account of the victimary process, tending to conceal the real guilt of the sacrificers, while transferring blame, implicitly and illegitimately, to the victim and convincing the community that this episode of crisis was a blessing in disguise. . . . The erstwhile victim becomes then the attributed divine origin of all the prohibitions and rituals instituted to prevent a recurrence of the same crisis.[26]

If you have ever paused to consider the prehistoric origins of human violence, most likely you thought first of *war*, or organized aggression of one group against another. But Girard insists that such organized intergroup aggression is a secondary phenomenon, because it requires that an aggressor group has already achieved a degree of internal group cohesion, through something like a scapegoat incident. Once a group has achieved that initial level of cohesion, threats from outside groups might then further increase group cohesion. Girard says that "the principle behind all 'foreign wars' [is that] aggressive tendencies that are potentially fatal to the cohesion of the group are redirected from within the community to outside it."[27] For Girard, the threat to the group from internal mimetic rivalry is primary, and its resolution through scapegoating violence must precede any effective response to danger from an external group.

Cultural anthropology indicates that religion in some form is ubiquitous among primitive humans, but standard evolutionary theory cannot account for its emergence. "From the standpoint of evolution, *religion ought not to exist*: it is costly in material sacrifices and in emotional expenditure; it imposes on us efforts to adhere to beliefs that defy common sense."[28]

One striking example of the "cost" of archaic religion is the archaeological site at Göbekli Tepe in southeastern Turkey, which dates back at least eleven thousand years, well before the emergence of agriculture or settled human communities. Over the course of at least a thousand years, large and complex stone structures were constructed and reconstructed,

---

26. Gifford, *Towards Reconciliation*, 38.

27. Girard, *Violence and the Sacred*, 249, quoted in Antonello and Gifford, *Can We Survive*, 101.

28. Scott Atran, *In Gods We Trust*, quoted in Gifford, "*Homo Religiosus*," 307. Emphasis added.

apparently only for ceremonial or ritual use. This would have required hundreds if not thousands of hunter-gatherers to work together cooperatively over long periods of time. What could have motivated such a cooperative endeavor? What would have been the evolutionary benefit? Excavations are ongoing, but the site seems to confirm what mimetic theory predicts: that ritual sacrifice and religion preceded all other aspects of emergent culture.[29]

By contrast to standard evolutionary theory, Girard's mimetic theory gives a convincing explanation for the emergence of archaic religion, as the "solution" to the problem of escalating mimetic violence. "The function of religion . . . [was] precisely to contain and control the violence that would otherwise engulf and destroy the community."[30] In other words, *it is not religion that caused violence* but *violence that caused religion.*[31] Archaic religion uses "good" violence (the scapegoating or sacrifice of a single individual) to overcome "bad" violence (the chaos of mimetic contagion), placating the gods and avoiding their wrath by sacrificing arbitrary victims.

Today, we are likely to find this account of human origins and the emergence of religion to be unduly dark and pessimistic. As one of Girard's collaborators has written, "The idea that human culture could be the product of endemic violence . . . is deeply unpalatable."[32] In particular, mimetic theory challenges Friends more optimistic view of human nature, with its fundamental belief of "that of God in everyone." We will be exploring this challenge further in subsequent chapters, but for now let me cite three lines of thought that together suggest we would do well to give mimetic theory our full consideration.

First, anthropology has given us increasing evidence of the stark reality of human violence in our evolutionary past: "The evidence is abundant, and archeology has simply demolished the myth of the peaceful savage. . . . The ethnographic record strongly suggests that violence is

---

29. Gifford and Antonello, "Rethinking the Neolithic Revolution." For the "well-nigh incredible" significance of Göbekli Tepe for confirming Girard's theory, including some preliminary evidence of human sacrifice, see also Gifford, *Towards Reconciliation*, 52–57.

30. Girard, *Evolution and Conversion*, viii.

31. Rabe, *Processing Mimetic Reality*, 61.

32. Antonello and Gifford, *How We Became Human*, xlii.

simply part of human behavior."[33] Any coherent theology must start with a credible anthropology—and so include an account of human violence.

Second, mimetic theory emphatically does *not* propose that humans are *genetically* preordained to violence. Instead, we are genetically programmed to *mimesis*, but as we shall see in part 3, mimesis can be redirected to positive ends. Violence may be our legacy from the past, but it need not be our fate in the future.[34]

Third, as we shall further explore in chapter 14, contemporary Friends optimistic view of human nature is a relatively recent development. As briefly touched upon in the introduction, early Friends had a robust view of the reality of sin, including violence, which they frequently suffered at the hands of their persecutors. We might even go so far as to say that contemporary Friends optimistic view of human nature is made possible by our relative privilege within society, privilege that can shield us from the reality of violence—an advantage that early (and some contemporary) Friends did not share.

Mimetic theory demonstrates that from an evolutionary perspective, archaic religion is all about group survival, about containing and controlling the violence that would otherwise destroy the community. But an important question remains: *Can religion itself evolve*, beyond its origins in mimetic crises and scapegoating violence, to become a vehicle of further revelation?[35] Girard answers that question with an emphatic *yes*—and exhibit A will be the Judeo-Christian Scriptures. It is to these we now turn.

---

33. Konner, "Violent Origins," 142, 144. See also anthropologist Ian Hodder's comment about "a long chronology of violence . . . stretching back at least 5 million years," quoted in Gifford, *Towards Reconciliation*, 50.

34. Bowles, "Conflict: Altruism's Midwife," 327.

35. Gifford, "*Homo Religiosus*," 323, 327.

2

Three Murders

> Once you have seen this way of reading the Bible, you can never go back.
>
> —Michael Hardin[1]

WE BEGIN OUR EXPLORATION of Scripture with an account of just three of those six hundred incidents of violence mentioned in the introduction to this section. All are murders of individuals; one is well known, and two are obscure. All three illustrate important aspects of mimetic theory.

The first is the familiar story of Cain and Abel, from Gen 4. In the garden of Eden, the Lord had warned Adam and Eve that "of the tree of the knowledge of good and evil you shall not eat, for in the day you eat it you shall die" (Gen 2:17). They ate—but they did not die; they were only expelled from the garden. The first death in Genesis is in fact a murder—the murder of Abel by his brother Cain, suggesting the possibility that the Lord's warning to Adam and Eve was not about natural death but violence and murder.

---

1. Michael Hardin, in Girard, *Reading the Bible*, 16. The full quote compares this to "swallowing the red pill," a reference to the movie *The Matrix* (1999) where the protagonist Neo is presented with a choice: swallow the blue pill and remain oblivious, or swallow the red pill, which will reveal the true nature of reality. Unfortunately, "swallowing the red pill" seems to have been appropriated by elements of the "New Right," so is omitted here.

Cain and Abel are trapped in a condition of rivalry. Each has made a sacrifice to God, Abel as "a keeper of sheep" from his flock and Cain as "a tiller of the ground" from his harvest. For reasons not explained, the Lord "had regard" for Abel's animal sacrifice but had "no regard" for Cain's grain offering. In their competing desire to obtain the Lord's favor, Cain and Abel provide an archetypal example of mimetic rivalry, which then quickly escalates to violence.

As the story is told, there is no attempt to hide Cain's guilt ("sin is lurking at your door" [Gen 4:7]). When Cain tries to conceal what he has done, the Lord responds, "Listen; your brother's blood is crying out to me from the ground!" (v. 10). God condemns Cain to become "a fugitive and wanderer on the earth" but does nothing to avenge Abel's murder. In fact, when Cain voices his fear that "anyone who meets me may kill me," the Lord gives him "the mark of Cain," which is meant to *protect* Cain from any human vengeance (v. 15). In this early story, the biblical God sides with an innocent victim—but at the same time rejects vengeance.

From this unpromising start, Cain goes on to establish the first city (v. 17). Cain's action is an explicit example of what Girard calls "the founding murder," a recognition that all civilizations are founded on violence. Although Cain's city apparently flourishes, it is also bedeviled by escalating mimetic rivalry, vengeance, and violence, as illustrated by the story of Cain's descendent Lamech, who seems to glory in revenge without constraint (vv. 23–24). By the time of Noah, "the earth was filled with violence" (6:11).

There follows the story of the great flood, so that by chapter 8 of Genesis, violence and revenge have been identified as the central problem. First humans (Cain and his descendants) and then God (in the flood) have tried to overcome violence with violence, with disastrous results. When the flood recedes, Noah's first act is to offer sacrifice:

> Then Noah built an altar to the Lord, and took of every clean animal and of every clean bird, and offered burnt offerings on the altar. And when the Lord smelled the pleasing odor, the Lord said in his heart, "I will never again curse the ground because of humankind, for the inclination of the human heart is evil from youth; nor will I ever again destroy every living creature as I have done." (Gen 8:20–21)

In response to Noah's sacrifice, God does not renounce all violence (9:5–6) but at least rejects any future divine attempts to destroy "every living creature" (9:12). But at the same time God sets limits on violence and vengeance, God also endorses sacrifice. Thus, with Noah, we enter "the age of sacrifice."

If we take these early chapters of Genesis literally, we are faced with all sorts of problems. For example, Cain's murder of Abel would leave just three humans on earth: Adam, Eve, and Cain. But then why would Cain be concerned that in his wandering "anyone that meets me may kill me" (4:14)? Who is this "anyone"? And how can Cain go on to establish the first city unless there are already other humans on earth?[2] Though not to be taken literally, the first few chapters provide an admirably concise account of the human predicament. The problem is identified as mimetic rivalry, violence, and revenge—and the solution is sacrifice.

The book of Leviticus is largely concerned with the laws and rituals governing the Levitical priesthood and their sacrificial duties, but it does contain a powerful account of scapegoating (one of only two narrative incidents in Leviticus). What is remarkable about this account is its direct, almost journalistic, style, without any attempt to hide or mythologize the violence that it describes. As one of Girard's interpreters comments, "Most of the mythical smoke around such [scapegoating] events has been blown away, and what we get is a very bare description."[3]

> A man whose mother was an Israelite and whose father was an Egyptian came out among the people of Israel; and the Israelite woman's son and a certain Israelite began fighting in the camp. The Israelite woman's son blasphemed the Name in a curse. And they brought him to Moses. . . . The Lord said to Moses, saying: "Take the blasphemer outside the camp; and let all who were within hearing lay their hands on his head, and let the whole congregation stone him. And speak to the people of Israel, saying: anyone who curses God shall bear the sin. One who blasphemes the name of the Lord shall be put to death; the whole congregation shall stone the blasphemer. Aliens as well as citizens, when they blaspheme the Name, shall be put to death." . . . And they took the blasphemer outside the camp, and stoned him to death. The people of Israel did as the Lord had commanded Moses. (Lev 24:10–16, 23)

---

2. Alison detects in the story of Cain and Abel as we have it "a later crystallization of an earlier account of a collective murder, a crystallization that occurred as the collective nature of the murder, and thus the universality of the responsibility, became obscured" (*Joy of Being Wrong*, 248–49).

3. Heim, *Saved from Sacrifice*, 75. I have borrowed from Heim's entire discussion of this incident, 74–75.

From a Girardian viewpoint, this has all the hallmarks of classic scapegoating: a marginal person (his father was Egyptian), a crisis (fighting in the camp), a horrible crime (blasphemy), and then collective violence (stoning) that is divinely sanctioned. Stoning is the archetypal fate of scapegoats; everyone participates and yet no one actually touches the impure victim. Everyone—and thus no one—is responsible for the death; the violence directed against the scapegoat unites the community (minus the scapegoat) in a common righteous cause. The account not only describes an incident of scapegoating but seems to endorse it. At least indirectly, Yahweh is responsible for the violence, through the command given to Moses. This incident is the epitome of *sacred violence*.

This episode leads to an explicit command that blasphemy is to be punished by stoning (Lev 24:16), but it also leads to a series of commands that have the effect of *limiting* vengeance. Unlike the situation in Gen 4, where Lamech brags about killing a man to avenge a minor injury, Moses tells the Israelites that "anyone who maims another shall suffer the same injury in return: fracture for fracture, eye for eye, tooth for tooth; the injury inflicted is the injury to be suffered" (24:20). To modern ears, this sounds harsh and punitive, but in its historical setting this should be read as progress toward the goal of restraining the human impulse to engage in unlimited vengeance, which inevitably leads to chaos and anarchy.

If this example from Leviticus is straightforward, by contrast our third example, from the book of Joshua, goes to great efforts to obscure and conceal the scapegoating mechanism and so demands some interpretive effort. In what follows, I am indebted to James Alison's brilliant insights, in his *Jesus the Forgiving Victim*.[4]

The story, which we find in Josh 7, under the NRSV chapter heading "The Sin of Achan and Its Punishment," requires some background. Moses has died, and the Israelites, now under the leadership of Joshua, have invaded "the promised land" of Canaan. They win a series of improbable military victories against the inhabitants, beginning with the destruction of Jericho in chapter 6.[5] Prior to the fall of Jericho, the Lord had instructed Joshua that any spoils of war were to be considered "devoted things . . . sacred to the Lord," and thus either destroyed or donated to "the treasury

---

4. Alison, *Jesus the Forgiving Victim*, 93–109.

5. The majority of biblical scholars believe that there was in fact no military conquest of Canaan by an outside invader; there is certainly no archeological evidence that Jericho was destroyed. Again, we are dealing with the text as it has come to us, not with events as they "actually" happened.

of the Lord" (6:18–19). We can perhaps rationalize this as an attempt to preempt Joshua's soldiers from "squabbling among themselves over spoils," which might threaten their solidarity.[6]

The victory at Jericho seems to have made Joshua a bit cocky; based on a scouting report that Ai was poorly defended, he sends a small force there, expecting an easy victory. But instead the Israelites are repulsed and suffer a humiliating defeat. Upon hearing the news, "Joshua rent his clothes, and fell to the ground on his face before the ark of the Lord until the evening" (7:6). But there is an explanation, an explanation that does not involve Joshua's poor military judgment: "But the Israelites broke faith in regard to the devoted things. . . . For thus says the Lord, 'There are devoted things among you, O Israel; you will be unable to stand before your enemies until you take away the devoted things from among you'" (7:1, 13).

To rectify the violation of the ban on spoils, the Lord instructs Joshua to organize a kind of lottery. Each of the twelve tribes is brought forward, and the guilty tribe is identified by lot. Then each clan in the identified tribe is brought forward, and the guilty clan is "taken," or identified by lot. Then each household in the identified clan, and then each family in the household, until finally Achan "draws the short straw" and is identified as the culprit (7:14–18). He confesses: "It is true; I am the one who sinned against the Lord God of Israel. . . . When I saw among the spoils a beautiful mantle from Shinar, and two hundred shekels of silver, and a bar of gold weighing fifty shekels, then I *coveted* them and took them" (7:20–21).

> Then Joshua and all Israel with him took Achan son of Zerah, with the silver, the mantle, and the bar of gold, with his sons and daughters, with his oxen, donkeys, and sheep, and his tent and all that he had; and they brought them up to the Valley of Achor. Joshua said, "Why did you bring trouble on us? The Lord is bringing trouble on you today." And all Israel stoned him to death; they burned them with fire, cast stones on them, and raised over him a great heap of stones that remains to this day. Then the Lord turned from his burning anger. (Josh 7:24–26)

On first reading, the plot seems reasonably straightforward: there is a divine command, a violation, identification of the guilty party, and subsequent punishment—even if the punishment seems a bit harsh to

---

6. Alison, *Jesus the Forgiving Victim*, 94.

us. The first step in "decoding" the story is to examine (and question) the method by which Achan is identified as the guilty party. To modern sensibilities, assigning guilt by a series of "drawing straws" seems, well, primitive. As Alison points out, "Lottery organization is in fact the only function of the word 'God' in our passage. It is the only thing God does."[7] But this brings up a host of theological difficulties. Does an omniscient God already know that Achan is guilty, and the lottery was just a charade, manipulated by God to give the preordained outcome? Or does God somehow "need" the lottery to identify the one who is guilty? And why does the account start with the assertion that "the *Israelites* broke faith in regard to the devoted things" (7:1)—but then goes on to finger Achan as the *individual* who is guilty? And how could several iterations of a basically random event possibly single out the one who was truly guilty?

If we read the story with the assumption that there is only one who is guilty (the narrator's assumption), then these questions are insoluble. But what if it was not *just* Achan? What if others also "disobeyed sacred orders by looting"?[8] In fact, what if most or even all of Joshua's several thousand soldiers pocketed some "souvenirs" from Jericho? Given the total destruction of Jericho, this is not an unreasonable assumption—and it changes everything about the meaning of the lottery.

Alison asks us to imagine a bag with twelve pebbles, one white and eleven black; one by one, the leader of each tribe picks a pebble from the bag:

> As each pebble is pulled out, so the relief starts to build. Each group whose name is not called—and that is the vast majority in each round of the lottery—experiences the feeling of being let off something terrible.... Your tribe is given a pass on whatever looting you might have engaged in.... So as tribe by tribe passes by, eleven tribes are relieved, only one is in trouble. As each clan then passes by, eleven clans are relieved, only one is in trouble. The group in trouble gets smaller and smaller each time, and the group feeling relief gets bigger and bigger, and more relieved, and more convinced of the rightness of the system. In the end, there is only one person who is not relieved (with of course his wife and children who didn't count as real people). You can see what has happened during this sacred time: a huge sense of relief has broken out, along with awe at the way that everyone is coming together and morale is being restored. Relief that they

---

7. Alison, *Jesus the Forgiving Victim*, 100.
8. Alison, *Jesus the Forgiving Victim*, 101.

are not going to be "got." That somebody is going to be "got" and it hasn't been them. . . .

> Unanimity is good, but unanimity minus one is even better, because the "one" is about to disappear, and the unanimity of the survivors will have been proven in a process, will have come to seem a foundational achievement.[9]

Suddenly, the story makes sense. Joshua, perhaps falling prey to overconfidence, has blundered into a military defeat, and the morale of his army has suffered ("the hearts of the people melted and turned to water" [7:5]). Joshua needs a fall guy, perhaps to take the heat off himself but certainly to restore morale. The elaborate lottery identifies hapless Achan, who is perhaps not innocent but at least no more guilty than thousands of others. Achan confesses his guilt, and the people (now a lynch mob) unite in first stoning and then burning him. All that remains is "a great heap of stones that remains to this day," a religious shrine to the now-restored morale of Joshua's army.

What is crucial to see is that the story as we have it is told from the perspective of the survivors, the persecutors, the lynch mob who engaged in stoning. From their perspective, the victim is assumed with utmost confidence to be truly guilty. This is Scapegoating 101. What remains hidden is the fact that the victim is innocent (or, in this case, no more guilty than everyone else).

Alison ends his discussion with the provocative question "Who in this story is the figure of Christ?" He suggests that it is *not* Joshua. "The obvious figure of Christ in this passage is Achan. The one who was put to death . . . the one being sacrificed."[10] As the story is told, what we don't hear is the voice of Achan, the victim (other than as reported by his persecutors). Alison emphasizes the crucial importance of this point:

> The only trouble is that the moment that the victim's story can be heard, it reveals that the other story is untrue. It is a lie. Its perpetrators need to believe it for it to work. They need to believe that they've really got the bad guy, and indeed in their account the bad guy even agrees with them. These are two entirely different perspectives on the same story. The perspective of the survivors and those who have benefitted from the lynching, which is a lie; and the perspective which is never normally heard, and

9. Alison, *Jesus the Forgiving Victim*, 101, 103.
10. Alison, *Jesus the Forgiving Victim*, 109.

starts to emerge into our world thanks to the crucified and risen Lord, the perspective which tells the truth and which reveals the official perspective to be a lie.[11]

As we progress through the Hebrew Scriptures, we will see that the voice of the victim gradually emerges, culminating in the gospel's revelation.

---

11. Alison, *Jesus the Forgiving Victim*, 110.

3

A Murder Averted
Abraham's (Non-)Sacrifice of Isaac

> There is a whole anthropology behind the word "sacrifice."
>
> —James Alison[1]

IN THE LAST CHAPTER, we looked at three episodes of apparently spontaneous violence, one between brothers locked in mimetic rivalry (Cain and Abel), and two that were portrayed as acts of divinely sanctioned mob violence resulting in stonings. All three resulted in the death of an individual victim—and in all three, benefits accrued to the perpetrators of violence.

A fundamental aspect of Girard's mimetic anthropology is that spontaneous acts of scapegoating violence can have *cultural* benefit, and in turn these can give rise to rituals, the purpose of which is to recapture that benefit. In its most archaic form, these rituals involve human sacrifice, and so we turn now to that challenging topic.

"The firstborn of your sons you shall give to me" (Exod 22:29). Although the exact meaning of "give to me" can be disputed, it is followed by the injunction to "do the same with your oxen and with your sheep" (22:30), so it seems likely that this is a command to sacrifice the firstborn son. Indeed, Hebrew Scripture contains "strong traces of an earlier practice

---

1. Alison, *Jesus the Forgiving Victim*, 380.

of child sacrifice."[2] To be fair, Israel is also commanded (in Lev 18:21 and 20:2) *not* to sacrifice its children—at least not to the pagan god Molech.

Israel's long struggle with child sacrifice is exemplified in the story of "the binding of Isaac" in Gen 22. In the traditional interpretation, Abraham is praised for being *willing* to do what he did not in fact do: killing his son (truly abhorrent to modern ears), but its real significance is in Abraham *not* doing what he *almost* did.[3] Gil Bailie underlines its central importance:

> Far more than we moderns generally realize, human sacrifice was a fact of life among the peoples in the ancient Near East [indeed, in archaic cultures worldwide], in tension with whom Israel first achieved cultural self-definition. Israel's renunciation of the practice of human sacrifice took place over a long period of time, during which periodic reversions to it occurred. No biblical story better depicts how the Bible is at cross-purposes with itself on the subject of sacrifice than does the story of Abraham and Isaac. . . . Abraham did the quintessentially biblical act: he renounced a form of sacrifice that had become morally intolerable, *and* he did so in the name of the God whom his contemporaries thought was requiring them to perform the outmoded sacrifice.[4]

The story is well known and powerfully depicted in various works of art, most memorably Rembrandt's 1635 *The Sacrifice of Isaac*. It is worth quoting the biblical account at some length. "After these things, God tested Abraham . . . [, saying,] 'Take your son, your only son Isaac, whom you love, and go to the land of Moriah, and offer him there as a burnt offering on one of the mountains that I shall show you'" (Gen 22:1–2).

> When they came to the place that God [*Elohim*] had shown him, Abraham built an altar there and laid the wood in order. He bound his son Isaac, and laid him on the altar, on top of the wood. Then Abraham reached out his hand and took the knife to kill his son. But the angel of the Lord [*Yahweh*] called to him from heaven, and said, "Abraham, Abraham!" And he said, "Here I am." He said, "Do not lay your hand on the boy or do anything to him; for now I know that you fear God, since you have not withheld your son, your only son, from me." And Abraham looked up and saw a ram, caught in a thicket by its

---

2. Quotation and examples from Williams, *Bible, Violence, and Sacred*, 117. See, e.g., 2 Kgs 3:27; 16:3; 23:10; Jer 7:31; 19:4–5; 32:35; Ezek 16:21; 20:26; 23:37.

3. Bailie, *Violence Unveiled*, 141.

4. Bailie, *Violence Unveiled*, 140, 141–42. Emphasis in original.

horns. Abraham went and took the ram and offered it up as a burnt offering instead of his son. So Abraham called that place "The Lord will provide," as it is said to this day, "On the mount of the Lord it shall be provided." (Gen 22:9–14)

The account as we have it was written more than a millennium after the events it depicts. Furthermore, the written account shows evidence of an earlier version that has been subsequently edited. Commentators note that after the sacrifice of the ram, the angel speaks a second time (v. 16), saying, "Because you have *done* this, and have *not* withheld your son." This at least implies that Abraham did in fact sacrifice Isaac; at the conclusion of the episode the text states only that "Abraham returned to his young men" (v. 19), with no mention of Isaac until he reappears again at the end of ch. 24. "*Abraham comes down from Mount Moriah on his own.*"[5]

But wait—there is more! The Hebrew text uses two different names for God, which is obscured in English translation. It is *Elohim* who commands Abraham to climb the mountain and sacrifice his son, but it is *Yahweh* (or the *angel of Yahweh*) who intervenes to prevent the act.[6]

The story of Abraham and Isaac is rich and can be interpreted in many ways, from veneration of Abraham's willingness to give up what was most precious to him in service of faithfulness to God, to our typically modern abhorrence that he would even consider murdering his young son.[7] We can never know what "really happened" on Mount Moriah over four millennia ago, but the story as it has come to us appears to reflect an important transition, from human sacrifice in the (hypothetical) earlier version, to substituted animal sacrifice in the later, edited version. As Mark Heim points out, "There could hardly be a more straightforward expression of the actual meaning of animal sacrifice: it is a replacement for human sacrifice."[8] This transition was so fundamental that it required a new name for the Divine.[9]

---

5. Alison, *Jesus the Forgiving Victim*, 133. Emphasis in original.

6. Alison, *Jesus the Forgiving Victim*, 130–33. See also Friedman, *Who Wrote the Bible?*, 256–57.

7. For a recent nuanced discussion of the story from a Quaker perspective, see Keeler, *Abraham, Sarah, Hagar*.

8. Heim, *Saved from Sacrifice*, 79.

9. The name of God in the first five books of the Hebrew Scriptures is a complicated subject, but oversimplified: the two main textual sources are called J and E. In the E source, God is referred to as Elohim (hence, E) *until* God reveals the name of Yahweh at the burning bush in Exod 3. In the J source, the name of God is Yahweh (J is Y in German), starting in Gen 2. Scholars have also described a third source, P or Priestly, as well as R, the Redactor who has skillfully woven the sources together. D, or

Whatever happened on Mount Moriah, generations later, Moses in the wilderness receives instructions for how animal sacrifices are to be conducted, constituting most of the book of Leviticus. The instructions are quite detailed and exact, covering various sacrifices necessary to atone for different transgressions; one gets the impression that it is critically important to get the details exactly right. The commandments culminate in ch. 16, with a description of the Day of Atonement. After offering "a bull as a sin offering for himself... Aaron shall cast lots on the two goats, one lot for the Lord, and one for the scapegoat" (Lev 16:8 KJV). The goat for the Lord is sacrificed on the altar and its blood sprinkled on the people, while the second, "the goat that escapes"—*scapegoat* in Tyndale's brilliant rendering[10]—is driven into the wilderness, taking with him the sins of the people (vv. 21–22).

The Israelites subsequently enter Canaan, and initially their system of animal sacrifice is somewhat portable. When the First Temple is eventually built in Jerusalem under King Solomon, an elaborate system of animal sacrifice in the temple becomes central to Hebrew practice, culminating each year in the Day of Atonement.[11] But it is also clear throughout the Hebrew Scriptures that a tension exists between the priests, concerned with the proper performance of sacrifices, and the prophets, who tend to be critical of the whole temple enterprise. Sometimes the prophets denounce animal sacrifice as simply a distraction:

> Even though you offer me your burnt offerings and grain offerings,
>   I will not accept them,
> and the offerings of well-being of your fatted animals,
>   I will not look upon.
> Take away from me the noise of your songs;
>   I will not listen to the melody of your harps.
> But let justice roll down like water
>   and righteousness like an ever-flowing stream.
> (Amos 5:22–24)

---

the Deuteronomistic history, is a later and independent source. See Friedman, *Who Wrote the Bible?*, 50–88.

10. You will not find "scapegoat" in the NRSV or some other modern translations but instead "Azazel." Modern scholars believe that Azazel in ancient Hebrew was the name of some kind of evil demon; William Tyndale mistakenly believed it referred to "the goat that escapes." Some errors are in fact fortuitous.

11. See Alison, *Jesus the Forgiving Victim*, 234–59, for a helpful discussion of the Day of Atonement as it was celebrated at the time of the First Temple, prior to the Babylonian exile; this is described in more detail below, in excursus 2.

> For you have no delight in sacrifice;
>> if I were to give a burnt offering, you would not be pleased.
> The sacrifice acceptable to God is a broken spirit;
>> a broken and contrite heart, O God, you will not despise.
> (Ps 51:16–18)

> "With what shall I come before the Lord,
>> And bow myself before God on high?
> Shall I come before him with burnt offerings,
>> With calves a year old?
> Will the Lord be pleased with thousands of rams,
>> With ten thousands of rivers of oil?
> Shall I give my firstborn for my transgression [an allusion to child sacrifice],
>> The fruit of my body for the sin of my soul?"
> He has told you, O mortal, what is good;
>> What does the Lord require of you
> But to do justice, to love kindness,
>> And to walk humbly with your God?
> (Mic 6:6–8)

At other times their denunciations can be quite strident:

> "What to me is the multitude of your sacrifices? says the Lord;
>> I have had enough of burnt offerings of rams and the fat of fed beasts;
> I do not delight in the blood of bulls, or of lambs, or of goats."
> (Is 1:11–17)

Hosea, in a passage quoted twice by Jesus in Matthew's Gospel ("go and learn what this means" [Matt 9:13; 12:7]), says, "For I desire mercy and not sacrifice, the knowledge of God rather than burnt offerings" (Hos 6:6). As we shall see, Jesus enters into a long-standing debate about the place of sacrifice—and chooses sides.

Jeremiah connects "burnt offerings and sacrifices" with the abomination of human sacrifice and goes so far as to state that the Lord never commanded these:

> For in the day that I brought your ancestors out of the land of Egypt, *I did not speak to them concerning burnt offerings and sacrifices*. But this command I gave them, "Obey my voice, and I will be your God and you shall be my people; and walk only in the way I that I command you, so that all will be well with you." Yet they did not obey or incline their ear . . . and they go on building the high place of Topheth . . . to burn their sons

and daughters in the fire—which I did not command, nor did it come into my mind. (Jer 7:22–24)

We started this chapter with oblique allusions to human sacrifice in the Bible, then moved on to consider Abraham's (non-)sacrifice of Isaac. We then examined how the story of Abraham and Isaac relates to the institution of animal sacrifice in the temple, as well as its critique by the prophets. What should be clear from this train of thought is the absolute centrality of *sacrifice* in the Hebrew Scriptures, and eventually in the New Testament.

When it comes to recognizing this, we children of the Enlightenment are at a disadvantage. We no longer live in a world where, when seeking protection from forces beyond our control, our first thought is to sacrifice a goat or ox. If we think of sacrifice at all, we tend to think of *self-sacrifice*, a noble willingness to forgo self-interest in the service of some greater good. What we miss is, first, how ubiquitous ritual sacrifice was in the ancient world—and not just the world of the Bible. "Ritual sacrifice has been a feature of virtually every human civilization. . . . [It is] found virtually everywhere in ancient religion."[12] Second, we miss the fact that in the ancient world, sacrifice required blood. To put it bluntly, in the ancient world the archetypal and most intense experience of the holy *came through killing*.[13] Again, *sacred* and *sacrifice* have the same Latin root.

Girard emphasizes this centrality of sacrifice: "Religion starts with sacrifice; sacrifice is the main thing about religion, because sacrifice saves the community from its own violence."[14] "Sacrifice does this by using 'good' violence to cast out 'bad' violence. The violence of reciprocal vengeance is to be cast out of the community through the violence done to a single victim."[15]

As we will see, the Bible will come to reject this logic, and it does so by first lifting up the voice of the victim. We turn now to the story of Joseph.

---

12. Heim, *Saved from Sacrifice*, 38.
13. Warren, *Compassion or Apocalypse*, 79.
14. Girard, *Reading the Bible*, 36.
15. Warren, *Compassion or Apocalypse*, 107.

4

Joseph and His Brothers
Deconstructing Myth

> [The Bible] is a text in which occurs the change from mythology to the biblical view, which is really the change from the guilt of the victim to the innocence of the victim.... *The Bible deconstructs mythology.*
>
> —RENÉ GIRARD[1]

THE STORY OF JOSEPH and his brothers is given prominence of place in the Hebrew Scriptures, occupying the final 25 percent of the first book in the Bible (Gen 37–50). It is a very human story; other than vague assertions like "the Lord was with Joseph" (39:3), no action is attributed to the intervention of God or the gods, which makes it virtually unique in the canon of ancient literature. As we will see, the story of Joseph also provides considerable validation for Girard's insights into the fundamental contrast between the Bible and myth.[2]

    1. Girard, *Reading the Bible*, 64. Emphasis added.
    2. Fundamental to understanding Girard is to realize that he uses the term "myth" in a way that is contrary to much of modern thought. Influenced by Carl Jung and Joseph Campbell, we think of myth positively, as something not literally but symbolically true, a reflection of timeless wisdom or universal archetypes. In stark contrast, Girard sees myth as a culture's attempt to hide the scapegoating violence against innocent victims. Girard says: "Not long ago in our society the word 'myth' was a synonym of 'lie.' Our intelligentsia has done everything it could since then to rehabilitate the myths at

Joseph was the second youngest of the twelve sons of Jacob and the older of the two sons of Rachel, Jacob's second but favored wife. "Now Israel [Jacob] loved Joseph more than his other children, because he was the son of his old age; and he had made him a long robe with sleeves [a coat of many colors (KJV)]. But when his brothers saw that their father loved him more than all his brothers, they hated him" (37:3–4).

At the beginning of the story, the sons of Jacob are immersed in a full-fledged mimetic crisis, consumed with envy and rivalry. They have already been implicated in a horrifically violent act of revenge against Shechem (34:25–31), and Judah has had a sordid encounter with Tamar, his own daughter-in-law (ch. 38). Joseph has made the mimetic rivalry worse by relating a dream that implied that he, the second youngest, would come to rule over his brothers.

Jacob sends Joseph out to join his brothers, herding their flocks: "So Joseph [followed] after his brothers. . . . They saw him from a distance, and before he came near to them, they conspired to kill him. They said to one another, 'Here comes this dreamer. Come now, let us kill him and throw him into one of the pits; then we shall say that a wild animal has devoured him, and we shall see what will become of his dreams'" (37:17–20).

In the end, Reuben pleaded with his brothers not to harm Joseph, if only because their father would not be able to bear it. Instead, Judah persuaded them to sell him to a passing caravan of Ishmaelites, and from there into slavery in Egypt. To make the "scapegoat" connection explicit, they then slaughtered a goat, dipped Joseph's coat with the goat's blood, and presented it to their father Jacob, who mistakenly concluded that his favorite son had been devoured by a wild animal.

Joseph ended up in the household of Potiphar, one of Pharaoh's top officials. Using his considerable native abilities, Joseph quickly rose to be overseer of the household, so that Potiphar "left all that he had in Joseph's charge" (39:6). But Joseph was "handsome and good-looking," such that Potiphar's wife repeatedly attempted to seduce him. He continually rebuffed her, but one day she grabbed a garment from the fleeing Joseph, raised the alarm, and loudly accused Joseph of attempting to rape her. Potiphar believed his wife's false accusation, and Joseph was cast into prison.

After languishing in jail for some years, Joseph was given an opportunity to demonstrate his gift for interpreting dreams. Eventually, this

---

the expense of the Bible, but in ordinary speech 'myth' continues to mean lie. Ordinary speech is right" (*I See Satan Fall*, 115).

talent brought him to Pharaoh's attention, and he foresaw in Pharaoh's dreams seven years of good harvests followed by seven years of famine. Joseph then proposed, and Pharaoh agreed, that he be placed in charge of buying and storing grain during the years of good harvest. Thus it was that Joseph rose from an enslaved foreigner to the most powerful official under Pharaoh.

When famine eventually struck not only Egypt but Canaan, Jacob sent ten sons (but not Benjamin, the youngest) to Pharaoh to purchase food. Joseph recognized his brothers, but they did not recognize him in his royal finery. He dealt harshly with them, accusing them of being spies, and told them that if he was to believe their story, they must return with the youngest brother, Benjamin. Upon their return to Canaan with the grain, Jacob refused to send Benjamin, fearing to lose the one remaining son of his deceased wife Rachel. But as the famine continued, he eventually relented and all eleven sons returned to Egypt, seeking again to purchase grain from Joseph. Eventually, there is a happy ending, but before we discuss the climactic final episode, we need to take an important detour.

In discussing the significance of Joseph's story, Girard often compared it to the Greek myth of Oedipus.[3] The story of Oedipus is perhaps the archetypal myth in our culture, owing first to Sophocles's *Oedipus Rex* and then to Freud's "Oedipus complex."

In the myth, Oedipus was born to King Laius and Queen Jocasta of Thebes, but the king learned through the oracle at Delphi that the child was destined to kill his father and marry his mother. Understandably, the king came to see the child as a rival, with the potential to usurp his father's throne. Attempting to thwart this prophecy, King Laius had the infant abandoned on a mountainside to die. But the infant was rescued by shepherds, passed through intermediaries, and eventually ended up in Corinth, where the childless King Polybus and Queen Merope raised him as their own son. As a young man Oedipus had his parentage questioned, and so he consulted the oracle at Delphi, who again warned that he was destined to kill his father and marry his mother. Horrified, and believing that Polybus and Merope were his true parents, he went into self-exile. Subsequently, while traveling in a chariot near Thebes, he quarreled with a stranger at a crossroads and ended up killing him (perhaps the earliest known incident of road rage).

---

3. Sources for this section on Oedipus and the comparison to Joseph are Girard, *I See Satan Fall*, 107–15; Girard, *Reading the Bible*, 82–86; Warren, *Compassion or Apocalypse*, 204–7; Williams, *Bible, Violence, and Sacred*, 54–60.

Continuing to Thebes, he found that the king had recently been killed and that the city was at the mercy of the monstrous Sphinx. Oedipus answered the riddle of the Sphinx correctly, defeating it, and winning the throne of the dead king and the hand in marriage of the widowed Jocasta. Years later, when Thebes was in the midst of a plague,[4] an oracle told Oedipus that the plague would abate only when the murderer of King Laius was brought to justice. He began a search for the one responsible—only to discover that it was he, in the altercation with the stranger at the crossroads years before. Jocasta, realizing that she had married her own son, hanged herself, and then Oedipus gouged out his own eyes, confessed his crimes, and was expelled from the city—whereupon the plague lifted.

At first reading, the two stories seem to have little in common, but Girard points out some striking structural similarities. Both start with a crisis of family rivalry that is "solved" by an expulsion: Oedipus by his parents as an infant, Joseph by his brothers as a boy. Both then rise to prominence, Oedipus as son to the king and queen of Corinth, Joseph as the overseer of Potiphar's household. Both then suffer a second expulsion: Oedipus to self-exile from Corinth, Joseph to prison. Both are then redeemed by demonstrating extraordinary abilities: Oedipus by solving the Sphinx's riddle, Joseph by interpreting dreams. Both rise again to positions of great authority, Oedipus as king of Thebes, Joseph under Pharaoh. Both subsequently confront a crisis, a plague in Thebes and a famine in Egypt. Finally, both are accused of horrific crimes, Oedipus of parricide and incest, Joseph of the equivalent of incest (Potiphar being "like a father" to him, an attempted rape of his wife would be comparable to actual incest).

Despite these structural similarities, Girard points to "an irreducible difference, an impassable gulf between the biblical story and the myth." In the myth, told from the perspective of the crowd, Oedipus is guilty of terrible crimes and is therefore the cause of the plague; no one, *not even Oedipus*, questions his guilt. In the biblical story, told from a perspective sympathetic to the victim, Joseph is unquestionably innocent. "In the myth, the victim is always wrong, the persecutors are always right. The reverse is true in the Bible: Joseph is right against his brothers as well as against the Egyptians."[5]

---

4. A *plague* in Greek literature is not necessarily due to an infectious disease, but could be a plague of violence, a breakdown of social order. Girard generally regards plague as referring to a mimetic crisis of "all against all."

5. Girard, *I See Satan Fall*, 109.

Both stories begin with rivalry and a mimetic crisis, resulting in collective violence and expulsion of a victim. The myth sides with the crowd against Oedipus; the Bible sides with Joseph as the innocent victim. Girard's insight is that the myth functions to *cover up the truth*: that Oedipus was in fact scapegoated by the mob, in a misguided effort to rid the city of the plague. This is a powerful example of Girard's main point: humans deal with their own internal rivalries and violence by projecting them on to a single victim and expelling or killing the scapegoat—and then concealing the evidence through a myth. It is worth emphasizing this by quoting James Warren at length:

> What is significant is that we allow the structural equivalence of the two stories to highlight the crucial difference between them, which is that *the two stories are told from completely different perspectives*. Oedipus is told from the perspective of the persecutors. It blames Oedipus for horrendous crimes. It even has Oedipus admitting to them himself, gouging out his eyes and accepting expulsion. Oedipus is therefore a quintessentially "mythical" story, for this is precisely what myth does, according to Girard: justify (albeit unconsciously) the scapegoating murders and expulsions that form the basis of community solidarity. The Bible, on the other hand, portrays Joseph as innocent. Joseph is decidedly *not* guilty of the crimes of which he is accused by Potiphar's wife.... With the story of Joseph, Genesis brings to a grand climax the rehabilitation of the victim.... Not only is the victim given voice and shown innocent, but Joseph forgives his persecutors.... It is precisely Joseph's refusal to avenge himself that allows the scapegoat mechanism to be exposed.... This story is therefore one of the Hebrew Scriptures' greatest triumphs over mythology and its power of illusion over all ancient peoples.[6]

Let us now return to the climactic final episode in the story of Joseph and his brothers. On their second journey to Egypt, the brothers as instructed have brought the youngest brother, Benjamin. They are in a weak position, reduced to obeisance before the powerful foreign ruler who alone can save their extended family from famine (43:26, 28). This time, Joseph treats them with lavish hospitality, astonishing the brothers by providing them with a banquet and then the requested grain. In a significant detail, Joseph directs that a fivefold larger portion of food be given to Benjamin (43:34)—showing favoritism to his younger brother, just as Jacob had once shown favoritism to Joseph. Still he does not reveal

---

6. Warren, *Compassion or Apocalypse*, 207. Emphasis in original.

his true identity to them—and then inexplicably hides a precious silver cup in Benjamin's grain bag. After their departure, Joseph's men pursue and overtake the brothers, demanding to search their bags, where they find the "stolen" silver cup. The brothers are ignominiously brought back to Joseph, expecting to all be thrown into prison. With feigned indignation, Joseph accuses Benjamin of stealing but announces that "only the one in whose possession the cup was found shall be my slave; but as for [the rest], go up in peace to your father" (44:17).

What is going on with all these twists and turns of the plot and with Joseph's seeming cruelty, toying with his brothers and keeping them ignorant of his identity? On first reading, we suspect that Joseph is finally avenging the wrong done to him those many years ago, but as Rabbi Jonathan Sacks points out, at every stage in the plot Joseph privately weeps (42:24; 43:30; 45:2), which would seem to rule out revenge as his motive.[7] On closer reading, we see that Joseph has engineered a moral test for his brothers. Benjamin has been unfairly accused; will the brothers abandon him to save themselves, just as they had abandoned Joseph those many years ago? Judah passes the test: in an eloquent speech, he offers himself as a slave in place of the innocent Benjamin (44:33).

Only now can Joseph reveal his true identity to his incredulous brothers: "I am your brother, Joseph, whom you sold into Egypt. . . . God sent me before you to preserve life" (45:4–5). Joseph forgives his brothers, but after Jacob's death some years later, they remain suspicious that he will "pay us back in full for all the wrong that we did to him" (50:15). They offer themselves as slaves to their powerful brother, in return for protection from his vengeance (50:18). But Joseph reassures them: "Do not be afraid. Am I in the place of God? Even though you intended to do harm to me, God intended it for good" (50:19–20).

Christians have long seen in the story of Joseph a foreshadowing of Jesus (one of Fox's "types, figures, shadows"). Joseph provides the biblical prototype of *the forgiving victim*, the type eventually fulfilled in Jesus. But Judah provides an equally important parallel, because in the end it is Judah who volunteers to suffer in place of the innocent Benjamin. Significantly, in both the Matt 1 and Luke 3 genealogies, it is Judah, not Joseph, who is the direct ancestor of the Christ.

We have in the story of Joseph and his brothers a narrative long recognized for its immense moral significance regarding scapegoats,

---

7. Sacks, *Not in God's Name*, 152.

innocent victims, forgiveness, and repentance. Perhaps no one has articulated this significance better than Rabbi Jonathan Sacks, whose reading is influenced by Girard but also by the deep well of Jewish wisdom:

> The source of violence lies in our need to exist in groups, which leads to in-group altruism and out-group hostility. The pathological form of this . . . is the dualism that divides humanity into children of light and children of darkness, the one all-good, the other all-evil. *It follows that the most profound moralizing experience, the only one capable of defeating dualism, is to undergo role reversal.* There can be no more life-changing trial than finding yourself on the other side. . . . That, in essence, is what Joseph is forcing his brothers to do. He is putting them through the intensely painful yet morally transformative ordeal of role reversal. They suspected him of ambition. Now they learn what it is to be under suspicion. They planned to sell him as a slave. Now they know what it feels like to face enslavement. They made Jacob go through the grief of losing a son. Now they must witness that grief again, this time through no fault of their own. Above all, they treated their brother as a stranger. *Now they must learn that the stranger,* Zaphenath-Paneah, ruler of Egypt, *is actually their brother.*[8]

Sacks continues by reflecting on Judah's action in the context of the Jewish concept of "perfect repentance," the idea that true repentance can only be demonstrated when one has an opportunity to repeat the original offence but chooses not to. Again, Rabbi Sacks:

> As soon as Judah has shown that, placed in the same situation, he has changed—he is now willing to sacrifice his own freedom rather than let his brother be enslaved—the trial is over and Joseph can reveal his identity. Judah has fulfilled exactly the requirements of perfect repentance. . . . The issue is repentance. Forgiveness is easy, repentance—true change of character—is difficult. Yet it is repentance, moral growth, on which the biblical vision depends. . . . *The way we learn not to commit evil is to experience an event from the perspective of the victim.* Judah's repentance—showing that he is his brother Benjamin's keeper—redeems not only his own earlier sin, but also Cain's.[9]

---

8. Sacks, *Not in God's Name*, 151–52. Emphasis in original.
9. Sacks, *Not in God's Name*, 153, 156, 158. Emphasis in original.

5

Job
A Failed Scapegoat

> What is going on in the book of Job is what is going on through the whole length of the Hebrew Bible: the very idea which humanity has of God is changing.
>
> —David Cayley[1]

OTHER VICTIMS IN THE Bible are not nearly as fortunate as Joseph; they are not always successful in prevailing against persecution and scapegoating. "More often than not, they perish."[2] The Psalms, for example, are filled with references to enemies and persecution. Some psalms read as if they were written by someone about to be lynched:

> For wicked and deceitful mouths are opened against me,
>   Speaking against me with lying tongues.
> They beset me with words of hate, and attack me without cause.
> (Ps 109:2–3)

---

1. Cayley, *Ideas of René Girard*, 40.
2. Girard, *I See Satan Fall*, 115.

> Deliver me, O Lord, from evildoers; protect me from those who are violent,
> Who plan evil things in their minds and stir up wars continually....
> Guard me, O Lord, from the hands of the wicked;
> Protect me from the violent who have planned my downfall.
> (Ps 140:1–2, 4)

> For dogs are all around me; a company of evildoers encircles me. (Ps 22:16)

> I am the scorn of all my adversaries, a horror to my neighbors....
> As they scheme together against me, as they plot to take my life....
> Deliver me from the hand of my enemies and persecutors.
> (Ps 31:11, 13, 15)

What is being described here are incipient scapegoat incidents: "evildoers" who surround and threaten violence, "without cause." These "scapegoat psalms" give voice to the victims, those about to be lynched. The book of Job carries this theme forward, with the story of the single most prominent victim in the Hebrew Bible. Girard calls the book of Job "an immense psalm,"[3] consisting of what amounts to an extended "interview with a scapegoat."[4] In the Psalms, victims generally appeal to the Lord for protection and vindication—but (mostly) blame the violence on humans. Job, in contrast, "raises his complaint directly to God.... God is the chief persecutor."[5]

Most of the book of Job consists of the dialogue between Job and his so-called friends (chs. 3–37), preceded by a prologue (chs. 1–2) and followed by God's answer out of the whirlwind (chs. 38–41), with a brief "happy ending" postscript (ch. 42). The book of Job can be perplexing, with a jumble of voices and perspectives; its meaning has been debated for thousands of years. Conventional readings, perhaps overly influenced by the brief prologue and postscript, emphasize Job's faithfulness and "patience." Tested by misfortune, Job complains mightily but passes the test and is rewarded by an encounter with the Creator. The lesson seems to be that Job's personal tribulations are insignificant in the face of the Creator's majesty. Job humbles himself, and in the end his fortunes are

---

3. Girard, *I See Satan Fall*, 115.
4. Heim, *Saved from Sacrifice*, 85.
5. Heim, *Saved from Sacrifice*, 87.

restored. As we will see, Girard offers a radically different reading, guided as usual by his insights into the victimary or scapegoat mechanism.

Anthony Bartlett helpfully places the book of Job in the wider context of the Deuteronomic worldview, which emphasizes that blessings flow from Yahweh when the community is faithful to the Lord's commandments, and disasters ("curses") ensue when the commandments are disobeyed. Life is characterized by strict cause and effect; ill fortune is always a consequence of previous sin. Specifically, the Deuteronomic history (the books of Deuteronomy through 2 Kings) comes to a climax with good King Josiah, who implemented a series of religious reforms before being killed in a battle with the Egyptians in 609 BCE. After his death, the kingdom of Judah rapidly declined, until Jerusalem was conquered and the temple destroyed by Babylon some twenty years later. Writing after the fall of Jerusalem, the task of the Deuteronomic historian is to "give some explanation for the horrendous collapse directly after the virtues of Josiah would seem to warrant the opposite."[6] The historian places the blame on the sins of a previous king, Manasseh (grandfather to Josiah), which evidently were of such magnitude that Josiah's reforms were too little and too late to avert Yahweh's wrath.

The book of Job pushes back against the logic of this worldview. Job suffers disaster after disaster; his "friends," immersed as they are in the Deuteronomic worldview, take this as irrefutable evidence that he has committed some especially grave sin. But Job stubbornly maintains his innocence throughout the dialogues—which leads him to directly challenge God's justice. Speaking from his own experience, Job perceives *no* connection between suffering and any previous offence.

The brief prologue sets the scene. Satan ("the accuser") puts into the Yahweh's mind that Job demonstrates admirable piety only because he has greatly prospered; take away his good fortune and Job will "curse you to your face" (2:5). God takes the wager and gives Satan free rein. A series of disasters then befalls Job, announced by a parade of messengers in quick succession: his multitude of oxen and donkeys were carried off by enemies, his servants were killed, his sheep and more servants were consumed when "the fire of God fell from heaven" (1:16); all his children were killed when a "great wind" collapsed their house (1:19); and finally Job was afflicted with "loathsome sores from the sole of his feet to the crown of his head" (2:7).

---

6. Bartlett, *Signs of Change*, 85–86; see 84–92 for fuller discussion.

Curiously, in the long dialogues that follow, Job nowhere complains of these serial calamities—not a word about his dead children or lost herds. As Girard points out, in the dialogues, "Job clearly articulates the cause of his suffering—the fact that he is ostracized and persecuted by the people around him.... He is the scapegoat of his community."[7] The words of Job echo the scapegoat psalms:

> All my intimate friends abhor me,
>   And those whom I have loved have turned against me.
> (19:19)

> They have gaped at me with their mouths;
>   They have struck me insolently on the cheek;
> They mass themselves together against me.
> (16:10)

> On my right hand the rabble rise up,
>   They send me sprawling, and build roads to my ruin....
> They promote my calamity; no one restrains them.
> (30:12–13)

Furthermore, this persecution at the hands of "the mob" represents a major change in status; until recently, Job was held in high regard by all. "When I went out to the gate of the city, when I took my seat in the square, the young men stepped aside, and the old men rose to their feet.... I was *like a king* living among his troops, and I led them wherever I chose" (29:7–8, 25 JB). Job is "the victim of a huge and sudden reversal of public opinion that is obviously unstable, capricious and void of all moderation." Only the "mimetic contagion of the crowd" can account for the shift between these two extremes. Job "seems hardly more responsible for the change in the crowd than Jesus is for a similar change between Palm Sunday and Good Friday."[8]

Job's sudden change in status is characteristic of the scapegoat mechanism, when a crowd under the influence of mimetic contagion can suddenly focus its hostility on a single victim. So Job is a scapegoat—but he is "a *failed* scapegoat." Girard again contrasts the biblical with the mythical: "Oedipus is a *successful* scapegoat, *because he is never recognized as such*," even to the point of accepting the crowd's accusations.[9] Job, by contrast,

---

7. Girard, *Job*, 4.
8. Girard, *Job*, 13.
9. Girard, *Job*, 35. Emphasis in original.

fails as a scapegoat because he continues to proclaim his innocence. For the scapegoat mechanism to succeed, there must be unanimity; even the scapegoat must accept his guilt. The process also must be unconscious: "In order to have a scapegoat, one must fail to perceive the truth, and therefore one cannot represent the victim as a *scapegoat*, but rather as a victim [of righteous judgment].... *To scapegoat someone is to be unaware of what you are doing.*"[10] Job fails as a scapegoat on both counts.

Satan plays a major role in the prologue—his only such role in all Hebrew Scripture.[11] But after 2:7, he completely disappears from the story. His role of "accuser" (the literal meaning of *Satan*) is taken up first by Job's three so-called friends (who represent the mimetic crowd) and ultimately by their God. As Job protests his innocence, he is drawn inexorably to the conclusion that it is God who is responsible for his suffering.

> Surely now God has worn me out;
>   he has made me desolate of all my company....
> He has torn me in his wrath, and hated me;
>   He has gnashed his teeth at me. (16:7, 9)

> He breaks me down on every side, and I am gone,
>   He has uprooted me like a tree.
> He has kindled his wrath against me,
>   And counts me as his adversary. (19:10–11)

If we follow the logic of the prologue, where Yahweh accedes to Satan's proposal to "test" Job, God is indeed ultimately responsible for Job's misfortune. But at this point, "there arises a sudden anomaly in the relentless language of protest."[12] Job now appeals to something else, some third party between him and God, or perhaps an appeal to God's better nature: "some parallel divine figure who would defend him and be an accuser of God."[13] He appeals to a "witness in heaven, he that vouches for me on high" (16:19), and declares that "I know that my Redeemer lives ... whom I shall see on my side" (19:25, 27). Job seems to be appealing to "a witness for the defense" (the literal meaning of the Greek *paraclete* in

10. Girard, *Evolution and Conversion*, 62. Emphasis added.

11. Satan (the accuser) in the prologue is portrayed as one member of "the heavenly council." Other than Satan's role here in the prologue, there are only two brief references to Satan in all of the Hebrew Scriptures (1 Chr 21:1; Zech 3:1). Contrary to popular belief, Satan is *not* present in the garden of Eden (it is "the serpent" who tempts Eve). As we will see in subsequent chapters, Satan is really a New Testament concern.

12. Bartlett, *Signs of Change*, 101.

13. Heim, *Saved from Sacrifice*, 89.

the New Testament), to defend him against God's accusations. This introduces a "dramatic new element—a redemptive *secondness* in God... [producing] a second iteration of God, one who *listens to victims*."[14] It is as if Job is groping toward something other than the violent and retributive God of his so-called friends.[15]

We can now see that what is at stake in the book of Job is the very character of God. Is Israel's Yahweh the god of the persecutors, the god who colludes with the accuser Satan, the god who demands sacrifice, the god who inspires the mob to lynch scapegoats?[16] Or is God on the side of victims, and thus opposed to a view of the "sacred" that endorses violence to persecute scapegoats? Heim elaborates:

> God [in Job's view] figures among the ranks of Job's enemies. The book of Job confronts directly—through its prologue (where Satan is a divine associate of some kind) and the extended argument of Job's friends—the presumption that the sacrificial [scapegoat] dynamic is itself God's work.... If "god" is in fact the divinity that requires the sacrifice of the innocent, then Job will appeal for justice against this god of the violent sacred. The book of Job can be read as a kind of struggle for the soul of the biblical God, a trial as to whether this is a divinity of the classic, mythical, sacrificial sort, or something different.[17]

Job, in his suffering and his protestations of innocence, is searching for a new vision, for a God who will side with victims. The answer provided by the book is ambiguous and not completely satisfying. Girard notes that when God finally speaks out of the whirlwind (chs. 38–41), God "does not make the slightest allusion to the questions posed by Job, or to Job's protestations of innocence." Instead, "this God takes refuge in nature," lecturing Job with "a little astronomy, a little meteorology, and a lot of zoology."[18] This God relies not on the threat of violence but "awe-

---

14. Bartlett, *Signs of Change*, 102. Emphasis added.

15. Girard, *Job*, 128.

16. See the prologue for more on the etymology of *lynching*. Girard uses the word very sparingly if at all in his early books (e.g., *Things Hidden*, 115), but in *Job* and subsequent books he describes the scapegoat mechanism as "lynching" dozens of times. For an account of Girard's personal acquaintance with racial discrimination and the legacy of lynching, see Haven, *Evolution of Desire*, 64–79 (based on Girard's year at Duke, 1952–53, early in his career).

17. Heim, *Saved from Sacrifice*, 86.

18. Girard, *Job*, 141.

struck wonder" to silence Job's questioning.[19] In response to this divine tour de force, Job acknowledges the inscrutability of God's purposes and seems to humbly accept the divine rebuke: "Therefore I despise myself, and repent in dust and ashes" (42:6).

Bartlett argues that the traditional translation of 42:6 is not consistent with the Hebrew text, and that a more accurate rendering would be something like, "I reject and regret dust and ashes."[20] Far from confessing and repenting, Job seems to be "repenting of repenting."

Regardless, the next verse is "remarkable" and even "astonishing."[21] Job 42:7 reads, "After the Lord had spoken these words to Job, the Lord said to Eliphaz, 'My wrath is kindled against you and your two friends; for you have not spoken of me what is right, as my servant Job has.'" Heim comments that "there is hardly a more amazing line in the Bible":

> Job, who has called God his persecutor and denounced God's injustice and indifference, has spoken what is right. . . . Job has seemed to talk of two different Gods—an adversary God for whom he is only a sacrificial target, and a divine vindicator, the God who sides with victims. And we may say that Job has spoken right about both of them. Some may see this as an incoherence in Job's position or as a conflict in the book's sources. In either case, it may reflect not merely a literary but a historical struggle between two religious realities, a sacrificial divinity and the God of victims.[22]

However ambiguously, the book of Job forces us to confront "the abyss between the God of executioners and the God of victims."[23] The author of Job intuitively senses that abyss, but the full articulation of it is not given to him: humanity is not yet ready. Job has glimpsed the truth that the accuser, the violent sacred, the god of the lynchers, is not the true God.

Hundreds of years after Job, Jesus of Nazareth is given a vision: "I saw Satan fall like lightening from heaven" (Luke 10:18 NIV). In this striking and mysterious image, Satan, the persecutor of Job, the accuser of scapegoats, "the ruler of this world" (John 16:11), the guardian of sacred

---

19. Bartlett, *Signs of Change*, 101.

20. Bartlett, *Signs of Change*, 104–5. Gutiérrez makes much the same point in *On Job*, 86.

21. Girard, *Job*, 144.

22. Heim, *Saved from Sacrifice*, 90–91.

23. Girard, *Job*, 145.

violence, is revealed as a false god. Sacred violence must be expelled from "humanity's very idea of God."

6

The Suffering Servant

> Remember not the former things, nor consider the things of old.
>   Behold, I am doing a new thing; now it springs forth,
> do you not perceive it?
>
> —Isa 43:18–19 RSV

THE FOUR SERVANT SONGS in Second Isaiah (Isa 40–55) are so familiar that it can be a challenge to read them with fresh eyes, to appreciate just how new and radical is their message. Christians have typically read these passages through the lens of substitutionary atonement theory (see excursus 2), seeing the servant's suffering as inflicted by God, thereby serving to atone for the sins of his persecutors—analogous to the literal scapegoat in Lev 16 and prefiguring Jesus's sacrifice on the cross. We begin, however, by initially setting aside any Christian implications and examining the text on its own merits.

As we saw in the previous chapter, Job vigorously resisted his scapegoating. The question in Job is: "When the innocent suffer, how can God be justified?" The Servant Songs tell the same scapegoat story but from a different perspective. Now it is crystal clear that the servant is suffering unjustly for the sins of others. The question then becomes: "How can those who do violence ever be justified?"[1]

The prophet Jeremiah, consistent with his Deuteronomic worldview, depicts God as punishing Israel through its exile to Babylon. By contrast, God in Second Isaiah is characterized by comfort, consolation, compassion, and tenderness. Anthony Bartlett claims that "Second Isaiah amounts to a full-scale redefinition of divinity itself . . . the breakthrough to true monotheism . . . [which goes] hand in hand with an organic separation of God from violence."[2]

As always, historical background is valuable. Jerusalem was destroyed in 587 BCE, and some portion of the Jewish population exiled to Babylon, where they stubbornly resisted assimilation. In 539 BCE, Babylon itself fell to Cyrus of Persia—without a battle, when the people of Babylon simply opened their gates to the conquering Persians. Cyrus, referred to as Yahweh's "anointed" (*messiah* in Hebrew; the only non-Jew in the Bible so designated),[3] is on his way to establishing the largest empire in the ancient world. He will permit previously conquered populations, including the Jews, to leave Babylon and return to their homelands. From the Jews' perspective, this "second exodus" was miraculous, and this time accomplished by God without any recourse to violence. Second Isaiah was composed amid these truly astonishing events.

In the first Servant Song (Isa 42:1–9), we are told that the servant "will not cry or lift up his voice . . . a bruised reed he will not break, and a dimly burning wick he will not quench." Bartlett elaborates: "The servant is to be a figure of judgement for the whole earth, but the method of achieving this is an extraordinary gentleness and nonaggression in relation to what is broken and close to extinction. . . . Instead of a pitiless quid pro quo [of vengeance], there is a compelling attitude of compassion and nonviolence."[4]

In the third Servant Song (Isa 50:4–11), the servant declares that the Lord God "opened my ear . . . to listen as those who are taught. . . . I was not rebellious. . . . I gave my back to those who struck me and my cheeks to those who pulled out the beard; I did not hide my face from insult and spitting." Yahweh is directly instructing his servant in nonviolence,

---

1. Heim, *Saved from Sacrifice*, 101.
2. Bartlett, *Signs of Change*, 120.
3. Bartlett, *Signs of Change*, 119–20.
4. Bartlett, *Signs of Change*, 129.

subverting "the calculus of vengeance" inherent in both Jeremiah and Deuteronomy.[5]

The fruits of the Lord's instruction in nonviolence are described in the fourth and most striking of the Servant Songs (Isa 52:13—53:12). The passage contains a jumble of different perspectives, which can make interpretation challenging: it bounces back and forth between a past violent event and the reassessment of that event in the present; and between Yahweh's perspective and the community's. It is not even entirely clear if the servant was killed (53:8b) or was given a long life (53:10). What is clear, though, is that events have led the community to a threefold insight. First, there has been an incident of violent scapegoating, during which the servant, as previously instructed, did not resist: "He was despised and rejected by others . . . wounded . . . crushed . . . he was oppressed, and he was afflicted, yet he did not open his mouth, like a lamb led to the slaughter . . . cut off from the land of the living" (53:3, 5, 7–8).

Second, the victim is innocent: "By a perversion of justice he was taken away . . . although he had done no violence, and there was no deceit in his mouth" (53:8–9). And third, despite and perhaps even because of the victim's innocence, there is a social benefit to the community: "Surely he has borne our infirmities and carried our diseases . . . upon him was the punishment that made us whole, and by his bruises we are healed. . . . The righteous one, my servant, shall make many righteous, and he shall bear their iniquities" (53:4–5, 11).

There has been endless scholarly debate about who the servant was and even if he actually existed or is simply a metaphor for the communal suffering of Israel. Regardless, the text as we have it signifies a remarkable breakthrough. James Warren observes that the main point is "how clearly the passage reveals the scapegoat mechanism. And the clarity of that revelation, it can be said, is directly due to the servant's nonviolence."[6] Heim comments:

> This is about as clear as it can be about religious scapegoating violence. It is an unequivocally bad thing. With undeniably good results. To perceive this sacrificial mechanism in others is unusual, a breakthrough. To face it explicitly in our own behavior may be, literally, a miracle.[7]

---

5. Bartlett, *Signs of Change*, 118.
6. Warren, *Compassion or Apocalypse*, 184.
7. Heim, *Saved from Sacrifice*, 98–99.

The text reveals the innocence of the servant, coupled with the social benefit that comes from his scapegoating. But there is potentially an additional and decisive insight: that the violence comes from humans and not from God. On this matter the text is somewhat ambiguous. "We *accounted* him stricken, struck down by God, and afflicted" (53:4b), which at least implies that the initial judgment of being struck down by God was wrong. Those responsible recognize their own guilt: "All we like sheep have gone astray; we have all turned to our own way" (53:6a); "by a perversion of justice he was taken away" (53:8a). But the text goes on to suggest, "The Lord has laid on him the iniquity of us all" (53:6b), and "it was the will of the Lord to crush him with pain" (53:10).

There are difficulties in the translation of these texts; notably the wording in the Greek Septuagint is much more open to attributing the violence to humans rather than to God.[8] Bartlett cautions that these texts unfortunately "seem automatically to produce the dynamic of an exchange—punishment in exchange for salvation."[9] This would be only a slightly refined version of the Deuteronomic worldview, now with an innocent third party suffering the required punishment for sin.

To "get us out of the bind of this interpretation," Bartlett directs us to the "transformative nonviolence" of the servant's response: an accurate understanding "depends on *the revolutionary empathy of nonviolence*."[10]

> The servant makes his body a nonretaliatory receptacle of violence. . . . The community grasps the nonretaliation as a true revelation of Godself, and its new, liberating, non-penal righteousness at once enters their souls. Seemingly out of nowhere, a new human coding is achieved, an anthropological and religious breakthrough of world-historical dimensions. "Who has believed what we have heard? And to whom has the arm of the Lord been revealed?"[11]

Perhaps the best way to understand the text's ambiguity about who bears ultimate responsibility for the described violence is to recognize

---

8. Bartlett, *Signs of Change*, 136–38. See also Ekblad: "The LXX translators' many differences with the [Hebrew text] can be interpreted as theologically motivated. They seek to disassociate God from the servant's suffering in verses where the [Hebrew text] could be (wrongly, I believe), and often has been, interpreted to support a notion of atonement through penal substitution" ("God Is Not to Blame," 200).

9. Bartlett, *Signs of Change*, 131.

10. Bartlett, *Signs of Change*, 132, 133, 134. Emphasis in original.

11. Bartlett, *Signs of Change*, 134–35.

that "there are two different things going on. . . . God is doing something different from what the persecutors are doing."[12] The community sees both the violence and the resulting social benefit, and at least retrospectively recognizes that the servant is innocent. But they still hold on to the belief that the servant's fate is somehow pleasing to God or even caused by God.

God, however, is "doing a new thing." The servant's willingness to suffer nonviolently changes the ancient scapegoating mechanism; "the servant is in league with God to change this dynamic."[13] Seeing this, however, may depend on answers to some very deep questions about the nature of God, and specifically how we believe God acts in the world. If we understand God as "sovereign," as the omnipotent cause of all things ("the omnicause"), a puppeteer pulling strings to control all that happens in the world, then it is hard to avoid the conclusion that God is in some way responsible for the servant's fate—either by actively willing it or passively allowing it.

But if instead we understand God's action in the world as never coercing but always inviting and persuading, a different conclusion emerges. God does not and cannot unilaterally control events but instead acts out of "uncontrolling love" (because genuine love never controls), honoring the freedom of creatures—even the freedom to make bad choices.[14] God is present in every moment, constrained by past and present realities but continuously offering new possibilities for human flourishing into the future. As the process theologians say, "God works with what is, to bring about what might be."[15] What actually happens depends on our human response to God's offered possibilities: perhaps nothing changes, perhaps there is incremental change, but occasionally there is a true breakthrough.

In the case of the suffering servant, the reality of "what is" is yet another episode of scapegoating, and that cannot be changed, but "what might be" is the revelation of a better, nonviolent way. This truly is a "new thing," made possible by the servant's obedient nonretaliation. It is as if the servant is saying to his community what Joseph said to his brothers:

12. Heim, *Saved from Sacrifice*, 100.

13. Heim, *Saved from Sacrifice*, 100.

14. For "uncontrolling love" and a cogent critique of God as "omnicause," see Oord, *Uncontrolling Love of God*, esp. ch. 4.

15. Suchocki, *God, Christ, Church*, 223. This paragraph reflects a process theology perspective. For a brief introduction to process thinking and its relevance to Quakerism, see Gates, *Reclaiming the Transcendent*. See excursus 1 below for the relevance of process theology to the theme of this book.

"Even though you intended it for harm, God intended it for good" (Gen 50:20). We have here in the suffering servant another prototype of "the giving and forgiving victim."

Despite this "anthropological and religious breakthrough of world-historical dimensions,"[16] subsequent Hebrew writers did not take up the theme of the suffering servant. For more than five centuries, the Songs of the Servant lie there, neglected or misunderstood. Schwager says that "not a single biblical author or Jewish writer referred to them explicitly."[17] But this will change in the Christian New Testament, where Isa 53 is prominently alluded to, as the church wrestles with the meaning of Jesus's passion and death. For example, in Luke 22:37 (KJV) Jesus himself quotes Isaiah: "And he was reckoned among the transgressors" (Isa 53:12). In all three Synoptic Gospels, Jesus three times predicts his suffering and death, and all seem inspired by the image of the suffering servant (Mark 8:31; 9:30–32; 10:33–34; and parallels). The second chapter of 1 Peter has several allusions: "He committed no sin, and no deceit was found in his mouth" (2:22; see Isa 53:9); "by his wounds you have been healed" (2:24; see Isa 53:5); "for you were going astray like sheep (2:25; see Isa 53:6).

The most explicit New Testament use of the suffering servant is in Acts, with the story of Phillip and the Ethiopian eunuch (8:26–39). The Ethiopian has been to Jerusalem to worship at the temple; Philip finds him in his chariot, puzzling over this very passage from Isaiah, which is quoted at some length. The Ethiopian asks, "About whom does the prophet say this, about himself or someone else?" Philip "began to speak, and starting with this scripture, he proclaimed the good news about Jesus" (8:34–35). Bailie comments: "When has one sentence summarized so much! From the grim story of persecution in Isaiah to the gospel in one sentence. From its effect on the Ethiopian, we are made aware of the shock that Phillip's interpretation delivered";[18] he immediately asks Phillip to baptize him. Even though his status as a eunuch made him ineligible to convert to Judaism, Phillip complies with the Ethiopian's request—prefiguring the early Christian church's acceptance of gentiles (made explicit in Acts 10).

The author of the Servant Songs has seen with unprecedented clarity both the innocence of the victim *and* the social benefit that comes from his victimization. In trying to reconcile these two insights, he seems

16. Bartlett, *Signs of Change*, 134–35.
17. Schwager, *Must There Be Scapegoats*, 135.
18. Bailie, *Violence Unveiled*, 43.

at times to fall back to the understanding of Job's so-called friends, that his suffering must be inflicted by God. But the passage itself contains evidence that this "solution" is unsatisfactory. Gil Bailie observes that "the moral and religious solution the text pronounces is an unstable one because these two forces—the empathy for victims and the need for rituals of victimization—are incompatible. Sooner or later, one of them will have to prevail over the other."[19]

Before we turn to the New Testament witness, we have one more story from the Hebrew Scriptures to explore—the remarkable story of Jonah.

---

19. Bailie, *Violence Unveiled*, 45.

7

Jonah
A Reluctant Prophet

> This generation ... asks for a sign, but no sign will be given to it except the sign of Jonah. For just as Jonah became a sign to the people of Nineveh, so the Son of Man will be to this generation.... Behold, something greater than Jonah is here!
>
> —Luke 11:29–30, 32

WE HAVE TAKEN A highly condensed and selective journey through the Hebrew Scriptures, highlighting stories of scapegoating and its "subversion from within."[1] Some of the stories give textual evidence of later editing, to better communicate an anti-scapegoating message (Abraham's non-sacrifice of Isaac, Joseph). Some convey a sense of authors unconsciously groping their way toward a new image of God, one that excludes divine violence (Job, Second Isaiah). We conclude our discussion of the Hebrew texts with the one book that gives every indication of having been consciously composed "with the express purpose of challenging sacred violence ... written for the purpose of criticizing a theology that represents God as a lover of vengeance."[2] The book of Jonah accomplishes

---

1. For Alison's notion of "subversion from within," see prologue, n8, xv.
2. Warren, *Compassion or Apocalypse*, 166–67.

this through a fable that is filled with irony, a parody of other prophetic texts, "a comedy if not a farce . . . hilarious from start to finish,"[3] an "outrageously tall tale," a "fireworks display of irony," a "semiotic transformation . . . a deliberate manipulation of biblical DNA to produce a remarkable new mutation."[4]

The book of Jonah comes to us with no clues as to when, where, or why it was written. The actual historical figure of "Jonah son of Amittai" (1:1) warrants only a single verse in the history of Israel (2 Kgs 14:25), with no mention there of a fish or a mission to Nineveh. The book appears to have been composed centuries after the historical figure, with the author using the name of Jonah to lend prophetic legitimacy to his fable. The author goes to great lengths to connect the story of Jonah with Israel's prophetic tradition, with at least twenty direct allusions to other prophetic texts. There is a particularly strong connection with the book of Nahum, the prophet who denounces Nineveh as the "city of bloodshed," offering the gruesome prophecy that the Lord's vengeance will produce "piles of dead, heaps of corpses, dead bodies without end" (Nah 3:1–7). One commentator says that "it is difficult to negate the impression that the writer of Jonah has deliberately constructed Jonah as a parody of Nahum, both a representation of his bitter spirit and a hilarious turning-it-on-its head." But in order to get a hearing for this outrageous parody, "a plot and a text must be produced which make an inversion of the popular viewpoint possible without lapsing into mere preachiness. A code transformation must be carried through with the reader hardly knowing it."[5]

Anthony Bartlett's important *Signs of Change: The Bible's Evolution of Divine Nonviolence* presents a "theory of semiotic transformation" that is directly relevant to the approach to the Bible advocated here. He argues that human nature does not change in response to rational deliberation or philosophical reasoning, but by "code transformations," changes in the deeply embedded cultural "signs" that come from shared narratives, are largely unconscious, and take generations to have their full effect. He compares these cultural code transformations to the genetic mutations in DNA that drive biologic evolution or, alternatively, to a new operating system in a computer: hidden from view but capable of producing profound new ways of understanding our world. Implicit in this is the sense that major code transformations might occupy a relatively small

3. Warren, *Compassion or Apocalypse*, 167.
4. Bartlett, *Signs of Change*, 207, 195, 198.
5. Bartlett, *Signs of Change*, 197.

portion of a sacred text but are still capable of producing major shifts in understanding. For Bartlett, the book of Jonah is exhibit A in the Hebrew Scriptures for his "semiotic theory," even as it prepares the way for an even greater semiotic transformation in the New Testament.[6]

The book begins with the word of the Lord directing Jonah to go to Israel's enemy, the Assyrian city of Nineveh, and prophesy its destruction. Jonah wants no part of this, so promptly boards a ship to take him in the opposite direction, as far away as possible, "away from the presence of the Lord" (1:3). Not a great plan: a violent storm promptly arises, threatening to swamp the ship. The sailors cast lots, seeking to identify who might be responsible for this natural calamity. "The lot fell on Jonah" (1:7), who confesses that he is in fact guilty of "fleeing from the presence of the Lord" (1:10) and invites the sailors to throw him overboard and save themselves (1:12).

At this point we seem to have a straightforward scapegoat tale: a crisis (the storm), identification of an arbitrary "guilty" party by lot, a confession by the designated scapegoat, and a plan to save the group by sacrificing the one. However, the sailors (gentiles all) are reluctant and half-hearted persecutors. They throw cargo overboard, attempt to row harder to bring the boat to shore, and plead not to be made "guilty of innocent blood" (1:14). Despite these attempts, the storm intensifies, and the sailors in desperation "picked Jonah up and threw him into the sea" (1:15).

The sailors' attempt at scapegoating sacrifice fails when "the Lord provided a large fish to swallow Jonah" (1:17). Jonah is angry at God, and in this type of story, "the raging forces of nature often divert attention from human rage."[7] The sea is quieted not by the sailors' reluctant attempt at sacrifice but when Jonah's rage is quite literally "swallowed."

The raging sea evokes the primal chaos, and the "great fish" (*not* a whale) recalls the primeval monster Leviathan (Job 41:1; Ps 74:13–14; Isa 27:1). In the upside-down telling of Jonah's story, Leviathan here is not an instrument of destruction but of redemption. In the abyss of the great fish's belly, "an enduring mythic image of violence and death . . . [is transformed into] one of hope and deliverance." God has given Jonah "an eruptive insight of nonviolence"[8]—but Jonah will prove to be a slow learner.

---

6. *Semiotics* is simply the study of signs and symbols and how they are used to construct meaning.

7. Schwager, *Must There Be Scapegoats*, 26.

8. Bartlett, *Signs of Change*, 203–4.

After three days in the belly of the fish (1:17), "the Lord spoke unto the fish, and it vomited out Jonah upon the dry land" (2:10 KJV). A chastened but still ambivalent Jonah is once again directed to Nineveh, where he delivers his terse message of judgment: "Forty days more, and Nineveh shall be overthrown!" (3:4). The Ninevites might be expected to respond by offering the usual sacrifices to their own protector gods, but instead the Ninevite king decrees that all residents—even the animals—must fast, don sackcloth and ashes, and "turn from their evil ways and *from the violence* that is in their hands. Who knows? God may relent and change his mind" (3:8–9). It seems that it is not Jonah's "minimalist, still hostile proclamation" that causes Nineveh to repent, but the manner of Jonah's deliverance from the great fish, which is why the king focuses on the issue of violence. The Ninevites' "sudden transformation is all one with the revelatory nonviolence of the great fish."[9]

With the Ninevites dramatic repentance, "God changed his mind [!] about the calamity that he had said he would bring down upon them; and he did not do it" (3:10). Bartlett says the Hebrew text is even clearer: when God "saw they turned from *the evil*, relented God of *the evil*." *Violence* is the evil from which *both* Nineveh and God relented. "We cannot avoid the impression that the meaning and identity of God are changed, from violence to nonviolence, by the change in humans."[10]

This turn of events "was very displeasing to Jonah, and he became angry" (4:1). He now claims that his initial flight to Tarshish was because he knew that Yahweh is "a gracious God and merciful, slow to anger, and abounding in steadfast love, and *ready to relent from punishing*" (4:2). From the beginning, he had feared being sent to warn Nineveh of its coming destruction, only to have God relent—exactly what has now happened. Jonah is here quoting Exod 34:6–7, but he has added the phrase about God being "ready to relent from punishing."[11] Again, Bartlett says the Hebrew text literally reads "ready to *repent* from *the evil*," using the same verb previously used to describe the Ninevites' repentance and the same noun previously used to describe the evil of violence.[12] Especially

---

9. Bartlett, *Signs of Change*, 204.

10. Bartlett, *Signs of Change*, 205.

11. Joel 2:13 also alludes to Exod 34:6–7, with the same addition as in Jonah, "and relents from punishing." Since neither the books of Jonah nor Joel can be accurately dated, it is impossible to say which was written first.

12. Bartlett, *Signs of Change*, 206.

from the original Hebrew, we are left with the distinct impression that *God*, like the Ninevites, is repenting of the evil of violence.

God may have changed his mind, but Jonah, despite his deliverance from the great fish, is still stuck in the paradigm of sacred violence. A sulking Jonah retreats to the outskirts of the city, still nursing his anger at God, "to see what would become of the city" (4:5). Jonah builds a booth for shade from the hot sun, but God upstages Jonah's work by "appointing a bush" to give Jonah better shade, which made Jonah "very happy." But the following day "God appointed a worm that attacked the bush, so that it withered" (4:7). Jonah was already angry with God for sparing the great city of Nineveh, but with the loss of shade from his bush, Jonah is now *really* angry.

In the remarkable final scene, God asks, "Is it right for you to be angry about the bush?" Jonah, his ego wounded, replies, "Yes, angry enough to die" (4:9). Yahweh then points out, "You are concerned about the bush, for which you did not labor and which you did not grow. . . . Should I not be concerned about Nineveh, that great city, in which are more than a hundred twenty thousand persons . . . and also many animals?" (4:10–11). The scene hearkens back to Gen 18, where Abraham bargains with Yahweh about the potential injustice of destroying all of Sodom, "the righteous along with the wicked." Abraham urges Yahweh to spare the city for the sake of even a few righteous, gradually bargaining Yahweh down from the presence of fifty righteous, to ten. In Genesis, it is *Abraham* arguing for mercy, for the sake of even ten righteous. But here it is *Yahweh* advocating for mercy, not for the sake of a few righteous but for the sake of all Nineveh—even the animals.

The book of Jonah, nowhere more than in this final episode, undermines the idea of sacred violence by making it look ridiculous. It is hard to avoid the conclusion that the whole business about destroying Nineveh is "little more than a pretext for teaching Jonah about mercy and compassion."[13] There could hardly be a more dramatic illustration of the Hebrew people's changing conception of their God; Jonah is "preparing the way for an eventual undermining of the entire sacred-violent concept of God."[14] From the testimony of the Gospels, it seems that Jesus meditated deeply on its meaning.[15] Girard comments that when the people ask for "a sign," Jesus "answers by telling them that the only sign is 'the sign of

13. Warren, *Compassion or Apocalypse*, 167.
14. Warren, *Compassion or Apocalypse*, 169.
15. Bartlett, *Signs of Change*, 207.

Jonah,' that is to say the sign of the scapegoat, the sign of the unfortunate wretch thrown to the whales by the sailors who hold him responsible for the storm."[16]

Before we finally turn to the New Testament witness, it is worth summarizing Girard's view of the Hebrew Scriptures with which we have been wrestling in the past several chapters:

> In the archaic world, every time the scapegoat mechanism works, a new god emerges. Judaism, since its inception, is the absolute refusal of this god-fabricating machine. In Judaism God has no relation to victimization, and victims are no longer divinized. That is what we call revelation, which, historically, unfolds in two stages. First of all, there is a shift from myth to the Bible, where . . . God is de-victimized and the victim is de-divinized; then you have the full evangelic revelation. God experiences the role of the victim, but this time deliberately, in order to free men from violence.[17]

In the view of his colleague Raymund Schwager, "Girard understands the Old Testament as a long and laborious exodus out of the world of violence and sacred projections, an exodus plagued by many reversals and one that does not reach its goal within the Old Testament writings."[18] In Girard's own words, "The Bible is a human text . . . in which occurs the change from mythology to the biblical view, which is really the change from the guilt of the victim to the innocence of the victim. . . . The Bible deconstructs mythology."[19]

We turn now to the second stage, "the full evangelic revelation," centered on the life and death of one who, let us not forget, was deeply immersed in his Jewish tradition: Jesus of Nazareth.

---

16. Girard, *When These Things Begin*, 119–20.
17. Girard, *Evolution and Conversion*, 143.
18. Schwager, *Must There Be Scapegoats*, 43.
19. Girard, *Reading the Bible*, 64 (cited previously as the epigraph to ch. 4).

8

"The Spirit of the Lord Is Upon Me"

How Jesus Read Scripture

> Go and learn what this means: I desire mercy, and not sacrifice.
> —Matt 9:13 (Jesus, quoting Hos 6:6)

As we turn from the Hebrew Scriptures to the Christian New Testament, we confront an important "hermeneutical question." When the New Testament refers to "the Scriptures," it is referring not to the New Testament (which did not yet exist) but to the Hebrew Scriptures. How were these to be interpreted? The nascent Christian church saw in the Hebrew Scriptures evidence that pointed to Jesus as the expected Messiah, despite his unanticipated fate. But rabbinic Judaism found in those same Scriptures multiple texts that explained why Jesus could *not* be the Messiah. The "hermeneutical question" then is this: How do we interpret the Hebrew Scriptures in light of Jesus of Nazareth?[1]

In the Gospel accounts of Jesus, we are given numerous instances of Jesus quoting or alluding to Scripture: clearly, Jesus was immersed in the worldview of the Hebrew Scriptures. In the temptation in the wilderness,

---

1. For the hermeneutical question, see Schwager, *Must There Be Scapegoats*, 136–49. For the question of how Jesus read Scripture, see Hardin, *Jesus Driven Life*, 65–91.

Jesus responds to Satan's temptations by quoting three separate times from Deuteronomy. In Matthew's Gospel, Jesus twice cites the words of Hosea, "I desire mercy and not sacrifice." When asked what he considered the greatest commandment, Jesus answers (in Matt 22:37–39) by quoting from Deuteronomy (6:5) and Leviticus (19:18). In explaining his parable of the wicked tenants, he appeals to the words of Ps 118. Even on the cross, his cry of distress is from Ps 22 ("My God, my God, why have you forsaken me?"). We could cite dozens of other examples, but the point is clear: Jesus knew the Hebrew Scriptures well, and he turned to them again and again to explain his mission.

We even have one account, from Luke's Gospel, where Jesus publicly *reads* from the Scriptures, from "the scroll of the prophet Isaiah":

> The Spirit of the Lord is upon me,
>> because he has anointed me to bring good news to the poor.
> He has sent me to proclaim release to the captives and recovery of sight to the blind,
>> to let the oppressed go free,
> to proclaim the year of the Lord's favor. (Luke 4:18–19)

In Luke, this is the first public event of Jesus's ministry, located in the synagogue of his hometown of Nazareth, immediately following his temptation in the desert and return to Galilee. The reaction to Jesus is most curious. Jesus declares, "Today this Scripture has been fulfilled in your hearing." Despite this rather grandiose claim, initially "all were amazed at the gracious words that came from his mouth."[2] Jesus is quoting a well-known passage from Isaiah, one that hearkens back to the practice of the Jubilee Year and at the same time looks forward to the liberation by the coming Messiah. But significantly, he has omitted the final line of Isaiah's text: "to proclaim the year of the Lord's favor, *and the day of vengeance of our God*" (Isa 61:2). He then goes on to elaborate on the Jubilee theme by giving examples of the prophets Elijah and Elisha helping and healing non-Israelites (4:27–29).

This evidently did not go over well: "When they heard this, all in the synagogue were filled with rage. They got up, drove him out of town, and

---

2. There is a technical issue in the translation of v. 22. The KJV reads: "All bore witness to him"; i.e., all were watching him attentively, neither positive nor negative. If the Greek is the *dative of advantage*, then the NRSV translation would be accurate: "All spoke well of him." But if the Greek is the *dative of disadvantage*, "All spoke ill of him" would be more accurate. Then "Is not this Joseph's son?" would be more like "Who does he think he is?" See Hardin, *Jesus Driven Life*, 67–68.

led him to the brow of a hill on which the town was built, so that they might hurl him off the cliff" (4:28–29). The allusion seems to be to Lev 16; during the time of the First Temple the scapegoat is sometimes said to have been hurled off a cliff (instead of driven into the wilderness). A crowd surrounds an individual (or goat), gradually closing in and forcing the individual to plunge off the cliff to his death. This is the equivalent of stoning, in that all participate but no one individual can be said to be responsible. So we have here at the very beginning of Jesus's public ministry an abortive scapegoat event, foreshadowing Jesus's eventual fate. "But he passed through the midst of them and went on his way" (4:30). Michael Hardin comments on this episode:

> In short, Jesus is saying to his synagogue hearers, "Jubilee is here, not only for you but also for those you hate; in fact God also goes to your oppressors with this message of jubilee, deliverance and salvation." Now we can understand why they got so mad at him.... By eliminating the phrase regarding God's vengeance, Jesus is removing the notion of retributive violence from the doctrine of God. He is in effect saying that God is not like you think, loving you [but] angry with those you hate.... Nothing irks some folks more than losing a God who is wrathful, angry, retributive and punishing.... We want so much to believe that God takes sides, and that side is inevitably our side.[3]

As presented in the Gospels, the main thrust of John the Baptizer's preaching was to warn about "the wrath to come" (Luke 3:7). After John was imprisoned by Herod Antipas, some of John's disciples came to Jesus and asked, "Are you the one to come, or are we to wait for another?" Jesus answered, "Go and tell John what you have seen and heard: the blind receive their sight, the lame walk, the lepers are cleansed, the deaf hear, the dead are raised, the poor have good news brought to them. And blessed is anyone who takes no offense [is not scandalized] at me" (Luke 7:19, 22–23).

Why would John's disciples be "scandalized" by Jesus?[4] Hardin points out that the list of miracles and good works that Jesus offers

---

3. Hardin, *Jesus Driven Life*, 68–69.
4. "Not scandalized by me" is the Rheims New Testament translation (1582). Girard notes that references to stumbling blocks, obstacles, etc. are all translations of the Greek *skandalon*, which he maintains is best translated as "scandal" (*I See Satan Fall*, 16–17). For more on the importance of scandal, see ch. 19.

contains allusions to several texts from Isaiah.⁵ But "the Isaiah texts all include a reference to the vengeance of God, *none of which Jesus quotes*."⁶ To cite just one of the texts Jesus alludes to:

> *Here is your God. He will come with vengeance, with terrible recompense.*
> He will come and save you.
> Then the eyes of the blind shall be opened, and the ears of the deaf unstopped;
> then the lame shall leap like a deer, and the tongue of the speechless sing for joy. (Isa 35:4–6)

John's disciples are at least potentially scandalized by Jesus's omission of all reference to God's vengeance. John the Baptizer, "like the prophets before him, believed that God was to bring apocalyptic wrath [but] nowhere in Jesus's preaching do we find such, and this is what confused John, just as it confused Jesus's synagogue hearers."⁷ John came preaching "the wrath to come"; Jesus came preaching the kingdom of God.

Virtually all New Testament scholars agree that Jesus's central message was "the kingdom of God is at hand; repent, and believe in the good news" (Mark 1:15). What Jesus actually meant by the kingdom of God has been endlessly debated, with no consensus among scholars more qualified than I to offer an opinion. But to my ears, there seem to be several key components. First, the kingdom is "at hand" and "among" (or within) you (Luke 17:21): whatever fulfillment awaits us in the future, the kingdom is also a present reality, breaking into history now. Second, although "kingdom" has fallen out of contemporary favor because of its patriarchal and hierarchical connotations, there is a distinct political edge to the kingdom of God. If God is king, then Herod (or Caesar) is not. The kingdom of God is radically subversive of the world's status quo. And third, the kingdom of God is "good news," characterized by grace, abundance, generosity, and forgiveness. God's blessings are bestowed on all: God "makes the sun to rise on the evil and the good, and sends rain on the righteous and on the unrighteous" (Matt 5:45). The human task is simply to respond to God's invitation and grace. To the extent that we fail to respond, we bring judgment on ourselves: "And this is the judgment,

---

5. Blind (Isa 29:18, 35:5; 61:1–2); lame (35:6); deaf (29:18; 35:5); poor (29:19).
6. Hardin, *Jesus Driven Life*, 69–70. Emphasis in original.
7. Hardin, *Jesus Driven Life*, 70.

that the light has come into the world, and people loved darkness rather than light because their deeds were evil" (John 3:19).

Raymund Schwager makes essentially the same point: the message of God's anger and vengeance, so prominent in the Hebrew prophets, was absent from Jesus's message about the kingdom of God. For the prophets, repentance comes first, which is then followed by salvation.[8] "Jesus broke with the religious thinking of Israel to the extent that for him *salvation and repentance exchanged places*, and he offered the sinner God's forgiveness, irrespective of whether the sinner was willing to repent, or unprepared to do so."[9] The offer of grace is extended to all without exception, as illustrated by Jesus's well-documented proclivity to "eat with sinners and tax collectors" (Mark 2:16). God's "offer of grace takes place in advance of human choice.... *Grace does not presuppose conversion*, but *wants to awaken it*." Conversion or repentance *follows* the experience of God's grace; only if "pure grace is rejected [does] a person fall prey to the consequences of his or her own decision."[10] God's grace is freely offered to all, but if we fail to respond to God's free offer, we bring judgment on ourselves.

We started this chapter with "the hermeneutic question" of how to interpret the Hebrew Scriptures in the light of Jesus of Nazareth. Both Girard and Schwager make the strong claim that Jesus himself provides the key, when in reference to himself he quotes Ps 118: "The stone that the builders rejected has become the cornerstone [or keystone]; this was the Lord's doing, and it was amazing in our eyes" (Matt 21:22; Ps 118:22–23).[11] The setting is important: in all three Synoptic Gospels, Jesus is teaching in the temple during the final climactic week of his life, when he relates his "parable of the wicked tenants" (Matt 21:33–42; Mark 12:1–12; Luke 20:9–19). A landowner leased his vineyard to tenants and went "to another country." After the harvest, he sent a succession of servants to collect his share, but his emissaries were beaten, stoned, and killed by

---

8. To some extent, Christians can be rightly accused of misinterpreting what Judaism actually believes. In *Paul and Palestinian Judaism*, E. P. Sanders has shown what is central to Jews is the covenant, which is initiated by Yahweh and reflects Yahweh's loving mercy. The law is given by Yahweh, and Jews strive to obey the law not out of "petty legalism" but out of gratitude to God for the covenant. For further discussion, see ch. 22.

9. Schwager, *Jesus in the Drama*, 55. Emphasis added.

10. Schwager, *Jesus in the Drama*, 56. Emphasis added.

11. Girard, *Reading the Bible*, 48; Girard, *Things Hidden*, 178; Schwager, *Must There Be Scapegoats*, 140–43.

the tenants. Finally, the landowner sent his own son, thinking "they will respect my son." But the tenants collectively "seized him, threw him out of the vineyard, and killed him." In Matthew's version, Jesus then asks his listeners what will happen when the owner of the vineyard comes, and they answer, "He will put those wretches to a miserable death" (Matt 21:41).[12]

In all three Synoptics, Jesus offers the verse from Ps 118 as a summary and interpretation of the parable. Spoken at the climax of his public ministry, the parable indicates that Jesus expected to suffer the same violent fate as the prophets and servants of God before him. The "stone that the builders rejected" will suffer a collective murder, with all the tenants participating—a clear example of the scapegoat mechanism. But the rejected stone will become the keystone of a new order, and this will be "the Lord's doing . . . amazing in our eyes." *This* scapegoat incident will bring something new. Schwager comments:

> If the parable served to sum up the whole dispute between Jesus and his opponents, then the concluding reference [to Ps 118] brings the parable to its ultimate significance. It is as if the passage about the rejected stone sums up the gospel. Thus it gains a central hermeneutic significance; it does indeed serve as a "keyword." . . . What constitutes the special hermeneutical value of the passage about the rejected stone is that if the parable sees in the material greed of the tenants the reason for the son's murder, the interpreting Psalm goes further. It shows that is it precisely through the rejection of the son that the hidden truth becomes visible. *[Their] collective blindness serves the process of revelation.*[13]

Further evidence for the importance of this interpretation comes from elsewhere in the New Testament. In Acts 4: 9–12, Peter, addressing the Sanhedrin, quotes this verse from Ps 118. He explicitly links the builders who reject the stone to Israel's religious authorities, and the rejected stone to Jesus. And in 1 Pet 2:4–8, in a dense passage weaving together several Old Testament references to stones, the author speaks of the cornerstone (Isa 28:16) and warns that "the stone that the builders rejected"

---

12. In Mark's and Luke's version, it is Jesus himself who says that the tenants will receive the landowner's vengeance, whereas in Matthew, this conclusion comes from the listeners.

13. Schwager, *Must There Be Scapegoats*, 141. Emphasis in original.

(Ps 118:22–23) will become "the stone that makes them stumble, the rock that makes them fall" (1 Pet 2:8; Isa 8:14).

In 1 Peter, the builders who reject the stone are not just the religious authorities ("the Jews") but "mortals" and "those who do not believe." Schwager comments, "This leads to the conclusion that the high priests, scribes and Pharisees of the synoptic Gospels and the people of Israel in Acts stand for all nonbelieving men and women. . . . The First Letter of Peter uses the same saying [from Ps 118] to refer to the behavior of all."[14] The stone is rejected by all—not just the religious leaders, not just Israel, but *all mortals*.

With an understanding of mimetic theory and informed by our exploration of specific Hebrew texts, we are now in a position to summarize our findings on Jesus's use of the Hebrew Scriptures. Jesus quoted the Scriptures frequently but selectively (as everyone does), conspicuously omitting references to God's vengeance. In continuity with the Hebrew prophets, he emphasizes the matter of collective violence (the scapegoat mechanism), foretelling that he himself will become "the stone that the builders reject." Somewhat in tension with the prophets, his preaching of the kingdom of God emphasizes God's generosity, grace, and forgiveness, rather than God's vengeance and wrath. References to judgment can at least partly be attributed to the self-judgment that comes from rejecting God's free offer of grace. And in the long-running dispute about the proper role of sacrifice, Jesus sides with the prophets, twice quoting Hosea: "Go and learn what this means: I desire mercy, and not sacrifice" (Matt 9:13; 12:7).

---

14. Schwager, *Must There Be Scapegoats*, 143.

9

Casting Stones

Let him that is among you without sin, cast the first stone at her.

—John 8:7 GNV

IN THE PREVIOUS CHAPTER, we looked at an incident in Luke 4, at the very beginning of Jesus's ministry, where a plain reading of the text suggests that something akin to a stoning nearly happened to Jesus. The Gospel of John briefly alludes to two other incidents where Jesus's opponents "took up stones again to stone him" (8:59; 10:31), but he either "hid himself" (8:59) or "escaped from their hands" (10:39), because his "time had not yet come" (7:6).

In perhaps the best-known biblical incident of near stoning, Jesus is not the target of a mob but rather the one who intervenes to avert a stoning. The incident, recounted in John 8:2–11,[1] is well known, but briefly: Jesus is teaching in the temple when the authorities bring to him a woman "caught in the very act of adultery." They point out that the law of

---

1. According to the NRSV textual notes, the earliest manuscripts do not include the story, and other early manuscripts place it elsewhere in John, or even in Luke. It may represent an independent early oral tradition that simply was too good a story to leave out of the Gospels, even if none of the writers knew it. Again, in this work I am primarily concerned with the text as we have it and less concerned with whether a specific text can reliably be traced back to the events of Jesus's life.

Moses "commanded us to stone such women," and, in order to test him, ask, "What do you say?" Jesus replies with one of the more memorable lines in the Gospels: "Let anyone among you who is without sin be the first to throw a stone at her." One by one, her accusers drift away.

Feminist scholars have pointed out all kinds of problems with the way this story is told.[2] "The law of Moses commanded us to stone such women"; what the law of Moses actually says is that "both the adulterer and the adulteress shall be put to death" (Lev 20:10; Deut 22:22). If the woman was truly "caught in the very act," why was her co-adulterer not also brought forward? According to tradition, there must be two witnesses to a capital crime, and these two witnesses initiate the execution by throwing the first stones. It is not clear who the witnesses are or even if they are present. Finally, this is a prominent example of the biblical text's tendency to preferentially scapegoat women for perceived sexual crimes, over the transgressions of men (sexual or otherwise).

Even allowing for all this, what is clear is that there is a mob thirsting for blood. Jesus himself is in a difficult position; if he forbids the stoning, the authorities will accuse him of disobeying the law of Moses. On the other hand, one wrong move in such a highly charged atmosphere could signal for the stoning to commence. Girard says that at this point, "the *first stone* is the *last obstacle* that prevents the stoning"; once the first stone is cast, we can be sure that others will imitatively follow.[3] Jesus kneels and writes with his finger in the sand, deflecting the crowd's attention away from the woman. When Jesus finally stands to speak, he explicitly calls attention to the first stone: "Let anyone among you who is without sin be the first to throw a stone at her." Jennifer Brashaw comments: "Jesus has shifted the accusations of the crowd away from the scapegoat and onto themselves. . . . The accusers, once united in a threatening mob, slowly disappear from view . . . no longer an intimidating force demanding death but now individuals distracted by their own guilt rather than obsessed with the guilt of another."[4]

Against all odds, Jesus has successfully defused a mimetic mob intent on scapegoating violence. Girard goes on to compare this incident from the Gospel with another incident described in ancient literature, an incident with a very different outcome.

---

2. See, e.g., Bashaw, *Scapegoats*, 65–78.
3. Girard, *I See Satan Fall*, 56. Emphasis added.
4. Bashaw, *Scapegoats*, 74.

Apollonius was a second-century wandering sage and miracle worker. Most of what we know about him comes from *Life of Apollonius of Tyana*, a biography written in the following century by the Greek author Philostratus. Apollonius's biographer clearly knew the Christian Gospels and thought the contrast between Apollonius and Christ was much to Apollonius's advantage: "Among the pagans, his miracles were viewed as superior to those of Jesus."[5] In Philostratus's telling, Apollonius's birth was accompanied by "unusual divine signs in the heavens." As an adult, he became an itinerant teacher and "gathered a number of followers around him who became convinced that he was no ordinary human, but the Son of God." He performed many healing miracles, including casting out demons. Eventually, he aroused the opposition of the Roman authorities, was put on trial, and was executed. After his death, he appeared to some of his followers, who were convinced that his soul had ascended to heaven.[6]

Perhaps Apollonius's most spectacular miracle was his healing of an unspecified plague in Ephesus. After their own attempts failed, the Ephesians summoned Apollonius. From Philostratus' account:

> "Take courage, for I will today put a stop to the course of the disease." And with these words he led the entire population to the theatre ... and there he saw what seemed an old mendicant artfully blinking his eyes as if blind, and he carried a wallet and a crust of bread in it; and he was clad in rags and was very squalid of countenance. Apollonius therefore arranged the Ephesians around him and said: "Pick up as many stones as you can and hurl them at this enemy of the gods." Now the Ephesians wondered what he meant, and were shocked at the idea of murdering a stranger so manifestly miserable; for he was begging and praying for them to take mercy upon him. Nevertheless Apollonius insisted and egged on the Ephesians to launch themselves on him and not let him go. And as soon as some of them began to take shots and hit him with their stones, the beggar who had seemed to blink and be blind, gave them all a sudden glance and showed that his eyes were full of fire. Then the Ephesians recognized that he was a demon, and they stoned him so thoroughly that their stones were heaped into a great cairn around

---

5. Girard, *I See Satan Fall*, 49. For the comparison of Apollonius with Jesus, see Ehrman, *How Jesus Became God*, 15–18.

6. Ehrman, *How Jesus Became God*, 11–15. Ehrman uses the example of Philostratus to illustrate that in the ancient world the idea of the divine man was not unique to Jesus. Tellingly, he does not mention the stoning at Ephesus.

him. After a little pause, Apollonius bade them remove the stones.... When therefore they had exposed the object which they thought they had thrown their missiles at, they found that he had disappeared and instead of him there was a hound who resembled in form and look a Molossian dog, but was in size the equal of the largest lion; there he lay before their eyes, pounded to a pulp by their stones and vomiting foam as mad dogs do.[7]

Philostratus evidently expected his readers to be impressed by this wonder. We, however, are appalled at his "horrible miracle."[8] Hearing this story from the perspective of the Gospels, we see (even if unconsciously) something that the ancient pagans could not: collective "sacred violence" against an innocent victim, the use of *good* violence to drive out *bad* violence.

It is hard to imagine a more definitive description of a scapegoat incident than Philostratus's account: a crisis (the plague), the identification of a marginalized victim (the blind beggar), the all-against-one violence of the mob (by stoning), and especially the overt dehumanization and demonization of an innocent victim. Furthermore, Girard comments that "the plague of Ephesus is not necessarily bacterial." Philostratus' account of the stoning is preceded by a description of rampant rivalry and disorder in the city. "It is an epidemic of mimetic rivalries, an interweaving of scandals, a war of *all against all*, which, thanks to the victim selected by the diabolical cleverness of Apollonius, is transformed 'miraculously' into a reconciliation of *all against one*."[9] The plague abates.

In comparing these two incidents, it becomes clear that Jesus in the encounter with the adulterous woman plays a role directly opposite that of Apollonius. "Apollonius's achievement is to incite the throwing of the first stone, and thus the unanimous violence. Jesus's achievement is to prevent it."[10] But at a deeper level, both incidents are about mimesis, the power of contagious imitation. Once Jesus convinces the first elder to walk away without casting a stone, the spell is broken and others follow suit. And once Philostratus convinces the reluctant Ephesians to *throw*

---

7. Quoted in Girard, *I See Satan Fall*, 49–50. Molossian dogs were a mastiff-type breed, noted for their fierceness and associated with the Bronze Age Molossus tribe of northwestern Greece.

8. Girard, *I See Satan Fall*, 49. The title of his ch. 4 is "The Horrible Miracle of Apollonius of Tyana."

9. Girard, *I See Satan Fall*, 53. Emphasis in original.

10. Heim, *Saved from Sacrifice*, 132.

the first stone, the others follow. As we will see in part 3, everything depends on the model we choose to imitate.

The comparison of the stoning at Ephesus with the averted stoning in John 8 is instructive, but Girard underscores that "the stoning of the beggar should also make us think of the Crucifixion. . . . The Cross is the equivalent of the Ephesus stoning. To say that Jesus identifies himself with all victims is to say he identifies himself not only with the adulterous woman or the suffering servant but also with the beggar of Ephesus. Jesus *is* this poor wretch of a beggar."[11]

In the process of stoning the blind beggar, "the Ephesians recognized that he was a demon." We turn now to an account of Jesus's own encounter with demons.

---

11. Girard, *I See Satan Fall*, 60–61.

10

Casting Out Demons

> But if it is by the Spirit of God that I cast out demons,
> then the kingdom of God has come upon you.
>
> —Matt 12:28 RSV

The stories of Jesus's miraculous healings, especially by casting out demons, are for many of us the single most challenging aspect of the Gospels. On this specific point, we cannot avoid the great gulf that separates the New Testament worldview from our own; these stories offend modern sensibilities.[1] The most spectacular of these stories is that of the Gerasene demoniac, told in all three Synoptic Gospels (Mark 5:1–20; Matt 8:28–34; Luke 8:26–39). This episode serves as a "test case" for our reading of the Bible: if mimetic theory can shed light on this enigmatic episode, then the case for its explanatory power will be greatly strengthened.

One way to understand demon possession is to view it as the psychological correlate to colonial occupation. Just as a colonial power comes in from outside and takes away a nation's self-governance, so too a demon is an unwelcome power that "invades" the personality, taking away the individual's agency. Under this reading, it is no wonder that

---

1. Girard, *Scapegoat*, 167.

demon possession is so common in Roman-occupied Galilee. That connection is made explicit in this episode, when the demon reveals its name as "Legion"—the designation for a Roman army regiment. The Roman military occupation certainly provides the background for this story, but Girard's reading goes well beyond this conventional understanding.

The key to a mimetic interpretation of the story of the Gerasene demoniac is to see its social aspect, and specifically to recognize that the demoniac plays the role of Gerasa's *scapegoat*. As James Warren comments, "Gospel texts are structured by the scapegoat mechanism and the victim, *even when these are not explicitly mentioned in the texts*."[2] What seems to be a straightforward (indeed, somewhat primitive) exorcism story turns out to be anything but.

For the Gerasenes, their demoniac seems to function like the town drunk or lunatic. They are good *because* he is bad; they are sane *because* he is crazy. Luke's account says, "For many times [the unclean spirit] had seized him: he was kept under guard and bound with chains and shackles, but he would break the bonds and be driven by the demons into the wild" (Luke 8:29). It beggars belief that a few sturdy men would not be able to restrain even the most violent individual or that stronger chains and shackles could not be found. The townspeople's efforts to restrain the demoniac seem to be half-hearted, suggesting that he plays some useful function for them. Instead of the usual stoning or once-and-done expulsion, *this* scapegoat is allowed to continue in an ongoing but unresolved relationship with the townspeople. We have every reason to suspect that the Gerasenes' treatment of their demoniac has become the glue that holds them together. *He is their scapegoat.*

But if the town needs the scapegoat, the scapegoat also needs the town. He reacts with genuine dismay when Jesus commands the unclean spirit to leave him. His role as the town scapegoat has become his identity; better to have this negative role than to have no role. He has internalized the punishment typically inflicted by a scapegoating mob. The text says he "was always howling and bruising himself with stones" (Mark 5:5); he was in effect *stoning himself*, or as Girard says, practicing "autolapidation."[3]

---

2. Warren, *Compassion or Apocalypse*, 242. Emphasis in original. My discussion of the Gerasene demoniac draws on Girard, *Scapegoat*, 165–83; Warren, *Compassion or Apocalypse*, 242–55, esp. 244; Alison, *Jesus the Forgiving Victim*, 273–80.

3. Girard, *Scapegoat*, 170.

When Jesus asks the name of the unclean spirit, the demoniac replies with a puzzling transition from singular to plural: "*My* name is Legion, for *we* are many." Just as in Matthew's account, the "whole town" will later come "as one" to "beg [Jesus] to leave their neighborhood" (Matt 8:34), so here Legion is one but also many. Indeed, as a demon who is both one and many, Legion is "the mirror image" of the city. "Legion is the satanic principle of the scapegoat mechanism, which is the very structuring principle of Gerasene society."[4]

The demon/demons sense that they cannot continue to exist in the presence of Jesus—"Son of the Most High God," as Legion addresses him (Mark 5:7). He (they) "begged him earnestly not to send them out of the country" (Mark 5:10) or, as Luke puts it, "not to order them back to the abyss" (Luke 8:31). So they beseeched Jesus to send them instead into "a great herd of swine" grazing on the hillside, and Jesus "gave them permission" (Mark 5:12–13).

So we have a whole legion of demons, mirroring the mimetic contagion of the Geresenes and now residing in a large herd of pigs. If the pigs had been human, they might have identified their own "scape-pig" to expel or force over the cliff and thus restore order. But because they are pigs and not humans, that option is not available to them, so "they all imitate each other in a frenzy, without any braking mechanism," rushing over the cliff to their demise.[5]

As in the episode from Luke 4, we note the symbolic meaning of plunging off a cliff: it is a common motif of collective murder, the equivalent of stoning. But this time, it is not the individual scapegoat (the demoniac or an individual "scape-pig") who goes off the cliff, but the mob, "Legion." Scapegoating violence has undergone a "subversion from within." Warren emphasizes the significance of this reversal:

> The text reveals the picture of a herd of pigs charging over a cliff and falling into the sea—the same thing that had happened countless times in the ancient world to countless victims of mob violence. The real excitement of Jesus's miracle, therefore, is that *for the first time in history it is the crowd, the mob, that is cast over the cliff, while the scapegoat goes free!* Rather than the scapegoat being cast out of the city, the city is cast out of the scapegoat, who now sits there "clothed and in his right mind." . . . The man who had been the legion, who had been the victim of the crowd, is

---

4. Warren, *Compassion or Apocalypse*, 247.
5. Alison, *Jesus the Forgiving Victim*, 276–77.

restored and healed, while the mob has unraveled, becoming a trampling chaos that undid itself by the force of its own violence.[6]

The story ends with the healed demoniac asking to accompany Jesus back across the Sea of Galilee. But Jesus refuses and says to him, "Go home to your friends, and tell them how much the Lord has done for you, and what mercy he has shown you" (Mark 5:19). We are given no further details—but we can well imagine that the healed demoniac would have been an unsettling presence in Gerasa, a constant reminder of the town's failed attempt at overcoming their disorder through scapegoating. All this anticipates what will happen in a few years, when the nascent Christian church ventures into gentile territory. James Warren comments that "the voice of the healed demoniac will continue to act like a thorn in Gerasene flesh, a herald of things to come . . . proclaiming the good news about a new way of being human, which understands life from the perspective of the victim, not the persecutor."[7]

In elucidating the role of Satan and his demons in the Gospels, Girard and his followers attribute outsized importance to another, earlier incident in Mark's Gospel. The story appears in all three Synoptic Gospels (Mark 3:21–27; Matt 12:22–29; Luke 11:14–23); here I quote Mark's version in full:

> When [Jesus's] family heard it, they went out to restrain him, for people were saying, "He has gone out of his mind." And the scribes who came down from Jerusalem said, "He has Beelzebul, and by the ruler of the demons he casts out demons." And he called them to him, and spoke to them in parables, "How can Satan cast out Satan? If a kingdom is divided against itself, that kingdom cannot stand. And if a house is divided against itself, that house will not be able to stand. And if Satan has risen up against himself and is divided, he cannot stand, but his end has come. But no one can enter a strong man's house and plunder his property without first tying up the strong man; then indeed the house can be plundered." (Mark 3:21–27)

The crucial question here is "How can Satan cast out Satan?" We tend to read that question as rhetorical, implying that of course Satan does not cast out Satan; otherwise his kingdom would be divided and "cannot stand." But Jesus is claiming that Satan's "end has come"; casting

---

6. Warren, *Compassion or Apocalypse*, 250–51. Emphasis in original.

7. Warren, *Compassion or Apocalypse*, 252–53. Warren credits a lecture by James Alison for these insights.

out demons is a demonstration of Jesus's superior power. Satan is the strong man and the demons are his property, but Jesus is about to "bind the strong man" and plunder his house (3:27 KJV).

What if Jesus is actually asking a different question: "*How is it* that Satan is able to cast out Satan; how does that work?" Rather than arguing that it is impossible for Satan to cast out Satan, "Jesus actually accepts the premise."[8] Girard elaborates:

> The true mystery of Satan, of his astonishing power, is that of expelling himself and bringing order back to human communities.... Accusing a rival exorcist of expelling demons by the power of Satan must have been a common accusation in that period.... Jesus wants to make his hearers reflect on its implications. If it is true that Satan expels Satan, how does he go about it?... Jesus does not deny the reality of Satan's self-expulsion; *he asserts it*. The proof that Satan possesses this power is the affirmation, frequently repeated, that this power is coming to an end. The imminent fall of Satan, prophesied by Christ, is one and the same thing as the end of his power of self-expulsion.[9]

So how does *Satan* cast out *Satan*? Girard notes that by repeating the word "Satan" a second time, instead of a pronoun, the text is emphasizing "the fundamental paradox" of Satan: he is the principle of both disorder and order.[10] As the personification of mimetic contagion, Satan sows disorder by arousing mimetic rivalries that threaten the community with "all-against-all" chaos and violence. But Satan is also "the accuser" who incites the scapegoat mechanism, transforming the disorder of "all-against-all" into the restored order of "all-against-one." By redirecting violence to a single innocent victim, Satan the accuser casts out Satan the sower of discord. In the midst of disorder, Satan "suddenly brings [it] to an end by expelling disorder.... Satan expels Satan by means of innocent victims whom he succeeds in having condemned. Satan is the master of the single victim mechanism, and so he is the master of human culture, whose origin is none other than this act of murder."[11]

Commenting on Girard, James Williams says that "in the language of the Gospels... this entire single victim process [the scapegoat

---

8. Heim, *Saved from Sacrifice*, 151.
9. Girard, *I See Satan Fall*, 34.
10. Girard, *I See Satan Fall*, 34.
11. Girard, *I See Satan Fall*, 87.

mechanism] is the work of Satan. *Indeed, it is Satan.*"[12] Girard says that "Satan has no actual being.... Christianity does not oblige us to see him as someone who actually exists."[13] Jesus himself describes his discourse about "Satan casting out Satan" as "a parable" (Mark 3:23). But by personifying Satan, the New Testament language serves to highlight the very real power of mimetic contagion and the victimary mechanism. Satan may not exist, but he is still the "ruler of this world," who is about to be "driven out" (John 12:31).

We turn now to the climactic event in that drama, the Gospel account of the passion and crucifixion.

---

12. James Williams, in Girard, *I See Satan Fall*, xii. Emphasis in original.
13. Girard, *I See Satan Fall*, 45.

11

Crucifixion as Revelation

> It is a collective murder if ever there was one. Jesus is obviously a scapegoat.
>
> —René Girard[1]

WE WILL HAVE MORE to say about Jesus's ministry in the next chapter and in part 3, but we come now to the cornerstone of our argument, "the stone that the builders rejected" (Ps 118:22): the events of the last week of Jesus's life, culminating in his crucifixion.

For Christians, the cross has significance as both *revelation* and *salvation*. These two aspects are of course connected: the cross saves precisely by revealing "things hidden since the foundation of the world" (Matt 13:35).[2] For Girard, the cross definitively reveals or unveils the scapegoat mechanism, which he argues is the hidden foundation of all human culture. In the Hebrew texts we have examined up to this point, the scapegoat mechanism is only obliquely or implicitly criticized, but here it is directly confronted.

After his triumphal entry into Jerusalem, riding on a humble donkey rather than a warhorse, Jesus instigated an action in the temple,

1. Girard, *Reading the Bible*, 48.
2. Not coincidentally, the title of Girard's major work, *Things Hidden*.

symbolically striking at the very heart of the sacrificial system. He taught "day after day" in the temple, including a series of rhetorical confrontations with the religious authorities. But his position rapidly became untenable.

He was betrayed by Judas (Mark 14:10–11), then abandoned by the rest of the disciples (Mark 14:50). Peter, perhaps his closest disciple, denied him not once but three times (Mark 14:66–72). Before the Jewish authorities, Jesus was accused of the highest *religious* crime of blasphemy (Matt 26:65–66). Before Pilate, he was accused of the highest *political* crime of sedition (Luke 23:2–3). "The crowd," which just days before had greeted him with adulation, now chose the violent insurrectionist Barabbas over Jesus (Mark 15:6–15). He was mocked, flogged, and tortured by the Roman soldiers (Mark 15:16–20; Matt 27:26–31). The Gospels, written decades later when it would have been prudent to avoid antagonizing Rome, are somewhat muted in this, but it is ultimately the Romans who executed Jesus. Crucifixion would have been available only to the Roman authorities, reserved for rebellious slaves or those guilty of insurrection against the empire. All four Gospels testify to the ironic inscription above the cross, "Jesus of Nazareth, the King of the Jews" (John 19:19).

Girard comments: "Jesus in not killed by the Romans alone, or by the Jewish priests alone, or by the crowd alone, but by everybody. It is a collective murder if ever there was one. Jesus is obviously a scapegoat."[3] As such, the passion account has the structure of countless myths before and since, but with one crucial difference: the Gospels clearly and repeatedly proclaim Jesus's innocence. The good thief (Luke 23:41), the centurion (Luke 23:47), a repentant Judas (Matt 27:3–4), even Pilate (Luke 23:4) all testify to Jesus's innocence. For the scapegoating dynamic to succeed, it must be unanimous. But as the passion narrative unfolds, there are immediate cracks in that unanimity, and of course with the resurrection the nascent Christian community becomes an outspoken dissenting minority.[4]

Caiaphas speaks for "the powers that be" throughout history: "It is better for you to have one man die for the people than to have the whole nation destroyed" (John 11:50). It would be difficult to articulate a more precise description of the "logic" of scapegoating. Jesus, like thousands before and since, was executed by the state, in the name of public order, to prevent "a riot that was beginning" (Matt 27:24). But in the crucifixion,

---

3. Girard, *Reading the Bible*, 48.

4. These three paragraphs borrow heavily from a previous article: Gates, "New Light on Atonement."

the scapegoat mechanism is decisively unmasked and revealed for what it is: unjustified human violence against an innocent victim. At least in this sense, Jesus can be said to have "died for our sins." Mark Heim summarizes this view:

> As surely as Jesus came between Barabbas and the cross, Jesus's death on the cross comes between us and one specific evil to which we are collectively in thrall, scapegoating sacrifice. . . . The death of Jesus set in motion a very concrete historical effect, the unveiling and undermining of sacrifice. Christ died for us, to save us from what killed him. And what killed him was not God's justice but our "redemptive violence." . . . Christ died for us to stop us from having people die for us. Scapegoats die for us because we make peace that way. Christ became one of those scapegoats and died so that we could live without them. . . . Jesus became a scapegoat for us, but Jesus is not our scapegoat.[5]

Going forward from the crucifixion, Girard says that the passion account will now "contaminate all scapegoats," as we discover that "all collective victims must be a little bit similar to Christ. . . . The Gospel undermines scapegoating."[6] As the scapegoating mechanism gradually becomes more visible, it also loses its effectiveness. Elsewhere Girard writes:

> What God demands is not a sacrifice of his son, not a perfect scapegoat, but *the unconditional refusal of scapegoating*, even if the price must be death, even if this very refusal, in a world such as ours, inevitably entails that we must be scapegoated. . . . In the long run, the hiddenness of scapegoating is everywhere uncovered and its power to persuade is gradually undermined.[7]

Thus, the cross functions first and foremost as *revelation*. At the moment of Jesus's death "the curtain of the temple was torn in two, from top to bottom" (Matt 27:51; Luke 23:45). This was probably never meant to be understood literally, but the symbolism is unmistakable. The temple curtain separated the innermost chamber of the temple from the people. Its tearing would have revealed for all to see: the holy of holies was empty. With Jesus's death on the cross, sacred violence is revealed to be an empty chamber. There is no divine being demanding blood but only mundane human violence.

---

5. Heim, *Saved from Sacrifice*, 305–7.
6. Girard, *Reading the Bible*, 76.
7. René Girard, in Williams, *Bible, Violence, and Sacred*, vi–vii. Emphasis added.

James Warren offers a useful parallel from *The Wizard of Oz*. When Dorothy and her companions return with the broom of the Wicked Witch, the wizard still resists their requests. As they cower before "the Great and Powerful Oz," Dorothy's dog Toto slips off to the side and pulls the curtain open, revealing a mere human manipulating knobs and levers and speaking into a microphone. "Pay no attention to that man behind the curtain," implores the terrifying image on the screen, but it is too late: the spell has been broken.[8] Likewise, the crucifixion breaks the spell of sacred violence.

Perhaps an analogy from real life would be helpful. On Memorial Day 2020, George Floyd was killed in the custody of the Minneapolis police. Anyone who had been paying attention should have known that this kind of police violence has been happening for decades, but something was different this time. With the stark and brutal video of Floyd's life ebbing away at the hands of a seemingly unfeeling officer, tens of millions of White Americans viscerally understood what they had not before. With that image, what became undeniable was not only the violence that African Americans continue to endure at the hands of police but also the countless ways in which structural racism has infected the soul of our nation. In a matter of days, tens of millions of Americans of all races took to the streets to express their outrage, in perhaps the largest civic protest in our history. With our hopelessly polarized politics, this movement eventually provoked a furious backlash. Two things can be true at the same time: with George Floyd's murder, something had irreversibly changed, and *at the same time*, our mimetic and scapegoating tendency remains with us.

As mentioned in the prologue, the African American theologian James Cone has written that "the cross and the lynching tree interpret each other."[9] To the extent that George Floyd's death was comparable to a lynching, let us examine how his death and the passion might interpret each other.

In the aftermath of Floyd's death, as the movement in his memory gathered momentum, his six-year-old daughter reportedly said, "My daddy changed the world." Undeniably, America's awakening to the reality of structural racism is a good thing. Does that mean that his death

---

8. Warren, *Compassion or Apocalypse*, 231–32.

9. Cone, *Cross and Lynching Tree*, 161. As mentioned in the prologue, n10, xvi, Cone acknowledges Girard as one of the very few scholars who have recognized this link between the cross and the lynching tree (171).

was itself good or that God permitted or even directed his death, in order to accomplish this good thing? Of course not: we intuitively understand that evil deeds can, contrary to their intention, ultimately lead to positive consequences.

In a similar way, we can see that the eventual consequences of Jesus's passion do not lessen the evil of his crucifixion. And we should be emphatic in rejecting the proposition that God intended, directed, or demanded Jesus's violent death. As Mark Heim says, the Gospels portray Jesus's death as "the good bad thing": Scripture affirms that "Jesus is supposed to die," that he goes "as it is written" in prophecy, that his death is necessary and inevitable, while *at the same time* "the Gospels are emphatic that Jesus is innocent, falsely accused, that his killing is unjust, that it is shameful for his friends to abandon him, that those who try and execute him are indifferent to truth, captive to evil."[10]

We have seen how the circumstances of Jesus's execution can be interpreted as a revelation of the scapegoat mechanism. But our larger concern throughout part 1 has been to demonstrate how Scripture works to undermine deeply entrenched beliefs about sacred violence, representing a "subversion from within."[11] It is therefore instructive to further examine just how deeply Jesus's actions seem to be influenced by an intentional "anti-violence" agenda, consistent with his earlier teachings about the kingdom of God.

In all four Gospel accounts of Jesus's triumphal entry into Jerusalem, Jesus is said to come mounted on a donkey or a colt; in both Matthew and John, this is explicitly tied to a verse from the prophet Zechariah. The actual text from Zechariah reads, "Lo, your king comes to you; triumphal and victorious, humble and riding on a donkey, on a colt, the foal of a donkey" (Zech 9:9). Neither Matthew or John continues the quotation: "He will cut off the chariot from Ephraim and the war-horse from Jerusalem; and the battle bow shall be cut off, and he shall command peace to the nations" (Zech 9:10). The king coming on a donkey evokes peace, the end of war.

New Testament scholars Marcus Borg and John Dominic Crossan speculate that on the same day and perhaps even at the very hour when Jesus was entering Jerusalem from the east, the Roman governor Pilate would have been entering Jerusalem from the west. He would have been

---

10. Heim, *Saved from Sacrifice*, 106–7.

11. On Alison's use of the phrase "subversion from within," see prologue, n8, xv. Alison, *Raising Abel*, 32–33, 96, 107, 138, 140.

mounted on a warhorse and leading a contingent of Roman troops from Caesarea, to reinforce the Roman garrison in Jerusalem in anticipation of possible trouble during Passover.[12] Jesus sent two disciples ahead to find a colt, ready and waiting in the next village. This is sometimes taken as an illustration of Jesus's clairvoyant power, but the incident instead suggests a planned and prearranged "counter procession," complete with secret passwords (Mark 11:3–6). As Pilate entered Jerusalem with all the military trappings of empire, Jesus entered, "humble and riding on a donkey," to proclaim the peaceful kingdom of God.

Many New Testament scholars consider the subsequent "temple incident" to provide the crucial context for Jesus's final week; a "Rosetta stone" that functions not only to interpret subsequent events, but also to suggest something of Jesus's intentions.[13] After scouting out the temple on Palm Sunday (Mark 11:8), Jesus returned the next day to carry out what can be only described as "nonviolent direct action." He disrupted the "money changers" and "those who sold doves"; John's account says that he made a "whip of cords" and used it to drive out "both the sheep and the cattle" (John 2:13–15).[14] On at least a symbolic level, it is clear that Jesus's intent was to stop the temple sacrifices.[15] The Gospel accounts seem somewhat hesitant to acknowledge this, so instead focus on the commercial aspect of buying and selling. But it is important to recognize that the work of the money changers and merchants was completely legitimate; their activities were an essential and accepted part of the sacrificial enterprise.

Because the temple complex was huge, covering many acres, Jesus could not possibly have prevented all sacrificial activity. "A continuous blocking of the sacrifices would have required an army, but Jesus's action *signified* the same thing."[16] The meaning of Jesus's action in the temple would not have been lost on either the authorities or the people. In

---

12. Borg and Crossan, *Last Week*, locs. 113–164 of 3354. Pilate was permanently stationed in Caesarea on the coast, but it is well documented that he often traveled to Jerusalem, esp. at the time of major festivals.

13. Bartlett, *Signs of Change*, 220.

14. John's Gospel places the incident in the temple at the beginning of Jesus's ministry, not the end. John A. T. Robinson argues for the historical validity of John's general outline of Jesus's ministry (including multiple trips to Jerusalem); it is possible that there were two separate temple incidents (*Priority of John*).

15. Bartlett, *Signs of Change*, 218–21. Borg and Crossan make essentially the same point (*Last Week*, locs. 817–829 of 3354).

16. Bartlett, *Signs of Change*, 220. Emphasis added.

late–Second Temple Judaism, there was a widespread belief that Herod's Temple needed to be restored to its original purity and that the first step in this purification would be the cessation of sacrifices. Furthermore, the predicted restoration of the temple came with the expectation of violence. The Essene War Scroll, dating from this same period, anticipates a seven-stage battle involving both men and angels, at the conclusion of which the temple would be restored and purified. "The goal of the [violent] apocalyptic conflict is restoration of the Temple, *and the latter does not happen without the former.*"[17]

In popular expectation, if the sacrifices were suspended, "that meant that the war had already begun"; Jesus was "detonating an anthropological timebomb."[18] But Jesus seems to have quite intentionally severed the connection between his actions in the temple and any hint of violence, apocalyptic or otherwise. Three days later, he will not resist but meekly submit to arrest. He rebukes the disciple who tries to defend him with a sword. He rejects the suggestion of apocalyptic violence: "Are you not aware that I can call on my Father, and he will at once put at my disposal twelve lesions of angels? But how then would the scriptures be fulfilled?" (Matt 26:53). Jesus's action in the temple was "a *sign*, an enacted parable" but without any trace of reciprocal violence or vengeance.[19] "Effectively, Jesus had announced the end of the temple but without provoking sectarian 'apocalyptic' violence, rather *bringing that violence down on himself.* Jesus consumed the 'cup of wrath' not as any kind of appeasement, but—as the image more radically suggests—to drain violence from human history."[20] Once again, we see a "subversion from within" of sacred violence, by Jesus's willingness to himself become the victim of violence.

It is worth noting that up to this point, the revelatory function of the cross—the definitive revelation of the scapegoat mechanism—has not depended on any theological assumptions. Following Girard, I have given a purely anthropological account; the passion and crucifixion can and should reveal the victimary mechanism to believers and nonbelievers alike. Girard elaborates:

17. Bartlett, *Signs of Change*, 222. Emphasis added. The Essenes were a Jewish sect who rejected the Jerusalem Temple and retreated to the desert to await its purification. We know of the Essenes primarily through the Dead Sea Scrolls, as well as the first-century Jewish historian Josephus. Some scholars hypothesize a connection between the Essenes and John the Baptist.

18. Bartlett, *Signs of Change*, 223.

19. Bartlett, *Signs of Change*, 224.

20. Bartlett, *Signs of Change*, 226. Emphasis added.

> From the anthropological aspect the Cross is the moment when a thousand mimetic conflicts, a thousand scandals that crash violently into one another during the crisis, converge against Jesus alone. . . . There is nothing in the Gospels to suggest that God causes the mob to come together against Jesus. Violent contagion is enough. Those responsible for the Passion are the human participants themselves, incapable of resisting the violent contagion that affects them all. . . . We don't have to invoke the supernatural to explicate this. The war of *all against all* that transforms communities into a war of *all against one* gathers and unifies them is not limited solely to the case of Jesus.[21]

In part 2, we will move beyond the realm of anthropology, by exploring accounts of the resurrection and the subsequent coming of the Spirit in the early church. But first, in the next chapter we will explore how Jesus's ministry during his life connects to the theme of scapegoats. Then in the following two chapters we ask if what we have learned thus far might inform our understanding of the experience of *conviction*, both for early Friends and for us.

---

21. Girard, *I See Satan Fall*, 21–22. Emphasis in original.

12

The Gospel of—and for— the Disinherited

> Christianity as it was born in the mind of [Jesus] appears as a technique of survival for the oppressed.... Wherever his spirit appears, the oppressed gather fresh courage; for he announced the good news that fear, hypocrisy, and hatred, the three hounds of hell that track the trail of the disinherited, need have no dominion over them.
>
> —Howard Thurman[1]

As will see in excursus 2, the church has tended to value the incarnation of God in Jesus solely from the standpoint of his *death*; put bluntly, the creeds imply that Jesus came to earth in order to die, and thereby "save" us. In the ancient Apostles Creed, there is only a simple comma that separates "born of the Virgin Mary" from "suffered under Pontius Pilate; was crucified, dead and buried," with no mention of *anything* about his ministry. Richard Rohr has called this *the Great Comma*: "Falling into that yawning gap, as if it were a mere detail, is *everything* Jesus said and did between his birth and death."[2]

1. Thurman, *Jesus and the Disinherited*, 29.
2. Rohr, *Universal Christ*, 103–4. Emphasis in original.

We have seen in the previous chapter how Jesus's passion and crucifixion can be viewed as a scapegoat incident gone awry. But before we leave the New Testament, and lest we commit the same error as the Creeds, we turn now to a fuller account of his ministry. As Jennifer Bashaw has argued, it is possible—and necessary—to read the Gospel accounts of Jesus's ministry through the eyes of victims. "The gospel story is a story *about* a victim, written *by* victims, and *featuring* victims. It is good news for victims; it is a scapegoat's gospel." However, it can be very difficult for us to recognize this, from our privileged position: "The Western church has been the victor for so long that we have stopped reading the Gospels from the victim's perspective."[3]

In recent decades, the various liberation theologies have begun to rectify this long-standing distortion, by lifting up individuals from various marginalized groups who play important roles in the gospel. Whether or not they are aware of it, all of these liberation theologies trace their origin to Howard Thurman's seminal 1949 book, *Jesus and the Disinherited*. Thurman begins his book with these words: "Many and varied are the interpretations dealing with the teachings and life of Jesus of Nazareth. But few of these interpretations deal with what the teachings and life of Jesus have to say to those who stand, at a moment in human history, *with their backs against the wall*."[4]

Jennifer Bashaw begins her account of "the gospel through the eyes of victims" (the subtitle of her book) with an examination of the prominent role of women in the Gospels. This is especially noticeable in Luke's Gospel, with forty-two passages about women, including twenty-three unique to his Gospel.[5]

Jesus's mother Mary is not only *Theotokos*, the mother of God, but a prophet in her own right (Luke 1:47–55). Bashaw engages in creative retelling of the stories of Mary, the widow of Nain (Luke 7:11–17), and the "sinful woman" who anoints Jesus (Luke 7:36–50), demonstrating that not only Jesus but also these women shatter stereotypes.[6]

We have already seen how Jesus intervened to save a woman from stoning, at some risk to himself (John 8; see ch. 9 above). There is also the story of Mary and Martha (Luke 10:38–42), which Bashaw describes

---

3. Bashaw, *Scapegoats*, 16. Emphasis in original.

4. Thurman, *Jesus and the Disinherited*, 11. Emphasis added. For the influence of Thurman, see Cone, *God of the Oppressed*, 29.

5. Bashaw, *Scapegoats*, 46. The section from 21–100 is called "Scapegoating Women."

6. Bashaw, *Scapegoats*, 39–64.

as "one of the most misinterpreted passages in the Gospels." Jesus affirms *both* Mary and Martha's roles, "expanding the roles of women with this story." Martha is faulted by Jesus not for performing her host role but only for her anxiety over "too many tasks."[7]

And then there is the remarkable story of Mary Magdalene. Diana Butler Bass, building on the work of New Testament scholar Elizabeth Schrader, shows how the story about the sisters Mary and Martha in John 11 is actually a story about Mary, Lazarus's sister (and not the Mary of Mary and Martha in Luke 10). "Martha" apparently was added to the story by an editor of Papyrus 66, the oldest version of John's Gospel that we have. The original manuscript makes it clear that there was only one sister, named Mary, and it is this Mary, not "Martha," who makes one of only two "Christological confessions" in the Gospels: "You are the Messiah, the Son of God, the one coming into the world" (John 11:27). And *this* sister is very likely Mary Magdalene, one of the Mary's at the cross (John 19:25), the Mary who was the first witness to the resurrection (John 20:11–18), Mary who became "the apostle to the apostles" by announcing that she had seen the Risen Christ.[8] This remarkable discovery has huge implications for our understanding of the role of Mary Magdalene, and for women generally, in the gospel story.

We could say more about Jesus's shattering of stereotypes and breaking of taboos around women in the gospel story: the menstrually impure woman who was healed when she touched Jesus's robe (Luke 8:43–48), the Syrophoenician woman who engaged with Jesus and convinced him to heal her daughter (Mark 7:24–30), and of course his extended conversation with the Samaritan woman at the well (John 4:7–30), who broke not just one but two taboos (against conversing with a man and with a Jew). Suffice to say that women, marginalized and often scapegoated from time immemorial, were given special prominence in the gospel stories—which makes them virtually unique in the canon of ancient literature.

Bashaw next turns her attention to gospel stories of those marginalized by illness or infirmity. Here she highlights Marks' Gospel, where roughly half of Jesus's encounters involve Jesus healing an illness or physical impairment.[9] Ancient societies generally attributed physical infirmity to an individual's sin, a kind of divine retribution for some moral

---

7. Bashaw, *Scapegoats*, 62, 64, 63.

8. Bass, "Mary the Tower," para. 1. The other Christological confession is of course from Peter, in all three Synoptic Gospels.

9. Bashaw, *Scapegoats*, 117.

failing. But Jesus "refutes this way of thinking" and the stigmatization to which it inevitably led. In both the healing of a paralytic (Mark 2:1–12) and the story of the man born blind (John 9), Jesus instead attributes infirmity to "Sin with a capital S—the evil at work in their environment, society, and world . . . and not this one man's sin."[10] The metaphorical significance of the healings is clear: "In the symbolic order of Judaism, illness was associated with impurity or sin, a state that meant exclusion from full status" in the community.[11] Once healed by Jesus, they were rendered worthy of reincorporation back into the community.

Mark's theme of healing ministry culminates in the stories of two blind men whose sight was restored by Jesus. These appear in Mark 8:22–25 and 10:46–52; the two healings bookend a series of incidents that highlight the disciples' misunderstanding of Jesus's mission. In the first story, there is a two-stage healing of an unnamed blind man. After the first attempt, he says, "I see people, but they look like trees, walking" (8:24). This partial healing seems to symbolize the disciples' only partial understanding. In the second stage, his sight was completely restored, foreshadowing that the disciples would eventually come to full understanding.

In the second healing, the final healing narrated by Mark, *this* blind man is named: Bartimaeus, son of Timaeus, "a blind beggar." When Jesus restores his sight, Bartimaeus proceeds to "follow him on the way." This blind beggar is not only named but is portrayed as a worthy disciple, perhaps even more "insightful" than the twelve. Bashaw comments: "People with sickness and impairments have emerged from the shadows, and Mark has drawn attention to their suffering—the poverty, exploitation, and invisibility they endure in society. . . . It is appropriate, then, that when Mark finally names one of these supplicants, he serves as the greatest example of a Jesus-follower."[12]

Like the prophets before him, Jesus taught that God had a special concern ("a preferential option") for the poor, who still today are often marginalized and blamed for their own poverty. This comes out most strongly in Luke's Gospel. Compared to Matthew, Luke's version of the Beatitudes (6:20–26) highlights the economics of the kingdom: "Blessed are you who are poor . . . are hungry now . . . who weep now . . . but woe

---

10. Bashaw, *Scapegoats*, 140–41.
11. Myers, *Binding the Strong Man*, 145.
12. Bashaw, *Scapegoats*, 148. Her discussion of the two healings is on 145–49.

to you who are rich now, who are full now."[13] Luke's Gospel has several direct warnings about the dangers of wealth and the necessary "reversal of fortunes" that will characterize God's reign. Jesus introduces the parable of the rich fool with this warning, "Take care! Be on your guard against all kinds of greed; for one's life does not consist in the abundance of possessions" (Luke 12:15), and ends the parable with "So it is with those who store up treasures for themselves but are not rich toward God" (12:21).

In his encounter with "a certain ruler" who asks what he must do to "inherit eternal life," Jesus teaches that following the commandments is not sufficient, but the rich ruler must "sell everything that you own and distribute the money to the poor." Jesus concludes: "How hard it is for those who have wealth to enter the kingdom of God" (Luke 18:18–25).

In Luke, Jesus's adage that "you cannot serve God and wealth" (16:13) serves as an introduction to the parable of the rich man and Lazarus, which vividly illustrates the reversal of fortune of the rich and the poor (Luke 16:19–31). In the story of the tax collector Zacchaeus (Luke 19:1–10), Jesus invites himself to dinner at Zacchaeus's home—and Zacchaeus responds by announcing that he will give half his possessions to the poor, and to anyone he has defrauded, he will pay back fourfold. It is this promise of redistribution and restitution of his ill-gained wealth, and not any confession of Jesus's messiahship, that causes Jesus to proclaim that "today salvation has come to this house."

In a discourse about "counting the cost," Jesus concludes by explicitly stating, "None of you can become my disciple if you do not give up all your possessions" (Luke 14:33). Bashaw comments, "Renunciation of wealth is the foundation of radical discipleship. . . . Discipleship without sacrifices and reversals is not discipleship at all."[14] These are difficult teachings, especially challenging to those of us who have benefitted from the current economic system.

The final category of marginalized or scapegoated persons to which the Gospels attend is the *outsider*. Jews in first-century Israel would have been highly suspicious of anyone outside of their own race and religion; much of Second Temple Judaism was premised on the idea that "purity" required separation from non-Jews. But there is a strand in the Gospels that undermines that. Here, Bashaw highlights the Gospel of Matthew. For example, when Jesus heals the Roman centurion's servant, the

---

13. Bashaw, *Scapegoats*, 170–71.

14. Bashaw, *Scapegoats*, 179, 176. I have borrowed heavily from her discussion of "Jesus and the Poor," ch. 9, 157–89.

centurion expresses faith that Jesus does not need to visit his home but asks Jesus to "only say the word." Jesus complies and adds, "Truly, I tell you, not even in Israel have I found such faith" (Matt 8:5–13).

In Matthew's version of the healing of the Canaanite woman's daughter (Matt 15:21–28), Matthew adds to Mark's account, "I was sent only to the lost sheep of the house of Israel." But despite Jesus's harsh words, the woman is still able to persuade him to heal the girl. And in the genealogy in Matt 1, only three women (other than Mary) are mentioned: Tamar, Ruth, and "the wife of Uriah." All three are foreigners, implying that "God's Kingdom is strengthened by outsiders."[15]

Jesus's conversation with the Samaritan woman at the well (John 4) as well as the parable of the good Samaritan (Luke 10) work to break down stereotypes and taboos against the Samaritans, the epitome of outsiders to Judaism. This will eventually culminate in Acts 10, when Peter, through a series of dreams and visions, is convinced to accept gentiles into the early church. "What God has made clean, you must not call profane" (Acts 10:16). The overall trajectory is to widen the circle of concern beyond one's own group, to include everyone. "For there is no longer Jew or Greek, slave or free, male and female; for you are all one in Christ Jesus" (Gal 3:28).

Bashaw lifts up one final outsider that enters into the gospel story: Simon of Cyrene, whom the Romans "compelled to carry [Jesus's] cross." This incident is mentioned in a single verse, in all three Synoptic Gospels (Mark 15:21; Matt 27:32; Luke 23:26). Cyrene is in present-day Libya; Simon is African, and so not surprisingly, his story has played a significant role in the Black church. Simon "serves as an archetype for oppressed people forced into the service of an exploitative empire."[16] Bashaw quotes a sermon by famed Black preacher Charles Adams:

> Simon represented Black humanity and oppressed humanity everywhere of whatever color. . . . He was given no freedom of choice whether or not to bear the cross. . . . The Black church is Simon—not Simon Peter—but Simon of Cyrene. It was compelled into existence. It is an involuntary institution, produced under the conditions of involuntary servitude. And that's why the Lord has called us out—in order to combat that heresy, to repudiate that terrible untruth, and to let the world know that

---

15. Bashaw, *Scapegoats*, 203–4.
16. Bashaw, *Scapegoats*, 253.

once you are in Christ, you can no longer be anybody's property but God's.[17]

In this chapter, we have seen how the idea of *scapegoating* elucidates not just Jesus's passion and crucifixion, but also his interactions with various marginalized groups: women, the sick and infirm, the poor, outsiders. With the exception of the woman caught in adultery, these are not classic Girardian scapegoats, in immediate danger of being stoned or crucified. They are more akin to Isabel Wilkerson's *scapegoat caste*, mentioned in the prologue. They are the stigmatized, the marginalized, the "other."

There is a deep-seated human tendency to define ourselves not just by the group or groups to which we belong but by our *opposition* to the groups to which we do *not* belong. Brian Zahnd has called this the "*us versus them* paradigm."[18] A certain amount of this is natural, but when we convince ourselves to *hate* "the other" *because God hates them*—then the way is open for the worst instincts of humanity: racism, war, genocide. This way of thinking believes that "*hating the other* (who is believed to be the enemy of God) *becomes a demonstration of your love for God*."[19] This *us* versus *them* paradigm is not foreign to the Bible. The psalmist writes, "Do I not hate those who hate you, O Lord? And do I not loath those who rise up against you? I hate them with complete hatred" (Ps 139:21–22).

In the Synoptic Gospels, the Pharisees are portrayed as Jesus's main opponents. Zahnd reminds us that the Pharisees were a conservative religious-political party concerned with *taking back Israel for God*; today we might say their program was to *make Israel great again*. "The Pharisees showed their faithfulness to God by hating the right people": the nonobservant, sinners, tax collectors, those blemished by physical infirmity, outsiders.[20] The Pharisees were convinced that God's reign would come only when Israel was sufficiently purified; their vision was founded on the need to exclude "the other." This is epitomized by the inscription on the stone wall within the Second Temple complex of Jesus's time, the wall beyond which gentiles were not permitted: "No foreigner is to be

---

17. Bashaw, *Scapegoats*, 253–54.
18. Zahnd, *Radical Forgiveness*, 131. Emphasis added.
19. Zahnd, *Radical Forgiveness*, 141. Emphasis added.
20. Zahnd, *Radical Forgiveness*, 139. It's important to recognize that the Pharisees are portrayed in the Synoptic Gospels as a kind of literary foil to Jesus; in some ways their piety is to be admired. In other words, we need to take care to not scapegoat the Pharisees.

beyond this wall. Whoever [enters] will have himself to blame for his death, which will follow." Zahnd interprets this warning, literally written in stone: "*We're chosen, and you're not. We're in, and you're out. If you cross this line, we will kill you.*"[21]

Jesus's vision of the kingdom of God was directly opposed to the Pharisees' vision of purity through exclusion. As we have seen in this chapter, he welcomed the very people whom the Pharisees sought to exclude. Zahnd summarizes: "Thus the battle lines were drawn between Jesus and the Pharisees. The fundamental disagreement was this—is the kingdom of God advanced through *erection* or *removal* of barriers?"[22] In today's parlance, we might ask: Through the practice of *othering* or *belonging*?[23]

---

21. Zahnd, *Radical Forgiveness*, 135–36. Emphasis in original.

22. Zahnd, *Radical Forgiveness*, 139. Emphasis in original.

23. The "othering" and "belonging" paradigm has been promoted by the Othering and Belonging Institute at the University of California at Berkley, and its director, John A. Powell. See https://belonging.berkeley.edu/. Though not working from a Girardian framework, it fits well with the theme of this book.

13

Conviction in the Experience of Early Friends

> For all are concluded under sin, and shut up in unbelief as I had been ... and this I knew experimentally.
>
> —George Fox[1]

IN THE PREVIOUS ELEVEN chapters, we have seen that alongside a prominent display of divine and human violence in the Hebrew Scriptures, the Bible at the same time functions to undermine the legitimacy of this violence, especially the "one specific evil to which we are collectively in thrall": scapegoating.[2] For Girard, the cross "constantly suggests that our scapegoats are nothing but innocent victims. . . . The discovery of the innocence of the victim coincides with the discovery of our own guilt. . . . [Conviction] is our discovery that *we are persecutors without knowing it.*"[3]

---

1. G. Fox, *Journal*, 11. The beginning of the quote is better known: "There is one, even Christ Jesus, who can speak to thy condition."

2. Heim, *Saved from Sacrifice*, 305.

3. Girard, *Evolution and Conversion*, 187, 152, 142. Emphasis added. I have substituted "conviction" for Girard's "conversion" to remain consistent with our terminology.

In the introductory chapter, I argued that conviction (in the sense of being found guilty) was often the entry into Quaker praxis, and to the extent that conviction suggests sin, it can be problematic for some Friends today. In this chapter, we further explore early Friends experience of conviction and sin, and then in the next chapter turn to ways that this experience might resonate with Friends today.

At its most basic level, *conviction* is simply the realization that one is on the wrong spiritual path. This should resonate with many contemporary Quakers, the majority of whom (at least among liberal Friends) come to the Society of Friends from some other spiritual tradition, or no tradition. Before one can embrace the Quaker way, one must first come to realize that one's previous path has not been helpful.

Historically, an important root of Quakerism is the seeker movement in northern England in the late 1640s and early 1650s, a time of intense disillusionment with Puritan orthodoxy. The seekers were not an organized sect but rather a loose gathering of individuals who rejected all sects. They recognized they were on the wrong spiritual path: seekers simply stopped going to church (any church), gathering in silence, without agenda, awaiting a further manifestation of the Spirit. They were "united by the sense of what they had *not* found."[4] We could say that the seekers were *convicted* of the futility of all the then-current sectarian options; theirs was a "spirituality of desolation."[5] Having gone through this long and often painful process of *conviction*, they were primed for *convincement* when George Fox first appeared among them in mid-1652.

But early Friends experience of conviction goes well beyond simply finding themselves in the wrong church. For most, the process of coming to Friends started with an intense, almost visceral experience of their own sinfulness, "a discovery of their inner inadequacy."[6] They were concerned not so much about *sins* (their individual transgressions) but rather *sin*—their complicity in a system of deceit and alienation from God that involved every aspect of society, including the established church. Again, the issue between Quakers and the Puritans was never the existence or even the relevance of sin: they agreed on this. But for early Friends, it was not so much that they *believed* in sin (as an abstract theological notion) but rather that they *experienced* sin (in the sense of alienation from God) as an existential reality. To repeat what we said in the introduction, for

4. Gwyn, *Covenant Crucified*, 89. Emphasis in original.
5. Gwyn, *Covenant Crucified*, 102–6, s.vv. "Spirituality of Desolation."
6. Barbour, *Quakers in Puritan England*, 97.

early Friends the first step in convincement was to feel themselves "convincingly convicted" of sin.[7]

Alan Kolp summarizes the importance of this broad understanding of sin for George Fox's spirituality, alluding to Fox's vision of "an ocean of darkness and death, but an infinite ocean of light and love, which flowed over the ocean of darkness":[8]

> At the heart [of idolatry] is the illusion that one's "self" is free and autonomous, that this "self" is independent. Life lived from these assumptions is a lie; it is life lived in sin. Sin is separation from God, alienation from the source of one's being and the resource of one's life. . . . Sin, then, is the primary theological truth of life found in the ocean of darkness and death. To be in this ocean is to be in sin—alienated from God. Although contemporary Quakers differ widely in assessing the meaningfulness of the concept of sin, it is unmistakable that Fox had a view of sin significant for his spirituality. Many contemporary Quakers and Christians have either ignored or underestimated the function of sin in Fox's thought and experience. . . . [Fox's spirituality is grounded in] the reality of sin. Sin is real because the ocean of death and darkness is real.[9]

This experience of sin was by no means confined to Fox. Quaker historian Hugh Barbour cites a typical account, from the journal of John Banks, describing his first experience at a Quaker meeting, at age sixteen in 1654:

> The Lord's Power in the Meeting so seized upon me, that I was made to cry out in the bitterness of my soul, in a true sight and sense of my sins. . . . And the same evening, as I was going to a Meeting of God's people . . . scornfully called Quakers, by the way I was smitten to the ground with the weight of God's judgment for sin . . . and oh, the Godly sorrow that did take hold of me, and seized upon me that night in the Meeting. [There followed for Banks several months and years of] Godly sorrow and Spiritual pain . . . but keeping close unto the power of God, in Waiting upon him in Silence among his people . . . I came to more Settlement and Weightiness in my Spirit, and Peace.[10]

7. Pickvance, "Conviction and Convincement," 10. Emphasis added.
8. G. Fox, *Journal*, 19.
9. Kolp, *Fresh Winds of Spirit*, 21–22.
10. Quoted in Barbour, *Quakers in Puritan England*, 96. Spelling and some capitalizations adjusted.

Barbour comments, "The Light that ultimately gave joy, peace, and guidance, *at first gave only terror*."[11]

One way to understand the experience of sin for early Friends is to relate it to their experience of the Light. For those first Quakers, the Light was not just a comforting warm glow, but was active and functional: it did things. The first function of the Light was to strip away all deceit and illusions about our own selves: "Therefore, I direct you to the Light, that with it you may see yourselves."[12] And when we see ourselves without deceit or illusion, we first see sin and alienation. From Fox's epistles:

> Wait in the Light that discovers sin and evil in you, and that will raise up a daily Cross to your own wills.[13]

> This Light shows you sin, the evil of the world, the lust of it and vain fashions that pass away, the unrighteousness and ungodliness of it.[14]

> This is the Light that shows you sin and evil, and shows you the deceit of your heart, and you that hate this Light your deeds are evil and goes in the broad way from God and Christ and from all the saints and children of God, and this light is your condemnation.... So the light you do see when you act contrary to it, and the judgement of God is upon you.[15]

Of course, this discovery of sin is only the first function of the Light, which if heeded then gives power to overcome sin—the crux of the Quaker disagreement with the Puritans.

> This Light ... is within you. If you stand still in the Light that comes from Christ ... Power will be given to you from him to forsake your evil deeds, which are contrary to the Light.... Wait in the Light that discovers sin and evil in you ... and a Power will arise within you to deliver you from temptations, to crucify sin, circumcise your hearts and work out the carnal part of you.[16]

---

11. Barbour, *Quakers in Puritan England*, 98. Emphasis added. Chapter 4 in his book is titled "The Terror and Power of the Light."

12. "Epistle 85," in G. Fox, *Power of the Lord*, 71–72.

13. "1654 Epistle," in G. Fox, *Power of the Lord*, 476.

14. "Epistle 85," G. Fox, *Power of the Lord*, 71–72.

15. George Fox, "1652 Epistle," quoted in T. Jones, "Nature and Functions of Light," 56.

16. "1654 Epistle," in G. Fox, *Power of the Lord*, 475–76.

> And as many as received the Light, Christ Jesus, the Power of God, which he has lighted you with . . . he will give you Power to become [children] of God.[17]

In all this, the first and second functions of the Light—first to show us our sin and then to empower us to overcome sin—closely parallel the experience of *conviction*, followed by *convincement*. They are describing the same two-stage process. To paraphrase Fox, the Light that troubles a person is also their salvation; that which shows people their sins is the same that takes their sin away.[18]

Early Friends, "Friends of Truth," spoke of Truth and Light interchangeably.[19] For them, the opposite of truth was not falsehood but deceit, and in particular self-deceit. The Light/Truth revealed sin not so much as disobedience but as "living in deceit" or what we might call living in denial. They were concerned not with truth in an abstract or philosophical sense but with "the truth of their lives."[20] Fox says that "the Light of God in you . . . shows you the deceit of your hearts."[21] Margaret Fell conveys a sense of this painful process of confronting self-deceit:

> Now Friends, deal plainly with yourselves, and let the Eternal Light search you . . . for this will deal plainly with you; it will rip you up, and lay you open . . . naked and bare before the Lord God, from whom you cannot hide yourselves. . . . Therefore give over the deceiving of your souls; for . . . all Sin and uncleanness the Light condemns.[22]

If the experience of early Friends began with Light/Truth convicting them of sin, understood largely as self-deceit, can we link this to the biblical themes of scapegoating violence that we have been exploring? We will have more to say about this in part 2, but one connection may be this: beyond their refusal to bear arms, the public witness of early Friends revealed the inherent violence underlying the prevalent social hierarchies of the day. In testifying to this, their most important resource was their

---

17. "Epistle 216," in G. Fox, *Power of the Lord*, 170. Following the KJV, the original reads, "to become sons of God" (John 1:12). The NRSV reads, "he gave power to become children of God."

18. G. Fox, *Journal*, 64. See also Barbour, *Quakers in Puritan England*, 108.

19. Guiton, *Early Quakers*, 307.

20. Ambler, *Light Within*, 10–17.

21. G. Fox, *Journal*, 135.

22. Margaret Fell, quoted in Barbour, *Quakers in Puritan England*, 98.

own experience of persecution by church and state. Early Friends willingness to suffer persecution demonstrates the same "self-sacrificial refusal of sacrificial violence" that led Jesus to the crucifixion.[23] Their suffering was a *convicting witness* to seventeenth-century English society.

Gerard Guiton, in his important *Early Quakers and the Kingdom of God*, has shown that the kingdom of God or its equivalent was "the central focus" of "almost all" of the thousand Quaker tracts published between 1650 and 1663.[24] Both the kingdom and the Lamb's war to achieve it were characterized by nonviolence. This was true from the beginning of the Quaker movement but came into sharper focus in what Guiton calls the "Quaker Pentecost" of 1659–61, when Quakers, during a time of intense political turmoil leading up to the restoration of the monarchy, published three remarkable declarations that "directly opposed the violence of Church and State."[25]

The well-known 1660 declaration asserts that "although we have always suffered, and do now more abundantly suffer, yet . . . when we have been wronged, we have not sought to revenge ourselves, we have not made resistance to authority, but wherein we could not obey for conscience' sake, we have suffered even the most of any people in the nation." The declaration then catalogues the various sufferings: "persecuted and despised, beaten, stoned, wounded, stocked, whipped, imprisoned, cast into dungeons where many have died."[26] Having searched inwardly and freed themselves from the "lusts" that "lead to wars and fightings among you" (Jas 4:1 KJV), Quakers now confronted the state with its own violence: their scapegoating of Quakers.

All Quaker historians acknowledge the persecution and suffering undergone by Quakers in the first several decades of the movement. This was hardly a peripheral issue; not only did persecution play a crucial role in their day-to-day lives, but it also was central to their theological stance. Quaker historian Rosemary Moore says that "Friends lived with persecution from the start," beginning in the Commonwealth period of the 1650s but greatly intensifying after the restoration of the monarchy in 1660.[27] Up to 15,000 were at one time or another imprisoned—a considerable proportion of the estimated 40–60,000 Friends in Britain at the

23. Cowdell, *René Girard*, 70.
24. Guiton, *Early Quakers*, 181.
25. Guiton, *Early Quakers*, 191. See extended discussion, 181–202.
26. G. Fox, *Journal*, 401; Guiton, *Early Quakers*, 426–27.
27. Moore, *Light in Their Consciences*, 155.

time.²⁸ As many as 450 died in appalling prison conditions.²⁹ Added to these imprisonments and deaths were exorbitant fines and confiscation of property, as well as frequent nonjudicial acts of harassment and persecution by mob violence. Fox, in addition to his many imprisonments, relates several instances of being beaten by irate mobs, which he suffered without resistance.³⁰

Becoming a Quaker came with the expectation of suffering, which was not sought out but also not avoided or resisted. Their first appeal to Parliament for relief from these "sufferings" dates from as early as 1653, and Friends quickly developed "a theology of suffering" and a "sufferings literature."³¹ By 1657, Friends were counseled to meticulously document instances of persecution. A Quaker broadside from 1659, titled *A Declaration of the Present Sufferings of the People of God Called Quakers*, counts 1900 imprisoned, including 26 who had died.³² Suffering was seen not as God's punishment but "as part of God's plan, so that Quaker faith and the Quaker experience of suffering were found to reinforce each other."³³ Suffering was for them "a way of participating in the passion and death of Jesus by dying to the particular shapes that sin took in their age." They were counseled to "rejoice that they are made worthy to suffer for the Lord's sake." Quaker suffering was "testimony of a most public kind ... a challenge to the Puritans."³⁴

Friends at the time did not refer to themselves as scapegoats or even as victims, but in retrospect these modern descriptors apply. A recent biographer of James Nayler observes that "the early Quaker movement ...

---

28. There are no accurate data on the number of Quakers in the seventeenth century, as membership statistics were not gathered until well into the following century. Braithwaite estimates that there were "30,000 to 40,000 Quakers at the time of the Restoration" (*Beginnings of Quakerism*, 512n1); Guiton gives an estimate of "possibly 60,000" (*Early Quakers*, 224). This is out of a total population of over five million, so Friends represented at most 1 percent of the English population.

29. Braithwaite, *Second Period of Quakerism* (1961), 114–15.

30. See G. Fox, *Journal*, e.g., 97, 98–99, 101, 112. See esp. 127–28, where Fox "stretched out my arms among them all, and said with a loud voice, 'Strike again, here is my arms and my head and my cheeks,'" an allusion to both the suffering servant in Isaiah and Jesus's Sermon on the Mount ("turn the other cheek").

31. Moore, *Light in Their Consciences*, 156–57.

32. Moore, *Light in Their Consciences*, 158–59. Moore says that up to 1660, 3179 had been imprisoned and 32 died (186). These numbers greatly increased after the Restoration.

33. Moore, *Light in Their Consciences*, 157–60.

34. Guiton, *Early Quakers*, 323–24.

played the role of *scapegoat* for the ascendant Puritans . . . [who] confirmed their righteousness by throwing Quakers in jail."[35] Douglas Gwyn says that "Quakers became the most visible *scapegoats* of the Restoration regime."[36] Hearkening back to what we said about "a scapegoat caste" in the prologue, a strong case can be made that early Friends played that role in England from the 1650s through the coming of toleration in 1688.

The most dramatic example of scapegoating of Friends was the hanging of four Quaker martyrs by Puritans in Boston, in 1659–61. Mary Dyer witnessed the execution of her colleagues William Robinson and Marmaduke Stephenson in October 1659, but she herself, blindfolded and on the scaffold about to be hanged, was given an unrequested last-minute reprieve. She was again banished but returned to Boston the following year. At her second trial, the prosecution charged that by returning "she was guilty of her own blood." She replied, "Nay, I came to keep blood guiltiness from you, desiring you to repeal the unrighteous and unjust law of banishment upon pain of death, made against the innocent servants of the Lord."[37] This time there would be no reprieve: she was hung on Boston Commons in June 1660.

Girard argues that "the scapegoating mechanism literally cannot be revealed" other than through the voice of the victim, the one scapegoated; persecutors are completely blind to their own actions.[38] This puts Quaker suffering and persecution in a new light: for their particular time and place in history, they were the innocent victims through whom revelation came. Quaker historian Douglas Gwyn describes this revelation at the beginning of Quakerism as "apocalyptic," in the original Greek sense of *apocalypse* as "that which reveals."[39]

---

35. Damrosch, *Sorrows of Quaker Jesus,* 14. Emphasis added. Nayler was arrested for blasphemy in 1656 and subsequently tried, convicted, and brutally punished by Parliament.

36. Gwyn, *Seekers Found,* 339. Emphasis added. Gwyn acknowledges Girard's contribution to the "scapegoating mechanism," n372.

37. Edward Burrough, "The Death of Mary Dyer," in Barbour and Roberts, *Early Quaker Writings,* 139. His written account of Dyer's death was presented by Burrough in person to the newly restored King Charles II, who issued a mandamus to the New England authorities, forbidding future executions. The king's edict arrived too late to spare the fourth Quaker martyr, William Leddra, who was hung in March 1661.

38. Girard: *One by Whom Scandal Comes,* 60; *Reading the Bible,* 117.

39. Gwyn, *Seekers Found,* 223. Chapter 8 in this work is entitled "The Quaker Apocalypse: From Seeking to Suffering" (213–64). His earlier work on the life and message of George Fox is *Apocalypse of the Word.* Gwyn's work endorses the view that the experience of early Friends was apocalyptic in the sense of revelational and that this

We have discussed the individual's conviction of sin by an encounter with the Light/Truth, but here we have added a new dimension to conviction. By their willingness to suffer publicly, Quakers were "convicting" their opponents of "the bloody spirit of persecution." The 1660 declaration explicitly states that the suffering of Friends functioned as "a witness for the convincing [convicting] of our enemies."[40] Willingness to suffer for their beliefs was taken as evidence that those beliefs were sincere—and true.

Many of Friends public testimonies, especially the insistence on "thee and thou" and refusal of hat honor to social superiors, were self-consciously meant to confront others with their own pride and vanity. These behaviors, especially when they resulted in suffering, were a "*witness to the unconvicted . . . an instrument of conversion.*"[41] In addition to being themselves convicted by the Light, early Friends set about to convict others, both by their words and by their willingness to endure suffering. By their actions, they were appealing to "the witness of God" in their persecutors. Although there was sometimes an "in your face" aspect to these actions, Quakers insisted that they were acting only out of "love for the lost."[42]

After the Quaker Act of 1662 and the Conventicle Act of 1664 (effectively outlawing Quaker and other nonconforming worship), "meetings were often broken up with violence and meetinghouses pulled down."[43] The most important Quaker testimony became the willingness to meet openly for worship, inviting arrest. In Reading in 1664, authorities "took thirty-four [adult male] Friends from meeting to prison on the Quaker Act." The women and children continued to meet, but over the next several weeks most of the women were arrested. But, as a correspondent later wrote to Fox, "our little children kept the meetings up, when we were all in prison."[44] Such willingness to suffer for the right to publicly worship eventually led to legal toleration of Quakers in 1688.

---

revelation had something to do with suffering. See also Douglas Gwyn, "Come Again? Early Friends as an Apocalyptic Movement," in B. Dandelion et al., *Heaven on Earth*, 90–106. Girard makes much the same point: "Apocalypse means revelation" (*When These Things Begin*, 9).

40. G. Fox, *Journal*, 401.
41. Barbour, *Quakers in Puritan England*, 160, 163. Emphasis added.
42. Nayler titled a 1656 tract *Love to the Lost*.
43. Punshon, *Portrait in Grey*, 88.
44. Braithwaite, *Second Period of Quakerism* (1961), 226.

In chapter 11, we saw that Jesus's crucifixion decisively unveiled and revealed the scapegoat mechanism. If, with Girard, we say that the crucifixion "contaminates" all future scapegoats,[45] can we then also say that early Friends willingness to suffer as scapegoats was likewise revelatory? Granted, in terms of absolute magnitude, the persecution of Quakers in the second half of the seventeenth century warrants barely a footnote in the long annals of human suffering, which includes medieval Crusades and anti-Jewish pogroms, the European religious wars in the hundred years prior to the rise of Quakerism, the genocidal colonization project of European nations, the African slave trade, and down through the multiple genocides of the twentieth century. Still, early Friends willingness to "suffer for truth" and to "bear the daily cross" was revelatory—even apocalyptic.[46] Perhaps this new/old revelation of the innocence of victims, "subverting from within" the ever-present scapegoat mechanism, can account for some of the heroic energy of the early Quaker movement.

In the next chapter, we turn to what conviction might mean for Friends (and others) today.

---

45. Girard, *Reading the Bible*, 76.
46. On "bearing the daily cross," see Luke 9:23; and, e.g., G. Fox, *Journal*, 18.

14

Conviction Today

> Quaker spirituality starts with two premises—that there is something good in creation, and that there is something amiss in creation (or at least in humanity). The thrust of all Quaker spirituality is that we can engage with that something good to overcome what is amiss.
>
> —Bill Taber[1]

WE HAVE SEEN THAT for early Friends, the process of *convincement* often started with a *conviction* of their own sinfulness, a felt sense of complicity in a wider system built on deceit and coercion—often resulting in violence directed at Friends. Given the Calvinist and Puritan presupposition of human depravity, this language of sinfulness is perhaps not surprising. What *is* surprising is that early Friends, through their experience of the power of the Light, managed to find a way out.

Today, most Friends do not share these presuppositions, and therefore language about sin and evil does not come easily. In a 1987 issue of *Quaker Religious Thought* dedicated to "Facing Sin and Evil," commentator Ann Miller sums up the several articles: "A summary response to the query: 'How do Friends face sin and evil?' might be, 'Not very well!'

---

1. Taber, "What Is Quaker Spirituality?," 27.

Friends find it difficult to face their involvement in both individual and social sin."[2]

Contemporary Quaker attitudes about sin probably owe more to Rufus Jones than to early Friends. Jones came into public life at the very end of the nineteenth century, a time of immense optimism about social and technological progress, when the world seemed to be steadily advancing toward the kingdom. His primary concern was to lift Quakerism out of the constraints of its original seventeenth-century prescientific worldview and bring it into the twentieth century, a task at which he largely succeeded. Although Jones is not much read today, his views continue to have tremendous influence among contemporary Quakers. Wilmer Cooper observes that Jones's "optimistic view of life was based on his belief in the fundamental goodness of human beings. He based this belief on his constant reference to George Fox's affirmation that there is 'that of God' in everyone":[3]

> In the final analysis Rufus Jones does not regard sin and evil as insurmountable, or even a major obstruction to human progress. It is therefore understandable why he placed so little emphasis on the need for repentance and redemption from human sin. He seems to conclude that growth in human goodness and freeing people from their base instincts and non-rational urges is a natural development in the evolutionary process.[4]

Subsequent events of the twentieth century—two world wars, the Holocaust, and all the rest—brought this optimism about innate human goodness into serious doubt. Though little noted, Jones himself, late in his long life (he died in 1948), questioned his earlier optimism. According to his biographer:

> On the whole, in his writings Rufus Jones had little to say about sin and evil. If his phrase "the divine movement toward holiness" . . . suggests the belief in inevitable progress which nineteenth-century liberals embraced as the accompaniment of evolution, he abandoned that point of view in later years, when he declared in several places that the "cosmic elevator" was no longer running. Evil, he said in *The Eternal Gospel*, arises as a result of man's freedom. But a few years later he was not sure of even that. "I cannot deny the fact of evil," he wrote in *New*

---

2. A. Miller, "Comments," 42.
3. Cooper, "Influence of Rufus Jones," 35.
4. Cooper, "Influence of Rufus Jones," 33.

Eyes for the Invisibles, "nor can I accept any of the explanations I have heard given of it. It remains an unsolved problem, a huge mystery."[5]

Rufus Jones's contribution to Quakerism was largely positive, but one part of his legacy is our modern reluctance to "face sin and evil." Many Friends today have an almost allergic reaction to language about sin, based, one suspects, more on negative experiences from their churches of origin rather than any appreciation of seventeenth-century Friends understanding. Nevertheless, since Rufus Jones's time, much Quaker scholarship has contributed to a more nuanced and balanced Quaker view of sin and evil and thus a reassessment of the role of *conviction*.[6]

Rex Ambler, a contemporary British Friend, has done as much as anyone in our generation to help Quakers today reclaim early Friends transforming experience of the Light, through extensive writing about early Friends as well as his "experiment with Light" practice. In his anthology of George Fox's writings, he helpfully translates seventeenth-century language into a more modern and accessible idiom. But in so doing, he almost completely avoids the language of sin. For example, Fox's advice to "mind the pure light of God in you, which shows your sin and evil" is changed to "pay attention to the pure light of God in you. It is this that makes you aware of what you have done wrong."[7] Similarly, in his *The Light Within: Then and Now*, I can find only two mentions of sin: one in a quote from seventeenth-century Friend Elizabeth Bathhurst and the second when he states that the light "freed a person from egocentricity and 'sin.'"[8]

Ambler has other ways of talking about "something amiss" in humanity: living in deceit, living in denial, the pretenses of the ego, egocentricity, the self-centered ego, typical ego-centeredness, the self (versus the deep self), the pretense of separation, and something in our lives that

---

5. Vining, *Friend of Life*, 107.

6. One of Rufus Jones's many contributions to twentieth-century Quakers was his central role in the Rowntree series of books on the origins and history of Quakerism. Jones himself wrote or co-wrote four of the six volumes; William Charles Braithwaite wrote the two specifically dealing with seventeenth-century Quakers. Jones interpreted the origins of Quakerism in the seventeenth century as in continuity with continental mysticism. Subsequent scholars of George Fox and Quakerism have found little evidence for this and have instead emphasized the Puritan roots of Quakerism (e.g., Lewis Benson, Geoffrey Nuttall, Hugh Barbour, Douglas Gwyn).

7. G. Fox, *Truth of the Heart*, 32–33.

8. Ambler, *Light Within*, 21, 16.

needs tending to.⁹ I don't wish to discredit Ambler's approach; indeed, I think he has made a very valuable contribution to our understanding of the Light in early Quaker experience. But I mention him for two reasons: first, he illustrates our modern reluctance to use the language of sin; and second, he shows that it is in fact possible to find alternative words to talk about the "something amiss."

My concern, however, is that something inevitably gets left out. When we use the language of psychology (ego, ego-centeredness, denial), we may miss the wider systemic connotations of *sin*. The traditional language of sin points to something larger than ourselves, "something amiss in creation," something we are "born into" and cannot easily escape. There is a systemic side to the reality of sin.

Ironically, contemporary Friends have been given ample opportunity to recapture this "larger than ourselves" dimension of "something amiss"—even if we don't call it sin. For example, over the last decade or more, white Quakers have started to grapple with the presence of systemic racism, in both the wider culture and our own Society of Friends. For many of us, this has involved not only an examination of our personal biases and unconscious attitudes ("the things we have done wrong"), but also a realization that racism so permeates our history and culture that we cannot escape its influence. Systemic racism is something we have been born into; it has been rightly described as "America's original sin."¹⁰ Many of us have come to feel *convicted* of our nearly unavoidable complicity in this systemic racism.

Another example might be the whole range of interconnected issues dealing with global climate change, ecological degradation, habitat destruction, and loss of biodiversity through species extinction. Part of this is a realization and conviction about our own individual contributions to these problems, contributions that at least in theory can be addressed by our individual choices. But part is the realization that at some deep level, we are complicit in a system based on an unsustainable exploitation of the earth and its resources. This is not anything we ever consciously chose or intended but something we are nevertheless part of, just by living at this particular time and in this particular economy. Yes, individual actions are important, but ultimately change will require collective action

---

9. Ambler: *Light Within*; *Quaker Way*.
10. Wallis, *America's Original Sin*, 8–11.

and systemic change. Unsustainable exploitation of the planet's resources could also be described as Western culture's "original sin."[11]

We could cite other examples: the ongoing consequences of colonization and the genocide of indigenous peoples, global economic inequality, runaway exploitive capitalism, political polarization, militarism. The underlying point is that the modern world gives contemporary Friends many opportunities to experience that sense of conviction that early Friends described. As eighteenth-century Quaker Job Scott said, in a characteristic understatement, "There is much to die to."[12]

In the previous chapter, it may have seemed that early Friends invariably experienced *conviction* first, with *convincement* coming later. To some extent that may be true, but I suspect that the two processes were more intertwined than what is conveyed by their retrospective accounts. Theirs was likely a more iterative process, conviction followed by convincement in a recurring cycle at ever-deeper levels. Gerard Guiton even speaks of George Fox emerging from his 1659 period of despair "*re-convinced*, but to a greater level of his being."[13]

This seems to be even more true for contemporary Friends. We may initially become a *convinced* Friend on a surface or intellectual level, and only later have one or more experiences of *conviction*. It is as if the initial convincement "tenders" us, as early Friends often said, opening us to experiences of genuine conviction. To quote again from Friend Eden Grace, true convincement obliges us to "become aware of all that is not right, of how far we and our human community have fallen from God's intended goodness. . . . If you're not heartbroken by the injustice and suffering of this world, *you're not paying attention*."[14] In our contemporary world, to pay attention leads inevitably to a sense of conviction.

In my first three decades or so as a Quaker, I rarely if ever heard Friends use "conviction" in the sense that we are using it here. However, over the last several years, this seems to be changing. At least occasionally, I hear Friends speak of "being convicted." Rarely, though, have I heard anyone speak of being convicted of *sin*—which is the implied and often explicit way that early Friends spoke of being convicted: convicted of sin.

---

11. See Gwyn, *Sustainable Life*, for a Quaker perspective on issues of sustainability.
12. Scott, *Journal*, 13.
13. Guiton, *Early Quakers*, 379. Emphasis added.
14. Grace, *Good News to Oppressed*, 21. Emphasis added. (Previously quoted in the introduction.)

Perhaps contemporary Friends reluctance to speak of sin comes not from some new revelation about human nature but from a too-narrow understanding of the traditional concept—a misunderstanding shared by the wider culture. Somehow, we have come to the mistaken belief that sin is primarily about behavior, or wrong actions. This leads to a legal or "juridical" view of sin: sin is analogous to committing a crime, for which we are tried, found guilty, and (eventually) punished.

But this is a very impoverished understanding. Sin is not primarily about behavior but about our *orientation*: about a turning away from God, the source of our being. "In spite of our penchant to focus on behavior, the doctrine of sin is not primarily moralistic at its heart. . . . It is [about] the orientation of the will—what it yields to, chooses, follows, or patterns itself after. . . . [Sin] begins when we face in the wrong direction."[15] One's orientation toward or away from the Divine of course affects behavior, but this is secondary. This deeper understanding resonates very much with the experience of early Friends, whose convincement represented a sometimes dramatic reorientation of their lives toward the Light, as inwardly experienced.

Even with this deeper understanding, we should acknowledge that "sin" can be a problematic word. "It is a fact that the doctrine of *sin* has been used *sinfully*, to separate, judge, and condemn."[16] After centuries of misunderstanding, misuse, and abuse, one wonders if we would be better off just finding a different word. "Sin" can even be a dangerous word, due to our propensity to project it onto others. It is so much easier to notice the speck in our neighbor's eye than the log in our own (Matt 7:3). Perhaps if we choose to continue using the word, we should restrict it to talking about our *own* shortcomings and not those of others. There is good scriptural warrant for this: when the woman caught in adultery is brought to Jesus, Jesus directs the mob's attention away from the woman's alleged behavior and proposed punishment, and toward a self-examination of their own experience: "Let the one who is without sin cast the first stone" (John 8:7; see ch. 9).

"Sin" may not be the word we choose—but at this point I do not have a better word, a word that expresses not just a sense of individual moral responsibility but also the deep structural reality that "sin" conveys. The Greek word that is translated as "sin" in the New Testament, *hamartia*,

---

15. Mercadante, *Victims and Sinners*, 28–29.
16. Mercadante, *Victims and Sinners*, 125. Emphasis added.

has the connotation of an archer "missing the mark," and that seems helpful.[17] A thesaurus gives several alternative words: iniquity, depravity, evil, immorality, wrongdoing, transgression, misdeed, fault, lapse. These alternative words all emphasize individual willfulness and so miss the sense of bondage or slavery that is part of the biblical understanding.[18]

Given the intense negative reaction "sin" elicits in many of us, perhaps this is a place where we simply await further revelation. I have no objection to finding other words to talk about the reality that "sin" conveys, but neither do I think that we should banish "sin" from our vocabulary. I note here that Girard himself used the word "sin" only sparingly, although some of his interpreters have made the connection between his ideas and sin more explicit.

In recent decades, one alternative way of talking about that "something amiss" has risen to prominence: addiction. With its origin in the emergence of Alcoholics Anonymous (AA) in the 1930s, *addiction* has come to be seen as an illness rather than a moral failing—a change in perspective that unquestionably has been liberating for millions addicted to alcohol and other substances. But the concept of addiction has gradually become all encompassing. An internet search of "addiction to" gives results for food, sugar, shopping, dieting, social media, video games, gambling, screens, smartphones, technology, sex, and even love. Linda Mercadante points out that "today an ever-expanding array of human difficulties is being categorized as forms of addictive disease. . . . It becomes, for many, a functional replacement for the concept of sin."[19] Addiction is seen as "the universal human predicament," expressed as "nearly everyone is addicted to something."[20] Some have even claimed that "to be alive is to be addicted"—with distinct echoes of original sin.[21]

The addiction-recovery model "implicitly copies, critiques, and challenges the Christian doctrine of sin. . . . [It stands in judgment against our] culture's rejection both of moral fault and of the unavoidable human inclination to turn from God—what theology has called sin."[22] But however helpful this has been for many, addiction is ultimately an inadequate

---

17. Biddle, *Missing the Mark*, 51, 64.
18. Biddle, *Missing the Mark*, 71–72. See esp. Rom 7:14–25, where Paul describes himself as "a slave to the law of sin." See also Mercadante, *Victims and Sinners*, 115.
19. Mercadante, *Victims and Sinners*, 80.
20. Mercadante, *Victims and Sinners*, 124.
21. May, *Addiction and Grace*, 11.
22. Mercadante, *Victims and Sinners*, 13–14.

model for the human condition. While the "addiction as disease" model has allowed us to move beyond simplistic, judgmental, and moralistic concepts of sin, it leaves us with a strong element of biological determinism, before which we are "powerless," as they say in AA. It offers coping skills but not transformation; one is "always an alcoholic." Some have even called it "Calvinism in disguise." In comparison to "a strong doctrine of grace," the addiction-recovery model offers "only a limited solution."[23]

This contemporary debate between sin and addiction has echoes in the seventeenth century. Early Quakers offered a genuine alternative to the Puritan understanding: Puritans offered "a coping strategy," but for Quakers, sin was paired with "a strong doctrine of grace," in the form of empowerment by the Light. Fox counseled that when the Light shows us our sins, we should focus not on what the Light shows, our "transgressions, confusions, and temptations," but on the "light that discovers them, that makes them manifest," and with that same Light "you will feel over them, to receive power to stand against them.... The same light that lets you see sin and transgression will let you see the covenant of God."[24]

In recent years, "complicity" has seen a major increase in usage, and is a word that may help convey some sense of the idea of sin.[25] One dictionary definition is "the condition of being involved with others in an activity that is unlawful or morally wrong." As commonly used, we can be said to be complicit in any number of "things that are amiss": systemic racism, our nation's involvement in unjust wars, environmental degradation, exploitive capitalism, or injustice towards indigenous populations. Indeed, complicity in these various ills seems to be almost an article of faith, at least on the progressive end of the political spectrum—in the same way that "original sin" was an article of faith among seventeenth-century Christians. *Complicity* in this sense, as unavoidable participation in societal evils, would seem to be sin by another name.

As we await further revelation about which words and metaphors are most helpful, perhaps we can learn from more recent nuanced and

---

23. Mercadante, *Victims and Sinners*, 14.

24. G. Fox, *Journal*, 347–48.

25. According to an online etymology resource, "complicity" came into English around 1650, from the French *complice*, meaning accomplice or comrade. The same source shows an exponential increase in usage, beginning in the 1950s. A word search of Fox's works failed to uncover any use of "complicit." See www.etymonline.com.

less moralistic discussions of the concept of sin, starting with a recognition that today, "there is widespread confusion about the concept of sin."[26]

Theologians, especially those who are male, white, and privileged, have often portrayed the essence of sin as the human tendency to overreach, to place ourselves in a position of rivalry with God. This is *the sin of pride*, "the denial of the inherent limitations of the human situation and a false absolutizing of the self."[27]

More recently, feminist and liberation theologians have pointed to a second and perhaps even more common sin: *the sin of hiding*, the inability or active refusal to live up to the image of God within oneself. Linda Mercadante helpfully names these two aspects of sin as "inordinate self-will" and "inordinate self-loss."[28] This helps us to recognize that the experience of sin can be very gender dependent: at least in our culture, inordinate self-will or pride is more typical of males, while inordinate self-loss or hiding is more typical of females. Mark Biddle summarizes these two aspects of sin:

> Some sin is wanting to be more than human, but much and even most sin stems not from egocentrism but from its polar opposite—the conviction that one is not or cannot or dare not be good enough to be authentically human. This is sin as the failure to embrace authentic freedom, as opposed to sin as a desire to be more than human. . . . Sin must be more complicated than the single "pride" definition of willful rebellion against God. . . . [This misunderstanding of] pride as the fundamental sin reinforces the status quo; those who seek liberation are [then] "guilty" of self-assertion rooted in pride.[29]

Biddle goes on to say that both aspects of sin have at their root in an even more basic attitude: "mistrust of God"[30] or what Mercadante would call "turning away from God." We are created from the dust of the earth (Gen 2:7) and thus subject to the limits of creaturehood; but we are also created "in the image of God" (Gen 1:27) and thus endowed with freedom and creativity. We can "miss the mark" in either direction, by emphasizing one aspect of our humanity to the exclusion of the other.

26. Mercadante, *Victims and Sinners*, 168.
27. Mercadante, *Victims and Sinners*, 35.
28. Mercadante, *Victims and Sinners*, 35–39, 148–49. See also Nelson, "Sin of Hiding."
29. Biddle, *Missing the Mark*, 49–50.
30. Biddle, *Missing the Mark*, 75–91.

We can sin by overreaching, denying our very real limitations; but we can also sin by underachieving, denying our limited but genuine freedom and creativity.

In the end, any meaningful doctrine of sin (as well as its younger sibling, addiction) will be helpful only when paired with "a strong doctrine of grace."[31] "The idea of sin only makes sense when placed within the framework of divine grace. . . . Starting with and focusing largely on [sin] can be devastating. Unless one starts from another premise [i.e., grace], it is difficult to come up with a thoroughly optimistic and healing alternative rather than simply a coping strategy."[32]

The idea of sin has largely been abandoned in our modern world, because at least since the European Enlightenment it is widely seen as providing an unduly pessimistic and fatalistic view of human nature. This rejection is certainly not based on empirical grounds—the evidence of human sinfulness is everywhere around us. But as H. Richard Niebuhr has written, "Though the doctrine of human sinfulness is apparently more pessimistic than rival theories, it is in fact more optimistic."[33] This is true, however, only when paired with a "strong doctrine of grace," grace that is universally available to the responsive soul.

Perhaps no one has said this better than the process-relational theologian, Marjorie Hewitt Suchocki. She sees "violence against creation" as the basic sin, and she argues that in the end, "sin is a salvific word":

> The critical importance of retaining the terminology of sin is that sin, unlike evil, entails human responsibility and human hope. Simply to call a situation evil can lead to passivity or paralysis with regard to that evil. Evil overwhelms us, often as an impersonal force of fate. But sin is a human category, created in, through, and by us—and therefore sin is potentially a reality that, no matter how intricate, can yield to transformation. To name something as sin is to say, "This ought not to be the case." Such a judgement witnesses to a better alternative, and offers the catalytic hope of transformation. . . . *Sin is a salvific word, a word of grace.* Sin can only be named as such when there is the possibility not simply of judgement, but of forgiveness and transformation. The naming of sin bespeaks a vision where

---

31. Mercadante, *Victims and Sinners*, 13.

32. Mercadante, *Victims and Sinners*, 30.

33. H. Richard Niebuhr, "Man the Sinner" (1935), quoted in Mercadante, *Victims and Sinners*, 173.

violence is not the norm; it bespeaks transcendence through the imagination of a new and different future.[34]

Our reflection on the Quaker sense of *conviction* has brought us inevitably to consider the place of *sin* in our contemporary discourse. We have examined why the terminology of sin has fallen out of favor and explored some alternative ideas. Even though none of those alternatives seems entirely satisfactory, nevertheless the concept behind the word "sin" remains important. Whatever we choose to call it, we cannot escape that we are born into systems larger than ourselves, systems of exploitation, oppression, and violence for which we share some responsibility, both individually and collectively.

In part 1, I have tried to make the case that Girard's mimetic theory (including the scapegoat or victimary mechanism) can help us to understand something important about what it is that is "amiss" in humanity, and that this connects to what Quakers have traditionally meant by "conviction." After a brief detour (in excursus 1) into the realm of process theology, in part 2 we will explore whether mimetic theory can also help us to find a way out of our predicament.

---

34. Suchocki, *Fall to Violence*, 129–30, 164. Emphasis added.

Excursus I

God in Process
The Slow Work of God

> Above all, trust in the slow work of God.
> —Pierre Teilhard de Chardin[1]

> There is a meaning in things, and perplexities can be unraveled—dimly, slowly, patiently.
> —Alfred North Whitehead[2]

RENÉ GIRARD CLAIMED THAT he was "not a theologian," by either training or inclination.[3] His interest was anthropology, what he sometimes described as "gospel anthropology."[4] He referred approvingly to Simone Weil's remark that before presenting a "theory of God," a *theology*, the Gospels offer a "theory of man," an *anthropology*, and he saw his unique task as explicating that "theory of man."[5]

---

1. Teilhard de Chardin, "Trust in Slow Work," line 1.
2. A. Whitehead, "First Lecture," 159.
3. Cowdell, *René Girard*, 85.
4. Girard: *When These Things Begin*, 93; *One by Whom Scandal Comes*, 34.
5. Girard, *I See Satan Fall*, 44, 182.

When Girard does venture into theology, it is usually in support of Christian and Roman Catholic orthodoxy. In various places, he affirms largely conventional beliefs in original sin, the incarnation, the resurrection, the Trinity, the virginal conception of Jesus, and even papal infallibility, all viewed through the lens of mimetic theory.[6] For Girard, "mimetic theory reassures him that his Christian inclinations are in tune with the truth.... It is not the whole of his faith, but it does confirm the heart of this faith."[7]

Girard's contribution has been called "a negative revelation": that the true God is "not to be identified as the violent god of scapegoating."[8] What at times seems to be missing from Girard is any positive sense of exactly who or what God is, and in what sense God can be said to be present and active in the world. "Mimetic theory ... does not make many explicit statements about God."[9] Beyond the basic affirmation that God has nothing to do with violence, any notion of exactly who or what God *is* lacks specificity in Girard's writings.

Both Raymund Schwager and Scott Cowdell have offered interpretations of Girard that advocate the category of theo-drama as the most useful way that theology might incorporate the insights of mimetic theory.[10] *Theo-drama* emphasizes the open-ended and improvisational nature of salvation history, as well as the profound relationality of God, which takes the form of successive rounds of divine initiative and human response. Thus, theo-drama would seem to fit comfortably under the umbrella term of "open and relational theology,"[11] which also includes "process theology."[12] I view process theology as compatible with theo-drama, and by offering more specificity about God's nature, it can

---

6. See, e.g., Girard, *When These Things Begin*, 91, 96, 100, 101; Cowdell, *René Girard*, 87–89.

7. Cowdell, *René Girard*, 85.

8. Rabe, *Processing Mimetic Reality*, 109.

9. Rabe, *Processing Mimetic Reality*, 11.

10. Schwager, *Jesus in the Drama*; Cowdell, *René Girard*. Both Schwager and Cowdell refer to Hans Urs von Balthasar, *Theo-Drama: Theological Dramatic Theory*, a four-volume tome (1976–83).

11. Oord, *Open and Relational Theology*. Open and relational theology affirms that the future is open (as opposed to predetermined by an omnipotent and omniscient God) and that God is intimately related to the world (as opposed to impassable and immutable, unaffected by the world).

12. For a brief introduction to process theology from a Quaker perspective, see Gates, *Reclaiming the Transcendent*.

be a useful adjunct to Girard's mimetic theory.[13] In our never-ending effort to comprehend the divine mystery, theo-drama gives poetic and dramatic expression to that work; open and relational theology lends a more pastoral viewpoint; and process theology provides the philosophical and metaphysical foundation. They can be considered compatible and complementary perspectives.

Briefly, process theology is based in the philosophy of Alfred North Whitehead (writing in the 1920s), who was attempting to answer basic metaphysical questions: Why does anything exist, instead of nothing; why is there order and continuity, instead of chaos; and why is there advance into novelty, instead of endless repetition? Influenced by both evolution and quantum theory, Whitehead began by analyzing the one thing in the universe of which we have firsthand knowledge: our own experience. He saw that the fundamental building blocks of reality are not "things" or substances but events: momentary "drops of experience," each with its internal process of becoming and change, and each intrinsically related to all other "occasions of experience." Each of these occasions begins by "feeling" the influence of past occasions (especially the immediate past), which are partially or even largely determinative. But each occasion of experience is also influenced by the realm of future possibilities, some of which may be quite novel. It is these future possibilities that entice or lure the actual occasions into its becoming.

At this point, Whitehead arrived at a philosophical impasse: *possibilities* do not actually exist and therefore (by his "ontological principle") cannot exert any real influence over present actualities. It is here that Whitehead famously invokes *God* as the "non-temporal actual entity" that mediates to every occasion, in the process of its becoming, the *relevant* possibilities for its future flourishing. God is thus the way in which future possibilities influence the present; nonexistent possibilities become real, influencing the becoming occasion through the mediation of God.

One way of understanding this is to imagine that all the infinite "possible possibilities" are present in "the mind of God," where they exist in some kind of "primordial harmony," what process theologians sometimes call the *Logos*, the ordering principle of the universe. Possibilities are infinite, but only a limited number are relevant to any actual occasion in the moment of its becoming; these limited and relevant possibilities

---

13. Foster has attempted a synthesis of mimetic theory and open and relational thought (*Theology of Consent*). More recently, Rabe has worked to harmonize mimetic theory and process theology (*Processing Mimetic Reality*). See below.

can be thought of as the *Logos incarnate*.[14] Furthermore, these limited possibilities are not just randomly given; some are more highly valued by God than others; and one, "the initial aim," is valued most highly. The initial aim is "God's prayer for the becoming actual occasion," which lends a moral dimension to the exercise of our agency in choosing between relevant possibilities: ideally, we will choose the possibility most valued by God. The Logos permeates all reality through the myriad of these initial aims, and so the basic structure of the universe is seen as incarnational or Christological.

In the moment of its becoming, each actual occasion exercises some degree of subjective agency, by selectively appropriating from past actualities and future possibilities and synthesizing these into a unified but fleeting whole. On the level of human experience, this subjective agency is experienced as real but limited freedom to choose between alternative future possibilities, but Whitehead envisioned that this subjective agency in fact extends all the way down to the quantum level (e.g., through "indeterminacy"). In this view, the universe is not a collection of objects but a community of subjects.[15]

In stark contrast to all preceding Western philosophy, Whitehead sees the human experience of freedom as but a special case of this subjective agency, which pervades all levels of reality. For Whitehead, *experience* does not require *consciousness*; to the extent that all actual occasions participate in reality, they can be said to have subjective *experience*.

All this may seem impossibly abstract, but it has two rather profound theological implications. First, it explains *how* God is everywhere and always present to each and every "drop of experience": as the relevant future possibilities that can promote individual flourishing and the overall well-being of creation. Second, God as the power of future possibilities cannot unilaterally cause any outcome but depends on the cooperation of the creatures, through the exercise of their agency. God acts in the world *only through persuasion*: inviting, suggesting, beckoning, luring us into God's desired future. God's nature is "uncontrolling love," which by definition cannot control or coerce but only persuade.[16]

In the realm of human experience, the presence and lure of God is normally far below the level of our conscious awareness. But on occasion,

---

14. Cobb and Griffin, *Process Theology*, 98–99; Cobb, *Christ in Pluralistic Age*, 82–83.

15. Swimme and Berry, *Universe Story*, 243.

16. Oord, *Uncontrolling Love of God.*

the lure may rise to the level of consciousness, what process theologian John Cobb has called "the call forward"—and which Quakers will immediately recognize as a *leading*.[17] For Cobb (and for Quakers), this is the most authentic way we experience God.

Marjorie Suchocki sums up this understanding of God: "God works with what is, to bring about what might be."[18] Or, expressed differently, "God influences everything, but determines nothing."[19] God cannot unilaterally "make things happen," but can only invite, suggest, and persuade an often-recalcitrant creation into God's desired future of mutual well-being and flourishing.[20] In an evolutionary universe, this can be a painfully slow process. We can now understand why it might take thirteen billion years for intelligent life to emerge in the universe and why it might take long millennia of struggle for humankind to rise above the sacred violence of archaic gods.

In process theology, God is not just the source of *leadings* or *the call forward*. God is also the constant and faithful companion, lovingly responding to how we have responded to the possibilities offered and then, in the next moment of experience, offering yet-new relevant possibilities, based on our new reality. We can think of this is an ongoing and intimate conversation or perhaps a divine-human dance. Marjorie Suchocki gives poetic expression to what is too often expressed in impossibly abstract language:

> Think of it as a dance, whereby at every moment of existence, God touches the world with guidance toward its communal good in that time and place . . . wooing the world toward richer and deeper modes of community.
>
> In this interdependent world, just as surely as we receive from God, God receives from us. Who we are, in every newly becoming moment, is received by God, known by God, felt by God.
>
> God gives to the world, and receives from the world; the world receives from God and gives to God. God gives creative and

---

17. Cobb, *Jesus' Abba*, 64–72.
18. Suchocki, *God, Christ, Church*, 223.
19. Griffin, "Panentheism," 43.
20. See Oord, *God Can't*, for a fuller discussion of what God can and cannot do in open and relational theology.

suggestive energy to the world, and the world gives the results of what it has done with this energy back to God.[21]

René Girard seems to have an intuitive understanding of this "slow work of God." Pressed by an interlocutor about "the mystery of an all-powerful and omniscient God who leaves his creatures free . . . who acts as if he doesn't know where they are headed," Girard urges us "to try to understand the relationship between *the call that comes from God*, on the one hand, and on the other, the interplay of mimetic desire and freedom."[22] Girard seems to be affirming that God acts in the world by means of "the call forward," but God's actions are constrained by our past inheritance as well as the present exercise of human freedom. Critics have sometimes interpreted mimetic desire as a kind a determinism in human affairs, but Girard always "insisted on human freedom alongside mimetic desire."[23]

A related criticism of Girard is why, if Jesus's passion and death was such a decisive revelation, so little has changed in the two thousand years since. Here again, Girard acknowledges that God can work only incrementally, by the slow work of persuasion, constrained by the free choice of humans:

> The disciples rightly saw that the Revelation [of Christ's crucifixion and resurrection] marked the end of the system of things of this world. But they got a little ahead of themselves. They thought that the world had been so profoundly changed by the death of Christ that the scapegoat mechanism would cease functioning immediately. In fact, *not even two millennia* have been enough for the influence of the Passion to really seep in, to penetrate men's minds to the point that this mechanism is disabled once and for all; for the non-guilt of the victims to be fully recognized, together with the illegitimacy of persecution and, more generally, of regimes based on exploitation of one group of people by another; in short, for all the systems of violence that have been breaking down for two thousand years to be exposed. The disciples' only error . . . was to believe all of this could be compressed into an instant, that one could pass from AD 37 or 38 directly to the year 2000.[24]

21. Suchocki, *In God's Presence*, 24, 69; 26; 24.
22. Girard, *When These Things Begin*, 120–21. Emphasis added.
23. Cowdell, *René Girard*, 101. See Cowdell's discussion on mimesis and freedom as a "test case" for Girard (93–102).
24. Girard, *One by Whom Scandal Comes*, 68. Emphasis added.

At first glance, Whitehead (and the process theologians) and Girard seem to be operating from completely different frames of reference, so much so that they would seem to have little in common. Girard's concern was "gospel anthropology," and what he calls *hominization*, the emergence of human nature from the animal world. By contrast, Whitehead's concern was metaphysics; the subtitle to *Process and Reality*, his magnum opus, is *An Essay in Cosmology*.

However, Andre Rabe in his important *Processing Mimetic Reality: Harmonizing Alfred North Whitehead and René Girard*, points out several areas of congruence. Both are heavily influenced by evolution, and both provide a narrative approach to "the big story." Both are highly relational; nothing (including our desires) exists in isolation but only in relation to its environment. And finally, "both Whitehead and Girard recognize that desire is formative of the self."[25] "Both Whiteheadian appetition and Girardian desire emerge in the space between what is and what could be; they can be understood as the tension created by the contrast between the actual and the possible." For both, "desire is how we feel the future—how we feel possibility."[26] Rabe concludes that "Girard enriches Whitehead through exemplification, and Whitehead enriches Girard through an expansion of the overall narrative and deeper ontological insights into the processes."[27]

Perhaps one way to think of all this is to see that Girard's mimetic theory provides a convincing anthropology, but for a complete picture, we need something more. Marcus Borg has written that "without a robust affirmation of the reality of God, Christianity makes no sense."[28] For me, that "robust affirmation of the reality of God" comes not from the "unmoved mover" of Aristotelian metaphysics (imported into classical Christian theology via Augustine and the other early church fathers), but from something like process theology, within the broader rubric of open and relational theology.

All language about God is necessarily metaphorical and therefore limited and inadequate, and so others may choose different ways to think about and talk about God. What is essential is that we do not confuse our *ideas about God* with *the reality of God*. In evaluating our theological metaphors and models, the proper question is not whether they are *true*

---

25. Rabe, *Processing Mimetic Reality*, 85.
26. Rabe, *Processing Mimetic Reality*, 84, 85.
27. Rabe, *Processing Mimetic Reality*, 10.
28. Borg, *Heart of Christianity*, 61.

or *false*, *right* or *wrong*, but, pragmatically, whether or not they are *useful*, *illuminating*, or *fruitful* for our understanding and for our living.[29] We will have more to say in the epilogue about process theology as a complement and corrective to mimetic theory, but for now: process theology for me provides the most useful and fruitful understanding of what we mean when we speak of *God*, filling out Girard's anthropology.

---

29. McFague, *Models of God*, 22–23; 192n37.

PART II

Convincement

> The supreme paradox of the Gospels is that the Resurrection, far from being the supreme mystification, as it is now almost universally interpreted, is the source of all demystification. It is the Resurrection that enables the disciples to say no to unanimity... the violent unanimity that is always visited upon the victim.
>
> —René Girard[1]

IN PART 1, I argued that *conviction* in the Hebrew Scriptures is tied to the issue of *violence*, and specifically, *sacred violence*. This is picked up in the Gospel account of Jesus's passion and crucifixion, which definitively unmask the dynamic of scapegoating violence—the one sin of which we are all guilty. Our perspective was largely anthropological, dealing with the dynamics of human violence. To quote Girard again: "There is nothing in the Gospels to suggest that God causes the mob to come together against Jesus; violent contagion is enough.... We don't have to invoke the supernatural to explicate this."[2]

But Christian faith has always gone beyond the proclamation of Jesus's death to include faith in his resurrection—however we might

---

1. Girard, *One by Whom Scandal Comes*, 61.
2. Girard, *I See Satan Fall*, 21, 22.

understand that. It is clear from the New Testament account that it was Jesus's post-resurrection appearances to his disciples that became the foundational experience for the early church. Something about those appearances was transformative for those who experienced them.

Given that we are all guilty, in one way or another, of the kind of scapegoating violence that killed Jesus, perhaps one way to convey the importance of the resurrection appearances is to imagine a courtroom scene, where we are all on trial for capital murder. The prosecution's case has hit a snag because they cannot produce a body, when into the courtroom strides the supposed victim, not only very much alive but willing to testify on our behalf: "Father, forgive them; for they do not know what they do" (Luke 23:34). Instead of a wronged victim seeking vengeance on those who betrayed and abandoned him, the Risen Christ comes speaking a word of peace: "Peace by with you" (Luke 24:36; John 20:19). So at this basic level, the resurrection not only vindicates Jesus from the charges against him but also acquits those who scapegoated him (which in the end is all of us).[3] For the disciples, the resurrection is experienced as *forgiveness*.[4]

In their separate accounts of the passion and crucifixion, the four Gospels are clearly telling the same story, even if the details differ. But when it comes to the post-resurrection appearances, the accounts diverge; it becomes difficult to say that they are in fact telling the same story. In Mark, the earliest Gospel, there is no account of any resurrection appearance, only an empty tomb, and a mysterious young man who tells the frightened women to go to Galilee, "where you will find him." Matthew records a brief appearance to women in the garden, and then an extended appearance on a mountain in Galilee, where Jesus charges the eleven to "go therefore and make disciples of all nations (Matt 28:19). In Luke, Jesus appears unrecognized to two disciples on the road to Emmaus, then to the disciples in the upper room, and then outside of Jerusalem, where he ascends. John, the latest source, describes an appearance to Mary Magdalene in the garden, then two separate appearances to the disciples in the upper room, and finally in a postscript a detailed description of an appearance to some of the disciples on the shore of the Sea of Galilee (but with no account of an ascension).

As we try to make sense of the diversity of stories concerning the post-Easter appearances, perhaps the best approach is to listen

---

3. Heim, *Saved from Sacrifice*, 145–46.
4. Alison, *Knowing Jesus*, 16.

parabolically, the way we listen to parables.⁵ When we hear the parables of the good Samaritan or the prodigal son, our first question is not "Did this really happen?" Rather, we ask, "Is this true?" Or even better: "*How is this true?*" We intuitively understand that the truth and meaning of a story do not depend on what "really happened." In any event, it seems clear that no amount of textual analysis or source criticism is likely, two millennia after the events, to reveal to us what "really happened."

In the end, perhaps all we can say with confidence is that *something* happened on Easter, something that transformed the frightened and dispirited disciples into bold apostles. What was muddled now became clear, what had looked like defeat now looked like victory, causing "our hearts to burn within us." Because of the resurrection appearances, the apostles gradually were given "the intelligence of the victim" that had previously belonged only to Jesus.

The apostle Paul at one point offers a rather minimalist explanation: that in death Jesus became "a life-giving spirit" (1 Cor 15:45). Elizabeth Johnson elaborates:

> The point of these stories, for all their bewildering diversity, is the same. The disciples are testifying that Jesus became present to them in a new way beyond the distance of time and space forged by death. He was not annihilated by death but transformed to new life by the Spirit, and able to inspire them with peace and boldness.⁶

In part 2, we turn now to convincement, in the Quaker sense of that word (what other traditions might call conversion). The scriptural template for this is *metanoia*, commonly translated as "repent," but conveying in the Greek a sense of turning around, "a dramatic change of direction," a "transformative change of heart."⁷ Jesus's initial proclamation is "The kingdom of God is at hand; repent [*metanoia*] and believe in the good news" (Mark 1:15). In the post-Easter appearances of the Risen Christ, the disciples experienced this *metanoia*. It also seems close to the response of many early Friends to George Fox's (and others') preaching, when, as Fox attests in numerous places in the *Journal*, "many were convinced." He seems to be describing "a transformative change of heart,"

---

5. Borg and Crossan, The Last Week, loc 2870–88 of 3354; see also Gwyn, *Apocalypse of the Word*, 114.

6. Johnson, *Creation and the Cross*, 96.

7. See https://www.merriam-webster.com/dictionary/metanoia.

catalyzed by an encounter with the Inward Light of Christ. One is reminded of contemporary Friend Paul Lacey's description of a Quaker not as someone who believes certain doctrines about Christ nor necessarily someone who follows the teachings of Jesus but someone who "has met the Inward Christ."[8]

We will begin in chapter 15 with a close reading of one of the paradigmatic stories of an encounter with the Risen Christ, Luke's account of the walk to Emmaus. In chapter 16 we will look at Paul's experience on the road to Damascus, anomalous because it is the one encounter with the Risen Christ that occurs several years after the first Easter. We will also explore how in both Acts and Paul's letters, these encounters with the Risen Christ are quickly supplanted by the experience of the Holy Spirit, beginning with Pentecost. In chapter 17, we will consider at some length early Friends experience of "the Inward Light of Christ" and how "Christ has come to teach his people himself," and how those experiences might help us to understand the experience that Friends described as "convincement." Chapter 18 will ask what relevance convincement has for Friends today.

---

8. Lacey, *Leading and Being Led*, 3.

15

The Road to Emmaus

> Were not our hearts burning within us, while he was walking with us on the road, while he was opening the scriptures to us?
>
> —LUKE 24:32

IN THE INTRODUCTORY FRAME to the parable of the good Samaritan, an "expert in the law" puts a question to Jesus: "Teacher, what must I do to inherit eternal life?" Jesus characteristically replies to the question with a question of his own: "What is written in the law? *How do you read it?*" (Luke 10:25–26 NIV, RSV).[1]

James Alison, in his discussion of the Easter story of the road to Emmaus, reminds us that at the time of Jesus, the Law and indeed virtually all Scripture was written in Hebrew. By the time of Second Temple Judaism, most Jews had lost their knowledge of written and spoken Hebrew, and so it had become a language accessible only to a small elite of "experts in the law." Furthermore, written Hebrew at that time contained no vowels, only consonants (the dots and squiggles indicating vowels were added only much later). This meant that "anyone picking up a text to read

---

1. The NRSV inexplicably renders this as "What do you read there?"

it aloud was going to have to supply the appropriate vowels in order to breathe life and meaning into the text."[2]

Alison offers the analogy that if in English we are given only the consonants *l* and *v*, we could read "love"; or "alive," "olive," "lava," "live," or "levee." The reading actually offered would depend on the context as discerned by the reader, but especially on how one had heard it read previously. Thus the tradition's great emphasis on who had been one's teacher. "How do you read it?" is really a question of "Who is your rabbi, your teacher? Through whose eyes do you interpret the text?" Luke has a sophisticated, almost postmodern understanding of *hermeneutics*: what is written on the page (or scroll) is not self-interpreting but is in need of an interpretive principle, "a hermeneutic key." Alison concludes:

> What we have here is something far richer, more sophisticated, more exciting, and indeed more miraculous than a mere miracle story. . . . [Luke] is not only telling a story, but he is giving in considerable detail the answer to a very sophisticated matter of interpretation, what we would call nowadays a hermeneutical question. He is setting out the framework by which Christians answer the question, "Through whose eyes do you read the texts that we call the Scriptures?"[3]

At the time that Luke wrote his Gospel, there were two competing answers to the question "Through whose eyes do you read this text?" In the aftermath of the destruction of the Jerusalem temple in 70 CE, the answer given by the rabbis who were regrouping and inventing rabbinical Judaism was "We read these texts though the eyes of Moses our rabbi." The other answer was the one given by "universalizing or New Testament Judaism, what we now call Christianity: we read the Scriptures through the eyes of Jesus our Rabbi."[4]

The story of the road to Emmaus is not the only warrant for interpreting Scripture through the eyes of "Jesus our rabbi." In the whole KJV, only two people are described as "meek": Moses (Num 12:3) and Jesus (Matt 11:29).[5] In a remarkable text later in Matthew, Jesus tells his disciples, "But you are not to be called 'Rabbi,' *for you have one Teacher, and you are all* [students]. . . . Nor are you to be called 'instructor,' for you

---

2. Alison, *Jesus the Forgiving Victim*, 45.

3. Alison, *Jesus the Forgiving Victim*, 43–44. For his discussion of "the hermeneutic question," see 44–48.

4. Alison, *Jesus the Forgiving Victim*, 48.

5. The NRSV renders both as "humble."

have one Instructor, the Messiah" (Matt 23:8–10 NIV). As will become clear on the road to Emmaus, the claim being made is that Jesus is "the living interpretive principle" through whom we are to read all Scripture.[6]

The road to Emmaus account is in Luke 24:13–35; no matter how familiar you are with the story, I encourage you to read it again. The discussion that follows is largely drawn from James Alison's brilliant essay "Emmaus and Eucharist."[7]

The story begins late on Easter day, with Cleopas and a second unnamed disciple leaving Jerusalem, bound for an otherwise unknown town named Emmaus—apparently running away from possible trouble in Jerusalem. On the road they are "talking and discussing about all these things that have happened" (v. 14) when a stranger approaches and asks them what they are "discussing." The Greek here is *antiballete*, from which we get the English "antiballistic": they are violently throwing opinions back and forth like missiles—having an argument.

The text (v. 17) says at this point the two "looked sad" (NRSV), "their faces downcast" (NIV). The Greek is *skuthropoi* (with downcast visage). Alison says that this is an unusual word in the Septuagint, the Greek translation of the Hebrew Scriptures that would have been familiar to Luke. The one place it does occur is in Genesis, when Joseph is in prison in Egypt. He approaches two fellow prisoners, Pharaoh's baker and butler, who are puzzled by dreams they have been having. Joseph asks them, "Why are your faces downcast today?" (Gen 40:7)—the same Greek word that Luke uses. In the Genesis story, "two people are discussing things which they are unable to interpret, and a third person turns up and offers the definitive interpretation from God. . . . [Luke is] putting a big red flashing light in his text, as if to say, 'Attention, attention, story about interpretation coming up.'"[8]

The named disciple, Cleopas, asks, "Are you the only stranger [visitor (NIV)] to Jerusalem who does not know the things that have taken place there in these days?" (v. 18). The Greek here is *paroikeis* (resident alien), from which we get the English "parochial." The stranger is recognized as someone who is "not from here"—presumably because he spoke with a (Galilean) accent. The two disciples seem predisposed to discount any explanation this stranger might offer—even though virtually *everyone* of

---

6. Alison, *Jesus the Forgiving Victim*, 48–49.
7. Alison, *Jesus the Forgiving Victim*, 43–79.
8. Alison, *Jesus the Forgiving Victim*, 55.

importance in the Hebrew Scriptures could be described as a "resident alien," starting with Abraham, Isaac, Jacob, Joseph, and Moses.

"He asked them, what things?" (v. 19). The two proceed with a confused jumble of explanations concerning Jesus of Nazareth: he was a "prophet mighty in word and deed" and yet was "handed over and condemned to death" by their leaders. Not only a prophet, but "we had hoped he was the one to redeem Israel"—the Messiah. But now, "on the third day, some women of our group have astounded us," finding the tomb empty and reporting a "vision of angels who said he was alive."

By asking "what things" the stranger gives the two disciples ample opportunity to reveal their own confusion—preparing them to now hear the better story about to be offered. The still-unrecognized stranger, "beginning with Moses and all the prophets, interpreted to them the things about himself in all the scriptures" (v. 27). The Scriptures here are of course the Hebrew Scriptures, the Christian Old Testament. *It is not that these Scriptures explain Jesus but that Jesus explains, or interprets, the Scriptures.* He is presenting himself as "the hermeneutic key" to our understanding. This is "the Emmaus way" of reading Scripture:[9] the "Word of God" is *not* the written word in the Bible, but the Word is Christ, the Logos, present from the beginning (John 1:1–2). It is Christ as the Word of God who reveals the meaning of Scripture, not the other way around. All Scripture is to be interpreted through the lens of God's revelation in Christ; this is "the Emmaus way" of reading Scripture.

We associate Christ as the Word (Logos) of God with the New Testament, but "the word of the Lord" is also a frequent theme in the Hebrew Scriptures. A KJV concordance gives hundreds of entries for "the word of the Lord," typically to introduce the authoritative pronouncement of a prophet. A representative example is Jer 1, where the prophet twice says that "the word of the Lord came to me" (1:4, 11) but elsewhere says "the Lord said to me" (1:7, 14). "The word of the Lord" seems to be not just a voice but a personal manifestation of Yahweh, simultaneously separate from, yet identified with, Yahweh. Eastern Orthodox biblical scholar Stephen De Young elaborates:

> What these various Old Testament visions and events indicate is that in pre-Christian Judaism, the Word of the Lord was perceived and understood as a divine Person who had appeared

---

9. Jersak, *More Christlike Word*, esp. 125–36.

and spoken to the prophets in bodily form. *This Person was both distinguished from and identified as Yahweh, the God of Israel.*[10]

Thus, when the prologue to John's Gospel identifies Christ with the Logos, the Word, there is no need to appeal to Greek philosophy to explicate; the "Word of the Lord" in the Hebrew Scriptures provides sufficient precedent.[11] By the time of the New Testament, the Word had long been understood within Second Temple Judaism as a manifestation or *hypostasis* of Yahweh; what was new was the suggestion that this Word had become incarnate in a specific person, Jesus of Nazareth, "the Word made flesh" (John 1:14).

Christ as the Word of God who interprets Scripture (literally, "that which is written") should sound very familiar to Quakers. George Fox referred to the Bible as "words" or "writings," but *Christ* was the Word of God. "For I told them what the Scriptures themselves said, that they were the words of God but Christ was the Word."[12] This view was decidedly controversial, as can be seen from Fox's interrogation after his 1653 arrest in Carlisle: "They asked me whether the Scripture was the word of God; I said God was the Word and the Scriptures were writings; and the Word was before the writings were.... And so after a long examination they sent me to prison as a blasphemer, a heretic, and a seducer."[13]

Fox was also adamant that it was not enough to simply read the words of Scripture. "The Scriptures were given forth by the spirit of God and all people must first come to the spirit of God in themselves by which they might know God and Christ . . . so that the spirit of God must be in them that come to know them [the Scriptures] again . . . and without it they cannot know neither God, nor Christ, nor the Scriptures."[14]

Fox and the early Quakers may have been lax when it came to the doctrine of the Trinity (even to the extent of not using the word, which they pointed out was not scriptural): Spirit, Word, God, Christ, and Light were used more or less interchangeably. Douglas Gwyn elaborates:

> It is perhaps Fox's most valuable contribution that he rejoins *the Spirit* and *the Word* in the prophetic experience of *the risen Christ*. While he presents Jesus *Christ as the one Word of God,*

---

10. De Young, *Religion of the Apostles*, 21. Emphasis added.
11. De Young, *Religion of the Apostles*, 21.
12. G. Fox, *Journal*, 146.
13. G. Fox, *Journal*, 159. See also Gates, *Opening the Scriptures*, 8–9.
14. G. Fox, *Journal*, 136.

present and teaching by his *Spirit*, he places scripture, the historical record of the Word's work, as the *words* of God. *The true Word is the Christ* who is speaking now.[15]

All of this strikingly resonates with "reading Scripture the Emmaus way." When we read "in the spirit by which they were given forth," with Jesus as our rabbi, the Word that is Christ can be seen prefigured and foreshadowed in the Hebrew Scriptures.[16] Fox speaks of the "types, figures and shadows" of the Hebrew Scriptures, contrasted with the "substance," which is Christ. The story is messy, with "texts in travail," because, as Peter Enns says, "God lets his children tell the story,"[17] and all too often the children's prejudices, unconscious projections, psychological shadows, and cultural biases get in the way. Scripture reveals to us both God and our humanity, in decidedly mixed proportions.

Returning to the road to Emmaus: the stranger appears to be ready to depart, "as if he were going on." But the two disciples invite him to stay and share a meal—the prototypical gesture of Jesus's entire ministry. The stranger quickly makes himself the host, taking the bread, blessing and breaking it, at which point "their eyes were opened, they recognized him, and he vanished from their sight" (v. 31). Or, as Alison renders the Greek, "he unappearing became," a "classic Yahwistic theophany."[18] It seems that the Risen Christ, our "living interpretive principle," our hermeneutic key, will "unappearing become" as soon as he is recognized.

Alison points out that what has been happening is that the two disciples have been walking and talking *with a dead man*. It is not that the Risen Christ has "recovered from a nasty bout of death." *He really is dead*. "Ordinarily being alive and being dead are two equal and opposite realities: you can only be one of them at a given time. We cannot easily understand the sort of 'being alive' that is able to assume within it, take inside itself, 'being dead.'"[19]

The nearest parallel we have for "dead men talking" would be ghosts. Indeed, later that same evening, when Jesus appears to the other disciples in the upper room, the disciples "were startled and terrified, and thought they were seeing a ghost" (24:37). But ghosts come seeking

15. Gwyn, *Apocalypse of the Word*, 122. Emphasis added.

16. Jersak, *More Christlike Word*, subtitle. See also his chs. 8, 11; above, pt. 1, "Conviction," for Fox's use of the same terminology.

17. Enns, "God Lets His Children," quoted in Jersak, *More Christlike Word*, 62.

18. Alison, *Jesus the Forgiving Victim*, 69.

19. Alison, *Jesus the Forgiving Victim*, 74.

revenge, and here "there is no request for vengeance." The stranger on the road to Emmaus is "seriously unbothered by what other people did to him. . . . Not only, then, is it a dead man talking, but it's a dead man talking without any rancor."[20] "*This is a victim telling the story, but it's not a victimary story.*"[21]

When the two disciples recognize their companion as the Risen Christ and he "unappearing became," they exclaim, "Were not our hearts burning within us while he was talking to us on the road, while he was *opening the scriptures to us*? That same hour they got up and returned to Jerusalem" (vv. 32–33). As a result of their encounter, the two disciples have a metanoia experience, "a transformative change of heart," quite literally a change in direction. They had been fleeing Jerusalem in fear; now they return to proclaim their experience to the other disciples.

By any measure, the road to Emmaus is an astonishing story. As Alison says, this is "something far richer, more sophisticated, more exciting, and indeed more miraculous than a mere miracle story." Written some fifty years after the events it describes, it demonstrates the community's deep reflection on the meaning and significance of the story. That process led to the conviction that the Risen Christ was their "living hermeneutic key" to reading the Hebrew Scriptures. Whatever happened on the road to Emmaus on that first Easter, clearly *something* happened.

We turn now to another encounter on another road: Paul's experience on the road to Damascus.

---

20. Alison, *Jesus the Forgiving Victim*, 75.
21. Alison, *Jesus the Forgiving Victim*, 76. Emphasis added.

16

Paul on the Road to Damascus

> The divine voice raises only one issue with Paul: violence.... For Paul, to accept Jesus is to be converted from scapegoating persecution to identifying with those against whom he had practiced it.
>
> —S. Mark Heim[1]

IN THE PREVIOUS CHAPTER, while considering the appearance of the Risen Christ to the two disciples on the road to Emmaus, we noted that the post-Easter appearance stories are a bit of a jumble: no two Gospel accounts agree on even the most basic details. Raymund Schwager remarks that all the recorded appearances occurred in the days and weeks immediately after Jesus's crucifixion and resurrection, and are characterized by fear and uncertainty on the part of the disciples.[2] In Mark, the women at the tomb were "alarmed" and "fled from the tomb [in] terror and amazement ... for they were afraid" (Mark 16:5, 8). In Matthew, the women at the tomb were told first by the angel and then the Risen Christ, "Do not be afraid," which implies that they were in fact afraid. Later, in Galilee, some of the disciples "doubted" or were "uncertain" (Matt 28:5, 10, 17).

---

1. Heim, *Saved from Sacrifice*, 139.
2. Schwager, *Jesus in the Drama*, 142.

In Luke, the disciples in the upper room were "startled and terrified, and thought they were seeing a ghost" (Luke 24:37). In John, the disciples on Easter evening were in a locked room "for fear of the Jews" (John 20:19).

With Pentecost (fifty days after Passover and the crucifixion) two things changed. First, further appearances of the Risen Christ ceased, replaced by the coming of the Holy Spirit. And second, instead of fear and uncertainty, the disciples began to demonstrate "boldness" (Acts 4:13, 29, 31) as they were "filled with the Holy Spirit" (Acts 2:4, 38; 4:8). Heretofore, the disciples had experienced Christ outwardly, either in the pre-Easter ministry of Jesus or in the post-Easter appearances. But with Pentecost, there is a shift to the inward experience of the Holy Spirit. Although the coming of the Spirit was accompanied by outward signs (rushing wind, tongues "as of fire"), these are divorced from any particular connection to the person of Jesus. The experience of the Holy Spirit was primarily an inward one, though now available to all; Peter quotes the prophet Joel, "I will pour out my spirit on *all* flesh" (Acts 2:17; Joel 2:28–32).

There is one major exception to this pattern: the appearance of the Risen Christ to Saul/Paul, on the road to Damascus, which occurred some years after Pentecost, well after the appearances had otherwise ceased. Paul himself, writing about twenty years before the earliest gospel, provides a cryptic list of several post-resurrection appearances and then claims, "Last of all, as to one untimely born, he appeared to me" (1 Cor 15:3–8). It is clear that Paul considered this a genuine appearance of the Risen Christ, which in turn gave him the authority of an apostle.

The actual description of this episode occurs in Acts 9:1–19 (subsequently repeated in Acts 22 and 26, when Paul narrates the story at his trials). Saul (his Hebrew name), "zealous for the law," had become one of the chief persecutors of the nascent Christian community. At this point, Saul is very much *unlike* the fearful and uncertain disciples on Easter: he is a self-righteous and fervent opponent of the new movement. However, on the road to Damascus, he is struck down by a blinding light and hears a voice: "Saul, Saul, why do you persecute me?" He asks, "Who are you, Lord?" and hears in reply, "I am Jesus, *whom you are persecuting*." The story goes on, but the result is that Saul, the chief persecutor of the early church, becomes Paul, its most important defender. Mark Heim emphasizes the importance of this unexpected transformation:

> The divine voice raises only one issue with Paul: violence. . . .
> The simple, original substance of Saul's conversion is his change
> from orchestrating violent animosity against a minority to

joining in community with those who were his victims. This is hardly a minor point. For Paul, to accept Jesus is to be converted from scapegoating persecution to identifying with those against whom he had practiced it. *There could hardly be more powerful continuity with the themes we have been exploring.*[3]

On the road to Emmaus, we heard the claim that Christ is the hermeneutic key that opens and interprets Scripture. On the road to Damascus, we receive confirmation that this interpretive key concerns violence, and specifically the violent scapegoating of innocent victims. In a flash of insight, Paul realizes that his zeal for the law has made him into a persecutor, an accomplice to murder, and he understands his violent persecution of the early church as identical to "the violence that killed Jesus and scapegoated the gentiles. . . . It was, for him, the violence of the Jewish community misusing the Law as a weapon of exclusion and persecution."[4]

Even a superficial reading of Paul's epistles (especially Galatians and Romans) shows his ambivalent and often negative assessment of the Jewish law. Commentators have not always been able to account for this;[5] some have even (illogically) accused Paul of anti-Judaism. But the specifics of his conversion experience provide a sufficient explanation: Paul saw that a certain (mis)interpretation of the law had made him into a violent persecutor. Any reading of Paul that does not take into account his previous violent persecution of the church, and his subsequent repudiation of that persecution, must be judged inadequate.

Even though Paul expresses a negative view of the law, he always insists that he "remains a Jew."[6] During his last journey to Jerusalem, he was in the temple to mark the "completion of the days of purification" with sacrifices when he was arrested (Acts 21:26)—even while advocating that gentile converts not be required to observe Jewish customs. His "conversion" on the road to Damascus is best understood not as a conversion from Judaism to "Christianity" but from one understanding of Judaism to a different understanding, free from the exclusionary and scapegoating propensities of the Mosaic law, as it was then commonly interpreted.[7] Recall here that Paul was opposed not to rabbinic Judaism, which

---

3. Heim, *Saved from Sacrifice*, 139. Emphasis added.
4. Hammerton-Kelly, *Sacred Violence*, 10.
5. Timothy Peat, in B. Dandelion et al., *Heaven on Earth*, 35–37. See ch. 22 below.
6. Hammerton-Kelly, *Sacred Violence*, 132, basing his argument on Rom 9:1–5.
7. More on this in ch. 22, where we will see that Paul's "conversion" is more

only emerged decades later, but to late Second Temple Judaism—which within a few short years would embark upon a disastrous and violent revolt against Rome, leading to the destruction of the Jerusalem temple in 70 CE.

We noted earlier that with the coming of the Holy Spirit at Pentecost, appearances of the Risen Christ ceased (with the exception of Paul). After Pentecost, the Holy Spirit continues to play an important if enigmatic role in the early church. As depicted in Acts, the coming of the Holy Spirit was a discrete, observable, and dramatic event; the Spirit is described as "falling upon" (10:44; 11:15) or "coming upon" (19:6) believers as a recognizable experience. On at least two occasions, believers who had "not yet received the Holy Spirit" despite having undergone "the baptism of John" (Acts 8:15–18; 19:2–6) subsequently received the Spirit through the laying on of hands from the apostles (Peter and John in Acts 8, Paul in Acts 19). On other occasions, the Holy Spirit is described as coming before water baptism (Acts 10:44–48). Such examples led early Friends to hold that water baptism was neither necessary nor sufficient to make a Christian but only "the baptism of the Spirit," which in their understanding was the same as the coming of the Holy Spirit.[8] The words of the Risen Christ (Acts 1:5) support this: "For John baptized with water but you will be baptized with the Holy Spirit not many days from now." The coming of the Holy Spirit at Pentecost (and subsequently) *is* the baptism of the Spirit.

The process theologian John Cobb, in his *Jesus' Abba: The God Who Has Not Failed*, maintains that in the Gospel account of Jesus ministry, God is present to Jesus as "Abba," an intimate and immanent divine presence that is like a nurturing and protective parent. In his second chapter, he asks (in the chapter title), "What Happened to Abba in Western History?" His first answer to that question is that Jesus's Abba became "the Spirit" in the early church, conveying that same intimate and immanent presence that Jesus experienced as Abba. Cobb continues:

> A fundamental characteristic of [Paul's] congregations was the experience of the Spirit. This could be thought of as the Spirit of God, but Paul never separated it from Jesus. The God of whom he speaks is emphatically the Abba of Jesus. When he speaks of the Spirit of God, Jesus is already implied. . . . He was speaking of the Spirit that was so powerfully felt by the participants in his

---

accurately understood as his "call" to become the apostle to the gentiles.

8. See Barclay, *Apology*, 301–26.

congregations that its reality was never in doubt. . . . Because this was the Spirit of Jesus and of Jesus' Abba, it was also first and foremost the Spirit of love.[9]

It is clear from Paul's epistles that it was this presence of the Spirit that characterized the New Testament church. Of dozens of references, here is a brief sampling: "You are in the Spirit, since the Spirit of God dwells in you" [plural "you"] (Rom 8:9).[10] "For all who are led by the Spirit of God are children of God" (Rom 8:14). "Do you not know that you are God's temple, and that God's Spirit dwells in you?" (1 Cor 3:16). "To each is given the manifestation of the Spirit for the common good" (1 Cor 12:7). "God has sent the Spirit of his son into our hearts, crying, 'Abba! Father!'" (Gal 4:6). "If we live by the Spirit, let us also be guided by the Spirit" (Gal 5:25). "Be filled with the Spirit" (Eph 5:18). "God who also gives his Holy Spirit to you" (1 Thess 4:8).

For Paul, the Spirit not only "gives life" (1 Cor 15:45; 2 Cor 2:6) but also leads us and guides us: it is functional. This resonates with Jesus's own words in the Gospel of John: the Holy Spirit, the Advocate, will "teach you everything, and remind you of all I have said" (John 14:26); "when the Spirit of truth comes, he will guide you into all truth" (16:13). Early Friends shared this functional view of the Spirit, which "speaks to our spiritual ear" as "an inward voice speaking to the ear of the soul."[11] "The Spirit of God is not a lazy, dumb, useless thing, but [it] moves, actuates, governs, instructs, and teaches him in whom he dwells."[12]

Can we say anything more about this functional role of the Spirit? I think we can, but it requires delving into some of the translation issues from New Testament Greek into English. For this I am dependent on the insights of Quaker New Testament scholar Timothy Peat.[13]

---

9. Cobb, *Jesus' Abba*, 37–38.

10. Note that in Rom 8 and generally throughout Paul's epistles, when the Spirit is described as "in you," the Greek specifies the plural and not singular *you*; the Spirit dwells in the community. See Hammerton-Kelly, *Sacred Violence*, 149. Modern English does not distinguish between the singular and plural forms of *you*, so this distinction is easily overlooked in English translation.

11. Barclay, *Apology*, 28.

12. Barclay, *Apology*, 36.

13. Peat, chs. 2–7, in B. Dandelion et al., *Heaven on Earth* (esp. ch. 3). Peat's analysis demonstrates how attention to the detail of the Greek text can bring out nuances of meaning that do not always come through in English translation. For a more detailed treatment of these same themes, see Ashworth, *Paul's Necessary Sin*. Note that in recent years Timothy Peat has chosen to go by Timothy Ashworth.

According to Peat (and many others), Paul contrasts "the law" with "faith" throughout his epistles. Law functions as an external constraint on our actions; faith for Paul is an internally experienced guide. Faith should be understood not as belief in doctrines (faith *in* Jesus) but as *faithfulness* to God's leadings, as *exemplified* by Jesus (the faith or faithfulness *of* Jesus; an alternative and legitimate translation of, for example, Rom 3:26; Gal 2:16).[14] Faith, according to Peat, is "living under direct guidance from God; living with confidence that God's word is active and can be discerned."[15]

In Galatians, Paul asks rhetorically, "Did you receive the Spirit by doing the works of the law or by *believing what you heard*? . . . Does God supply you with the Spirit and work miracles among you by your doing the works of the law, or by *believing what you heard*?" (Gal 3:2, 5). The Greek phrase translated as "believing what you heard" is *akoe pisteos*. The second word is straightforward: it is the genitive (possessive) of the noun "faith," so the "*x* of faith" or "faith's *x*." The first word is more problematic: it is a noun that is derived from the verb "to hear." In English, we can speak of hearing a voice, a bird, a song—but there is no noun to indicate "something heard" without specifying *what* is heard. So translators must make an assumption about *what* was heard, and the assumption is usually that it was something like "the Gospel message" (REB) or "believing what you heard" (NIV, NRSV). Peat, however, proposes translating the phrase as "faith's 'heard thing,'" which is clumsy in English but better expresses the nuances of Paul's Greek.[16]

Peat is suggesting that with "faith's heard thing" or "God's heard thing" (1 Thess 2:13), Paul is speaking not of the Gospel message as preached, but "something heard within the believer. . . . What is heard in association with the coming of the Spirit is the prophetic word from God, guiding the actions of those who receive it."[17] Paul is describing a life guided not by the external law but by "this voice from God which sounds within . . . faith's inner voice."[18]

---

14. Timothy Peat, in B. Dandelion et al., *Heaven on Earth*, 54, 59. The alternative translation is given as a footnote in the NRSV. For a discussion of the relevant point of Greek grammar, see Campbell and DePue, *Beyond Justification*, 309–14. See also ch. 22 below.

15. Timothy Peat, in B. Dandelion et al., *Heaven on Earth*, 19.
16. Timothy Peat, in B. Dandelion et al., *Heaven on Earth*, 28–32.
17. Timothy Peat, in B. Dandelion et al., *Heaven on Earth*, 32.
18. Timothy Peat, in B. Dandelion et al., *Heaven on Earth*, 27, 32.

This "heard thing" connects directly with the "word of prophecy." Peat reminds us that although we often think of prophecy as foretelling the future, the broader and richer meaning is "to speak by divine inspiration."[19] In 1 Cor 14, Paul discusses the ways in which the Spirit "speaks" within the community, in contrast to their former worship of "idols that could not speak" (12:2). He compares "speaking in tongues" with those who "prophesy." "Those who speak in a tongue do not speak to other people but to God, for nobody understands them." But "those who prophesy speak to other people for their upbuilding and encouragement and consolation. . . . Those who prophesy build up the church. . . . One who prophesies is greater than the one who speaks in tongues" (14:2–5).

As Paul continues in 1 Cor 14, he gives perhaps the fullest description we have of worship in the early church:

> When you come together, each one has a hymn, a lesson, a revelation, a tongue, or an interpretation. Let all things be done for building up. . . . Let two or three prophets speak, and let the others weigh what is said. If a revelation is made to someone else sitting nearby, let the first person be silent. For you can all prophesy one by one, so that all may learn and be encouraged. (1 Cor 14:26–31)

Prophets speak to the community what they have heard within: "God's heard thing." The others "weigh what is said," presumably to discern if it is truly from God. It is impossible to read Paul's description without thinking of Quaker waiting worship—at least on our better days.

Paul sees the presence of the Spirit as fundamentally transforming, a kind of liberation, now universally available to all through Christ's crucifixion and resurrection. The believer is liberated from sin, and from the law: "But if you are led by the Spirit, you are not subject to the law" (Gal 5:18). Those in the Spirit "have died to the law" (Rom 7:4); "the law of the Spirit of life in Christ Jesus has set you free from the law of sin and death" (Rom 8:2). To those guided by the Spirit, by "faith's inner voice," the external constraint of the law is not only unnecessary but counterproductive.

And yet: despite Paul's lofty vision of the Spirit bringing universal transformation, his correspondence with his churches frequently alludes to controversies, conflicts, and divisions. Reality seems to fall far short of his ideal. How does he explain this?

---

19. Timothy Peat, in B. Dandelion et al., *Heaven on Earth*, 19.

Peat notes that Paul often qualifies the implications of the coming of the Spirit: he speaks of "we who have the *first fruits* of the Spirit" (Rom 8:23) and of God through Christ "giving us his Spirit in our hearts as a *first installment*" (2 Cor 1:22).[20] More explicitly, Paul says that now "we know only in part, and we prophesy only in part, but when the complete comes, the partial will come to an end. . . . For now we see in a mirror, dimly, but then we will see face to face. *Now I know only in part; then I will know fully*" (1 Cor 13: 9–10, 12).

Paul is speaking here of "a change that is still to come."[21] In his earliest letter, Paul describes what eventually became the conventional understanding of Christ's second coming: "For the Lord himself, with the archangel's call and with the sound of God's trumpet, will descend from heaven. . . . Then we who are alive, who are left, will be caught up in the clouds together with them [those in the church who have died] to meet the Lord in the air" (1 Thess 4:16–17). Over time, Paul's description of "the change that is still to come" becomes less definite and more inclusive. He declares in Galatians, "I have been crucified with Christ, and it is no longer I who live, but it is Christ who lives in me" (Gal 2:19–20). Paul is making the "extraordinary suggestion"[22] that just as God was incarnate in Jesus of Nazareth, Christ could be incarnate in Paul, and by extension in others, through "the faith *of* the Son of God" (Gal 2:20). According to Peat, the same faithfulness that was in Jesus was now a possibility for all, "so that now there might be a second incarnation: the whole of humankind as the incarnation of God." Paul's mature "view of the Second Coming of Christ was not of an individual returning, but an incarnation of God in all humanity."[23]

The fullness of that possibility lies in the future. Paul describes the church in Corinth as "infants in Christ . . . not yet ready for solid food" (1 Cor 3:1–2). Unlike Paul, the early church has not yet grown to adulthood; they have received only "the first installment" of the Spirit; they know "only in part." In the next chapter, we turn to the convincement experience of early Friends—who believed that they were receiving the next installment.

---

20. Timothy Peat, in B. Dandelion et al., *Heaven on Earth*, 73.
21. Timothy Peat, in B. Dandelion et al., *Heaven on Earth*, 70.
22. Timothy Peat, in B. Dandelion et al., *Heaven on Earth*, 63.
23. Timothy Peat, in B. Dandelion et al., *Heaven on Earth*, 63, 238.

17

Convincement in the Experience of Early Friends

> Then, oh then, I heard a voice ... and this I knew experimentally.
>
> —GEORGE FOX[1]

GEORGE FOX IN HIS *Journal* often uses a formula statement to summarize how his preaching was able to *convince* others: "And so I *opened the Scriptures* to them and our principles, and *turned them from darkness to the light* of Christ and his spirit by which they might know the Scriptures."[2] There could hardly be a more powerful illustration of the continuity between early Friends and the topic of the last two chapters. "Opening the Scriptures" is how the two disciples on the road to Emmaus described their encounter with the Risen Christ (Luke 24:32): "Were not our hearts burning within us while he was talking with us on the road, while he was *opening the scriptures* to us"? The second part of Fox's formula, "turned them from darkness to light," echoes the account Paul gave to King Agrippa concerning his encounter on the road to Damascus, and his subsequent call to spread the gospel to the gentiles, "to open their eyes

---

1. G. Fox, *Journal*, 11.
2. G. Fox, *Journal*, 352. Emphasis added. For variations of this, see 89, 109, 152, 271.

so that they may *turn from darkness to light*, and from the power of Satan to the power of God" (Acts 26:18).

In using these words to describe his mission, Fox of course never quotes "chapter and verse"; it is possible that his choice of words was on some level unconscious. This is an example of how, as Douglas Gwyn puts it, Fox does not so much *cite* Scripture as *breathe* it.[3] We see Fox here adopting the biblical language of the apostles because he, like them, has had his own encounter with the Risen Christ, experienced inwardly. Fox sees his mission in continuity with that of the apostles, and so he is drawn to their words in describing his mission.[4]

Fox describes the pivotal experience in his own convincement in a well-known passage from the *Journal*:

> But as I had forsaken all the [parish] priests, so I left the separate preachers [separatists], and also those called the most experienced people; for I saw that there was none among them that could speak to my condition. And when all my hopes in them and in all men were gone, so that I had nothing outwardly to help me, nor could tell what to do, then, oh then, *I heard a voice* which said, "There is one, even Christ Jesus, that can speak to thy condition," and when I heard it my heart did leap for joy. Then the Lord did let me see why there was none upon the earth who could speak to my condition, namely that I might give him the glory; for all are concluded under sin and shut up in unbelief, as I had been, that Jesus Christ might have pre-eminence, who enlightens, and gives grace, and faith, and power.... And this I knew experimentally.[5]

Fox here provides a summary of his long process of *conviction*, not so much of any specific sin but of a general state of alienation and of the radical inadequacy of all the varieties of religion on offer to him. He is describing what in other settings might be called the dark night of the soul: "All my hopes ... were gone, so that I had nothing outwardly to help me." His *convincement* begins when he "hears a voice." It is not the voice *of* Christ but a voice directing him *to* Christ, as inwardly experienced. Would it be too much of a stretch to say that Fox, like Paul, is describing an experience of *God's heard thing*?

---

3. Gwyn, *Apocalypse of the Word*, 146. See also Guiton, *Early Quakers*, 122; Gates, "George Fox and Bible."

4. Gates, *Opening the Scriptures*, 2–3.

5. G. Fox, *Journal*, 11. Emphasis added.

Other early Quakers had similar experiences. William Dewsbury (1621–88) was three years older than Fox; if anything, his journey among the various sects was even more tortured than Fox's. He relates that his journey started at the tender age of eight, when he became aware that "the light in my conscience did witness against me . . . against my pride, pleasures, lightness and vanity."[6] Over many years, he earnestly traveled among various denominations "who were seeking the Kingdom of God in outward observations, as I had done."[7] Eventually he joined Parliament's army, to "fight for the Gospel," but there found only "as much ignorance of the Gospel as I was in."[8]

> Then my mind was turned within, by the power of the Lord, to wait in his counsel [for] the light in my conscience, to hear what the Lord would say; and *the word of the Lord came unto me* and said, "put up thy sword into thy scabbard; if my kingdom were of this world, then would my children fight" . . . and [I] discovered the mystery of iniquity, and that the Kingdom of Christ was within; and the enemy was within and was spiritual, and my weapons against them must be spiritual, the power of God . . . but then the Lord discovered to me the deceits of all the men in England, that were seeking the Kingdom of Heaven in outward observations . . . [which caused me] to yield in obedience, to put up my carnal sword into the scabbard, and to leave the Army.[9]

As with Fox, note "the word of the Lord came unto me" ("God's heard thing"). Dewsbury's "resolution to turn inward changed everything. . . . It redirected the focus of struggle from outward, political, and miliary warfare to inward, spiritual warfare." This pivotal event occurred in about 1645, but "his discovery of inward spiritual authority only deepened his turmoil at first."[10] It was not until several years later, in late 1651, that he connected with George Fox, becoming one of the most important and influential of those "convinced of the truth." Like several others, "it appears likely that Dewsbury had found his way to a Quaker-like faith before he met Fox."[11]

---

6. Dewsbury, *Discovery of Great Enmity*, 12.
7. Dewsbury, *Discovery of Great Enmity*, 14.
8. Dewsbury, *Discovery of Great Enmity*, 16.
9. Dewsbury, *Discovery of Great Enmity*, 16–17. Emphasis added.
10. Gwyn, *Seekers Found*, 224–26.
11. Moore, *Light in Their Consciences*, 12.

James Nayler, second only to Fox in his influence among early Friends, had likewise spent several years in Parliament's army, where he was known as a radical and charismatic preacher. He, too, eventually left the army and returned to his Yorkshire farm. At his 1653 trial for blasphemy, he relates that the critical incident in his own convincement also involved hearing a voice:

> I was at the plough, meditating on the things of God, and suddenly *I heard a Voice* saying unto me, "Get thee out from thy kindred and from thy father's house" [see Gen 12:1]. And I had a promise given in with it. Whereupon I did exceedingly rejoice, that I *heard the voice* of that God which I had professed from a child, but had never known him.[12]

Asked by the justices whether this was an *audible* voice, Nayler replied, "No, Friend, it was not a carnal voice, audible to the outward ear."[13] He was then asked what the nature of the promise was. "That God would be with me: which promise I find made good every day."[14] Further questioned whether by speaking of this "Inward Christ" he was denying the sacrificial death of the historical Jesus in Jerusalem, he memorably replied, "If I cannot witness Christ nearer than Jerusalem, I shall have no benefit by him: but I own no other Christ but that who witnessed a good confession before Pontius Pilate; *which Christ I witness in me now*."[15]

Isaac Penington's convincement offers somewhat of a contrast to Fox, Nayler, and Dewsbury. Like them, Penington had years of seeking and spiritual desolation, well documented in his pre-Quaker writings. In a "letter to an intimate friend," published in 1650, he describes his state: "everything is darkness, death, emptiness, vanity, a lie. . . . I am weary of all things, of religion, reason, sense, and all the objects that these have to converse about."[16] But unlike Fox, Dewsbury, Nayler, and many Friends described in *The First Publishers of Truth* (see below), Penington's convincement was slow and gradual, extending over most of two years. For Fox, the experience of the light was "powerful, overwhelming, irresistible." But Penington emphasizes "the smallness of the light" and the need

12. Nayler, "Saul's Errand to Damascus," 1:29. Emphasis added.
13. Frances Higginson, "The Irreligion of the Northern Quakers" (quoting Nayler), in Barbour and Roberts, *Early Quaker Writings*, 68.
14. Nayler, "Saul's Errand to Damascus," 1:29.
15. James Nayler, in Barbour and Roberts, *Early Quaker Writings*, 261. Emphasis added.
16. Penington, *Knowing the Mystery*, 9.

for "lowliness and humility of thy heart"—exceedingly difficult for a man of such intellect and learning. This smallness makes it easy to overlook the presence of the light, "this little weak thing of God." Instead, Penington was (mistakenly) "believing that my condition required the manifest appearance of a very great power to help me."[17]

Isaac and Mary Penington were "not favorably impressed" with their first contact with Quakers, in 1656. Isaac later wrote that "the more I conversed with them, the more I seemed in my understanding and reason to get over them, and to trample them under my feet, as a poor, weak, silly, and contemptible generation, who had some smatterings of truth . . . but very far from the clear and full understanding of his way and will . . . and therein I daily more and more despised them."[18] But by 1658, the Peningtons were known to have attended a series of Quaker meetings. On May 31, at a large meeting attended by Fox, other leading Friends, and as many as three thousand Quakers, Isaac Penington "definitely decided for Quakerism"; likely it was Fox's preaching about the seed of Christ that "thrust Isaac over the precipice."[19] For Penington, it seems it was not so much "hearing a voice" as "feeling the life." He elaborates:

> After a long time I was invited to hear one of them. . . . And indeed, when I came, I felt the presence and power of the Most high among them, and words of truth from the spirit of truth reaching to my heart and conscience. . . . I did not only feel words and demonstrations from without, but I felt the dead quickened, the seed raised; insomuch that my heart said, This is he, there is no other: this is he whom I have waited for and sought after from my childhood; who was always near me, and had begotten life in my heart; but I knew him not distinctly, nor how to receive him, or dwell with him. . . . And I was given up to the Lord, to become his, both in waiting for the further revealing of his seed in me, and to serve him in the life and power of the seed.[20]

By contrast, Barbara Blaugdone, in her account of her convincement in the mid-1650s, does not emphasize any strong pre-Quaker sense of sin

17. Penington, *Works*, 2:290, quoted in Halvorsen, "Day of Small Things," 122.

18. Penington, *Knowing the Mystery*, 16.

19. Gwyn, *Seekers Found*, 286. Gwyn gives a fine summary of Penington's journey to convincement (265–98). Fox gives a brief summary of his preaching ("the Seed is Christ") before "three or four thousand people" that day (*Journal*, 339).

20. Penington, *Knowing the Mystery*, 17; 14–20 also gives a succinct account of Penington's prolonged experience of convincement.

and alienation. She says only that in her youth, she "feared the Lord . . . and was zealous and diligent . . . and sought the Lord earnestly, although I knew not where to find him." When traveling ministers John Audland and John Camm came from the north to Bristol, she relates that their "behavior and deportments were such, that it preached before they ever opened their mouths . . . and when they did open their mouths . . . and directed my mind unto the Light of Christ, therein to wait, which I was diligent to do, and found the virtue of it; and as the evil was made manifest, I departed from it, and willingly took up the Cross." After adopting "plainness in speech and in my habit," as well as preaching "in their public places and steeple-houses," she lost her employment as a schoolteacher and suffered several imprisonments while traveling in the ministry.[21]

Perhaps the most complete account of convincement among the early Quaker leaders was that of Francis Howgill, in his 1656 "The Inheritance of Jacob Discovered." Like the others, Howgill spent years moving through various denominations and sects. By age twelve, he was a scrupulous young Puritan, "setting my heart to know the God which the world professed," praying three or four times a day, and reading the Bible, but "in my imagination I imagined God at a distance." Over several pages, he describes his journey from Puritans, to Independents, then Anabaptists, and finally to seekers. Through it all, he "could not see how [Christ] had died for me, and had taken away my sin: for the witness in my conscience told me I was a servant of sin. . . . So being overcome by sin, I had no justification witnessed in me, but condemnation. . . . And I said to myself, this was a miserable salvation."[22] Despite (or perhaps because of) these doubts, by 1652 Howgill had emerged as an influential leader of the large group of Westmoreland Seekers.

Eventually, "there was something revealed in me, that the Lord would teach his people himself."[23] The critical event was hearing Fox preach for three hours on Firbank Fell. "As soon as I heard him declare that the Light of Christ in man was the way to Christ, I believed the eternal word of truth, and that of God in my conscience sealed to it. . . . And so not only I, but many hundreds more" were convinced.[24]

Despite this breakthrough, Howgill continued to struggle with a sense of judgment. Even after his encounter with Fox, he says that "all

21. Blaugdone, "Account," 275.
22. Howgill, "Inheritance of Jacob Discovered," 170, 172, 171.
23. Howgill, "Inheritance of Jacob Discovered," 172.
24. Howgill, "Inheritance of Jacob Discovered," 173.

that I had ever done was judged and condemned, all things were accursed. . . . I was accursed. . . . My eyes were dim with crying, my flesh did fail of fatness, my bones were dried and my sinews were shrunk."[25] It is not clear how long this state lasted, but it seems to have been some weeks. Eventually, Howgill came to a place where he was able to declare, in much-loved words, "The Lord of Heaven and earth we found to be near at hand. . . . The kingdom of Heaven did gather us and catch us all, as in a net. . . . We came to know a place to stand in and what to wait in; and the Lord appeared daily to us, to our astonishment, amazement, and great admiration."[26]

Howgill goes on to offer this advice to others: "All, therefore, that see the darkness that you live in, return home . . . and be not forward nor rash, but stand still in quietness and meekness, that *the still voice you may hear*, which till you come down within, you cannot hear. . . . So be low and still, *if you would hear his voice* . . . that which you must wait in is near you, yes, in you."[27]

As with the other early Quakers, Howgill's convincement seems initially to have only increased his sense of judgment and conviction. As Douglas Gwyn said of Penington's convincement, so also with Howgill: "He felt much worse before he felt better."[28] We might then well ask: So what is it that changed?

Perhaps one way to understand what changed with the convincement of these first Quakers is from the perspective of "narrative psychology." Over the last few decades, this emerging field has, with some solid empirical evidence, shown that the "life stories" we tell ourselves are crucial to our identities, lending a sense of unity, coherence, and purpose to the events of our unfolding lives. These life stories or narratives are often heavily influenced by the surrounding culture and tend to first emerge in late adolescence or early adulthood, though open to revision as life proceeds.[29]

One can easily imagine that those who went on to become the first Quakers found themselves immersed in a life story heavily influenced by the surrounding Calvinist and Puritan culture. This story told them

25. Howgill, "Inheritance of Jacob Discovered," 174.

26. Francis Howgill, "Testimony Concerning Edward Burrough," in Britain Yearly Meeting, *Quaker Faith and Practice* 19.08.

27. Howgill, "Inheritance of Jacob Discovered," 176. Emphasis added.

28. Gwyn, *Seekers Found*, 286.

29. McAdams, "Psychology of Life Stories."

they were totally depraved, "sinners in the hands of an angry God," what narrative psychology calls a "contamination story." Their only possible escape from this Puritan dilemma was being somehow included in the minority predestined for salvation—but this was something they could not know or experience but only infer. For sensitive souls, this could not help but produce alienation and anxiety.

With their convincement, they came to experience the Light of Christ inwardly. Convincement was an awakening to the Inward Witness, present in all.[30] Their experience of the Light could mean only that God in fact loved and accepted them, willed their salvation, and provided the means—available to all, awaiting only their response. *They now found themselves in a new and radically different story,* a story not of contamination but *redemption*.[31] Their sense of conviction and judgment did not immediately disappear (and indeed for many only increased), but now it was not coming from the Puritan story of original sin and utter depravity. Now, conviction came from the Light—and so came with a reassurance, "the promise," as Nayler says, that there was a way forward, grounded in God's immediate presence, guidance, and love. "The essence of pain was to know one's sin and self-will, but the source of the pain was [now] the Light itself . . . [but] the Light that ultimately gave joy, peace, and guidance gave at first only terror."[32] This was indeed an *apocalypse*, in the original sense of *revelation*, experienced as "the terror and power of the Light."[33]

Although narrative psychology may lend insight into the experience of convincement, I want to emphasize that my intention is not to psychologize or "explain away" the experience. At bottom, convincement was based on a real experience, which in turn produced a real change in the lives of early Friends. However described, *this experience led them to see God in a different light* (pun intended). Instead of God as distant, judgmental, and punitive, the Light showed them that God was near at hand, available to all, concerned for their salvation, and most of all loving—but

---

30. "Awakening the witness" is esp. prominent in Isaac Penington, e.g., *Works*, 1:108; 2:461; 3:19. See also Rosen, "Awakening the Witness."

31. McAdams, "Psychology of Life Stories," 113. See also podcast at Hidden Brain Staff, "Healing 2.0." Contamination and redemption stories were originally described in ex-addicts and ex-convicts.

32. Barbour, *Quakers in Puritan England*, 98.

33. "The Terror and Power of the Light" is the title of ch. 4 in Barbour, *The Quakers in Puritan England*, still an invaluable source for understanding the experience of convincement.

loving with a kind of "tough love" that required them to honestly, even ruthlessly, confront their own deceit and complicity.

These are the convincement experiences of a few prominent leaders, but, wanting to know more about the experience of convincement for "ordinary" Quakers, I turned to *The First Publishers of Truth*, edited by Norman Penney and published in 1907. It seems that as early as 1676 (and again in 1680 and 1704), London Yearly Meeting had directed all its constitutive meetings to compile records of how "truth" (i.e., the Quaker message) first arrived in their locale, who were the "first publishers of truth" (the first traveling ministers who visited and preached), who were those first convinced, and the sufferings they underwent during the decades of persecution. Answers to these queries filtered in over several decades, and the collected documents were placed on a shelf in Devonshire House, only to be rediscovered almost two centuries later.[34] As published, the accounts are arranged by county and make for somewhat tedious reading, as they are mostly secondhand accounts that were written several decades after the events described. Often, there are just lists of names of the "first publishers" and the dates of their visits, as well as lists of those convinced. Accounts of suffering and persecution are more extensive; it is clear that beatings, fines, and imprisonment were not confined to the leaders of the movement but were suffered by many and maybe even most ordinary Quakers.

The First Publishers of Truth contains disappointingly little by way of description of the subjective experience of those convinced. A summary statement might be: the first publishers came, published or declared truth, or bore a testimony to truth. Several or many were convinced, convinced of the truth, or convinced and received truth, or received truth in the love of it. In most of the ninety accounts, beatings, stonings, and imprisonments followed in short order.

There are, however, a few hints of what the subjective experience might have been like. In Chesire, Thomas Yarwood preached to a "considerable assembly" in 1652. "Many of them were convinced and as with one mouth confessed that it was the Truth which had been declared that day, being that *which they had long waited for*."[35] As with the leaders, convincement often followed a time of intense spiritual disillusionment. In Cumberland, some "had separated themselves from the national worship

---

34. Penney, *First Publishers of Truth*, preface, 1–4.
35. Penney, *First Publishers of Truth*, 19. Emphasis added.

before the coming of Friends, and kept meetings in their houses . . . but when the Truth appeared, they readily did embrace it."[36]

Sometimes convincement appeared to be quite sudden and dramatic. George Canby gives an account of his own convincement in Yorkshire, in 1652:

> William Dewsbury was then a blessed instrument in the Lord's hand of my convincement. . . . [I] was wild and wanton in that day, though not outwardly profane. . . . And the power of God was mightily upon William, and fixing his eyes upon me, declared what the Lord had put into his mouth to me in particular, and I did truly witness the Word of the Lord to be quick and powerful, which cut me to the heart, that I fell down [to the] floor as dead to all appearances as any clod or stone. When I came to sense once again, he got me up in his arms . . . so that I can truly say I was smitten down to the ground by the living power of the Lord, as sure as ever Saul was, on his way to Damascus.[37]

Sometimes convincement came not as a result of preaching but in a silent meeting. "John Grave, received truth in the year 1654, being invited by a friend to a silent meeting, in which God's power broke in upon him, whereby he was wonderfully shaken, insomuch as he was constrained to cry out against the many gods in Egypt."[38] The convincement of traveling minister John Hall (1637–1719) was later described by his son: "Presently the power of the Lord seized upon him and broke him down so that he was fully convinced of the blessed truth in that silent meeting."[39] Howard Brinton, in his *How They Became Friends*, cites many examples of early Friends attributing their convincement at least in part to silent meetings, including Edward Burrough, Luke Howard, and George Whitehead. John Burnyeat's account from his *Journal* is typical: "We met together and waited together in silence; it may be sometimes not a word was spoken in our meetings for months; but everyone that was faithful waited upon the living word in our own hearts."[40]

One of the more remarkable accounts of convincement comes from Thomas Camm, from Preston Patrick, in 1652, when he was one of several hundred at a public meeting attended by George Fox and other

36. Penney, *First Publishers of Truth*, 73.
37. Penney, *First Publishers of Truth*, 290.
38. Penney, *First Publishers of Truth*, 43.
39. Quoted in Brinton, "Stages in Spiritual Development," 393.
40. Brinton, *How They Became Friends*, 8–11.

leaders of the nascent movement. Camm, from a vantage point several decades later, recalls that Fox was invited to sit in front near the pulpit, but he declined and "took a back seat near the door." After about a half hour of silent waiting, Fox stood and opened his Bible several times, but each time sat down again, as "a dread and fear being upon him that he durst not begin to preach." Finally, as reported by Camm, Fox rose again and spoke:

> In the mighty power of God . . . was his mouth opened to preach Christ Jesus, the Light of life, and the way to God, and savior of all that believe and obey him, which was delivered in that power and authority that most of [those present], which were several hundreds, were effectually reached to the heart and convinced of the truth that very day. . . . A notable day indeed, never to be forgotten by me . . . I being present at the meeting, a school boy but about twelve years of age . . . in which my soul, by that living testimony then borne in the demonstration of God's power, was effectually opened, reached, and convinced, [and] many more . . . were convinced, and turned from darkness to light and from Satan's power to the power of God.[41]

At the risk of oversimplification, perhaps we can summarize the experience of convincement for early Friends—though obviously, there was great variation. Most would have already gone through "a full conversion experience of the Calvinist type, in which they learned to trust in the vicarious atonement of Christ for salvation."[42] But for whatever reason, they found this "vicarious atonement" inadequate, which left them longing for a more authentic spirituality. This often led to a period of disillusionment and "desolation," with a long journey through the various sects and denominations. Their Quaker convincement could be sudden or gradual, but when it came, it represented a dramatic reorientation of their lives. It did not initially bring an end to their struggles; one early Friend said that convincement resulted only in "sin appearing exceedingly sinful."[43] "It was the beginning, not the end, of struggle."[44] But they found themselves in a new story, a story of redemption rather than contamination.

---

41. Penney, *First Publishers of Truth*, 244–45.

42. Barbour and Roberts, *Early Quaker Writings*, 155.

43. William Crouch (1628–1710), quoted in Brinton, "Stages in Spiritual Development," 392.

44. Barbour and Roberts, *Early Quaker Writings*, 155.

Time and again, the key seems to have been an *experience* of the Inward Light of Christ in their consciences, sometimes described as "an inward voice" or "witness" but always carrying the persuasive certainty of *Truth*. As Fox says, "this I knew experientially"—by experience. The Light, the seed, truth, the Spirit, Christ (terms used more or less interchangeably) was experienced inwardly but as something *other than* or even *alien* to what we would call the ego or self. With the dualistic assumptions of the time, if it was not "self," it must be "of God." And being divine, it was crucial not to resist, but to "give over" or "submit," sometimes spoken of as "carrying the daily cross"—often leading to persecution and suffering. Beyond the conviction of sin, this Light provided guidance and power. However described, these experiences were self-validating, "possessing their own clarity and serving as their own evidence."[45]

We began part 2 with a consideration of how *convincement* for the two disciples on the road to Emmaus, and for Paul on the road to Damascus, came from an experience of the resurrected Christ. Gerard Guiton connects this resurrection experience in the New Testament with the experience of early Friends:

> To summarize, acceptance of the Light heralded a state of justification and sanctification in which God was now fully present within.
>
> The complete convincement process . . . was a Gethsemane-Golgotha-Easter experience. . . . According to their tracts, convincement demanded a descent into their inmost depths to identify, confront and then drive away impulses separating them from God. . . . Convincement enabled the immediate forgiveness of their sins as the power of the Kingdom revealed itself in creative love.
>
> *Through convincement, an individual was resurrected*, inwardly "mortified" (purified) and redeemed whole (returned to the love of God) and thus turned to the joy of belonging "to a fulfillment beyond all greedy human fears and dreams."[46]

---

45. Barclay, *Apology*, 16.
46. Guiton, *Early Quakers*, 275, 268–69, 275. Emphasis added.

18

Convincement Today

> Reading these convincement narratives [of early Friends] has allowed me to better understand my own story and to frame it within the tradition.... It has allowed me to own the power of religious experience.
>
> —Ben Pink Dandelion[1]

DELVING INTO THE EXPERIENCE of convincement for seventeenth-century Quakers brings to mind the aphorism that "the past is a foreign country; they do things differently there."[2] Early Friends intense preoccupation with all things religious, their profound experience of sin and alienation, and their willingness to suffer and even die for matters of belief, are foreign to us. And so it remains to be seen: How is this relevant to the experience of Friends today? What can *we* say about convincement?

Obviously, people today can still have transforming experiences, marked by sudden or gradual reorientation of their life's direction. But in general, as described in the introductory chapter, *convincement* for many Friends today "can seem a rather bland affair . . . not so much an experience of transformation, but more the finding of a comfortable home." In

---

1. B. Dandelion, *Convinced Quakerism*, 20.
2. The first line of L. P. Hartley's 1953 novel, *The Go-Between*.

Quaker by Convincement, Geoffrey Hubbard goes so far as to say that today Friends become Friends by "becoming convinced that one *should* be a Quaker and *by convincing a Monthly Meeting* of this," which seems a far cry from the seventeenth-century experience.[3] Ben Pink Dandelion has observed that as sin and salvation have disappeared from our religious discourse, Friends today find it easier to fall into "cozy complacency," because "the stakes are far less high than they were in the seventeenth century, when probably the most important question was how to be in right relationship with God, how to achieve salvation."[4]

Dandelion has given a compelling account of his own convincement, "on a Greyhound bus just outside St. Louis," in 1986, when he had a "powerful experience of being held by God, and being told I was not alone." Elsewhere, he has described this as "being taken beyond myself, of being lifted up by what I have called God, of being forever-after accompanied, loved, and guided. . . . It was an unbidden experience." Notably, this occurred well *after* he was accepted into membership; in retrospect he says, "I think they never should have let me in."[5]

Marcelle Martin gives another contemporary account of convincement, although she does not use that word. In her chapter "One Friend's Spiritual Journey," she describes a decades-long process of longing, seeking, and turning within; followed by openings, the refiner's fire, leadings, and the cross—all categories that she gleaned from her reading of early Friends. She does relate a pivotal experience in this long journey, in her late twenties, before she found Friends, and after she had concluded that she had arrived at "the end of my spiritual life." While walking under a starry night sky, she was "by grace" given a glimpse of "what George Fox called 'the hidden unity in the Eternal being'":

> From deep within me, I suddenly knew that the stars and I are part of one vast oneness. A divine Light flows through us and through all things. I felt this Light flowing through me. . . . I was changed forever by this glimpse of the invisible, divine Reality that undergirds everything and of which I am a part. It took time before I could use the word *God* for the oneness and the Light I had experienced, but from that moment onward, I no longer doubted that I am part of an eternal spiritual reality.[6]

3. Hubbard, *Quaker by Convincement*, 213. Emphasis added.
4. B. Dandelion, *Open for Transformation*, 28–29.
5. B. Dandelion, *Convinced Quakerism*, 14.
6. Martin, *Our Life Is Love*, 181, from the chapter "One Friend's Spiritual Journey," 178–89.

Matt Rosen has argued that in our present changed circumstances, it may be helpful to distinguish between *membership* and *convincement*. He starts by observing that for eighty years after Quakers first appeared, there was no formal membership process and no official membership rolls. One became a Quaker, and was known to be a Quaker, by the public keeping of the testimonies. Yet during this time, clearly individuals became convinced Friends in the fullest sense of the word. He offers the examples of James Parnell and Elizabeth Fletcher, both of whom were teenagers when they were first convinced in the early 1650s. Both publicly preached the Quaker message, were arrested and jailed for their witness, and both died at the age of nineteen from their maltreatment in prison. There can be no doubt that they were both genuinely *convinced*, yet neither were official members—because that category did not yet exist.

Conversely, it is possible today to become a member and not be convinced, as Ben Pink Dandelion's experience illustrates. Rosen encourages us to think of membership as a form of belonging and that convincement is *not* a prerequisite for this belonging. One can belong or be in membership without having been convinced; and one can be convinced without being in membership.

Rosen dates his own convincement to a time before he even knew who or what Quakers were. He describes as a teen struggling with debilitating anxiety and depression, but having several experiences of sensing "the presence and power of God; I started to feel just held and cared for and accompanied." He emphasizes that this was not a comfortable experience; as a "devout atheist" and "proud rationalist," these experiences were "profoundly unwanted." Nevertheless, as he gradually gave way to these experiences, and surrendered his sense of self-sufficiency and control, he began to change. "I found a guide who could show me what I needed to do and say, and more than that, a guide who could empower me and energize me, who could befriend and accompany me."[7]

Another modern-day account of convincement comes from Gerald Hewitson, in his 2013 Swarthmore lecture, *Journey into Life: Inheriting the Story of Early Friends*. Hewitson became a Quaker in his early thirties, based largely on a favorable impression that two Friends made while they were working overseas, at a school in Turkey. When he later first attended Quaker meeting, he saw words on the meetinghouse door, words

---

7. Rosen, "Awakening the Witness." See also Rosen, "Light Will Be Shining." Rosen's thinking about conviction, convincement, and conversion closely parallels my own, but a draft of this current work was largely complete before I heard his talk.

that at the time impressed him as pleasantly open and inviting: "Quakers are people of different beliefs, lifestyles, and social backgrounds. What we have in common is an acceptance that all people are on a spiritual journey. We hope that we are indeed a real society of Friends, open to the world and welcoming everyone." But from a perspective of thirty years on, he finds these same words to be "bland, anodyne":

> In attempting to exclude none, to be inoffensive, to convey no hint of dangerous fervor or undesirable conviction, they said little that was not trite or commonplace. Was this what we contemporary Quakers had created? A belief-free zone into which anyone could step without any sense of conviction? A group of well-meaning friends who spoke of friendship, but not of commitment? Who offered a spiritual journey without indicating the inevitable concomitant sacrifice? What had changed in me that I should find those words so difficult now—words which I would have found attractive all those years ago?[8]

What had changed is that he himself had gone through what he describes as "my convincement process, which began in 2008"—after at least two decades as a member.

> The starting point was to hear, truly hear, the words of George Fox: "Now I was come up in spirit through the flaming sword into the paradise of God. All things were new, and all the creation gave another smell, beyond what words can utter." These words acted as a spark to a flame. In seeking to understand what they meant in the lives of other early Friends and the origins of Quakers, it seemed as if I was following a thread in a labyrinth. As I penetrated deeper and deeper, more seemed to be revealed. . . . I saw early Quakers as offering insight into my state of mind and where I was in my life—that which Quakers call "my condition." . . . [Early Friends] describe for us our capacity to be human. So if we can hear them, their words offer a strength and a vigor, a depth and clarity of spiritual awareness and understanding which can offer us insights in our own condition, and thereby into the human condition. And it is by seeing their world as fully as we can that we can begin to hear what they have to say to us today.[9]

---

8. Hewitson, *Journey into Life*, 1.
9. Hewitson, *Journey into Life*, 4–5. Quote is from G. Fox, *Journal*, 27.

In a similar vein, Ben Pink Dandelion affirms the importance of preserving Quakerism's "primal language.... We need to mind our language and find together a primal tongue."[10] It is striking to me that those modern-day Friends who can describe a convincement process or experience so often depict it as stemming from an entry into the words and experience of early Friends. The words of those first Quakers often act as a catalyst to our going deeper. Elsewhere, Dandelion elaborates on this primal language:

> For me, the accounts of early Friends, even if they are different from my story, give me a starting place, a set of phrases and meanings against which I can better understand my own experience. It is part of the culture in which I try to understand my spiritual journey.
>
> There is something in these accounts of Fox and Penington and Crisp and Howgill which speaks to my condition. It is not the same condition, but I recognize the elements of their story in mine ... the unmediated experience which doesn't require a priest but requires us each to take on that priestly role for one another, the conviction of sin and the ensuing spiritual warfare, the sense of regeneration, the value of sinking down to the seed in silent worship and being fed by the Inward Light.... Reading these convincement narratives has allowed me to better understand my own story and to frame it within the tradition. It has given me a language to state to myself and to the world what I found within myself, what had grown in me and what has since grown in me, my failings in the past and my sense of possibility for the future.... It has allowed me to own the power of the religious experience I have felt weave through my life and my Quakerism since that moment outside of St Louis.
>
> Reading the lives of early Friends has transformed my self-understanding.[11]

In the previous chapter, I suggested that one way to understand early Friends experience of convincement was from the perspective of narrative psychology: convincement represented a radical change in their "life story," from a story of *contamination* to one of *redemption*. Contemporary accounts of convincement can likewise be seen as a shift in one's

---

10. B. Dandelion, *Open for Transformation*, 62, 72.
11. B. Dandelion, *Convinced Quakerism*, 19, 20, 22.

life story, but in contrast to the mid-seventeenth century, the story that we are shifting away from, the story we imbibe from the surrounding culture, is very unlikely to be a story of original sin and human depravity. Rather, the story we are born into in our modern and postmodern secular culture is almost the opposite. The "self" is no longer regarded as suspect, as it was until the end of the nineteenth century.[12] Instead, we celebrate the inherent goodness of the self, "that of God in everyone," and largely place our trust in our own freedom, rationality, and autonomy. Ben Pink Dandelion speaks of our "sacro-egoism, the way in which we become our own sacred authorities and take charge of our spiritual lives."[13]

That may be true for some, but another common story we receive from our secular culture is what Hewitson calls the "deficit model," the idea that "we are lacking something, or need something extra for our existence to be validated: that we need to believe something, or do something, and then we will be worthy of existence."[14] We receive from the surrounding culture a story of competition and rivalry, rather than belonging; of scarcity rather than abundance; of autonomy and independence, rather than relationality and interdependence; of conditional love based on achievement, rather than unconditional love grounded in divine grace. Sometimes these two stories coexist: we are simultaneously our own sacred authorities, *and* we lack something essential.

In our changed circumstances, where we no longer define ourselves within a cultural story of sin and human depravity, it is perhaps inevitable that convincement stories in our own time will be more muted. And in our setting of religious pluralism, the actual content of our convincement stories is likely to be less specific and more varied than it was in the seventeenth century. They are more likely to be kept private, perhaps not even very noticeable in a society that celebrates pluralism and diversity. Dandelion notes this same tendency and asks, "Does our silence or reticence to voice our own experience, however limited the language we use may be in the final analysis, undermine the power of the experience, both for ourselves and those hearing of it? . . . Is it not better to hear each other's versions of our convincement narratives, for them to be voiced and heard, than not?"[15]

12. B. Dandelion, *Open for Transformation*, 47.

13. B. Dandelion, *Open for Transformation*, 30. He is referencing an unpublished PhD dissertation by Knox, "Sacro-Egoism."

14. Hewitson, *Journey into Life*, 19.

15. B. Dandelion, *Convinced Quakerism*, 21.

Despite our changed circumstances, and the less intense form that convincement often takes today, it is important that we not lose sight of the central role that convincement plays, or should play, in a vital Quakerism. Ben Pink Dandelion, using transformation as a synonym of what I have been calling convincement, says that we need to recognize that "transformation is still the heart of Quakerism.... We are personally and collectively transformed and in turn seek to transform." And even more explicitly: "If as Quakers we are not open to transformation, or do not understand that Quakerism is centered on that kind of experience, *we misunderstand Quakerism*."[16]

If it is true that convincement or transformation should continue to play a central role in Quakerism, and I think it is, then how can we learn to talk more openly about our experiences? There is, as I have tried to show above, at least a modest literature describing convincement experiences, even if that is not always the language used. But I wonder if for the average Quaker, in the average meeting, we might do a better job in finding opportunities to give expression to these intimate experiences; in Dandelion's words, "to own the power of religious experience." My sense is that many of us, given the opportunity, could describe one or a very few profound spiritual or quasi-mystical experiences that were pivotal to our formation.

In my own meeting, we have a long tradition, four or five times a year, of inviting a Friend to "share their spiritual journey." The venue for these spiritual journeys is the forty-five-minute after-meeting "forum," and invariably they are among the best attended of our biweekly forums. Not infrequently, Friends will reveal previously unsuspected depths of wisdom, life-changing experiences, or crucial episodes in their earlier lives. Over time, this practice has built a web of connection and spiritual depth in our meeting community, as we come, in Fox's words, "to meet together, and know one another in that which is eternal."[17]

No doubt there are other possible venues, other formats, for Friends to share such experiences. Some will be more comfortable sharing these experiences in smaller, more intimate settings. But if "transformation is still the heart of Quakerism," then we will need to find ways to "nurture personal transformation and affirm convincement in its traditional meaning when it occurs, not find it an embarrassment or an awkwardness."[18]

16. B. Dandelion, *Open for Transformation*, 18–19. Emphasis added.
17. "Epistle 149," in G. Fox, *Power of the Lord*, 114.
18. B. Dandelion, *Open for Transformation*, 18, 90.

Psychologist Dan Gottlieb has written that there are "four words that could change the world: *Tell me your story*."[19] Quakerism at its root is not about doctrines, beliefs, or ideas but about spiritual experience, and so it is incumbent upon us to find ways to share and nurture those experiences of transformation. Quaker convincement is still important.

---

19. Gottlieb, "Tell Me Your Story," paras. 1–2. Emphasis added.

Excursus II

New Light on Atonement

> Whatever it meant in the past... in the future the atonement must be vital and dynamic. It must be put in language which grips the heart, convinces the mind, and carries the will.... It will cease to signify a way by which God was appeased and it will come to express, as it did in apostolic days, the identification of God with us in the person of Christ, and the identification... of ourselves with [God].
>
> —Rufus Jones (1906)[1]

CONTEMPORARY FRIENDS, AT LEAST of the liberal variety, do not often speak of "atonement."[2] For many, the word has the worn-out feel of a previous era's dogmas and doctrines, the very essence of what George Fox derided as "airy notions." But the language of atonement was not unknown among early Friends—usually with a characteristic inward emphasis. Fox wrote that "none know this atonement of Christ but by the light within."[3] William Penn testified that "I never experienced real

---

1. R. Jones, *Double Search*, 82–83.
2. This discussion of Quakers and atonement borrows from a previous article, Gates, "New Light on Atonement."
3. "The Great Mystery of the Great Whore Unfolded," in G. Fox, *Works*, 3:120. Fox's few references to atonement seem to be exclusively in his so-called doctrinal works,

Atonement . . . but by the reproofs of that Light, wherewith Christ has enlightened me."[4]

Etymologically, atonement is *at-one-ment*, the state of being at one, in unity.[5] A foundational Quaker experience is that the Inward Light of Christ, when attended to, can bring us into unity with the Divine, and with one another. George Fox counseled, "Mind the *oneness*, and that which keeps you in the *oneness* and unity. . . . This one light leads you out of darkness and into the everlasting day."[6] So in this non-doctrinal sense, *at-one-ment* expresses an essential belief and experience of Quakers.

"To atone" belongs to a nexus of words that refers to the change that God can bring to our lives; as we saw in the previous chapter, "transformation" might be a modern equivalent. In Christian experience and teaching, this change is intimately connected with the life, death, and resurrection of Jesus, but it is important to recognize that the New Testament does not present a single "theory of atonement." Instead, it offers "a rainbow of metaphors": salvation (originally, to heal or make whole), liberation (alluding to the Exodus story of escape from slavery in Egypt), new birth (or "born from above"), redemption (to purchase the freedom of a slave), adoption (of a favored slave into one's family), justification (to be found innocent at trial), military victory (over sin and death), and reconciliation (negotiated peace between enemies). These metaphors *describe* the *experience* of atonement; the problem comes when we invent theories to *explain* that experience.[7]

Theologians see atonement as "the core of the Christian gospel"; a workable definition would be "the claim that through Jesus's life, death, and resurrection we are saved from sin and reconciled to God."[8] That claim may or may not involve belief in an afterlife, but it certainly involves a belief that humanity is in a state of separation or alienation from God, and in need of reconciliation. It is instructive to follow various theories of atonement as they developed chronologically though Christian history.

---

rather than in his *Journal* or epistles.

4. Penn, "Spirit of Truth Vindicated," 2:122.

5. According to De Young, "at-one-ment" was coined by Wycliffe for his medieval translation of the Bible into English; it has no earlier etymological history. By the sixteenth century, it had been shortened to "atonement" (*Religion of the Apostles*, 167–68).

6. "Epistle 46," in G. Fox, *Power of the Lord*, 39. Emphasis added.

7. De Young, *Religion of the Apostles*, 169–70.

8. Collins, "Girard and Atonement," 133.

The first serious attempt to explain atonement is the so-called *Christus Victor* or "classic" model, going back to the early church fathers. With his crucifixion, descent into hell, and subsequent resurrection, Christ was said to have won a great victory over Satan. Satan's defeat was sometimes attributed to trickery (with Christ compared to bait on a fishhook, and Satan the hungry fish who swallows the hook along with the bait, leading to his defeat) or sometimes to a ransom paid to Satan, in exchange for freeing sinful humanity. Numerous variations in the early church fathers have this common theme: the atonement is the result of Christ's victory over Satan. The iconography of the resurrection in the Eastern Orthodox Church reflects this: the Risen Christ emerging from the tomb, with a defeated Satan under his foot, broken locks and chains scattered about, and Christ reaching down with his right arm to grasp Adam and Eve (representing all humanity) and lead them out of Hades.[9]

The Christus Victor image of atonement reflects the early church's experience of confrontation with the world and specifically with the Roman Empire. Eventually, with Constantine's embrace of Christianity, that stance of confrontation shifted toward accommodation with empire, and Christus Victor gradually lost its potency as an image of atonement. Perhaps also the idea that God had to stoop to trickery or payment to the devil, elevating the status of Satan to near equal with God, became objectionable.[10]

A second theory of atonement eventually came to displace Christus Victor and continues to cast a very long shadow: the *satisfaction theory*, first articulated by Anselm of Canterbury (1033–1109). Most Christians today, regardless of whether they have ever heard of Anselm, implicitly accept some variation of the satisfaction theory—to the general detriment of Christian spirituality.

Writing at the time of the First Crusade and working from a medieval framework of honor and shame, Anselm argued that God was something like a feudal lord whose honor has been offended by the disobedience of his vassals. The lord's honor can be restored only by the offender paying a price, either by monetary payment or by appropriate punishment. Likewise, when God's honor is offended by human sin, God's perfect justice requires that a price must be paid in order to restore the moral order. But it is impossible for humans to pay that price, since we already

---

9. Crossan and Crossan, *Resurrecting Easter*, see esp. images on 15, 22, 146. Crossan and Crossan emphasize that Adam and Eve are being led out of *Hades*, not *hell*.

10. Weaver, *Nonviolent Atonement*, locs. 257–265; 1366–1442 of 5050.

owe the Creator everything, including our very lives—we have nothing to give that would satisfy. Only God can provide satisfaction, restoring the moral order by offering the divine Son who is without sin to suffer and die in our place. Jesus's death by crucifixion "pays the price" for human sin, which God's honor demands. For Anselm, atonement requires punishment.

The early Protestant Reformers (primarily John Calvin) took this one step further, with their *penal substitution theory* of atonement: penal, because it involves a deserved legal punishment for breaking God's law; and substitution, because Jesus substitutes for us, by suffering the death we deserve as the penalty for sin. This is simply a variation of Anselm's satisfaction theory, with Jesus's death now satisfying God's demand for justice, rather than God's offended honor.

Whatever value it might have had in its original medieval context, the shortcomings of the satisfaction theory leap out to most contemporary seekers. It portrays God as sadistic, so concerned with God's own honor or justice that God needs to be placated by the death of the innocent Son—the theological equivalent of child abuse. It makes Christ into a passive victim of divine justice, crucified to satisfy the terms of some inscrutable heavenly transaction. It places the sole emphasis on Jesus's death, entirely omitting both his ministry and his resurrection, as though his life's entire purpose was simply to die. By turning salvation into a legalistic transaction, it divorces salvation from the radical ethics of the kingdom. It ignores the role of the "powers that be," who after all were responsible for Jesus's crucifixion—turning them instead into agents of God's will. It sacralizes violence; God uses violence for a good purpose, why shouldn't we? It encourages a morbid spirituality that glorifies suffering. Finally, it seems to encourage passivity in the face of injustice. How many abused women and oppressed minorities have been counseled to "imitate Christ" by submitting to unjust suffering?[11]

Girard says of the penal substitution theory, "This line of reasoning has done more than anything else to discredit Christianity in the eyes of people of goodwill in the modern world. However acceptable to the medieval mind it might have been, it has become intolerable for us, and it

---

11. Criticisms of Anselm have become ubiquitous over the last several decades. For one particularly convincing example, see Johnson, *Creation and the Cross*, "Wrestling with Anselm," 1–30.

forms the major stumbling-block for a world that is entirely (and justifiably) hostile to this idea of sacrifice."[12]

The third major theory of the atonement is usually referred to as the *moral influence model*, first articulated by Peter Abelard (1079–1142) a generation after Anselm. He rejected the idea that Jesus's death was either a ransom paid to the devil or a payment demanded by God to restore God's honor. Jesus's death saves us not by placating God but by subjectively changing us, inspiring us by his example of sacrificial love and obedience. "For Abelard, the problem of atonement was not how to change an offended God's mind toward the sinner, but how to bring sinful humankind to see that the God they perceived as harsh and judgmental was actually loving. Thus for Abelard, Jesus died as the demonstration of God's love."[13] Abelard's moral influence theory has functioned throughout subsequent history as a persistent critique of the mainstream view, but it has been decidedly less influential than the predominant penal substitution model.

Abelard's model is sometimes criticized as "subjective," by which critics seem to mean that it works by effecting a change in us (subjective) rather than a change in God (objective). As Robin Collins points out, "The accusation that moral influence theory is subjective is really no objection at all, but a merit of the theory": it is the only theory that posits a real change in us.[14] This echoes early Friends claim, against the Puritan belief in penal substitution, that the Light does not save us *in* our sins but *from* our sins. An adequate model of atonement should show how we are *made* righteous, not just how God is persuaded to overlook our unrighteousness. The moral influence theory at least points us in that direction.

J. Denny Weaver helpfully points out that the major difference between these three models is to whom or what Jesus's death was directed, and therefore how that death can be said to be saving. In Christus Victor, "*Satan* is the object of Jesus' death; Jesus' death is directed toward [tricking, ransoming or defeating] the devil." In Anselm, Jesus's death is directed at *God*, in effect an offering to God, to restore God's honor or satisfy God's justice. Jesus's death in effect changes God's opinion toward humans—without necessarily changing us ("imputed righteousness"). For Abelard, *humanity* is the target of Jesus's death, which becomes "a

---

12. Girard, *Things Hidden*, 182.
13. Weaver, *Nonviolent Atonement*, loc. 295 of 5050.
14. Collins, "Girard and Atonement," 138.

way for God to get our attention," inspiring or influencing us to imitate Jesus's sacrificial love, and thus changing us.[15]

The past few decades have seen the emergence of new ways of understanding atonement, many of which reflect the perspectives of historically oppressed or disadvantaged groups. Most of these start by rejecting Anselm's satisfaction theory, which is rightly criticized as serving the interests of a hierarchical and oppressive status quo. These new models seek to reconnect our understanding of atonement with the radical ethic of love, service, and nonviolence demonstrated in Jesus's ministry, a connection completely lost by Anselm. Theologians influenced by Girard have made important contributions to this dialogue, articulating new ways of thinking about atonement.[16]

Robin Collins says Girard and his followers offer two related and complementary models of atonement: the *unmasking theory* and the *imitation theory*, both of which are variants of the moral influence theory.[17] The unmasking theory emphasizes how the crucifixion was revelatory, definitively unmasking and revealing the scapegoat mechanism, which we have explored in chapter 11. As James Warren has pointed out, "After Jesus, we have not been able to hide the innocence of the victim."[18] Once the innocence of the victim and the underlying violence has been revealed, we are inspired to then live without scapegoating violence.

The imitation theory emphasizes that Jesus, in his faithfulness and nonviolence, "even unto death on the cross," provides an alternative model for us to imitate. In effect, Jesus as model redirects our desires away from the "social other" of mimetic rivalry and scapegoating violence, and toward the "good mimesis" of imitation of Christ. We will explore this further in chapter 21.

But is this enough? Is Jesus as a model to inspire us and for us to imitate sufficient to account for the "new creation" that Paul and other early Christians believed they were living into? Defenders of Anselm and Calvin have traditionally criticized the moral influence theory as being "too weak" to account for humanity's changed status and for its tendency to attribute salvation to the creature's initiative rather than to God's grace.[19]

---

15. Weaver, *Nonviolent Atonement*, loc. 303 of 5050.
16. See Jersak and Hardin, *Stricken by God?*
17. Collins, "Girard and Atonement," 135–39.
18. Warren, *Compassion or Apocalypse*, 280.
19. Collins, "Girard and Atonement," 136. Moral influence is often criticized for

Girard himself seems to incorporate elements of Christus Victor into his account of the cross, over and beyond moral influence. Here it is critical to remind ourselves of what we said in chapter 10, that when Girard (as opposed to the early church fathers) speaks of Satan, he is not talking about an actual being but the personification of mimetic contagion and the single victim (or scapegoat) mechanism. Understood in this way, Girard believes that the cross does indeed represent the defeat of Satan.

In his chapter on "The Triumph of the Cross,"[20] Girard directs our attention to a somewhat enigmatic text from Paul's letter to the Colossians: "[Christ has] cancelled the accusation that stands against us with its legal claims. He set it aside, nailing it to the cross. He thus disarmed the principalities and powers and made a public spectacle of them, [triumphing over them by the cross]" (Col 2:13–15).[21] The allusion here is to a military procession, *the triumph*, a reward bestowed on victorious generals by the Roman Empire. Preceded by his triumphant troops, the general (often the emperor himself) entered Rome riding in a chariot, to receive the acclamation of the crowd, while the leaders of the vanquished foe followed behind in chains, as they were led to their public execution. Girard comments:

> This metaphor of triumph contains a paradox so evident that it has to be deliberate, and it must stem from irony. Military violence is as alien as possible to the intention of the letter to the Colossians. The victory of Christ has nothing to do with the military triumph of a victorious general: rather than inflicting violence on others, Christ submits to it. . . . Christ does not achieve his victory through violence. He obtains it through a renunciation of violence so complete that violence can rage to its hearts content without realizing that by so doing, it reveals what it must conceal.

Pelagianism, the view that humans are able to save themselves through their own efforts. The term reflects a misunderstanding of what Pelagius actually taught. Pelagius was a fifth-century contemporary of Augustine who opposed Augustine's doctrine of original sin.

20. Girard, *I See Satan Fall*, ch. 11, 137–53.

21. It is not clear which translation Girard (or his translator) is using here. I have substituted for his final clause, "drawing them along in his triumph," the NIV's "triumphing over them by the cross." "Powers and principalities" is the KJV wording; contemporary translations speak of "rulers and authorities."

> By nailing Christ to the Cross, the powers believed they were doing what they ordinarily did in unleashing the single victim [scapegoat] mechanism. They thought they were avoiding the danger of disclosure. They did not suspect that in the end they would be doing just the opposite: they would be contributing to their own annihilation, nailing themselves to the Cross, so to speak. They did not and could not suspect the revelatory power of the Cross.

> Though ordinarily the accusation nails the victim to a cross, here by contrast the accusation itself is nailed and publicly exhibited and exposed as a lie. The Cross enables the truth to triumph because the Gospels disclose the falseness of the accusation; they unmask Satan as an imposter.[22]

Girard refers approvingly to a thesis he attributes to Origen and the Greek fathers, that Satan was "duped" by the cross; that the cross is "a kind of divine trap, a ruse of God that is even stronger and cleverer than Satan's ruses."[23] Satan is "the great mystifier caught in the trap of his own mystification." Girard goes on to say that this ruse does not involve any violence or deception on the part of God but simply "the inability of the prince of the world to understand divine love."[24]

Over and above the moral influence theory, this begins to sound like Christus Victor. In this view, an objective change is indeed introduced into the human condition: "As a result [of the cross] the world looks completely different." The major difference from the early church fathers is that Girard does not see Satan as a literal being. "All we need to make the thesis of Satan duped by the Cross intelligible is a clear definition of what imprisons human beings in the realm of Satan: mimetic contagion and its outcome in the victim mechanism have provided that definition."[25]

Of course, the empiric evidence for this "triumph of the cross" is decidedly mixed. It is historically true that wherever Christianity was introduced, ritual sacrifice (human or animal) quickly died out. There is some evidence that the world has gradually become less violent.[26] In addition, as we will see in part 3, a "global concern for victims" has gradually emerged, which was simply absent in the pre-Christian world. On

22. Girard, *I See Satan Fall*, 140, 142, 138.
23. Girard, *I See Satan Fall*, 149.
24. Girard, *I See Satan Fall*, 151, 152.
25. Girard, *I See Satan Fall*, 151.
26. Pinker, *Better Angels*, chs. 2–4.

the negative side of the ledger, we can point to the Crusades, medieval pogroms, witch trials, colonial Europe's genocide of indigenous populations, the enslavement and transport of millions of Africans, the twentieth-century's world wars, and the Holocaust and other acts of genocide. One need only read the morning newspaper to see that scapegoating violence is still very much with us.

So a crucial question remains: If the events of the passion, crucifixion, and resurrection represent a decisive change in our relationship with God and our understanding of violence, *why has it seemed to make so little difference*? Why do we still live in a "world of crucifixion," suffering so much hatred and "unnecessary violence"?[27]

In other words, in light of the current state of the world, how should we think of "the triumph of the cross"? James Alison offers a useful analogy. Imagine yourself living in 1989 in, say, rural Albania. For forty years, you have suffered under a brutally oppressive totalitarian regime, but one morning you hear through the static on your transistor radio that a certain wall many miles to the north, in Berlin, has been torn down. "You know exactly what this means: it means that it's over, the beast which ran your lives is mortally wounded, has lost its transcendence, is dead. . . . It may take some time for the thrashing about of the beast in its death throes . . . but fundamentally it's over."[28] The beast of mimetic contagion and scapegoating violence is in its death throes, still very dangerous, but it has been mortally wounded. Victory is assured—but has not yet fully arrived.

So many theories! Perhaps we should end where we started, with the observation that the problem comes when our theories try to *explain* the *experience* of atonement. James Alison says that "the principal problem with this conventional account [of atonement] is that it is a *theory*, while atonement, in the first place, was a *liturgy*": something we undergo, something we experience, something we participate in.[29] He follows this observation with a brilliant analysis of the liturgy of the Day of Atonement in First Temple Judaism (i.e., prior to the Babylonian exile), which we know only from fragments. The liturgy culminates with the high priest entering the holy of holies and sacrificing one of the two goats, the goat chosen by lot to *represent* Yahweh. He then emerges from behind the veil in a brilliant white robe, the high priest himself now "acting in the person of

---

27. Both phrases from Baker-Fletcher, *Dancing with God*, 37, 39, 48.

28. Alison, *Undergoing God*, 40–41.

29. Alison, *Undergoing God*, 52. Alison's essay also appears in Jersak and Hardin, *Stricken by God?*, 166–79.

Yahweh." He proceeds to sprinkle the blood of the sacrificed goat—*Yahweh's own blood*—onto the people, signifying that their sins are forgiven. At this point, the second goat, the "escape goat," is driven into the wilderness, removing the people's sins (already forgiven) from the community.

This, Alison says, is worlds away from what he calls the "Aztec" notion of sacrifice, where a priest offers a sacrifice to placate an angry God. There, it is humans taking the initiative in an attempt to influence or manipulate their god. In the Jewish Day of Atonement, it is *Yahweh* who takes the initiative; Yahweh who is making the offering, sacrificing God's own self for the people; Yahweh who emerges from the holy of holies into the world, offering forgiveness through the shedding of Yahweh's own blood. Here it is God's own self that is the "giving and forgiving victim." In this liturgy of atonement, forgiveness comes *before* repentance; *repentance is not the prerequisite for forgiveness but its consequence.*

Alison sums up: "We are talking about a liturgy rather than a theory, something we undergo over time as part of a benign divine initiative towards us."[30] This view represents what Alison elsewhere calls a "subversion from within" of the usual notion of sacrifice: "not a human sacrifice to God, but God's sacrifice to humans."[31] This subversion from within will ultimately culminate in the New Testament account of the passion and crucifixion. Indeed, for Alison the expression "subversion from within" serves as a succinct summary of how the Bible addresses the issues of both sacrifice and sacred violence.[32]

In the usual understanding, atonement is something that occurred in the past, a completed divine transaction between the persons of the Trinity. Perhaps this alternative idea of atonement as something "we undergo over time as part of the divine initiative towards us" is close to what George Fox meant when he spoke of an "inward atonement." For the early Quakers, atonement was something we *participate* in, not through an outward liturgy, but inwardly, through our ongoing experience of the Light. Not surprisingly, these early Friends were much more interested in this inward experience than any theory or "notion" of atonement.

The title of Douglas Gwyn's third book in his trilogy on early Quaker history is *Seekers Found: Atonement in Early Quaker Experience*. He traces not the doctrine but the experience of atonement in the lives of several seekers, many of whom became Quakers. He writes that their

---

30. Alison, *Undergoing God*, 55.
31. Alison, *Raising Abel*, 45, 46.
32. For Alison's "subversion from within," see prologue, n8., xv.

stance "implied a Copernican revolution regarding the usual understanding of atonement in Christ. . . . It must be known within, through the individual's death to self and the raising of Christ the seed within. . . . Quakers insisted [that] saving knowledge [must be] inwardly received and morally expressed."[33] In the same vein, Gerard Guiton observes that for early Friends, "through their convincement, Jesus' atonement was *internalized*. . . . Convincement meant that Friends internalized the atonement and resurrection."[34]

This perspective represents a potential sea change in our understanding of atonement. Gone is Anselm's medieval idea of atonement as a legalistic transaction to appease God's need for retribution, miraculously removing the consequences of human sin but without changing us ("imputed righteousness"). Instead, we begin to see atonement as an ongoing process of revealing and unmasking the universal human propensity to scapegoat innocent victims, attempting to achieve social cohesion by demonizing some "other." God comes to us offering not retribution but forgiveness, forgiving our trespasses as we forgive others—even our enemies. *At-one-ment* is not our individual ticket to heaven but the progressive enlargement of the human circle of care, from family to tribe to ethnic group to nation to world, and finally to all life—all the while resisting the temptation to create more victims.

With these observations that atonement is best understood not as a "theory" but something ongoing, something we undergo as an inward experience, something we participate in, we are now ready to move on to part 3, the experience of the lifelong "conversion of the heart." How is it that *convincement* changes us?

---

33. Gwyn, *Seekers Found*, 301. Gwyn's view of atonement in early Quaker experience is summarized in 299–305.

34. Guiton, *Early Quakers*, 248, 254. Emphasis added.

PART III

Conversion of the Heart

> Their Quaker "convincement," when it came, was neither a conversion to new doctrines nor completed inward change.... It was a commitment to accept what the Light showed. *It was the beginning, not the end, of struggle.*
>
> —Hugh Barbour and Arthur Roberts[1]

RECALL FROM THE INTRODUCTION that we are using the term "conversion" not as it is usually used in Protestant and Evangelical Christianity, as a sudden and dramatic change; for Quakers, that is closer to convincement. We speak rather of *conversion* in the sense of "continuing conversion," what in the monastic tradition is the ongoing "conversion of manners," through both an active cultivation of spiritual practices and habits and a passive surrendering or giving over to God. It is perhaps best thought of as "the conversion of the heart," in the spirit of the promise given to Ezekiel: "A new heart I will give you, and a new spirit I will put within you" (Ezek 36:26). For early Friends, their convincement marked the beginning of this lifelong process of continuing conversion, as in the words from Barbour and Roberts above.[2]

---

1. Barbour and Roberts, *Early Quaker Writings*, 155. Emphasis added.
2. I owe the phrase "conversion of manners" to L. Wilson, *Essays*, 37. "Conversion of

Howard Brinton, in a 1938 essay, delineates ten stages in Quaker spiritual development, as recorded in the journals of seventeenth- and eighteenth-century Friends. The fourth stage is convincement, followed by the fifth stage of conversion. Brinton describes *convincement* as "the intellectual acceptance of the Quaker interpretation of Christianity," which we saw in chapter 17 may not be adequate to account for the intensity of the convincement experience of early Friends. But Brinton does show that even in the early years, convinced Quakers saw that there was still something lacking. He quotes George Whitehead (1636–1723): "The Lord by his Light and Grace fully persuaded me that without being *converted as well as convinced* and without being regenerated, sanctified and born again I could not enter his kingdom." More poetically, William Crouch "saw that a distance is set between seed-time and harvest."[3]

Likewise, Robert Barclay testifies that convincement is not sufficient: "Even if thousands were to be convinced intellectually of the truths we maintain, if they could not feel this inward life, and their souls did not turn away from unrighteousness, they would add nothing to us."[4] Daniel Wheeler expresses optimism that conversion will follow convincement: "An individual thoroughly *convinced* or our principles and keeping close to that which has convinced him will undoubtably, as he continues faithful, be *converted* by it."[5]

In 1692 John Bank (1634–1710) wrote "An Epistle to Friends Shewing the Great Difference Between a Convinced Estate and a Converted Estate and the Profession of Truth and the Possession Thereof." Following George Fox, Bank distinguished between the "profession" of truth and its "possession"—but with the distinction now applied to his fellow Quakers. The difference between the convinced and converted estates comes down to "obedience" in the latter, which is learned "by degrees," i.e., gradually.[6]

Brinton goes on to claim that "*conversion* was the central event in the spiritual progress of the Quaker journalist. The word itself, however,

---

the heart" I first heard from Rosen, "Awakening the Witness." It seems that both phrases are common in the monastic and Catholic tradition; "conversion of the heart" seems less likely to cause confusion. "Continuing conversion" comes from Father Dan Horan, discussing Thomas Merton in a conversation with Ilia Delio (Center for Christogenesis, "What Thomas Merton").

3. Brinton, "Stages in Spiritual Development," 392. Emphasis in original.

4. Barclay, *Apology*, 255.

5. Quoted in Brinton, "Stages in Spiritual Development," 394. Emphasis added.

6. Brinton, "Stages in Spiritual Development," 392, referencing John Bank, "An Epistle to Friends" (1692).

is seldom found in the journals, probably because it tends to imply the kind of sudden change which is not stressed by Quaker theory to the same degree that is stressed by some others, for example the Methodist."[7] Interestingly, in his 1972 book *Quaker Journals*, Brinton does not speak of either convincement or conversion. Instead of convincement, he describes "the divided self," which becomes "unified through silence" (perhaps an admission that his earlier view of convincement as "intellectual acceptance" was inadequate). And instead of conversion, he has chapters on "appearing in the ministry" and "adoption of plain speech and dress," evidently the two most common struggles for Friends in the eighteenth century (or at least those Friends who left journals).[8]

In part 3, we will explore this "conversion of the heart" in both the New Testament and in the experience of early Friends, concluding with how that might look today. Chapters 19 through 22 explore discipleship and the imitation of Christ in the New Testament, through our Girardian lens, which in my experience leads to a much deeper understanding of the New Testament perspective. Chapters 23 through 26 explore the experience of conversion of the heart for early Friends. Chapter 27 returns to Girardian themes of scapegoats, sacrifice, and victims, but in our modern context. Chapter 28 explores what conversion of the heart might mean for Friends today.

---

7. Brinton, "Stages in Spiritual Development," 394. Emphasis in original.
8. Brinton, *Quaker Journals*, chs. 4–7.

19

The Scandal of—and in— the Gospels

> Woe to the world because of scandals. For it must be that scandals come: but nevertheless woe to the one by whom scandal comes.
>
> —MATT 18:7 RHEIMS[1]

IN HIS FIRST LETTER to the Church in Corinth, the apostle Paul famously describes his message of "Christ crucified" as a scandal or stumbling block to the Jews and foolishness or even lunacy to the Greeks (1 Cor 1:23).[2] With all our various fine-sounding theories of atonement, the church has largely lost that sense of scandal.

---

1. The Rheims New Testament is an English translation of the Latin Vulgate dating from 1582. Modern translations translate the Greek *skandalon* variously: "offence" (KJV), "stumbling blocks" (NASB, NRSV), "things that cause sin" (NAB, NIV), "sin" (RSV), "causes of falling" (NJB). However, Greek has perfectly good words for sin and temptation; Girard contends that modern translations obscure the meaning of the Greek *skandalon*. See below.

2. Green and Baker argue that "foolishness" is too weak a translation of the Greek. Citing Justin Martyr, they offer "madness" or "lunacy" as more accurate (*Recovering the Scandal*, 14).

As portrayed in the Gospels, Jesus was reluctant to accept the title of Messiah (Mark 8:33; Matt 16:20; Luke 9:21), perhaps because of the militaristic connotations it had for his listeners. Instead, he seemed to interpret his mission in terms of the suffering servant in Isaiah and Ezekiel's "Son of Man."[3] When Jesus predicts his own suffering and death, Peter rebukes him, which in turn provokes harsh words from Jesus: "Get behind me, Satan! You are a stumbling block to me; for you are setting your mind not on divine things but on human things" (Matt 16:23). One of Girard's insights is to see that the Greek word *skandalon*, variously translated as "stumbling block," "obstacle," or "hindrance," has a precise meaning in the Gospels: the state of being in mimetic rivalry with another. James Warren explains:

> We see that Jesus says Peter is a scandal to him because Jesus is repelled by Peter's suggestion—and at the same time attracted to it and tempted by it. Were Jesus not able to overcome this temptation, and put it decisively "behind" him, he would fall into what Girard calls a state of scandal; that is he would be "scandalized." . . . To be scandalized is thus to be in a double-bind state: both attracted and repelled at the same time.[4]

Recall from chapter 1 that in Girard's anthropology, humans learn what to desire by imitating the desire of others: "We desire according to the desire of the other." This mostly occurs far below the level of conscious awareness; we *believe* that we are autonomous, uninfluenced by others, choosing to desire an object only because of its inherent value. In other words, we are largely blind to the influence of others in forming our desires. Beneath the level of our awareness, our desire is shaped by a *model*, someone we imitate by desiring what they desire. But if the two of us desire the same object, the *model* can easily become a *rival* for the possession of whatever object we both desire. And therein lies the challenge to human society: the mimetic nature of our desires can easily lead to escalating rivalries, which often enough spiral out of control. Hence the Tenth Commandment: "Thou shalt not covet . . . *anything* that belongs to your neighbor" (Exod 20:17).

The nature of this rivalry is the double bind of which Warren speaks: we are both attracted to our model and repelled by our rival—even though they are one and the same person. This is the double bind:

---

3. Wink, *Human Being*.
4. Warren, *Compassion or Apocalypse*, 55.

"Imitate me! Don't imitate me!"⁵ Girard describes scandal as "a paradoxical obstacle that is almost impossible to avoid: the more this obstacle, or scandal, repels us, the more it attracts us."⁶ Jesus sees and names this double bind as *scandal*, not in the modern sense of an action that causes public outrage or strong moral disapproval but in the Greek sense of *skandalon*, the double bind of being simultaneously attracted to and repelled by one's model/rival. Part of Jesus wants—desires—what Peter wants: a triumphant Messiah, not a suffering one. Jesus is truly tempted by Peter's desire but also sees that the "human things" that Peter desires pose a threat to the "divine things" of his mission. Thus his vehement reaction to Peter's suggestion: "Get behind me, Satan!" Once again, mimetic rivalry is explicitly named as *Satan*.

Author Luke Burgess reminds us that "mimetic tension is present even in relations that are, on the whole, healthy: between spouses, parents and children, or colleagues. . . . Even your relationship with your best friend might be—and probably is—*tinged by mimesis*."⁷ As I examine my own life, I can see the truth in this statement. I am aware of a deep and pervasive sense of competition and rivalry, mostly subtle, mostly unconscious, mostly not directed at specific individuals but the generalized "social other." Even when I do something "good," there is a part of me trying to show that I am "better." I want to think I am not susceptible to the mimetic influence of consumer advertising, yet somehow, I have accumulated the usual array of modern conveniences. Having participated in sports in high school and college, I am more susceptible than some to the "fanaticism" of mimetically rooting for a favorite team.

In my medical practice at a community health center, I was known to write very detailed and complete patient notes. Mostly that was just good medical care, the way I had been trained—but a small part of me was demonstrating to my colleagues (and myself) that I was a better physician than them. At a couple points of my career, I spent extended time in Africa, providing medical care among some of world's poorest and medically underserved people. Mostly I was acting out of a genuine desire toward service—but if I am honest, I also recognize that some part of me *wanted to be seen by others* as the kind of person who went to Africa to work with the poor. Even when I offer vocal ministry in meeting for

---

5. Alison, *Jesus the Forgiving Victim*, 194–95.
6. Girard, *I See Satan Fall*, 16.
7. Burgis, *Wanting*, 202. Emphasis added.

worship, I aspire to share a divinely inspired word that may be helpful, comforting, or challenging to others, but is there not a small part of me that also aspires to be the esteemed Quaker minister, perhaps just a little bit more spiritual or eloquent or profound than the previous speaker? When we look closely, mimetic rivalry is everywhere, deeply pervading our social life.

Matthew 18:1–9 contains Jesus's most explicit teaching on *skandalon*: "Woe to the world because of scandals. For it must be that scandals come: but nevertheless woe to the one by whom scandal comes" (v. 7 Rheims). Girard comments that "scandals are so formidable that to put us on guard against them, Jesus resorts to an uncharacteristic hyperbolic style: 'If your hand scandalizes you, cut it off; if your eye scandalizes you, pluck it out.'"[8] Modern translations render the Greek *skandalon* here as "stumbling block," "temptation," "causes of falling," or "sin," because "translators have not grasped that *skandalon* had its own special meaning for Jesus, being his way of speaking about the mimetic double-bind."[9]

Jesus's teaching on scandal was prompted by the disciples' question (v. 1), "Who is the greatest in the kingdom of heaven?" James Warren points out that "the context is the theme of *rivalry*; Jesus' disciples are competing with one another for the position of greatest in the kingdom of heaven." Jesus answers by calling forward a child, telling his disciples that they must "become like children" in order to enter the kingdom. He is calling attention to the child's quality of humility—and humility means "not being in rivalry with the other." Jesus is advocating a return to a childlike "non-rivalrous trust," where children can imitate their models without falling into a state of rivalry.[10] His harshest warning is to those who draw one of these innocent and trusting children into a state of scandal: "It would be better for you if a great millstone were fashioned around your neck and you were drowned in the depth of the sea" (v. 6).

And yet, "scandals must come." Given that mimetic desire and rivalry seem so ubiquitous, does Jesus offer an alternative?

Matthew 6:1–18, part of the Sermon on the Mount, contains Jesus's explicit teaching on the standard religious duties of almsgiving, prayer, and fasting. He warns against acting out of a desire for approval of (or competition with) others: "Beware of practicing your piety before others

---

8. Girard, *I See Satan Fall*, 17.

9. Warren, *Compassion or Apocalypse*, 58. Emphasis in original. See also n1 above, 187.

10. Warren, *Compassion or Apocalypse*, 59.

in order to be seen by then; for then you have no reward from your Father in heaven" (v. 1). To the almsgiver, he says, "Do not let your left hand know what your right hand is doing" (v. 3). Those who fast are advised not to make a public show, "so that your fasting may not be seen by others but by your Father who is in secret" (v. 18). Instead of comparing ourselves to others, Jesus challenges us to seek approval of God, and three times repeats the refrain that "your Father who sees in secret will reward you" (vv. 4, 6, 18).

On prayer, Jesus cautions his disciples not to "heap up empty phrases as the Gentiles do; for they think they will be heard because of their many words" (v. 7). He then follows with a very enigmatic statement: "Do not be like them, *for your Father knows what you need before you ask him*" (v. 8). James Alison points out that the logical conclusion from Jesus's statement is *to stop praying*. "There is literally no point in expressing your desire, since it is [already] known independently of its expression, and its expression makes no difference at all."[11] This cannot possibly be what Jesus means—especially since it is immediately followed by the Lord's Prayer (vv. 9–13).

This seeming contradiction can be resolved only when we realize that as moderns, we read this with an assumption of "the authentic self," the autonomous self which has desires independent of and uninfluenced by what others desire. This is the "blob and arrow" model of desire from chapter 1, what Girard has called "the romantic fallacy." Mimetic anthropology holds that this model of "the authentic self" is false; in reality, we "desire according to the desire of the other." We are given our desires by *the social other*: "To a large extent our desires are not simply our own but rather a sort of common property that gets passed around among members of a community.... We *participate* in the desires of the community, instead of merely generating or having them individualistically."[12] We live in an ecosystem of desire, a cloud of free-floating desires from which we derive "our" desires by imitation. This is much closer to the worldview of the New Testament, and as we will see, Jesus is expressing a rather sophisticated view of the dangers of *the social other* as the source of our desires. Read again Jesus's instruction on how we are to pray:

> And whenever you pray, do not be like the hypocrites; for they love to stand and pray in the synagogues and at the street

---

11. Alison, *Jesus the Forgiving Victim*, 399.
12. Collins, "Girard and Atonement," 134. Emphasis added.

corners, so that they might be seen by others. Truly I tell you, they have received their reward. But whenever you pray, go into your room and shut the door and pray to your Father who is in secret; and your Father who sees in secret will reward you. (Matt 6:5–6)

Alison points out that the Greek word translated here as "your room" is the word for pantry or larder; it was a room in the interior of the house that was used to protect perishable food from the extremes of heat and cold. This room of course had no windows; once you shut the door you could neither see others nor be seen by them. You were isolating yourself from the social other: this is the proper setting for prayer.[13]

Jesus here is demonstrating an astute understanding of the nature of desire. He understands that "we are all immensely needy people who long for approval and rewards."[14] Alison says:

> What people really want is approval, a particular reputation in the eyes of others and this leads them to act in such a way that they will get that approval.
>
> The trouble with seeking the approval of the social other is that you will get it! You will act in such a way as to get that approval, and *then become its puppet*.[15]

But Jesus does not tell us just to grow up and get over our desire for approval, to strive for the modern "autonomous self," which, as we have seen, is illusory. Given that "we desire according to the desire of the other," the critical question becomes "*Which other?*" Alison answers with a question: "We know that there is a *social* other which gives us desire and moves us this way and that. But is there *Another other*, who is not part of the social other, and who has an entirely different pattern of desire into which it is seeking to induct us?"[16]

Rather than persuading us to outgrow our need for approval, Jesus is instructing us to attend to *where* we seek our approval. Instead of looking to the *social other*, we can look to *Another other*—to God. Alison goes on to say that for Matthew "your Father who sees in secret" and "your heavenly Father" are code words for this *Other other*, the transcendent

---

13. Alison, *Jesus the Forgiving Victim*, 411.
14. Alison, *Jesus the Forgiving Victim*, 408.
15. Alison, *Jesus the Forgiving Victim*, 409, 408. Emphasis added.
16. Alison, *Jesus the Forgiving Victim*, 403. Emphasis in original.

God who is above any rivalry with human beings. To imitate God rather than the social other means: avoid mimetic rivalry and scandal, which so often leads to violence; avoid comparison, competition, or the need for approval. We can now see that Jesus's injunction to "be perfect, therefore, as your heavenly Father is perfect" (Matt 5:48) means "take God as your model, not one another."

Here is Jesus's alternative to the scandal of mimetic rivalry, an essential aspect of the intelligence of the victim: receive your desires not from the social other, but from the *Other other*, which leads to what James Warren calls "the transformation of desire."[17] But *how* is this possible?

---

17. Warren, *Compassion or Apocalypse*, 67. Burgis, *Wanting*; and Swartley, "Discipleship and Imitation" also speak of the "transformation of desire."

20

The Transformation of Desire

> We don't become better because we acquire new information. We become better because we acquire better loves.
>
> —David Brooks[1]

In the Gospel of John, immediately after the magnificent prologue with its theme of the universal Word incarnate, the actual narrative starts with a telling incident (1:35–39). John the Baptizer is with two of his disciples, when, "watching Jesus walk by, he exclaimed, 'Behold the Lamb of God.'" John's two disciples, evidently curious, set out to trail Jesus. Sensing that he is being followed, Jesus turns to face the two. "What do you want?" (NIV, NET); "What are you looking for?" (NRSV, NEB); "What are you seeking?" (KJV). The two seem taken aback; instead of a coherent reply, they can manage only to stammer, "Teacher, where are you staying?" Jesus responds to their non sequitur with an invitation: "Come and see."

What do you want? What are you seeking? What are you longing for? What is your deepest desire? In a word, *what do you love?* James K. A. Smith, in *You Are What You Love*, writes, "That's the question. It is the first, last, and most fundamental question of Christian discipleship."

---

1. Brooks, *Road to Character*, 211.

Jesus does not ask these two would-be disciples, "What do you *know*?" or even "What do you *believe*?" He asks only, "What do you *want*?"[2] *What do you desire?*

Readers can be forgiven if up until now they have thought of mimesis and mimetic desire as something bad, perhaps even akin to "original sin." As we have seen, mimetic desire can easily become mimetic rivalry, which all too commonly leads to violence and scapegoating. But there is another aspect of mimesis. In a 1993 interview, Girard clarifies his earlier view, which he says had been misinterpreted as calling for a "renunciation of mimetic desire." After noting that what Jesus advocates is in fact mimetic desire, "imitate me, and imitate the Father through me," he goes on to state that "mimetic desire, even when bad, *is intrinsically good*, in the sense that far from being merely imitative, it's the opening of oneself, opening to others. . . . Mimetic desire is also the desire for God."[3]

Many of Girard's commentators have picked up on this second aspect of mimetic desire. James Alison speaks of "pacific mimesis" and "loving imitation," as opposed to acquisitive or conflictual mimesis.[4] Marlin Miller speaks of "nonviolent mimesis" or imitation of the nonviolent God.[5] Michael Hardin speaks of positive, healing, or restorative mimesis.[6] Petra Steinmair-Posel speaks of "positive mimesis."[7] Rebecca Adams speaks of "constructive" and even "loving" mimesis.[8] Girard himself, in a late publication, speaks of "good" and "bad" mimesis. "There is good mimesis, which is called the imitation of Christ; there is bad mimesis, which I see as imitation of a human model. . . . Satan in a way is a symbol of this bad mimesis."[9]

Girard's key insight (not original to him) is that "our neighbor is the model for our desires; this is what I call mimetic desire. . . . The principal source of violence between human beings is mimetic rivalry, the rivalry resulting from imitation of a model who becomes a rival or of a rival who

---

2. Smith, *You Are What You Love*, 1. Emphasis added.

3. Adams and Girard, "Violence, Difference, Sacrifice," 23–25.

4. Alison, *Joy of Being Wrong*, 12–13. For loving imitation, see Alison, *Knowing Jesus*, 107.

5. M. Miller, "Girardian Perspectives," 45.

6. Hardin, *Mimetic Theory*, 77, 85, 94.

7. Steinmair-Posel, "Original Sin, Grace."

8. Adams, "Loving Mimesis."

9. Girard, *Reading the Bible*, 111, 146.

becomes a model."[10] But Girard is adamant that any predisposition toward violence is *not* genetic; there is no "instinct of aggression or aggressive drive."[11] And if violence is not genetically determined, it is possible to rise above it. We have a choice, and "choice always involves choosing a model. . . . True freedom lies in the basic choice between a human or divine model."[12]

We might say that humans are *inescapably mimetic*, but we are capable of a certain degree of choice about who or what we will imitate. The question then becomes *which* "other" will be the model of our desires: the social other or the *Other other*, in James Alison's language. The moral life is a matter of the proper ordering of our desires, not by renouncing all models but by choosing a model worthy of imitation. The "conversion of the heart" thus comes to us through a "transformation of desire."[13]

There are echoes here of a great debate among the early church fathers about the proper role of "the passions" or desires in the moral life, and specifically how the passions or "affections" relate to the Christian virtue of love. The fathers were often well versed in Greek philosophy and were eager to find commonalities with Greco-Roman thought. Mainstream Greek philosophy, represented by Plato and Aristotle, held that for a moral life, reason must be primary, functioning to strictly bridle the passions and affections that were seen as suspect.

Stoic philosophy (perhaps the main rival to the early Christian worldview) goes even further: the passions—desires—were not just to be controlled but overcome. "According to the Stoics, the life of virtue required detachment from the passions. . . . The sage strives to be totally self-sufficient, free of the disordered impulses that deflect one from pursuing what is good and noble. . . . The passions were not to be moderated or channeled, but rather rooted out, or, in the language of the Stoics, extirpated."[14] The Stoic ideal was *apatheia*, a life of indifference to the passions.

Desire or passion is of course closely connected to love, and "the language of love permeates the Scriptures."[15] For the early church fathers, this language of love could be problematic, especially in light of the

10. Girard, *I See Satan Fall*, 10, 11.
11. Girard, *I See Satan Fall*, 11.
12. Girard, *Deceit, Desire, and Novel*, 58.
13. Warren, *Compassion or Apocalypse*, 67.
14. Wilken, *Spirit of Early Christian*, 295.
15. Wilken, *Spirit of Early Christian*, 293.

Stoic challenge of *apatheia*. The fathers "could not avoid the language of love ... [but] how could love be a matter of indifference? ... The key failing of the Stoic doctrine was that it could not give an adequate account of what moved the soul to act."[16]

Over several centuries, various Christian thinkers (e.g., Lactantius, Gregory of Nyssa, Augustine, and Maximus the Confessor) struggled to clarify the place of desire and its relation to the primary Christian virtue of love.[17] The Greek language of the New Testament famously has three separate words that translate into English as "love": *agape, eros*, and *philia. Agape* (charitable love or love that is unmerited) predominates in the New Testament and describes God's love for us, as well as the ideal of human charity toward our fellows. *Philia* (friendship) is also frequently used in the New Testament (some forty times), at times interchangeably with agape. However, *eros* (erotic love or, more generally, attraction and desire to be united with that which is considered valuable) does not appear at all in the New Testament, perhaps out of a concern to avoid confusion with sexual indulgence.[18]

Eventually, eros entered the Christian lexicon, primarily to express the human longing or desire for God. Church historian Robert Louis Wilken describes the evolving position of the early church fathers: desire is "a yearning to possess what we do not have, but our desire for God is unlike desire for things in the world. ... Our yearning for God will be satisfied only by knowing God more fully and intimately"; i.e., by love.[19] According to Gregory, "The passions prepare the way for the love of God."[20] Desire or eros "draws us to God ... but desire is self-centered and acquisitive. ... As one comes into the presence of God *desire gives way to love*, and what was formerly sought by desire is now possessed in love. ... Desire is a restless activity, a yearning for something one craves but does not possess."[21] "Desire feeds on absence, love lives off presence."[22] For Maximus, "In the devout person the passions become good when they prudently turn away from earthly things and put themselves at the

---

16. Wilken, *Spirit of Early Christian*, 296, 298.
17. Wilken, *Spirit of Early Christian*, 297–311.
18. Oord, *Pluriform Love*, 73–76.
19. Wilken, *Spirit of Early Christian*, 299, 301.
20. Wilken, *Spirit of Early Christian*, 298.
21. Wilken, *Spirit of Early Christian*, 301. Emphasis added.
22. Wilken, *Spirit of Early Christian*, 302.

service of possessing heavenly things. . . . Desire brings about an insatiable spiritual movement that drives us toward divine things."[23]

It is this desire or eros that motivates the soul toward acts of love and charity (agape). According to these church fathers, the human problem is not the presence of passions or desires, as the Stoics claimed, but "disordered love." Their solution to our problem is to direct our love only toward that which is "ultimately desirable," to God.[24] This is the "transformation of desire," away from "earthly things" and toward "heavenly things."

In the Western tradition, this view is primarily associated with Augustine, who "has probably influenced more Christians than anyone whose writings are not in the Bible."[25] Augustine thinks of love exclusively as desire for God, or eros. What gets lost in Augustine is the commonsense conviction that love in the biblical sense is more than a *feeling* of desire, that it has to do with "*acting* intentionally, in response to God and others, to promote overall well-being."[26] To paraphrase the apostle James, "love without works is dead" (Jas 2:17).

It is not so much that Augustine is wrong but that his exclusive focus on love as eros, desire directed to God, leads him to strange places. Augustine's philosophical conviction, borrowed from the Greeks, is that God is beyond time, eternally and perfectly unchanging, entirely self-sufficient, radically transcendent to and unmoved by anything creatures do or experience. These convictions, combined with his "theology of desire,"[27] lead Augustine to the untenable and ultimately incoherent position that all *human* love is misdirected love of God, who, as perfect, unchanging, and lacking nothing, neither needs nor values human love. Augustine's God "does not love the world," at least in any usual sense of the word "love" as presupposing a mutual and responsive relationship.[28]

To return now to Girard, we have seen in part 1 that mimetic theory provides a compelling account that explicates the human tendency

23. Maximus the Confessor, quoted in Wilken, *Spirit of Early Christian*, 306.

24. Wilken, *Spirit of Early Christian*, 307. See also Oord, *Pluriform Love*, 108–9.

25. Oord, *Pluriform Love*, 104. Oord presents a persuasive critique of Augustine's view of love, as well as his doctrine of God, which depends heavily on Greek philosophical notions (104–55).

26. Oord, *Pluriform Love*, 35; this is Oord's overarching definition of love. Emphasis added.

27. Oord, *Pluriform Love*, 83.

28. Oord, *Pluriform Love*, 119, 121. Process theology in general has been very critical of "classical theism," rooted in Augustine's neoplatonic metaphysics.

toward violence and explains how, through the scapegoat mechanism, a certain type of "sacred" violence played a crucial role in allowing human culture to emerge and progress. We have also seen that Girard himself (as well as his interpreters) has drawn attention to a more positive role for mimetic desire, but this has remained relatively undeveloped.[29]

It is as though Girard has given us a diagnosis, but the cure remains elusive. As Rebecca Adams has written, when it comes to understanding why there is violence in our world, "we need more than a theory of violence: we need an alternative vision of what human beings could be, or are meant to be."[30] We turn now to an exploration of how Scripture envisions this "conversion of the heart" or "transformation of desire," through discipleship and the "imitation of Christ."

---

29. Swartley, "Discipleship and Imitation," 218, 218n2.
30. Adams, "Loving Mimesis," 277.

21

Discipleship as Imitation

> For I have set you an example, that you also should do as I have done to you.
>
> —John 13:15

> Be imitators of me, as I am of Christ.
>
> —1 Cor 11:1

Girard scholar Willard Swartley says that "the pattern of mimesis appears to permeate New Testament thought" and that the neglect of this theme constitutes "the mimetic error in New Testament scholarship."[1] Jesus invites us to join him "on the way" by becoming his disciples; we become disciples by imitating him, and specifically by imitating his suffering and servanthood.[2] Discipleship *is* imitation: the prototypical example of "good" or "positive" mimesis.

This emphasis on mimesis is there from the very beginning. In what is likely the earliest extant Christian text, Paul tells the Thessalonian church, "You became *imitators* of us and of the Lord, for in spite of

---

1. Swartley, "Discipleship and Imitation," 234, 220.
2. Swartley, "Discipleship and Imitation," 222.

persecution you received the word with joy inspired by the Holy Spirit, so that you became an *example* to all the believers in Macedonia" (1 Thess 1:6–7). Later in the same letter, Paul adds that the Thessalonian church has not only provided an example for others to imitate, but itself has imitated the churches in Judea: "For you, brothers and sisters, became *imitators* of the churches of God in Christ Jesus in Judea, for you suffered the same things from your compatriots as they did from the Jews" (1 Thess 2:14–15).[3] Swartley says this text stands in the tradition of Hebrew prophetic critique ("killing the prophets") and "denotes suffering as the identifying mark of Christian experience."[4]

Paul's letters are filled with exhortations to imitate him (Paul), and through that, to imitate Christ. "Brothers and sisters, join in imitating me, and observe those who live according to the example you have in us" (Phil 3:17). "I appeal to you, then, be imitators of me" (1 Cor 4:16). "Be imitators of me, as I am of Christ" (1 Cor 11:1). In Ephesians, we are urged to "forgive one another, as God in Christ has forgiven you"; i.e., to follow the example of Christ (Eph 4:32). We are even urged to imitate not just Paul, not just Christ, but God (Eph 5:1).

Beyond these exhortations to imitation, the whole Pauline theme of "in Christ" implies not only imitation but *participation*. "In Christ" or its close equivalent appears over 160 times in Paul's letters.[5] We are baptized with Christ, suffer with him, crucified with him, die with him, and are raised with him "in newness of life" (Rom 6:3–6). "I have been crucified with Christ; it is no longer I who live, but it is Christ who lives in me" (Gal 2:19–20).

Although imitation is not an explicit theme in the Gospel accounts, the idea of becoming disciples by following Jesus "on the way" is implicitly mimetic. In John 13:15, Jesus "sets an example" for us by washing the disciples' feet. And in the synoptic accounts, Jesus instructs his followers "on the way," even as he warns them of what is about to happen in Jerusalem (see, e.g., Mark 10:52; Luke 17:11).

---

3. Passages like this can all too easily lend support to Christian anti-Semitism. Recall that Paul always considered himself to be a Jew, but he also knew from personal experience that the law was capable of becoming an instrument of violence and death. References to "the Jews" refer either to the religious leaders of the Jews or to Paul's "Judaizing" opponents in Galatia. Much more on Paul, "the Jews," and anti-Semitism in the next chapter.

4. Swartley, "Discipleship and Imitation," 222.

5. Campbell and DePue, *Beyond Justification*, 86; Guiton, *Early Quakers*, 162n138.

We have already seen (in ch. 19) Jesus's reaction when Peter tries to dissuade him from the way of the suffering servant. As Swartley says, "It is clear that two opposing views of Messiahship have locked horns,"[6] and Jesus will become increasingly insistent about his view of the Messiah as suffering servant, with three separate incidents of misunderstanding by the disciples, followed by three separate discourses from Jesus on genuine discipleship. The first is here, after Peter rebukes Jesus and Jesus responds by rebuking Peter: "Get behind me, Satan!" This is immediately followed by Jesus's instructions to his disciples, "If any want to become my followers, let them deny themselves and take up their cross ("daily cross" [Luke 9:23]) and follow me; for those who want to save their life will lose it, and those who lose their life for my sake and the sake of the gospel will save it" (Mark 8:34–35).

The second incident, in Mark 9:33–37, is prompted by the disciples arguing "on the way" about "who was the greatest." Once again, Jesus calls together his disciples, saying "whoever wants to be first must be last and servant of all." To make the point even clearer, he calls forward a child, offering the child as an appropriate model, which is then followed by his warning about scandal (see ch. 19). Jesus is "turning aspirations to greatness upside down.... To follow Jesus on the way requires, absolutely and thoroughly, a revisioning of greatness."[7]

The third incident follows the request of John and James to be seated on his right and left hand when he "comes in glory." Jesus responds with his third prediction of suffering, this time combined with an explicit warning that his disciples will also be asked to suffer. "The cup that I drink you will drink; the baptism with which I am baptized, you will be baptized" (Mark 10:35–39). This is followed by Jesus's third and most extensive discourse on discipleship. "You know that among the Gentiles those whom they recognize as their rulers lord it over them, and their great ones are tyrants over them. But it is not to be so among you; but whoever wishes to become great among you must be your servant, and whoever wishes to be first among you must be slave of all. For the Son of Man came not to be served, but to serve, and to give his life a ransom for many" (Mark 10:42–45).

Willard Swartley summarizes what he calls the "mimetic pattern that lies at the heart of the New Testament":

---

6. Swartley, "Discipleship and Imitation," 231.
7. Swartley, "Discipleship and Imitation," 231.

The "in Christ" person dies to the old *acquisitive mimetic pattern of desire* and lives by the power of a new mimesis, *imitating the pattern of Jesus Christ and seeking to be conformed to his image*.... We learn a new pattern of mimetic desire, one that leads not to rivalry and violence, but to building others up, avoiding scandal, preferring one another, empowering the other, and nonretaliation against evil in order that as members of the community of the new creation we break the spiral of violence and become the strands of yarn that by God's Spirit are knitted into the display of love, justice, and shalom.[8]

James Alison puts it this way: "The new heart is created in us by the old heart . . . being broken. Conversion works as we recognize our complicity in creating victims, cease to see ourselves as a victim, and begin to see ourselves as co-victimizers."[9]

But how exactly do we "imitate Christ"? Is it as easy as consciously *choosing* a new and better model to imitate? Does this imply that we can bring about our own salvation—the classic conservative critique of the moral influence view of the atonement? Is this just a fancy variation of the popular slogan "What Would Jesus Do?"[10]

Jim Fodor, in his endorsement/critique of discipleship as imitation, suggests that "Girard's thesis is articulated at such a high level of abstraction, it is difficult to see precisely what Jesus' preaching of the kingdom could really amount to, what positive content it might convey, other than the negative gesture of refusal of acquisitive desire."[11] After again noting the strong connection in both Paul and the Gospels between discipleship and suffering, he observes that "mimesis is not something that Christians *do* as much as it is something that Christians *undergo*; mimesis is

---

8. Swartley, "Discipleship and Imitation," 238–39. Emphasis in original.

9. Alison, *Joy of Being Wrong*, 62.

10. See Wikipedia, "What Would Jesus Do?," for the details of this fascinating story. Briefly, the idea of "what would Jesus do" goes back to Paul's letters, Augustine, and esp. Thomas a Kempis's fifteenth-century *The Imitation of Christ*. The specific phrase was the subtitle of a wildly popular novel first published in 1896 by Charles Sheldon, *In His Steps*, which in turn helped to inspire the social gospel movement. It had a resurgence among Christian youth in the 1990s, often in the form of a distinctive wristband, designed to keep the reminder physically close. James Alison says the fad faded quickly after 9/11, when presumably it was obvious to everyone that Jesus would *not* engage in a war of retribution. See Alison, *Jesus the Forgiving Victim*, 522–27.

11. Fodor, "Christian Discipleship," 249.

something they *suffer*." Following Jesus is "less a matter of choosing than of being chosen."[12] "You did not choose me, but I chose you" (John 15:16).

James Alison gives us perhaps a place to start. He notes that the phrase "What Would Jesus Do?" leaves unspoken the second half of the question, *"if he were here now."* There is a *presumption of absence*, that Jesus is *not* here and that we are left on our own to figure out what to do. Alison instead proposes that we start with a *presumption of presence*, so that the question changes from "What *would* Jesus do, if he was here?" to *"What is Jesus doing, here and now?"* By beginning with this presumption of presence, we "develop a habitual sensitivity to a certain form of imitation, of being challenged by the mode of Jesus's presence that we saw on the Road to Emmaus." We are "drawn into a flexible imitation of him"; not a mechanical imitation but a creative one, in the very changed circumstances that we find ourselves."[13]

By way of illustration, Alison cites Jesus's new commandment, "that you love one another; even as I have loved you, that you also love one another" (John 13:34 RSV). Alison observes that "just telling someone to love someone [else] is not very useful"; everything then depends on our (notoriously undependable) will.[14] So, an example is given, "even as I have loved you." And how does Jesus love the disciples? "No one has greater love than this, to lay down one's life for one's friends" (John 15:13). Jesus's self-giving love *is the same as* his new commandment; "something done *for us* becomes a defining source of our acting *for others.*"[15] Love is not a commandment in the usual sense, but something we imitate: "We love because he first loved us" (1 John 4:19).

In the Sermon on the Mount, Jesus offers an even more difficult commandment, to "love your enemies . . . so that you may be children of your Father in heaven" (Matt 5:44–45). Alison emphasizes that this is not a suggestion that Jesus wants you as a doormat. Rather, in the context of the entire passage (5:43–48), Jesus is offering a contrast between "two different patterns of desire."[16] Normally, we desire according to the desire of the other, defining ourselves over and against a social other, and in particular against our enemies. "One of the things we pick up from our social group with astonishing ease, is enemies: the one who is not like

12. Fodor, "Christian Discipleship," 250, 251. Emphasis added.
13. Alison, *Jesus the Forgiving Victim*, 526. See 524–27 for fuller discussion.
14. Alison, *Jesus the Forgiving Victim*, 551.
15. Alison, *Jesus the Forgiving Victim*, 552. Emphasis added.
16. Alison, *Broken Hearts and New Creations*, 166.

us and, by comparison with whom, we know who we are."[17] But God's desire is different: "God is able to be *towards* each one of us without ever being *over against* any one of us. God is in no sort of rivalry at all with any one of us."[18] God "makes his sun rise on the evil and the good, and sends rain on the righteous and unrighteous" (Matt 5:45). And through the experience of God's love, we can "come to love other people without any over against them.... We can become a different sort of imitator, one who receives being from another [the *Other* other, which is God], without any grasping of it at all by rivalrous comparison with anyone else."[19]

Rebecca Adams has given what may well be the deepest interpretation and critique of Girard's notion of mimetic desire. She begins by noting that Girard has overly emphasized the negative aspects of mimetic desire, while neglecting "the primordial goodness of human beings, as represented by their biblical creation in the image of God."[20] Late in his career, Girard "admits that he has at times split and verbally as well as conceptually scapegoated the term *mimetic desire* itself by forgetting to stress that mimetic desire is also sometimes, or even fundamentally, good."[21] She goes on to elaborate that splitting "involves dividing a concept in half, then expelling the undesirable half," while at the same time obscuring or mystifying what remains. "The term *mimesis* or *mimetic desire* or even *acquisitive mimesis* has *already* undergone a process of splitting and expulsion revealed by contradictory uses in the same text."[22]

Adams further notes that Girard's "solution" to the problem of violence—renunciation of acquisitive desire through the imitation of Christ—speaks mostly to those in a position of power, those who are "unconsciously informed by a persecutor/powerful perspective." What actual victims of violence, especially those who belong to historically victimized groups, need to renounce is *not* their own agency but their "*lack* of will to *appropriate* subjectivity, desire, and agency as those made in the Image of God":[23]

---

17. Alison, *Broken Hearts and New Creations*, 169.
18. Alison, *Broken Hearts and New Creations*, 166. Emphasis in original.
19. Alison, *Broken Hearts and New Creations*, 168, 171.
20. Adams, "Loving Mimesis," 279.
21. Adams, "Loving Mimesis," 282. Emphasis in original.
22. Adams, "Loving Mimesis," 283. Emphasis in original.
23. Adams, "Loving Mimesis," 288. Emphasis in original.

> The reality is that some people are genuinely more victimized than others. Such people have a different and positive relationship to this desire for selfhood, power, agency. . . . This means that the solution to the problem of violence must centrally include an account of constructive desire, the taking on of *a new, nonvictimizing*, and *nonvictimized* perspective. . . . The imitation of Christ thus must mean something strong, active and liberative, simply to include, let alone privilege, the perspective of those who have been real victims. . . . A complete theory of violence must not only *tell* us that we can take on this new perspective, but it must also *show us how* those who have been victims can actually cease to be victims *by ceasing to identify with their victim position*.[24]

This directly relates to the point we made in chapter 14, about the distinction between the sin of pride and the sin of hiding, between inordinate self-will and inordinate self-loss. *Both* are sins.

Rebecca Adams says that the crucial question, one that "Girard never explicitly asks, is this: 'What does *God* desire?'"[25] For Adams, the answer is that God desires our *subjectivity*: our sense of selfhood, agency, creativity, and our flourishing within a community of other subjects. But human desire too easily derails God's desire. We desire some object through the mediation of a model, but this dynamic quickly turns the *model* into an object and a rival. In turn, the model, through the mutually desired object, transforms the original desiring subject (the "protosubject") into an object, and we are quickly in the realm of escalating rivalry. She elaborates:

> Violence is somehow bound up with the nature of *objects*, or the nature of *turning [subjects] into objects*, a process of "object-ifying." . . . The essence of the scapegoating process is that someone or something is turned into an *object*. This temptation to turn things into objects instead of subjects, even ourselves or God, might be called Idolatry.[26]

Adams goes on to ask, "What happens if the *object* desired by the mediator is the *subjectivity* of the proto-subject? . . . If the proto-subject were [then] to imitate the desire of the mediator, then the proto-subject would desire his or her own subjectivity." Instead of a cycle of escalating rivalry

---

24. Adams, "Loving Mimesis," 288–89. Emphasis in original.
25. Adams, "Loving Mimesis," 290.
26. Adams, "Loving Mimesis," 293, 295. Emphasis in original.

between proto-subject and model, we would then have a virtuous cycle where both participants desire the *subjectivity* of the other. If as the mediator I desire not some object but your own subjectivity, "it enriches *both* of us . . . it is *both* selfless and self-interested to desire the subjectivity of the other, since I am desiring my own subjectivity in the process. . . . In desiring your subjectivity I get or acquire an intersubjective relationship with you, the proto-subject, but I do so without acquiring you as an *object*."[27]

Perhaps more poetically, this contrast can be understood as the difference between "gazing at the world with a loving eye" (which *requires* seeing the subjectivity of the other) and looking with an "arrogant" or "acquisitive" eye (which is premised on the other as object). The loving eye "does not try to reduce or simplify the other to something more manageable or usable. The loving eye is not invasive, coercive, or acquisitive in relation to the other."[28]

Adams goes on to say that desiring the subjectivity of the other can only be described as love:

> This new paradigm of mimetic desire describes genuine love.
>
> If I as a proto-subject imitate the mediator's desire [for my own subjectivity] . . . I end up desiring not only myself but others and indeed potentially *everything around me* as a subject—as something alive with its own irreducible being, yet in dynamic, loving, intersubjective relation with me . . . adopting the same unconditional relation of love that Christ exemplifies in relation to the Father, or *imitating* him.[29]

Because we habitually experience our own subjectivity over and against others *as objects*, this "change in perspective involves a type of conversion," but a type of conversion that simply "recognizes the *already existing reality* of the deeply intersubjective, interdependent, and unfolding nature of human relationships and life."[30] Adams suggests that "subjects need not be conceived as emerging out of an inevitably violent

---

27. Adams, "Loving Mimesis," 294. Emphasis in original.

28. Case-Winters, *God Will Be All*, 158. See 158–60 for fuller discussion. Winters writes from the perspective of process/relational theology, which strongly resonates with Adams's point that "God desires our subjectivity." In process theology, subjectivity is not confined to humans but "goes all the way down." See epilogue.

29. Adams, "Loving Mimesis," 296, 295. Emphasis in original.

30. Adams, "Loving Mimesis," 299. Emphasis in original. Note how the "deeply intersubjective, interdependent, and unfolding nature of human relationships and life" resonates with process theology, as described in excursus 1.

opposition and exclusion, but could be understood as the creative product of the dynamic loving mimesis itself."[31] Because this conversion involves letting go of our old ways of selfhood, the change in perspective may well be experienced as a kind of death: losing our (old) life in order to gain (new) life, "for the sake of the gospel."

With her "creative reassessment of mimetic desire," Adams goes a long way toward bringing "the imitation of Christ" and the commandment to "love one another" back down to earth. We are not likely to have opportunities to imitate Jesus of Nazareth by healing lepers, casting out demons, cleansing the temple, or dying on a literal cross. But through this "conversion of the heart," this loving mimesis, we can perhaps die to the old self and come to a new way of living in the world, a way that does not involve defining our self over and against "the other." Perhaps we can even learn to "provoke one another to love and good deeds" (Heb 10:24).

Before leaving the Bible and turning to the experience of early Friends, we have one more task: coming to terms with the apostle Paul.

---

31. Adams, "Loving Mimesis," 295.

22

"In Christ"
Paul's Gospel of Participation

> I have been crucified with Christ, and it is no longer I who live, but it is Christ who lives in me. And the life I now live in the flesh I live by the faith of the Son of God, who loved me and gave himself for me.
>
> —Gal 2:19–20

> There is no longer Jew or Greek, there is no longer slave or free, there is no longer male and female, for all of you are one in Christ Jesus.
>
> —Gal 3:28

The apostle Paul has previously entered into our discussion, primarily in chapter 16, in terms of the role of the Spirit; and chapter 21, in terms of discipleship "in Christ." In this chapter, we delve more directly into Paul's contentious legacy.

It is sometimes said that Paul was the "first Christian," transforming the religion *of* Jesus into a religion *about* Jesus. In an understatement, Marcus Borg and John Dominic Crossan write that Paul "is not universally well regarded, even among Christians."[1] He is variously accused of opinions that support slavery, anti-Semitism, homophobia, patriarchy, and

---

1. Borg and Crossan, *First Paul*, 1.

misogyny. As read through the lens of the sixteenth-century Protestant Reformers, his theology appears to support the penal substitution view of atonement as well as double predestination. Karen Armstrong entitled her biography *St. Paul: The Apostle We Love to Hate*; Borg and Crossan's first chapter is "Paul: Appealing or Appalling?," and an early chapter in Pamela Eisenbaum's study of Paul is "Paul the Problem."[2]

On the other hand, Quaker authors John Punshon and Alan Kolp both observe that "Fox loved the apostle Paul." Kolp says that "Fox is Pauline even when he may be explicitly citing a text from John's Gospel or some other New Testament writing. . . . One cannot really understand Fox unless one understands Paul."[3] For Quakers, and indeed for all Christians, it is incumbent to come to some understanding of the thought of this pivotal figure.

Borg and Crossan helpfully divide Paul's writings into "the radical Paul" (the seven undisputed genuine letters), "the conservative Paul" (Ephesians, Colossians, and 2 Thessalonians: contested but probably from later followers writing in his name), and "the reactionary Paul" (from 1 and 2 Timothy and Titus: "definitely not Paul").[4] Most—but not all—of what we dislike about Paul is from these post-Paul writings, likely written at least a generation after his death. Borg and Crossan make the case that in the genuine letters of Paul, we find a "radical visionary" whose primary dispute is with the "imperial theology" of the Roman Empire.

Pamela Eisenbaum, writing as a Jewish scholar teaching at a Christian seminary, argues that our basic problem with Paul is our insistence on seeing him as "Paul the convert." In this near-universal view, Paul starts out as a zealous Jew, has a dramatic experience of the Risen Christ, and promptly "converts" to being a Christian. "Paul the convert" abandons a "bad form of religion" (legalistic Judaism) in exchange for a good one (the Christian gospel of grace). The implication is that by becoming Christian, Paul's Judaism is thereby superseded: at best, no longer relevant, and at worst, something to be vigorously opposed.

Eisenbaum points out that this view of "Paul the convert" is misleading. First of all, from his letters it is clear that Paul never stopped considering himself to be a Jew. And second, "Christianity" in Paul's time did not exist as something separate and distinct from Judaism. Eisenbaum

---

2. Eisenbaum, *Paul Was Not Christian*, 10–31.

3. Kolp, "Fox Loved Apostle Paul," 10; see also Punshon, *Testimony and Tradition*, 14.

4. Borg and Crossan, *First Paul*, 13–16.

argues that we should see Paul's experience on the road to Damascus not as a *conversion* but as a *call*. Specifically, Paul is called to become "the apostle to the gentiles." In his own description of that event (Gal 1:13–17), he uses language that echoes the call of the prophet Jeremiah (compare Jer 1:5 with Gal 1:15). His epistles are addressed to gentiles, and we should read everything he says about the Jewish law as applying specifically (and only) to gentiles. In his calling as the apostle to the gentiles, Paul is seeking to bring gentiles into the family of God but without burdening them with strict Torah observance.[5]

I owe my own deeper engagement with Paul, at least in part, to the Quaker New Testament scholar Timothy Peat and his discussion of some of the nuances of translating from the original Greek, which I touched on in chapter 16.[6] Peat also pointed me to the so-called new perspective on Paul, which dates to the 1977 publication of E. P. Sander's monumental *Paul and Palestinian Judaism*.[7]

Peat observes that "you do not need to read very far in Paul to find that he says some negative things about the Jewish law, in particular contrasting it detrimentally with faith."[8] Luther and the other Protestant Reformers saw this as Paul's attack on the presumed "petty legalism" of Judaism and assumed that prior to his conversion, Paul was tortured by his futile attempts to live up to the demands of the law. Sanders points out that there is nothing in Paul's letters to support this: with no evidence of Paul's pre-conversion "tortured conscience," it seems to be something that the sixteenth-century Reformers read into Paul, based on their *own* experience.

Through an exhaustive review of the contemporaneous Jewish literature, Sanders also shows that Judaism of the time was *not* characterized by "petty legalism"; no Jew believed that salvation could be "earned" through their own works. Rather, Jews viewed the Torah as a gift from God, one part of their covenant with Yahweh; *salvation came from being part of the covenant*. Out of gratitude for the gift of Torah, they owed

---

5. Eisenbaum, *Paul Was Not Christian*, 132–49. See also Stendahl, *Paul Among Jews*, 7–23. Stendahl was one of Eisenbaum's teachers at Harvard.

6. Timothy Peat, chs. 2–7, 9, in B. Dandelion et al., *Heaven on Earth*. In more recent years, Timothy Peat goes by the name Timothy Ashworth. See also his more complete treatment of these issues (Ashworth, *Paul's Necessary Sin*).

7. Although Sanders himself says he is picking up on work by G. F. Moore and Albert Schweitzer (*The Mysticism of Paul the Apostle*, 1931), both writing in the 1920s and '30s. See Sanders, *Paul and Palestinian Judaism*, 33–36.

8. Timothy Peat, in B. Dandelion et al., *Heaven on Earth*, 34.

obedience to the law, but there was no belief that anyone could perfectly obey, and the law itself provided for various rituals and prayers of atonement to renew the covenant whenever it was violated. Sanders calls this position "covenantal nomism," as opposed to the "petty legalism" that Luther and others saw in ancient Judaism.[9]

If this is true (and Sanders's conclusions are now widely accepted) then we are still left with the question: Where does Paul's animus toward the Jewish law come from? Sanders's own answer is that while we usually argue in terms of "plight" (universal original sin) to "solution" (faith in Christ), in Paul's case the argument goes in the opposite direction. Here is Peat's summary of Sanders's position:

> What Sanders discovers is that Paul's thought, his understanding, moves "from solution to plight." Paul has a dramatic experience, a transforming experience, in which Jesus Christ and in particular the death and resurrection of Christ are central. It is an experience of reconciliation and liberation. Paul comes to new life. This is reflected in the language he uses: death to rebirth; liberation from slavery; a new creation. It is this experience that is the starting point of Paul's understanding, his theology. He has a dramatic and positive experience. He experiences what he feels is the solution to the whole world's suffering and sin. It is only from that perspective that he then describes "the plight," "the problem" of which the law is a significant part.... There was something wrong with the law, [but] only in relation to what he had now come to.[10]

In their recent book, Douglas Campbell and Jon DePue extend Sanders's argument by presenting Paul's interpretation as a "model that 'thinks backwards,' understanding the plight in the light of the solution.... The solution, which has been gifted to us, reveals with true clarity our plight."[11]

Campbell and DePue maintain that the major part of Paul's authentic writings convey a positive "gospel of participation, transformation, and resurrection."[12] This "gospel of resurrectional participation" is succinctly summarized by Paul's frequent reference to our life "in Christ,"

---

9. Sanders, *Paul and Palestinian Judaism*, 75, 422.
10. Timothy Peat, in B. Dandelion et al., *Heaven on Earth*, 36–37.
11. Campbell and DePue, *Beyond Justification*, 133.
12. Campbell and DePue, *Beyond Justification*, 87.

"IN CHRIST" 213

which we explored in chapter 21.[13] For Paul, our ongoing life is lived *in Christ*. We are crucified *with Christ*, baptized *into* Christ's death, raised *in Christ*, justified *in Christ*. We are one body *in Christ*; the Spirit of Christ is *in us*; Christ lives *in us*. We access this life *in Christ* through the faithfulness *of* Christ—Campbell and DePue's preferred translation of what has traditionally been rendered as faith *in* Christ.[14] By imitating Jesus's faithfulness, even unto death on a cross, "we *participate* in the death and resurrection of Jesus, die and rise with Christ, and thereby enter a new life *in Christ*."[15]

Borg and Crossan call this life *in Christ* "the participatory atonement."[16] In their striking metaphor, life *in Christ* is the result of "a spirit transplant," the Spirit of Christ coming to replace our own spirit, as in Gal 2:20.[17]

Campbell and DePue hold that this "gospel of resurrectional participation" accounts for at least 90 percent of Paul's genuine letters. The problem some of us have with Paul comes from the remaining 10 percent, which has been used over the centuries to support what Campbell and DePue term "justification theory." Briefly stated, this "minority opinion" within Paul seems to *start* with the "plight" of universal or original sin and the futility of "salvation by works of the law" and then proceeds to the solution of faith in Christ, by way of penal substitution atonement.

Campbell and DePue show that this 10 percent of Paul, which has for centuries been read as supporting justification theory, is not actually Paul's position but the position of his *opponents*. They refer to these opponents as "the teachers";[18] Paul himself refers to them as "the circumcision faction" (Gal 2:12). From what we can understand, these were very real opponents who were raising havoc in the Galatian church. They seem to have been messianic Jews who believed that Jesus was indeed the Messiah but that gentile converts needed to undergo circumcision, keep the

---

13. Campbell and DePue, *Beyond Justification*, 86, 125. They state that "in Christ" or its equivalent occurs "upward of 160 times" in Paul's letter (86).

14. Campbell and DePue, *Beyond Justification*, 306–23 (ch. 14, "The Faith of Jesus"). See ch. 16 above. See also Eisenbaum, *Paul Was Not Christian*, 191–95, for a clear discussion of the Greek grammar. According to her, "a majority of New Testament scholars now favor this translation" (i.e., "faithfulness of Christ" rather than "faith in Christ").

15. Borg and Crossan, *First Paul*, 137. Emphasis added.

16. Borg and Crossan, *First Paul*, 137, 166. See also their ch. 7, "Life Together 'In Christ,'" 185–213.

17. Borg and Crossan, *First Paul*, 183–84.

18. Campbell and DePue, *Beyond Justification*, 254.

Sabbath, and follow kosher dietary restrictions—basically become Jews, which was anathema to Paul's position of maximal inclusiveness.[19]

Romans is the one Pauline epistle written to a church he had never visited, and it seems to have been written at least in part to warn the Roman church to be on the lookout for these "teachers" (see Rom 16:17–18). According to Campbell and DePue, the epistle (esp. chs. 1–3) should be read as Paul carrying on a vigorous but hypothetical debate with one of these teachers and point by point refuting his teaching. For our purposes, there are two important conclusions. First, Paul is accusing these opponents—*but not all Jews*—of "petty legalism" and "salvation by works."

Second, what has been read for centuries as Paul's "justification theory" is actually the position of his *opponents*, which Paul is refuting—so it can sometimes seem that Paul is arguing with himself. Campbell and DePue point out that such a hypothetical debate was a common rhetorical device in the ancient world (as, for example, in Plato's Socratic dialogues) but is difficult for us to recognize because the text does not clearly identify who is speaking. They hypothesize that the letter was meant to be read out loud to the Roman churches, possibly by Phoebe (Rom 16:1); a reader familiar with its purpose could easily have "play-acted" the two roles.[20]

One of the pernicious effects of justification theory is its portrayal of "the Jews." Anyone rejecting "faith in Christ" is, by the logic of justification theory, "immoral, irrational, hypocritical, legalistic, and mercantile . . . negative descriptors that apply above all to unconverted Jews."[21] Justification theory leads Christians to "the teaching of contempt" toward Jews, and as history has amply shown, "when we are convinced that God will punish and execute recalcitrant Jews on the day of judgement, we have few qualms about seeing them punished and executed in advance of that date."[22]

In the background of justification theory is the image of the divine as a God of retribution, punishing those who don't live up to the legalistic terms of a contract. It "defines non-Christians essentially as cosmic felons—by criminalizing them. And this characterization applies above all

---

19. Campbell and DePue, *Beyond Justification*, 266–305. For Paul's Galatian opponents, see 254–59.

20. Campbell and DePue, *Beyond Justification*, 269. Chapters 12 and 13 (266–305) gives their reconstruction of a dialogue between Paul and one of these opponents.

21. Campbell and DePue, *Beyond Justification*, 160.

22. Campbell and DePue, *Beyond Justification*, 162. See their ch. 7, "The Teaching of Contempt," 152–68.

to recalcitrant Jews."[23] This simply cannot have been Paul's intention, and given the appalling historical consequences of Christian anti-Judaism, it is incumbent on all Christians to resist this line of thinking—which ultimately means rejecting justification theory. The presence of anti-Judaism within Christianity becomes "a litmus test for the presence of a sinister 'othering' program that is operating with theological cover, as 'the will of God.'"[24]

There is one more perspective on Paul that bids for our consideration, Robert Hammerton-Kelly's study of Paul's "hermeneutic of the cross," which examines Paul's theology from the framework of Girard's mimetic theory. In some tension with E. P. Sanders, Hammerton-Kelly starts by insisting that Paul's vision on the road to Damascus was not just "a dramatic and positive experience" but instead a "double realization" that "fused the negative and positive."[25] On the negative side, Paul was *convicted* of his own role in scapegoating violence, arising out of his zeal for the law ("Why do you persecute me?"). In 1 Corinthians, after alluding to his Damascus road experience, Paul writes that he is "the least of the apostles, unfit to be called an apostle, because I persecuted the church of God" (1 Cor 15:9). But beyond his personal actions, Paul also came to see that his persecution of the nascent Christian movement was all of a piece with the authorities' crucifixion of Christ, manifesting the exact same underlying dynamic of sacred violence (hence, the title of Hammerton-Kelly's book, *Sacred Violence*).

On the positive side, Paul's Pharisaic worldview *convinced* him that the Risen Christ's appearance meant that the promised resurrection at the end of time was beginning: Jesus, whom he had been persecuting, was in fact the Messiah. Paul, with some urgency, saw that it was now time for Israel to inaugurate the long-prophesied "ingathering of the nations," that all people might come to worship the one true God.[26] Again, recall that Paul was not *converted* to Christianity but rather *called* to be the apostle to the gentiles (Rom 1:5; Acts 26:17; Gal 1:16).

Hammerton-Kelly claims that Paul saw in the death of Christ on the cross "an epiphany of sacred violence."[27] He saw that the Jewish law could and did lead to a variety of exclusionary rites and practices, resulting in an unnecessary wall of separation between Jews and gentiles. Eventually, these

23. Campbell and DePue, *Beyond Justification*, 166.
24. Campbell and DePue, *Beyond Justification*, 166.
25. Hammerton-Kelly, *Sacred Violence*, 67, 68, 67.
26. Eisenbaum, *Paul Was Not Christian*, 241–49.
27. Hammerton-Kelly, *Sacred Violence*, 63. His broader argument is found in 63–87.

practices end in scapegoating violence on the part of those who, like him, had been "zealous for the law." Paul came to believe that this was a misinterpretation of Torah, so he can say that it was "through the law [properly understood] that I died to the law [as misunderstood]" (Gal 2:19).

Admittedly, this ambiguous status of the law led to Paul's sometimes tortured arguments about its proper role (e.g., Rom 7:7-25; Gal 3:19-29): he struggled mightily to reconcile his Pharisaic conviction that the law was God's infinitely valuable gift to the Jewish people with his own experience that the very same law had made him into a violent persecutor. Christianity has tended to emphasize Paul's negative evaluation of the law, but we should not ignore his many positive comments. We should understand his negative remarks not so much as Paul's rejection of Judaism, as his rejection of *all* religion based on exclusion and sacred violence.[28]

Hammerton-Kelly's analysis of Paul's apparent animus toward the Jewish law is firmly grounded in Girard's mimetic theory.[29] He starts with the assertion that the law—all law—derives from sacred violence. Recall that in Girard's primal scene, an archaic group of hominids overcomes its internal strife and mimetic rivalry by arbitrarily choosing and killing a scapegoat. The unity that results is then attributed to the power that the (now-dead) victim must have had; the experience of this power leads them to (mistakenly) conclude that the victim must have been divine. A system of prohibitions and taboos arises, to prevent mimetic rivalry from recurring. In all cultures, the price of violating these taboos is divine vengeance: sacred violence. "Law is, therefore, essentially mimetic violence transformed into divine vengeance and then rationalized as retributive justice.... In Paul's Judaism, Law had not yet been fully rationalized and so still rested on the idea of divine vengeance."[30]

In order to explain how God's gift of the law became enmeshed in sacred violence, Paul turns in Rom 5 to the figure of Adam. In Hammerton-Kelly's interpretation, Yahweh's "primal prohibition" ("of the tree of the knowledge of good and evil you shall not eat" [Gen 2:17]) was given to *protect* Adam and Eve from mimetic rivalry; trusting in Yahweh's beneficence, they would know only good. "The purpose of the primal

---

28. Hammerton-Kelly, *Sacred Violence*, 9.

29. Recall here again that Paul is writing at the time of late Second Temple Judaism, twenty years before the Jews' violent and disastrous revolt against Roman rule, ending with the destruction of the temple. Subsequent rabbinic Judaism comes to its own accommodation with the Mosaic law.

30. Hammerton-Kelly, *Sacred Violence*, 150.

prohibition was to ensure that the relationship between creature and creator would be one of trust . . . [but] desire [symbolized by the serpent] misinterpreted the divine motive and misused the Law to incite envy."[31] Acting on the "suspicion that the prohibition guards God's privilege rather than our paradise,"[32] Adam and Eve "entered into mimetic rivalry with God."[33]

Hammerton-Kelly says that Paul regards the Torah of Moses to be "enduringly valid when properly interpreted, because it contains the primal prohibition": in a negative form, as the tenth commandment against envy and covetousness; and in a positive form, as commandments to love God and love the neighbor (see Rom 13:9–10). But "the Law was hijacked by sin to the service of sacred violence."[34] Thus, Paul's argument with the Jews was over the proper interpretation of Torah. In Hammerton-Kelly's interpretation of Paul:

> Despite its misuse by sacred violence, the Law in its essence is not alien to the divine purpose; therefore it must be fulfilled, but in a sense different than the [then] current Jewish way. Faith is the way to fulfill the essential purpose of the Law.
>
> Thus the fulfillment of the Law is the faith that trusts God and restores the primal prohibition to its true role as the guardian of creaturehood, by inhibiting mimetic rivalry with God. At issue, therefore, are two different interpretations of Torah, one that caused the death of Christ and one that prevents such violence. They are respectively the Mosaic reading and the reading through faith in the Cross of Christ. Therefore, faith is the fulfillment of Torah also in the sense that it provides a way to read it according to its real intention.[35]

This very definitely resonates with what we said in chapter 15, about the "Emmaus way" of reading Scripture, with Christ as the "hermeneutic key" to interpretation.

Hammerton-Kelly further elaborates on Adam and the primal prohibition by contrasting eros with agape. *Eros* is desire structured by lack; it seeks to acquire and appropriate the other as an object. By contrast,

---

31. Hammerton-Kelly, *Sacred Violence*, 158.
32. Hammerton-Kelly, *Sacred Violence*, 158–59.
33. Hammerton-Kelly, *Sacred Violence*, 158.
34. Hammerton-Kelly, *Sacred Violence*, 158.
35. Hammerton-Kelly, *Sacred Violence*, 158, 159.

agape is "desire flowing from the divine plenitude that fulfills our lack"; its desire is not to acquire but "to give of itself generously."[36] This relates to the Genesis story:

> *Agape* is also the prelapsarian [i.e., before the fall] innocence of Adam, when the prohibition defended him from the knowledge of evil and kept access open to the tree of life, while *eros* is the knowledge of good and evil. Agape trusts the God of the prohibition, puts hope in place of rivalry, and thus fulfills the Law. Eros suspects the prohibition of excluding it from an entitlement and so has deformed itself into rivalry with the divine, and the prohibition into a principle of competition in the mimetic game.[37]

Hammerton-Kelly holds that "sacred violence and deformed desire need to be redeemed; eros is the desire that needs reformation and agape is the redeeming action of God." In the triangular structure of desire (lover/beloved/model), the model/obstacle in eros comes to be replaced in agape by the divine victim, in whom there is no rivalry. By imitating this divine model, we transform eros into agape: the conversion of the heart. Agape involves "renouncing rivalry," as Paul points out in Rom 14.[38]

Unlike the other Pauline interpretations we have examined, Hammerton-Kelly does not minimize the conflict between Paul and the followers of Moses. He acknowledges that this poses a distinct danger: his reading can easily be seen as just another way to scapegoat "the Jews." He counters this potential criticism by showing that Paul's critique of Torah is a critique of sacred violence; properly understood, this gives a built-in safeguard to prevent it from any reversion to scapegoating. Simply put, Paul's criticism of Torah is that when misunderstood it leads to scapegoating and sacred violence; for Christians to then use Paul as justification for scapegoating Jews is anathema to his purpose.

Paul's "exposition of faith [is] precisely the taking of responsibility rather than scapegoating others." In multiple ways, Paul "specifically undermines the possibility that his theology and his churches might become instruments of the primitive sacred. To the extent that subsequent generations have allowed them to be used for that purpose, they have

---

36. Hammerton-Kelly, *Sacred Violence*, 166, 170.
37. Hammerton-Kelly, *Sacred Violence*, 166–67.
38. Hammerton-Kelly, *Sacred Violence*, 181.

been misused."³⁹ Sadly, early Friends were among those who misused Paul's theology in their largely negative view towards Jews.⁴⁰

If Paul's disagreement with the Judaism of his time centers around its misinterpretation of the Mosaic law, leading to exclusivism, scapegoating of gentiles, and ultimately to violence, we might well ask: Who are "the Jews" in our time? Are they not the Christian church (or at least much of it) that excludes, scapegoats, and dreams of retributive violence? For Hammerton-Kelly, "The moment at which the church identified itself as 'the new Israel' marks the moment at which it reveals its fall from grace and the deformation of its self-understanding as part of the new creation, to a structure of sacred violence." Too often, the church has become just "another exclusive structure [that] is undermined by its own gospel of the Cross."⁴¹

Hammerton-Kelly sees in Paul "a radical critique of culture." Paul's disagreement with Judaism is "the spearhead of his attack on the structures of this world," which is everywhere characterized by sacred violence. Having seen this violence revealed in the cross, Paul realizes that *"the antidote to sacred violence is identification with the victim.... Rather than sacrifice the victim, agape wants to sacrifice itself on behalf of the victim."*⁴² It is this that allows him—and us—to live "in Christ."

Commentaries and interpretations of the apostle Paul abound and could fill a small library; we have sampled a few that seem especially relevant to our theme. From our survey, we can say with some confidence that the church (and especially the heirs of the Protestant Reformation, including Quakers) have misinterpreted Paul for centuries. Paul did not "convert" to Christianity but continued to consider himself a Jew and a Pharisee, with all the apocalyptic presuppositions that involved. His experience on the road to Damascus is best understood as a "call" to become the apostle to the gentiles, and all his writings should be understood as addressed to gentiles who are in the process of coming to understand their changed relationship to both to Judaism and polytheism.

39. Hammerton-Kelly, *Sacred Violence*, 184.

40. See, e.g., "A Visitation to the Jews," in G. Fox, *Works*, 4:56; "The Jew Outward," in Penington, *Works*, 1:286. All Jews were expelled from England in 1290, and it was not until 1656 that Cromwell allowed Jews to return, so it is unlikely that early Friends had much firsthand knowledge of Judaism. Instead, they were likely following Luther and other early Protestant Reformers, even if unconsciously.

41. Hammerton-Kelly, *Sacred Violence*, 187, 185.

42. Hammerton-Kelly, *Sacred Violence*, 188, 175, 178, 177. Emphasis added.

His sometimes strident comments about the Jewish law must be read in the context of the wider issue of sacred violence (which is by no means unique to Judaism). His argument with his Jewish coreligionists was not for or against Torah but about its proper interpretation, especially as it applied to new gentile converts. His opposition to circumcision and kosher dietary restrictions for gentile converts was in the service of breaking down artificial barriers between communities. Finally, and most importantly, when Paul is used to justify Christian anti-Judaism, it is a red flag that we have misunderstood Paul as well as our own gospel.

What should stand out in this brief survey is the degree to which Paul emphasized a "participatory gospel" of "life in Christ," what Albert Schweitzer nearly a hundred years ago called "the mysticism of the apostle Paul." As we shall see, this will have important resonance with early Friends experience. We are now ready to turn to early Quaker language and metaphors for the conversion of the heart.

23

The Two Seeds and the Refiner's Fire

> Sink down to the seed which God sows in the heart, and let that grow in thee, and be in thee, and breathe in thee and act in thee.
>
> —Isaac Penington[1]

I ARGUED IN THE introduction to part 3 that early Friends quite explicitly saw their convincement not as an end but as the beginning of a lifelong process, what we might call "the conversion of the heart," or "continuing conversion." Here I want to explore two common Quaker metaphors for that process, the "seed" and the "refiner's fire"; we will explore other metaphors in the two subsequent chapters.

Quaker historian Douglas Gwyn states that "the image of God's seed was particularly important to Fox—it suggests a fundamental new being and will, *a transcendent subjectivity*."[2] But the use of "seed" by Fox and other early Friends can be quite confusing, so some background is in order.[3]

---

1. "Some Directions to the Panting Soul," in Penington, *Knowing the Mystery*, 141.

2. Gwyn, *Seekers Found*, 243. Emphasis added. Note the similarity of "transcendent subjectivity" with Rebecca Adams, ch. 21.

3. The following paragraphs concerning the seed draw heavily on a previously

My Bible dictionary gives at least six different meanings of the word "seed" as it is used in the Bible, and early Friends at various times allude to all six of these meanings. Biblical (and Quaker) use of seed can be roughly divided into two classes: the botanical metaphors, rooted in the plant kingdom; and the zoological metaphors, rooted in the animal kingdom. Fox in particular seems drawn to the zoological meanings. "Seed" in the Hebrew Scriptures can mean semen and so, by extension, the power of procreation, and by further extension, it comes to mean offspring, descendants, or progeny. Thus, from Genesis, "the seed of Abraham" means Abraham's descendants. Because Fox considered Quakers to be the *spiritual* progeny of Abraham, he sometimes referred to Quakers as the seed: "the elect seed of God called Quakers."[4]

Much more commonly, however, Fox talked about "the seed of the woman," which would "bruise the head of the serpent" (Gen 3:15). Following Paul, Fox identifies this seed of the woman (as well as the seed of Abraham) as Christ (Gal 3:16). Thus, for Fox, the seed is primarily Christ, but with typically Quaker stress that the "imperishable seed" (1 Pet 1:23) that is Christ dwells in us: "because God's seed abides in them" (1 John 3:9). Much of this in Fox can be completely lost on us, largely because our modern Bible translations of these passages use words like offspring or progeny, instead of the somewhat archaic "seed."

Quakers today are likely more drawn to the botanical metaphors, in part because this is how Jesus talked of *seed* in the Gospels. At least four of Jesus's parables employ seed as a botanical metaphor: the good seed and the weeds (Matt 13:24–30), the mustard seed (Matt 13:31; Mark 4:30; Luke 13:18), the seed growing secretly in the night (Mark 4:26–29), and finally the seed and the sower (Matt 13:3–9; Mark 4:3–9; Luke 8:4–15). The parable of the sower is one of the few parables where we have Jesus's own interpretation: when asked by his disciples for its meaning, he begins his explanation with "now the parable is this: *the seed is the word of God*" (Luke 8:11).

The Epistle of James picks up on this theme: "Submit to God and accept *the word that God plants in your heart*, which is able to save you" (Jas 1:22 GNB). This is immediately followed by the admonition, often cited by early Friends, "Be not hearers of the word only, but doers" (1:22 KJV). The "word of God" here is obviously not a book, a point early Friends

---

published work, "Metaphors of Transformation: The Seed," in Gates, *Opening the Scriptures*, 39–48.

4. G. Fox, *Journal*, 281.

never tired of making: the word of God is the seed, Christ, planted in our heart. Fox writes that "there is no true seed but what Christ has sown in the heart."[5] Like the tiny mustard seed, it can be small and inconspicuous, easy to miss, yet when the soil is good and the seed nurtured and watered, it can grow and flourish.

Early Friends often spoke of *two* seeds, which contend for preeminence; progress in the spiritual life involves tending to the one while resisting the other. Alluding to Gen 3:15 and the enmity God places between the serpent, the woman, and their respective seeds, Fox writes: "All Friends everywhere, know the *seed of God* which bruiseth *the seed of the serpent*, and is a-top of the seed of the serpent, which seed sins not but bruiseth the serpent's head which tempts to sin and doth sin . . . which seed is one in the male and in the female."[6]

Isaac Penington is even more explicit: "This is the sum or substance of our religion; to wit, to feel and discern the two seeds: the seed of enmity, the seed of love; the seed of the flesh, the seed of the Spirit; the seed of Hagar, the seed of Sarah; the seed of the Egyptian womb, the holy seed of Israel; and to feel the judgments of God administered to the one of these, till it be brought into bondage and death; and the other raised up in the love and mercy of the Lord to live in us, and our souls gathered into it, to live to God in it."[7] Penington goes on to elaborates on the importance of the two seeds:

> So that this is our religion, to witness the two seeds, with the power of the Lord bringing down the one, and bringing up the other; and then to witness and experience daily the same power, keeping the one in death, and the other in life, by the holy ministration of God's pure living covenant. . . . Here are the two seeds (the seed of the serpent, the seed of the woman) whose striving and fight is in man, when God awakens the soul; the one whereof hath a nature, a desire, or lust contrary to the other. Now as the one of these prevails in any heart, so the other goes down. As the one gains life and power, so the other is brought into death and captivity.[8]

---

5. "Epistle 230," in G. Fox, *Power of the Lord*, 188.

6. G. Fox, *Journal*, 174.

7. "Concerning the Sum and Substance of Our Religion," in Penington, *Works*, 2:441.

8. Penington, *Works*, 2:443–44.

James Nayler likewise speaks of two seeds: the seed of enmity, the evil seed, the seed of the evildoer, which is opposed to the holy seed, the seed of the covenant, the righteous seed, or simply the seed of God. He speaks of this latter "good" seed as being "in bondage" or "imprisoned."[9] Fox also speaks of the world having "oppressed and grieved the tender seed."[10]

John Whitehead, in his 1655 pamphlet *The Enmity Between the Two Seeds*, captures this sense of conflict and striving between "the seed of the serpent" and "the seed of God." Whitehead relates in unusual detail his spiritual journey, from his "day of visitation" at age fifteen; his journey through various sects, including what sounds like time among Ranters (when he says he was "ignorant of the daily cross of Christ"); a stint in Cromwell's army, and his eventual convincement by the preaching of William Dewsbury in 1652, at about age twenty-two.[11]

The seed as a metaphor for the "conversion of the heart" is an image of something small, even insignificant, but which, given time, grows from within. Gradual and continuing growth is especially emphasized by Penington:

> The true sanctification consists in the *growth* of the seed, and its spreading, like a leaven, over the heart . . . [but] the appearance of the power at first is small, and contemptible. . . . All lies in one little seed, where the day of small things is known . . . and in receiving that little thing, all is received; and in the growth of that, all grows up . . . and when it is received, is but like a little seed, even the least of seeds; and when it grows up, it is a long while like a child.[12]

The growth of this seed is not unimpeded, and so it can remain oppressed, in bondage. Two seeds are in conflict with one another; and before one can prevail, we must recognize the conflict. In this "conversion

---

9. Nayler, "Door Opened."

10. "Epistle 371," in G. Fox, *Power of the Lord*, 397.

11. J. Whitehead, "Enmity Between Two Seeds." The pamphlet includes a detailed account of his 1654 trial and subsequent imprisonment in Northampton Jail, for refusing the oath of abjuration. My thanks to Mary Crauerhauf of the Haverford Quaker Collection for finding a pdf of this somewhat obscure work, which is referenced in Brinton ("Stages in Spiritual Development," 390; Brinton gives the date as 1665). John Whitehead (not George) is mentioned in Fox's journal as the bearer of the order from the king, releasing Fox from Scarborough Castle in 1666 (G. Fox, *Journal*, 501).

12. "The Way of Life and Death Made Manifest," in Penington, *Works*, 1:43, 77.

of the heart," as Alan Kolp notes in his book on Fox's spirituality, *"the key to the conversion journey is to be brought to the place of inner conflict."*[13]

The gentle, organic image of the growing seed is in some tension with the image of *two* seeds in conflict, which may strike contemporary Friends as too stark, too dualistic. But is it too much of a stretch to relate these "two seeds" to James Alison's point (in ch. 19) about the choice we face, of which "other" to imitate, the social other or the *Other* other?

The image of the refiner's fire underlines this sense of inner conflict so prominent in the lives of early Friends. The image comes from a passage in Malachi:

> The Lord whom you seek will suddenly come to his temple. . . . But who can endure the day of his coming, and who can stand when he appears? For he is like a refiner's fire and like fuller's soap. . . . He will purify the descendants of Levi and refine them like gold and silver. (Mal 3:1b, 2–3)

Metal-bearing ore is refined by fire; only when the temperature is sufficiently high do all the impurities separate out, leaving behind pure silver or gold. Margaret Fell speaks of "the living principle of God in you" as a "consuming fire," burning away all impurities (alluding to Heb 12:29: "Our God is a consuming fire").[14] George Fox testifies to his experience of the refiner's fire:

> As the Light appeared, all appeared that is out of the Light, darkness, temptations, the unrighteous, the ungodly; all was manifest and seen in the Light. Then after this there did a pure fire appear in me; then I saw how he sat as a refiner's fire and as the fuller's soap; and then the spiritual discerning came into me, by which I did discern my own thoughts, groans and sighs, and what it was that did veil me, and what it was that did open me. And that which could not abide in the patience nor endure the fire, in the Light I found . . . [that which] could not give up self to die by the Cross, the power of God . . . and that which would cloud and veil from the presence of Christ, that which the sword of the Spirit cuts down and which must die, [and] might not be kept alive.[15]

---

13. Kolp, *Fresh Winds of Spirit*, 24. Emphasis added.

14. Fell, "Epistle to Friends," 458. "Consuming Fire" also appears in G. Fox, Nayler, and Penington.

15. G. Fox, *Journal*, 14–15.

Marcelle Martin, in her helpful chapter on "The Refiner's Fire in the Seventeenth Century," points to the essence of the refiner's fire as the individual becoming "acutely aware of the inward struggle," sometimes, as we have seen, described as the struggle between two seeds.[16] "The Refiner's Fire continued for years and decades, purifying mind and heart until every distraction and sinful tendency was removed . . . making possible the full growth of the inner divine Seed."[17] She quotes William Smith (1661) as a typical example: "In the Refining Fire," every form of corruption

> is purged and consumed; and as man abides the Fire, and waits in the Judgment, he puts off the Old in which he hath lived, and puts on the New and is translated; and *here truly man dies to himself*, and receives Christ the Seed of Life, and putteth him on."[18]

The refiner's fire purifies by consuming all that is impure, and so, as both Fox and Smith suggest, can be experienced as a kind of death. As such, both the seed and the refiner's fire, as used by early Friends, hearken back to Jesus's words: "Unless a grain of wheat falls into the earth and dies, it remains just a single grain; but if it dies, it bears much fruit" (John 12:24).

Alan Kolp observes that the inner conflict, to which both the two seeds and the refiner's fire testify, is "a struggle between two wills: the earthly, fleshy will and God's will. It is a struggle between the false self and the possibility of an emerging true self."[19] In language that echoes Thomas Merton, Kolp continues:

> The problem is that so often this selfish, earthly self will seem like the only "person" one knows. It is taken for one's real self; in fact it is *real*, but it is one's false self. The real, *authentic* self can only be known by seeing the real, false self put to death. Most people . . . prefer to ignore or deny truth: that they are a false self. . . . As God begins to call one, this wrestling with the truth of one's false self is a *struggle*. "It is the struggle to die to the false self."

Our "dying," then, has to do with the stripping away of illusions.[20]

16. Martin, *Our Life Is Love*, 61.
17. Martin, *Our Life Is Love*, 64.
18. Martin, *Our Life Is Love*, 64. Emphasis added. Quoting William Smith, "The New Creation Brought Forth, in the Holy Order of Life."
19. Kolp, *Fresh Winds of Spirit*, 30.
20. Kolp, *Fresh Winds of Spirit*, 30, 20. Emphasis in original. Internal quote from "The Way of the Heart," in Henri Nouwen, *The Spiritual Life: Eight Essential Titles*.

We turn now to another metaphor for the conversion of the heart, common for early Friends and even more direct about the need for "a kind of death": the way of the cross.

24

The Way of the Cross

> The bearing of the daily cross is the only true testimony.
>
> —William Penn[1]

THE WRITINGS OF EARLY Friends are saturated with the language of the cross, which represents for them a central metaphor for "the conversion of the heart." George Fox repeatedly describes the cross of Christ as the power of God,[2] alluding to the apostle Paul, who says that "the preaching of the cross . . . is the power of God" (1 Cor 1:18). Fox speaks of the inward cross of Christ, keeping to the daily cross, living in the cross, and the fellowship of the cross. The cross functions as "a cross to their own will," and "crucifies you from the state that Adam and Eve were in in the fall, and so from the world."[3] He counsels Friends to "keep in the daily cross, the power of God, by which ye may witness all that is to be crucified which is contrary to the will of God, and which shall not come into

---

1. Spencer, "Quakers in Theological Context," 143. Quoting Penn, *No Cross, No Crown* (1682 ed.).

2. G. Fox, *Journal*, 174. See also 205, 283, 338, 341; "Epistle 222," in G. Fox, *Power of the Lord*, 176. See Pickvance, *Readers Companion*, 64–66, for many and varied references to the cross.

3. G. Fox, *Journal*, 365, 283.

his kingdom."[4] The cross can signify a willingness to suffer; we are not only to "live in the cross of Christ" but to "rejoice in it."[5]

For Isaac Penington, the cross is likewise the power of God, experienced inwardly. "This I have experienced concerning the cross of our Lord Jesus Christ; that it is an inward and spiritual thing, producing inward and spiritual effects in the mind . . . which slays the enmity in the mind, and crucifies to the world, and the affections thereof . . . that which is contrary to the world, and crucifies to the world: that is the cross."[6] Penington also ties the cross to suffering and persecution. To Friends suffering persecution, he counsels, "He on whose back the Lord lays the cross, and crucifies him every day; his self-will and self-wisdom, with all the conceitedness and stiffness which arise therefrom, must needs be broken in him."[7]

Margaret Fell touches upon many of the same themes, including the cross as the power of God. In a passage that ties the Quaker theme of waiting in the light to Paul's words about the cross (1 Cor 1:23–24) she tells Friends to "wait here in the light, and you will come to know and see the Cross of Christ, which is the power of God unto salvation, which is foolishness unto the world, but unto them that believe, it is the Power of God, and the Wisdom of God."[8] She advises Friends to "abide in the cross, so that you may come to witness the enmity slain . . . and nailed to the cross, and you crucified to the world, and the world to you."[9]

We could cite many other examples from the writings of virtually all seventeenth-century Quakers; William Penn wrote an entire book on the central place of the cross in Quaker spirituality, with its "invitation to take up the daily cross."[10] The point is clear: early Friends commonly spoke of the cross of Christ—in ways that may be difficult for contemporary Friends to appreciate or even understand.

We saw in chapter 21 how Jesus in the Gospels urged his disciples to follow him by "taking up the cross," explicitly linking this to a willingness to accept suffering. Imitation is likewise an important theme in Paul, and it is closely tied to themes of suffering, of being "crucified with Christ" (Gal 2:19).

4. G. Fox, *Journal*, 18.
5. "Epistle 216," in G. Fox, *Works*, 7:218.
6. "The Naked Truth, or Truth Nakedly Manifested," in Penington, *Works*, 3:368.
7. Penington, *Knowing the Mystery*, 200–201.
8. Fell, *Call unto the Seed*, 35.
9. M. Fox, *Life of Margaret Fox*, 92.
10. Penn, *No Cross, No Crown*, 5.

For early Friends, one important aspect of the way of the cross was self-denial, the cross as "a cross to our wills." Penn's *No Cross, No Crown* is illustrative: "The work of the cross of Christ in man is self-denial. . . . [It is] the denial and offering up of ourselves, by the same Spirit [that was in Christ] to do or suffer the will of God."[11] Our model in this, what Penn calls our "best example," is Christ's prayer in Gethsemane: "Not my will, but thine, be done" (Mark 14:36). "[Jesus] did not suffer that we might avoid it; he suffered that we might deny ourselves and so be the true followers of his example."[12]

Contemporary Friends may well see danger in these sentiments. If we are prone to "the sin of pride," what we described in chapter 14 as "inordinate self-will," self-denial is a necessary and constructive strategy. But if our temptation is instead "the sin of hiding" or "inordinate self-loss," self-affirmation and even assertion might instead be called for. The danger is that the cross, thought of as "a cross to our wills," may encourage victims of oppression to see their suffering as some kind of spiritual duty, encouraging submission when resistance is instead called for. But if Penn and his generation could be blind to the "sin of hiding," our own generation may be blind to the legitimate place of self-denial. Commenting on Penn's title, *No Cross, No Crown*, twentieth-century Quaker Henry Cadbury wrote:

> Modern taste does not like to think in terms of the cross. The need for sacrifice, for renunciation, is certainly, even in some religious circles, unpopular. Self-affirmation, self-expression, is much in vogue and the restrictive features of self-denying discipline are anathema to those worldlings who would please themselves. . . . William Penn's classic still reminds us of a feature of Quakerism that ought not be forgotten in our generation.[13]

Penn testifies to the cross in its "inward" sense, as self-denial, renunciation, and sacrifice. The "outward" cross was equally important to early Friends: the cross experienced as suffering and persecution at the hand of authorities. In chapter 13 we saw that "becoming a Quaker came with the expectation of suffering, which was not sought out but also not avoided or resisted." This was hardly a peripheral issue; the fact of suffering in the face of state persecution was foundational for the first generation of

---

11. Penn, *No Cross, No Crown*, 22.
12. Penn, *No Cross, No Crown*, 29.
13. Henry Cadbury, quoted by Ronald Selleck, in Penn, *No Cross, No Crown*, xvi.

Quakers. "Bearing the cross" of arrests, beatings, fines, and imprisonment constituted a central aspect of Quaker spirituality for early Friends.

Even though they never used this language, early Friends were victims of state oppression—they were what today we would readily identify as scapegoats. We concluded in chapter 13 that in a very real sense, Quakers functioned as a "scapegoat caste," first for the Puritans in the Commonwealth period and subsequently for the reestablished Anglican Church and restored monarchy. Even so, their identity did not come from being victims; though *victimized*, they did not see themselves as *victims*. What James Alison has said about the Risen Christ on the road to Emmaus could also be said about early Friends: they were victims, but theirs is not a victimary story.[14] For the first Quakers, suffering was seen as *redemptive*: salvation was not *from* their suffering but *through* their suffering.

While meticulously documenting and publicizing their various sufferings, they could also, through their "theology of suffering," see their experience of persecution in a positive light. Instead of seeing suffering as God's punishment for sin, as their contemporaries often did, suffering was part of God's plan and indeed "a privilege, evidence of their election."[15] Suffering represented a crucial testing of their faith; "it was a way of participating in the passion and death of Jesus by dying to the particular shapes that sin took in their age."[16]

Margaret Fell urged imprisoned Friends to "rejoice in that they are made worthy to suffer for the Lord's sake."[17] In their 1660 declaration to King Charles, Quaker leaders claimed that "we have suffered even the most of any people in the nation . . . yet we know it is for righteousness' sake . . . which for us is a witness for the convincing [convicting] of our enemies."[18] Suffering, like their other testimonies, was "an instrument of the gospel" and so came in part from an *evangelical* intent, by unmasking the "bloody spirit of persecution" in their opponents.[19]

Quakers today are no longer beaten, fined, or thrown in jail—or worse—for our beliefs. We are fortunate to live in a much more tolerant and diverse culture. Having climbed the ladder of social respectability,

---

14. Alison, *Jesus the Forgiving Victim*, 75–76.

15. Moore, *Light in Their Consciences*, 160. The phrase "theology of suffering" is hers.

16. Guiton, *Early Quakers*, 323.

17. Margaret Fell, letter to Nayler and Howgill (1653), quoted in Guiton, *Early Quakers*, 324.

18. G. Fox, *Journal*, 401.

19. Punshon, *Testimony and Tradition*, 33.

our various countercultural quirks are mostly met with indifference rather than opposition. Despite this, perhaps early Friends attitude toward suffering still has lessons for us and for our wider culture.

Early Friends did not engage in violent resistance to their persecutors—but neither did they passively acquiesce. They did not shrink from the suffering of persecution, and in some ways they went out of their way to provoke it. They wore their suffering as a badge of honor, an assertion of the truth. In this, they were aligning with Jesus's teachings—perhaps more than they realized.

In a well-known passage from the Sermon on the Mount (Matt 5:39–41), Jesus advises his followers to turn the other cheek, go the second mile, and give those who sue for your coat your cloak as well. Too often this has been interpreted as a call to docile *nonresistance* to evil, a "doormat" or masochistic mentality. But Jesus's instructions to "not resist an evildoer" (Matt 5:39) are better translated as "don't react *violently* against the one who is evil."[20] Walter Wink has shown that Jesus is actually teaching a "third way," between *nonresistance* and *violent resistance*.[21]

By detailed exegesis of the Greek text, Wink shows that "if anyone strikes you on the right cheek" describes how a person in a position of power might strike a subordinate with the *back* of the right hand, a gesture intended to humiliate. By "turning the other cheek," the recipient is resisting this gesture of humiliation and instead inviting the attacker to strike him on the offered left cheek with the right *fist*—to fight him as an equal rather than insult him as an inferior. Without violently striking back (a response that would be sure to end poorly), the recipient has nevertheless managed to assert his (or her) dignity.

Likewise, the context of "go also the second mile" is the Roman military occupation. A Roman soldier had the absolute right to impress any civilian to carry his heavy pack to the next milepost—but no further. To avoid antagonizing the local population, the code of military conduct forbade soldiers from forcing civilians to carry their burden beyond one mile. If a soldier did go beyond that limit, he could be subject to harsh discipline. Thus, "going the extra mile" would place a Roman legionnaire in the impossible situation of asking—begging—a Jewish civilian to relinquish the load he had just forced him to carry, lest he be punished for "breaking the rules."

---

20. Wink, *Powers That Be*, 101.
21. Wink, *Powers That Be*, 98–111 (ch. 5, "Jesus' Third Way").

The third example, "give your cloak as well," refers to the all-too-common event of a creditor taking an impoverished person to court for an unpaid debt. The creditor is entitled to a destitute person's coat as collateral, but the coat had to be returned every evening (Deut 24:12–13). To counter this pretense of charity, Jesus advises the debtor to "give your cloak too." The cloak was the innermost garment—underwear—so Jesus was suggesting that the debtor make his point by stripping naked in court. Nakedness of course was taboo in that culture, but "the shame fell less on the naked party than the person viewing or causing the nakedness."[22] One can well imagine the scenario Jesus paints would have elicited guffaws from his audience, who knew all too well the burdens of an unjust legal system.

Wink says that "the logic of Jesus' examples in Matt 5:39b–41 goes beyond both inaction and overreaction, to a new response, fired in the crucible of love, that promises to liberate the oppressed from evil even as it frees the oppressor from sin. Do not react violently to evil, do not counter evil in kind, do not let evil dictate the terms of your opposition, do not let violence lead you to mirror your opponent."[23]

Note here the parallel between Jesus's third way and early Friends response to persecution. Wink says Jesus showed how "the oppressed can recover the initiative and assert their human dignity in a situation that cannot for the time being be changed . . . by taking the law and pushing it to the point of absurdity."[24] This is an accurate description of how Friends met their persecution head on: subverting legalized cruelty by provoking it, so that it became visible to all.

Could we go even further and say that for early Friends, "living in the cross" was the equivalent to "the intelligence of the victim" described in the prologue? I think we can, and to further explore this, I want to go into some detail, to see if this intelligence of the victim might resonate with the experience of early Friends. Recall that the phrase comes from Girardian theologian James Alison, whose primary concern is to explain what happened to the disciples, those "apostolic witnesses" on whom all subsequent Christianity depends, when they became witnesses to the resurrection.

In the resurrection, the disciples experienced Jesus as *crucified* yet *risen*. Alison describes this as an entirely gratuitous experience—unexpected, freely given, unmerited. Resurrection would have been experienced as forgiveness: Jesus appeared not as a ghost seeking vengeance,

---

22. Wink, *Powers That Be*, 104.
23. Wink, *Powers That Be*, 110–11.
24. Wink, *Powers That Be*, 107, 110.

but instead offering peace and forgiveness ("peace be with you" [Luke 24:36]). Alison says, "The resurrection *is* forgiveness.... The simple fact of Jesus' appearance to his disciples ... was the presence of forgiveness."[25] What the disciples gained in these experiences, as well as their subsequent long reflection on them, is what Alison means by "the intelligence of the victim":

> As a result of the resurrection of Jesus, the disciples underwent a profound shift in their understanding, such that they were able to understand something about human life that had never really been understood before. That something was, to put it simply, the relationship between God and victims.[26]

> They had understood something radically new about the whole way in which God makes [Godself] manifest to humanity ... enabling them to go back in their memories and [now] tell the story of Jesus as that of the self-giving and self-revealing victim.[27]

> [The Easter event] was in fact the condition which made it possible for God to be revealed for what [God] really is: the forgiving victim.[28]

Alison cites many examples of how Jesus seemed to understand this "intelligence of the victim" from the beginning of his ministry. Here two will suffice. The Beatitudes list all the ways that the downtrodden and disadvantaged are "blessed," culminating in the last one: "Blessed are you when people revile you and persecute you and utter all kinds of evil against you falsely on my account. Rejoice and be glad ... for in the same way they persecuted the prophets who were before you" (Matt 5:11–12). And in the parable of the sheep and goats, Jesus makes clear that in the end we will be judged on one thing only: our attitude toward victims (Matt 25:31–46). Alison comments, "Human society is a violent place, which makes victims, and *the revelation of God is to be found in the midst of that violence, on the side of the victims.*"[29]

Alison emphasizes that he is not celebrating victimhood, not claiming that "to be a victim is in itself a good thing."[30] This intelligence of

---

25. Alison, *Knowing Jesus*, 16. Emphasis added.
26. Alison, *Knowing Jesus*, 34.
27. Alison, *Knowing Jesus*, 36–37.
28. Alison, *Knowing Jesus*, 39.
29. Alison, *Knowing Jesus*, 43. Emphasis added.
30. Alison, *Knowing Jesus*, 46.

the victim is "a consequence of something that precedes it": the freedom that comes from an identity that is dependent not on comparison and rivalry with the *social* other, but is freely given by God, the *Other* other.[31] Human societies normally work "by basing their social order on victims," on building our identities on "a series of exclusions."[32] Jesus modeled a different way: a society built not on rivalry, but on self-giving, in response to the freely given gifts from God. "The intelligence of the victim comes from the freedom in giving oneself to others, in not being moved by the violence of others, even when it perceives that this free self-giving is going to be lynched as a result."[33]

> It was not . . . having been killed that made Jesus special, or even having been killed and raised again. It was what, for want of a better term, I call the self-giving of Jesus, which led to his being crucified.

> In the intelligence of the victim, the self-giving is prior, anterior to the sacrifice, and the sacrifice is incidental, accidental, to the self-giving. So, Jesus did not give himself [in order] to be a victim; he gave himself, in the full awareness that he was to be a victim, but did not want this at all. There was no death-wish in Jesus.[34]

In words that could well describe early Friends willingness to suffer (think, for example, of Mary Dyer returning to Boston), Alison says, "The free self-giving is not a seeking to be lynched, but is completely open-eyed about the probability of just that happening. . . . This sort of open-eyed freedom-towards-being-lynched . . . [starts by] siding with the victims and those who can easily be victimized, even though, as an inevitable consequence of this breaking out of the violent determinism of the world, they would be liable to become victims themselves."[35]

Alison goes on to make a somewhat startling claim. From the perspective of the disciples, having now witnessed the Risen Christ:

> The resurrection of the crucified and risen one had given the complete background to the self-giving victim, showing everything as depending on the self-giving and revealing of God. *It is this movement, and this alone, that made possible the emergence*

31. Alison, *Knowing Jesus*, 48.
32. Alison, *Knowing Jesus*, 47, 45.
33. Alison, *Knowing Jesus*, 45.
34. Alison, *Knowing Jesus*, 48, 49.
35. Alison, *Knowing Jesus*, 45.

> *of the discovery that God is Love.* It was this which made it possible that Jesus' self-giving as victim came to be understood to be part of the self-giving of God, which hugely anteceded it. . . . It is the revolution wrought by the intelligence of the victim that was made available to the disciples after the resurrection of the crucified and risen Lord that made it possible for the discovery to be made that God is love. That phrase, "God is love," is only possible within the intelligence of the victim.[36]

Is it possible that early Friends, through their encounter with the Inward Light of Christ (an *apocalypse* or revelation, parallel to the disciples' original encounter with the Risen Christ), were given some sense of this intelligence of the victim that Alison describes? Of course, they did not use Alison's language, but if we can say that through their suffering they gained some inkling of this intelligence of the victim, it might help explain their attraction to the language of the cross, as well as their remarkable willingness to endure suffering and persecution. If suffering was seen as redemptive, as a participation in the work of Christ, then they could say with Paul that by "sharing abundantly in Christ's sufferings" (2 Cor 1:5 RSV) they could "complete what is lacking in Christ's afflictions" (Col 1:24 RSV).[37]

We saw with our discussion of Penn's *No Cross, No Crown* that there might be potential pitfalls to considering the inward cross as involving only self-denial and sacrifice, pitfalls that cause contemporary Friends to shy away from the language of the cross. Likewise, there are perils to this outward sense of the cross, if we see it as an unambiguous endorsement of suffering and persecution. There is an important difference between choosing to lay down one's life for one's friends as opposed to having one's life involuntary taken away, between choosing the cross and having it imposed.

An additional danger for those suffering persecution and oppression is the temptation to divide the world neatly into two: victims and victimizers, persecuted and persecutors, oppressed and oppressors. Early Friends were not immune to this temptation—and our modern world seems especially prone to it.

We will defer a fuller discussion of these issues to chapter 26, where we will revisit sacrifice, victims, and scapegoats from a contemporary perspective. But first, we turn to a final image early Friends employed for "the conversion of the heart": the Lamb's war.

---

36. Alison, *Knowing Jesus*, 50. Emphasis added.
37. See Fodor, "Christian Discipleship," 255, for this insight.

25

The Lamb's War

> And now his appearance in the Lamb... is to make war with the god of this world, and to plead with his subjects concerning their revolt from their creator... [who have] also become open enemies to every check and reproof of that Spirit which should lead them to God, and does testify against their evil deeds.... Now against this evil seed, and its whole work brought forth in that nature, does the Lamb make war.
>
> —James Nayler[1]

The Lamb's war seems to have been a common way for early Friends to describe what they were about. The term comes from James Nayler's 1658 pamphlet *The Lamb's War Against the Man of Sin*; ultimately it refers back to the book of Revelation, where the "Lamb slain from the foundation of the world" (Rev 13:8 KJV) figures prominently in that book's symbolism. Although Fox himself seems not to have used that exact phrase, Lewis Benson counts at least fifteen times in Fox's writings when he says that "the Lamb and the saints shall have the victory."[2] In one of his doctrinal works, Fox gives a chapter-by-chapter commentary on the book of

---

1. Nayler, *Lamb's War*, 105.
2. Benson, *Catholic Quakerism*, 55.

Revelation—according to Douglas Gwyn, "the only book in the Bible to receive an extended, point-by-point interpretation in [Fox's] writings."[3]

Interestingly, Braithwaite's *The Beginnings of Quakerism* (1912) does not list "the Lamb's war" in its index; neither does Brinton in *Friends for 300 Years* (1952). The renewed prominence given to the Lamb's war seems to have started with Hugh Barbour's *The Quakers in Puritan England* (1962), where he titles his chapter 2 "The Lamb's War: The Quaker Awakening." Subsequently, Barbour and Roberts reprinted Nayler's original pamphlet in their *Early Quaker Writings* (1973). Most recent Quaker historians have given prominence to "the Lamb's war" in their account of early Friends.[4]

The term "the Lamb's war" is used in a variety of ways. Nayler's original tract, while alluding to the book of Revelation, mostly emphasizes the inward and spiritual struggle, closely akin to the enmity between the two seeds (see ch. 23). For Nayler, "the true warfare" is fought with spiritual weapons, to "cast down the strong holds of the man of sin in you." The preferred weapons are "much long suffering . . . the Lamb has prevailed unto suffering with much weakness and patience."[5] Recall that a chastened Nayler wrote this tract during his long imprisonment, a few months after suffering near-fatal punishment, subsequent to his conviction by Parliament for blasphemy.

For many Friends, the Lamb's war began as an inward struggle but then grew to have wider social implications. Brian Drayton and Bill Taber summarize this progression:

> Although at first [the Lamb's war] may be experienced as a process of personal purification, the inward struggle against "the Man of Sin" sooner or later leads us to engage outwardly with the powers of culture, custom, and the over-reliance on human reason and competence. The Lamb that suffers conquers not only the inward kingdom, but moves ultimately to transform the society that is the fruit of the human heart.[6]

---

3. Gwyn, *Apocalypse of the Word*, 186. Fox's treatment of Revelation is in G. Fox, *Works*, 5:127–41.

4. See esp. Gwyn, *Apocalypse of the Word*, 179–207 ("The Lamb's War and the Consummation of History"); Barbour and Roberts, *Early Quaker Writings*, 25–38 ("The Lamb's War and the Wakening of the North of England"); Guiton, *Early Quakers* (forty-two references to "Lamb's War" in the index).

5. Nayler, *Lamb's War*, 113, 106, 110.

6. Drayton and Taber, *Language of Inward Landscape*, 139.

The Lamb's war can also serve as a convenient shorthand designation for the turbulent first decade of the Quaker movement, marked by explosive growth and frequent confrontation with the persecuting powers of church and state. All observers agree that this early phase of marked growth ended after a few short years, when, in the face of withering persecution, attention turned from converting the world to the more modest goal of survival.[7]

All of these various connotations are surely interconnected, but what concerns us here is the Lamb's war as an image for "the conversion of the heart," that lifelong process that follows convincement and holds the promise of "perfection." Any strict separation between inward and outward is artificial, but by all indications early Friends saw the process as beginning with an inward struggle against "the man of sin" or "the seed of the serpent."

This struggle inevitably had outward implications for Friends conduct in the world—and the persecution they in turn suffered was then reflected back to become part of their ongoing inward struggle. In other words, even though the Lamb's war began with the inward struggle of individual Friends, it nevertheless had major social and cultural implications. Quaker historian Douglas Gwyn describes it as a "covenantal conflict" and "a cultural revolution." The Lamb's war went far beyond the preceding Puritan Revolution, which was largely a political conflict among elites:

> Many common people were not affected by the advanced political ideas of the Levellers and other radical Puritans. But nearly everyone was affected and moved (either toward convincement or reaction against) by the Lamb's War. There was probably no parish in England left untouched by the mercurial Quaker preachers and agitators of the 1650s. . . . While the Lamb's War was consistently nonviolent on the part of Friends, it was often decidedly violent on the part of those they confronted. The church and state reacted with alarm and vengeance upon the Quakers' interruptions of parish services, street preaching for social justice and reform, and their scathing diatribes against the government. Clergy, magistrates, gentry, and Parliament took a variety of legal and illegal measures to fine, imprison, and silence Friends. . . . Sometimes

---

7. As an example of "the Lamb's war" as shorthand for the first period, see Buckley, *Quaker Testimony*. Buckley breaks down the evolution of Quaker testimony into three stages: the Lamb's war (roughly the first decade); living under persecution (1660s to 1680s); and being in the world but not of it (following toleration in 1689).

the most dangerous violence came from the common people, through spontaneous mob actions against Quaker preachers or entire gathered meetings of Friends.[8]

The very language of "the Lamb's war" may strike Friends today as overly martial, too similar to "spiritual warfare" language common among some segments of the contemporary evangelical church. It can seem to reflect a dualistic "us-against-them" mentality. Two things should be noted in defense of the language of the Lamb's war. First, for Friends it always started with that inward struggle, where individuals were moved to first confront their own complicity in systems of violence and oppression. The inward struggle was always near at hand, which helped to make the Lamb's war "us against evil" rather than "us against them." Second, with its symbolic roots in the book of Revelation, one could argue that Friends nonviolent interpretation of that most violent of biblical books is actually closer to the original spirit of Revelation, as amply confirmed by contemporary scholarship. Let us now examine some of that scholarship and how it bolsters early Friends interpretation of Revelation.

Over the last 150 years or so, the book of Revelation in popular imagination has come to be seen as a "code book" that foretells the future end of the world in great detail—even though such interpretations have proved notoriously inaccurate, going back at least as far as "the Great Disappointment" of 1844, when William Miller's proclamation of the imminent second coming proved to be premature.[9] More recently epitomized by Hal Lindsey's *Late Great Planet Earth* (1970) and the wildly popular *Left Behind* series, these interpretations often highlight "antichrist" and "the rapture" (even though neither term actually appears in the text of Revelation) and invariably come with lots of violence.[10]

Contemporary Evangelical Brian Zahnd claims that "the book of Revelation is easily the most misunderstood book in the Bible . . . regularly shanghaied as a polemic against enemies and as a warrant for violence." Instead, Revelation is "perhaps the most important text for the American church right now . . . written specifically for Christians living as citizens in a superpower."[11] It is, he argues, a book written for Christians resist-

---

8. Gwyn, *Covenant Crucified*, 106–7.

9. Wikipedia,"Great Disappointment." Some of Miller's disappointed followers went on to form the Seventh-day Adventist Church, now with twenty-two million adherents worldwide.

10. Lindsey with Carlson, *Late Great Planet Earth*; LaHaye and Jenkins, *Left Behind*.

11. Zahnd, *Sinners in the Hands*, 149–50.

ing persecution and assimilation into empire. Biblical scholar Michael Gorman says, "Nearly all interpreters of Revelation recognize that the entire book is a critique and parody of the Roman Empire and the cult of the emperor . . . [even though] the word 'Rome' does not appear in the document."[12] The "crisis" depicted in the book is complacency about Rome—the crisis of "ordinary empire."[13]

One of the popular misconceptions about Revelation is that it describes a violent and inevitable "apocalypse" at the end of the world, foretelling a time when God finally gives up on Jesus's message of peace, "the ultimate endorsement of an angry, violent, retributive God."[14] But "Revelation isn't about the violent end of the world; it's about the end of the evil of violence."[15] The sometimes wild symbolism acts always to undermine the ideology of empire. Although Fox's seventeenth-century reading of Revelation is somewhat idiosyncratic, with the various beasts and dragons representing the persecuting church-state alliance of his time, we can say that at least he got the part about nonviolence right.

A full interpretation of Revelation is beyond the scope of my purpose here, but highlighting some of John's creative symbolism is perhaps in order.[16] The first thing that should be said is that virtually everything in Revelation is communicated by symbols, but in our completely different cultural context, the symbolism may be lost on us. Both Zahnd and Gorman compare the images in Revelation to political cartoons, full of "symbolism, exaggeration, and fantasy." If we see a cartoon with a donkey and elephant facing off with boxing gloves, we know immediately that the subject is partisan political conflict. But two thousand years from now, future readers are very likely to miss that symbolism.[17]

The crux of the book is chapter 5. John has been transported into the heavenly realm where he is granted a vision of "the one seated on a throne." A scroll, evidently depicting God's plan for salvation, is sealed, and there is no one who can break the seven seals to open it. "Who is

12. Gorman, *Reading Revelation Responsibly*, 62.
13. Gorman, *Reading Revelation Responsibly*, 54.
14. Zahnd, *Sinners in the Hands*, 178.
15. Zahnd, *Sinners in the Hands*, 154.
16. A partial list of contemporary interpretations of Revelation: Gorman, *Reading Revelation Responsibly* (2011); Schüssler Fiorenza, *Revelation: Vision of a Just World* (1991); Peterson, *Reversed Thunder: The Revelation of John & the Praying Imagination* (1991); Howard-Brook and Gwyther, *Unveiling Empire: Reading Revelation Then and Now* (2010); (from a Quaker) Daniels, *Resisting Empire: The Book of Revelation* (2019).
17. Gorman, *Reading Revelation Responsibly*, 36; Zahnd, *Sinners in the Hands*, 153.

worthy to open the scroll and break its seals?" (v. 2). John weeps, because there is no one on heaven or earth worthy to open the scroll, but an elder tells him: "Do not weep. See, the Lion of the tribe of Judah, the Root of David, has conquered, so that he can open the scroll and its seven seals" (v. 5). "When John looks, expecting to see a fearsome lion, he doesn't see a lion but a lamb—a little slaughtered lamb."[18] The Lamb proceeds to break the seals and open the scroll, and the multitude breaks into worship of the Lamb. Here recall the etymological connection between *worthy* and *worship*: "Myriads of myriads and thousands of thousands proceed to sing with a full voice: *Worthy* is the Lamb that was slaughtered" (vv. 11–12).

The elder tells John to look for a lion, a symbol of the military and political messiah that so many longed for and expected. But a lion never appears and is never mentioned again, while the Lamb appears twenty-eight more times. Symbolically, John is saying that Rome will be conquered not by another superpower beast but by a little Lamb, the Lamb "slain from the foundation of the world" (Rev 13:8 KJV). "Jesus advances his empire by being the slaughtered Lamb.... The kingdom of God does not conquer the world by the violent means of the beast but by the self-sacrificing way of the Lamb."[19] The image of the Lamb is the controlling metaphor of the book of Revelation, and it is simply impossible to make a lamb (especially a slaughtered lamb) into a symbol of violence and retribution.

In the popular misinterpretation of Revelation, much emphasis is given to the alleged "final battle" of Armageddon. Gorman says that "despite the vast amount of speculation regarding the time and location of this battle, Revelation mentions it only [once] in passing" (Rev 16:16).[20] Armageddon literally means "the mountain of Megiddo," an actual place in central Palestine and now a World Heritage archaeological site. The city is in a broad and fertile valley that for centuries functioned as a superhighway for invading armies. The "mountain" is an artificial mound two hundred feet high; archaeological excavations have shown that the city was destroyed and rebuilt twenty-six times over the centuries. John's first readers would have recognized the place as "an apt symbol for endless war ... an icon of war."[21] Too often, Armageddon has been portrayed as the necessary "final battle" prior to Christ's return, a requisite stop on

---

18. Zahnd, *Sinners in the Hands*, 159.
19. Zahnd, *Sinners in the Hands*, 161. See 159–62 for fuller discussion.
20. Gorman, *Reading Revelation Responsibly*, 189.
21. Zahnd, *Sinners in the Hands*, 168.

the way to the new Jerusalem of chapters 21 and 22. But a more nuanced reading suggests that Armageddon represents a choice:

> John's apocalyptic vision doesn't predict an inevitable war where two hundred million people [see Rev 9:16] will be killed in the Middle East; rather, John presents us with our choices. Either we follow the Lamb into the Shalom of New Jerusalem, or we follow the Beast into the horrors of Armageddon. . . . If we reject the way of the Lamb, we get Armageddon. This is the "wrath of God," wrath as a consequence [of our own choices], not retribution.[22]

One final example will suffice. One of the best-known scenes from Revelation is from chapter 19:

> Then I saw heaven opened, and there was a white horse! Its rider is called Faithful and True, and in righteousness he judges and makes war. . . . He is clothed in a robe dipped in blood, and his name is called the Word of God. . . . From his mouth comes a sharp sword with which to strike down the nations. (Rev 19:11, 13, 15)

There follows a description of the "armies of heaven" and "the kings of the earth and their armies" amassing for battle—but no actual fighting occurs, only that the beast and the false prophet are thrown into the symbolic lake of fire. *There is no actual final battle in Revelation.* "The images of battle are supposed to suggest the *promise* and *reality* of God's defeat of evil, but they are not the *means* of that defeat."[23]

The rider on the white horse is "clothed in a robe dipped in blood," but this is *before* any battle begins. "Jesus's robe is soaked in *his own* blood. [He] doesn't shed the blood of enemies; Jesus sheds his own blood."[24] The sword coming from his mouth is obviously not a literal sword: the Lamb triumphs not by the sword of Caesar but by his word and his own suffering. Zahnd adds a telling detail: the rider "is called Faithful and True" (19:11). The motto of Sixth Roman Legion, stationed at Megiddo after the Jewish revolt against Rome in 66 CE, was *Fidelis et Constans*: faithful and true. John's original readers would have immediately seen the intended parody of Rome's military power.[25]

---

22. Zahnd, *Sinners in the Hands*, 169–70.

23. Gorman, *Reading Revelation Responsibly*, 203. Emphasis in original.

24. Zahnd, *Sinners in the Hands*, 175. Emphasis added. See also Gorman, *Reading Revelation Responsibly*, 203.

25. Zahnd, *Sinners in the Hands*, 178.

Revelation closes with a vision of the new Jerusalem; the faithful are not transported to a distant paradise, but heaven comes down to earth (21:10). "See, the tabernacle of God is among mortals. He will dwell with them as their God; they will be his peoples, and God himself will be with them" (21:3). The dimensions of new Jerusalem are given as fifteen hundred miles in both length and width—the approximate dimensions of the Roman Empire (21:16).[26] "The Roman Empire is to be replaced by the Empire of the Lamb."[27] There is no temple in the new Jerusalem, "for its temple is the Lord God Almighty and the Lamb" (21:22). Neither is there sun or moon, "for the glory of God is its light, and its lamp is the Lamb" (21:23). The river of the water of life flows from the throne of God and the Lamb, and on either side is the tree of life (22:1–2), which had been kept from Adam and Eve when they were banished from the garden (Gen 3:22) but is now finally given "for the healing of the nations."

George Fox offered an interpretation of the book of Revelation for his time; we can do the same, but we must start with the fact that *Revelation was not written for us*. It was written for first-century Christian communities facing persecution and the threat of assimilation into empire, and any coherent interpretation must be rooted in their historical situation. Gorman says that "the purpose of the book of Revelation is to persuade its hearers and readers, both ancient and contemporary, to remain faithful to God in spite of past, present, or possible future suffering."

If that is true, then we can readily understand why early Friends would be attracted to its language and symbolism. Quaker Wess Daniels adds that Revelation is "meant to spark the imagination of nonviolent resistance. . . . The central image is the lamb that was slain, the lamb that did not fight back, who was crucified, and who God honored as the innocent victim." In keeping with the theme of this book, "this is a total reversal from humanity's constant effort to project blame on to the scapegoat."[28]

Today, as in the seventeenth century, the book of Revelation is too often read as a prediction and warrant for religious violence as the necessary means to usher in God's kingdom, "foretelling a time when God

---

26. In his commentary on Revelation, George Fox discusses these dimensions and quotes the Greek from "Arias Montanus' interlineary Translation" (*Works*, 5:139). I know of no other place where Fox delves into New Testament Greek; presumably he had some scholarly help.

27. Zahnd, *Sinners in the Hands*, 188.

28. Daniels, *Resisting Empire*, 57. See also 24–26, where Daniels argues that "enemies and the scapegoat mechanism" is one of four explanatory themes that are key to our interpretation of Revelation.

finally gives up on Jesus's message of peace." Early Friends, by attending to the central image of "the lamb slain from the foundation of the world," saw instead a manifesto of nonviolent resistance to "the god of this world."

Let us close with James Nayler's "last words," written in 1660, after he was released from prison, only later to suffer fatal injuries at the hands of unknown assailants. See if you can detect in his words what James Alison calls "the intelligence of the victim":

> There is a spirit which I feel that delights to do no evil, nor to revenge any wrong, but delights to endure all things, in hope to enjoy its own in the end. Its hope is to outlive all wrath and contention, and to weary out all exaltation and cruelty.... As it bears no evil in itself, so it conceives none in thoughts to any other.... Its crown is meekness, its life is everlasting love unfeigned; it takes its kingdom with entreaty and not with contention, and keeps it by lowliness of mind.... It's conceived in sorrow, and brought forth without any to pity it, nor doth it murmur at grief or oppression. It never rejoiceth but through sufferings; for with the world's joy it is murdered.[29]

---

29. James Nayler, *A Collection of Sundry Books, Epistles and Papers*, quoted in Britain Yearly Meeting, *Quaker Faith and Practice* 19.12.

26

Truth in the Heart

> They must come to the spirit in themselves, and the truth in the inward parts.... If they be worshippers of God in the truth and in the spirit ... they must come to the truth in the heart.
>
> —GEORGE FOX[1]

WE HAVE PREVIOUSLY SEEN that early Friends often claimed a unique relation to "truth"—which can be unsettling to our postmodern ears. Those convinced were often said to have been convinced of the truth, or convinced and received truth, or received truth in the love of it. The first to bring the Quaker message, the first publishers of truth, were described as having published or declared truth, or bore a testimony to truth. Indeed, early Friends sometimes referred to themselves as Friends of Truth.[2]

Contemporary British Friend and theologian Rex Ambler has offered a compelling reading of early Friends, focusing on the relationship of their experience of the Inward Light to truth and culminating in his

---

1. "Epistle 222" (1662), in G. Fox, *Truth in the Heart*, 62. The title of the present chapter is the same as Ambler's excellent anthology of Fox's writings.

2. Griswold, "Friends of Truth." "Publishers of Truth" would appear to be much more common than "Friends of Truth," as a way that early Quakers referred to themselves.

"experiment with Light."[3] For Ambler, the most important feature of early Friends understanding of truth was that it was not about propositional or doctrinal truth, as in the creeds of the churches; nor was it about the objective truth of science, dealing with facts in the external world. Rather, truth for early Quakers meant "personal truth": "*Truth* as the Quakers understood it and pursue it is *the reality of our own life.*"[4] In Fox's words, everyone must come to "truth in their own particulars . . . the truth in their own hearts,"[5] or, in the words of the psalmist, "truth in the inward parts" (51:6 KJV).

This sense of inward or personal truth is perhaps best understood by considering its opposite: deceit, and especially self-deceit.[6] For early Friends, the process of discovering or being convinced of truth was thus a process of *un-deceit*: confronting what "we are already in some sense aware of, but have denied and repelled from our consciousness."[7] Ambler describes this as a confrontation with "the pretenses of the ego," our "idea of ourselves" . . . which is "bent on bolstering our self-image," and replacing these instead with "reality itself."[8] "Truth was the reality of one's own life which is always there to be experienced if only one is open to it. The only trouble is that people won't or can't face the truth and so opt for a make-believe world instead, which they then become so attached to that they are no longer aware of the reality they are denying."[9]

In this process of coming to the truth of their lives, the light functions as "the God-given capacity to see things as they are, without the distortions of the self."[10] The light is not something we see but the *means* by which we see. In Fox's words, "The light is that by which ye come to see. . . . For with this light man *sees himself.*"[11] This "inward light" (as op-

3. See esp. Ambler, *Light to Live By*, as well as numerous other publications, cited below. See also https://experiment-with-light.org.uk/.

4. Ambler, *Quaker Way*, 13, 26. Emphasis added. See also Ambler, "Darkness and Light," 200.

5. G. Fox, *Truth of the Heart*, 16.

6. G. Fox, *Truth of the Heart*, 179; Ambler, *Light Within*, 11; Ambler, "Talks on the Experiment," 10.

7. Ambler, *Quaker Way*, 26.

8. Ambler, *Light Within*, 15–16, 12.

9. Rex Ambler, in G. Fox, *Truth of the Heart*, 182–83. Ambler notes that "the word 'reality' hardly existed in the seventeenth century. . . . What we understand by the word was covered then by the word 'truth.'"

10. Rex Ambler, in G. Fox, *Truth of the Heart*, 188.

11. G. Fox, *Truth of the Heart*, 28, 32. Emphasis added. See Ambler, *Light Within*, 5–6.

posed to the outward lights of the sun and moon) was *not* identified with reason or even conscience (though it was experienced *in* the conscience), which were too tied up with the concerns of protecting one's ego or self-image. The light was "an awareness [that] arose within them [but] which seemed to come from outside them."[12] For early Friends:

> "The true light within" was a capacity to see things as they are, to see reality, that was beyond their normal capacity to think or discern. Human reason was too biased in favor of the self for authentic discernment. They needed a source outside their normal self . . . that challenged the normal self and enabled them to get beyond it. *It had to be a light from God.* . . . It required them to give up their familiar sense of self and trust a source within them that was apparently beyond their control.[13]

But what was this "reality of their lives" that the light revealed? The light, in its initial appearance, showed *darkness*. Fox says, "As the light appeared, all appeared that was out of the light; darkness, death, temptations . . . all was manifest and seen in the light."[14] We should understand darkness not as some metaphysical reality, but as "the condition of not being aware of the truth. . . . Just as 'the light' made people aware of reality, 'darkness' was the state of *not* being aware of it, of not being able to recognize the truth or live one's life in accordance with truth."[15]

This capacity to see their inward reality clearly and without illusion gave them a new perspective on evil. Ambler quotes a "remarkable passage" from Fox's *Journal*, which he says "must be the first time, historically, that this insight was given expression":

> I saw the state of those, both priests and people, who, in reading the scriptures, cry out much against Cain, Esau, Judas and other

---

12. Ambler, *Quaker Way*, 27.
13. Ambler, *Light Within*, 23. Emphasis added.
14. G. Fox, *Journal*, 14.
15. Ambler, "Darkness and Light," 201. I am aware that some Friends, including some Friends of Color, advocate avoiding all references to light and darkness because of perceived racial connotations. However, the language of early Friends is so saturated with light and darkness, clearly referring not to race but to moral categories like "truth" and "ignorance," that I think it would be more misleading to eliminate such language from our contemporary discourse. Ultimately, this language goes back to the Bible, esp. to John's Gospel, so one could argue that it is wrong to superimpose our current debates about race onto ancient texts. However, it is incumbent on all of us to use such language with great care and to make it clear that we are not using light and darkness as a proxy for racial distinctions—which I agree can be hurtful.

wicked men of former times mentioned in the holy scriptures, but do not see the nature of Cain, of Esau, of Judas and those others, in themselves. These said it was they, they, they that were the bad people, putting it off from themselves, but when some of these [later] came, with the light and spirit of truth, to see into themselves, then they came to say, I, I, I, it is I myself that have been the Ishmael, the Esau, etc. . . . When these, who were so much taken up with finding fault with others and thought themselves clear from these things, came to look into themselves with the light of Christ thoroughly to search themselves, they might see enough of this in themselves; then the cry could not be that it is he or they, but I and we are found in these conditions.[16]

As Fox says elsewhere, "The nature of these I saw within, though people had been looking without."[17] He is giving a surprisingly precise description of the psychological phenomenon of *projection*, our very human tendency to project negative aspects of ourselves on to others as a way of preserving our own positive self-image.

But beyond a description of projection, Fox is describing a very definite view of evil. Evil is not illusion, as some Eastern religions would have it; nor is evil a "substance," originating in some supernatural being like Satan and conveniently found only in "those other people." Instead, evil can be found within every individual, including ourselves, in the refusal to face up to our own reality. Human evil comes from the absence of light ("darkness")—it is very real but can be overcome by our openness and response to the light.[18] Fox's insight is that the line separating good and evil is not *between* people, tribes, or nations, but *within* every human heart. We must first acknowledge and confront our own darkness before we can address evil in the world.

The sense we get from Ambler is that in response to the inevitable anxiety and insecurity of human life, we set about constructing a "false self," a self-image that we can present to ourselves and others. This false self is based in a lie, but can we now be more specific about the *nature* of this lie? And, in light of the general theme of this book, can we connect this with Girard's mimetic theory? I think we can, and the clue for this is that both Ambler and Girard quote the same passage from John's Gospel:

16. G. Fox, *Works*, 1:87; also in *Journal*, 30–31. Quoted in Ambler, "Darkness and Light," 196.

17. G. Fox, *Journal*, 19.

18. This is the "evil as privation" view, with a long history in Christian spirituality. For a thorough discussion from a Quaker point of view, see Beals, "Evil."

> You are from your father the devil, and you choose to do your father's desires. He was a murderer from the beginning and does not stand in the truth, because there is no truth in him. When he lies he speaks according to his nature, for he is a liar and the father of lies. (John 8:44)[19]

By way of explanation, Ambler then states, "*The primal fault*, the origin of all the suffering that we cause one another, is a refusal to accept the reality of life as it presents itself to us. . . . Both Fox and Jesus [are referencing] our primal history, when humans first developed *the capacity to lie and live their lives on the basis of a lie*."[20] In words written by Girard but echoing Ambler, "Everybody is lying but no one is aware of it."[21]

What if this lie is not just our general response to human anxiety but a more specific lie, the lie that denies the mimetic nature of our desires, what Girard calls "the romantic lie"? Recall from chapter 1 that for Girard the romantic lie is our insistence that our desires emerge from an autonomous and independent self, whereas in fact we desire what others desire, simply because they desire it.[22] In mimetic theory, the self is not *independent* but *interdependent*, inextricably linked with others—a fact we constantly seek to deny. For Girard, this is the underlying deceit of our human condition, which in turn leads to all manner of mimetic rivalries and violence. Ambler gives similar (though less specific) recognition to our *interdependence*: "We claim to be independent, but in fact depend a great deal on others."[23]

In an unpublished manuscript, Ambler seems to come close to a mimetic understanding of our underlying condition. He speaks in several places of "the bad feeling" early Friends expressed about their pre-convincement lives, the inner despair and anxiety that provides a near-constant undercurrent to our lives. He elaborates: "Often feeling bad about themselves, though they don't know why, *they look to other people and things out there to make them feel good*. They may buy goods, so-called, associate with outwardly impressive people, or . . . look to

---

19. Quoted in Ambler, "Darkness and Light," 200; and Girard: *Things Hidden*, 161; *Scapegoat*, 196; *One by Whom Scandal Comes*, 40.

20. Ambler, "Darkness and Light," 200. Emphasis added.

21. Girard, *Evolution and Conversion*, 131.

22. Reeve, "Mechanisms of Internal Cohesion," 163. On the romantic lie or myth, see Girard, *One by Whom Scandal Comes*, 7; *Evolution and Conversion*, 123; and Warren, *Compassion or Apocalypse*, 22–25.

23. Ambler, *Light Within*, 23.

religious objects and religious people."[24] This is a description of mimetic rivalry, sublimated as it so often is today by our consumer mentality. I am proposing that one aspect of "the reality of our lives" that Ambler speaks of is the mimetic nature of our desires, which so often puts us in a position of competition, envy, and rivalry with our fellows, leading to this "bad feeling about our lives."[25]

All of this can sound quite gloomy, not much of an improvement on the "utter depravity" of the Puritans. Recognizing this, Ambler asks, "How can a revelation of our darkness lead to such a positive outcome?" His answer is that by simply recognizing and accepting the reality of our lives, we experience a kind of acceptance and empowerment that can lead to real change. "With the help of this light that they have discovered in themselves, they can now see through the deceit and recognize the truth . . . with the surprising sense that in this moment of acceptance, *they find themselves accepted.*"[26]

Ambler often describes the positive outcome of this process as *peace*. "You start with an experience of ill-ease and inner conflict, and you end with an experience of peace."[27] He quotes George Fox: "Through the light that enlighteneth them they have life . . . they have salvation, they have truth, they have peace with God."[28] In perhaps his most extended description of this positive outcome, he emphasizes the gradual nature of this change—what we could reasonably identify as *the conversion of the heart*:

> Instead of being fundamentally anxious about life, they can relax and trust. They also sense a kinship with other people. Having dropped the mask, and all defenses with it, they can see others more clearly and recognize themselves in others, and others in themselves. An habitual attitude of self-concern gives way, slowly perhaps, to a desire to help others. This is not a desire to prove themselves good, or to make up for their half-acknowledged selfishness or to win others' approval, all of which will be recognized as subtle forms of selfishness. Feelings and desires that are freed from self-anxiety will now be spontaneous and natural, generous and unmeasured. Goodness will be found to be the core of their nature, obscured and restricted only by the false

24. Ambler, "Talks on the Experiment," 8. Emphasis added.
25. Ambler, "Talks on the Experiment," 10.
26. Ambler, "Darkness and Light," 203. Emphasis added. Ambler attributes this insight about acceptance to a sermon by Paul Tillich, "You Are Accepted" (203n13).
27. Ambler, "Talks on the Experiment," 12.
28. G. Fox, *Works*, 4:219; quoted in Ambler, *Light Within*, 20.

image of themselves that arose from their fear. It is the natural response of their hearts to a world they feel they belong to.[29]

Rex Ambler's "experiment with Light" and René Girard's mimetic theory have obvious differences, but there are some notable similarities. As above, both begin their analysis with "the lie" that underlies our human condition—even if their understanding of that lie is somewhat different. For both Ambler and Girard, the convincement process starts with a searching introspection into our own individual complicity with evil. We have seen how Fox discovers "the nature of Cain, Ishmael, and Esau" in himself and directs others to the light by which they might make this same discovery. Ambler says that the initial experience of the light "is an experience of evil as well as good, and indeed the experience of evil is in some sense prior to the experience of good."[30]

Girard in turn writes that our "understanding of mimetic theory presupposes that we acknowledge our own mimeticism."[31] Even beyond that, he maintains that "conversion means to become aware that we are persecutors. . . . Conversion is the discovery that we have always, without being aware of it, been imitating the wrong kind of models who lead us into the vicious circle of scandals and perpetual frustration."[32] In Fox's language, the nature of Cain, Ishmael, and Judas is within all of us.

Girard maintains that all humans (and all human cultures) are so entangled in the victimary mechanism that it is only a revelation from God that is able to extricate us. "The scapegoat mechanism literally cannot be revealed without Christ. . . . For anthropological truth to be unveiled, the Cross was necessary. It was the gift of the Spirit: only the Cross could make the victim's innocence visible."[33]

Ambler seems to have a more optimistic view of human capabilities, holding that humans have the capacity to penetrate "the lie" and come to the liberating truth, albeit after a prolonged and deep struggle. But here it is important to remember that for early Friends, the Inward Light is not a "natural" light but the Light of *Christ*. As above, Ambler says, "It had to be a light *from God*."

---

29. Ambler, "Darkness and Light," 204.
30. Ambler, "Darkness and Light," 195.
31. Girard, *Evolution and Conversion*, 122.
32. Girard, *Evolution and Conversion*, 160.
33. Girard, *One by Whom Scandal Comes*, 60.

Compared to Girard, the first Quakers to varying degrees de-emphasized the historical Christ event, speaking instead of an "inward atonement" (see excursus 2). But here again, recall the words of James Nayler at Appleby: "If I cannot witness Christ nearer than Jerusalem, I shall have no benefit from him: but I own no other Christ but that witnessed a good confession before Pontius Pilate, *which Christ I witness in me now.*"[34] For early Friends, their experience of the Inward Light of Christ was the functional equivalent of the resurrection appearances to the apostles. The experience of early Friends can extend Girard's insights by affirming that the liberating truth that reveals "the lie" can be inward as well as outward. The cross is inward as well as outward; both can lead to Alison's "intelligence of the victim."

Ambler suggests that by simply recognizing and accepting the reality of our lives, that reality can and does change. The truth has a kind of inexorable power: "Truth itself will change things."[35] Girard seems to hold a similar belief but emphasizes the sociological dimension more than the individual: the passion and crucifixion unveil or unmask the truth of the scapegoat mechanism, with irreversible consequences. "When the single victim mechanism is correctly nailed to the Cross . . . everything based on it gradually loses its prestige, grows more and more feeble, and ultimately disappears."[36]

The historical evidence in support of this is, of course, decidedly mixed. Perhaps Girard interpreter James Alison can again be helpful here. Even after the truth is revealed, we remain inescapably mimetic, still prone to mimetic rivalry. It is only by directing our mimetic desire away from the social other to the "*Other* other," to God in whom there is no rivalry, that our condition can change. "Jesus asks us to imitate him, rather than our neighbor, *in order to protect us from the mimetic rivalry.*"[37]

My aim in this preliminary dialogue between Rex Ambler's experiment with Light and Girard's mimetic theory has been to test whether they can mutually inform and enrich each other. They are not the same, but they are complementary and in dialogue can deepen and enrich our understanding. Girard's observations on the pervasive nature of mimetic rivalry can lend more specificity to Ambler's analysis of "the bad feeling" with which we all struggle. Ambler can help us put Girard's insights into

---

34. Nayler, in Fox and Nayler, "Saul's Errand to Damascus," 261. Emphasis added.
35. Ambler, "Talks on the Experiment," 34.
36. Girard, *I See Satan Fall*, 139.
37. Girard, *Evolution and Conversion*, 46. Emphasis added.

a specifically Quaker context. Most importantly, both see the critical role of *truth* in exposing *the lie*, in the ongoing process of the conversion of the heart.

27

Scapegoats, Sacrifice, and Victims

> God reuses the scapegoat mechanism, at his own expense, in order to subvert it.... It may be thought of as slow and terrible voyage from the first sort of sacrifice toward the second.
>
> —René Girard[1]

BEFORE WE TURN TO the forms that *conversion of the heart* might take in our own times, we need to revisit Girard's mimetic theory, specifically around the three related concepts of *scapegoat, sacrifice, and victim*. We have seen how mimetic theory can be a powerful interpretive lens through which to view the past: the primeval role of the scapegoat mechanism in limiting intragroup violence, the role of ritual sacrifice in creating group cohesion, the emergence of archaic forms of religion, the Hebrew people's gradual recognition of the innocence of the victim, all culminating in the gospel revelation. But how does mimetic theory contribute to our understanding of the contemporary world? And how might mimetic theory help us in the conversion of the heart for this new day?

---

1. Girard, *One by Whom Scandal Comes*, 43–44.

Girard and his interpreters contend that the passion and crucifixion definitively unveil the scapegoating mechanism. And yet, undeniably, scapegoating still occurs—and occurs within ostensibly Christian (and post-Christian) cultures. It is not necessary here to cite all the historical and contemporary evidence that confirms this. Suffice to say that the power of scapegoating, of using "good" violence to control "bad" violence, continually reasserts itself. Recognizing this, Girard says that the first Christians were naïve in thinking that the world, "the powers and principalities" that are sustained by violence, would suddenly change. "In fact, *not even two millennia* have been enough for the influence of the Passion to really seep in, to penetrate men's minds to the point that this mechanism is disabled once and for all; for the non-guilt of victims to be fully recognized."[2]

One factor contributing to this delay is that, according to Girard's original description, scapegoating in the ancient world was a totally unconscious process. "To scapegoat someone is to be unaware of what you are doing . . . unaware that you have a scapegoat, to think he is really guilty. . . . Scapegoating is effective only if it is nonconscious."[3] By contrast, the modern world at some level understands scapegoating—largely, Girard contends, under the influence of the gospel revelation. Today, when someone is referred to as "a scapegoat," we immediately understand that they are innocent but unjustly accused, an understanding that the ancients simply did not have. This is not to deny that we still have our blind spots: "We ferociously denounce the scapegoating of which our neighbors are guilty, but are unable to do without our own substitute victims."[4]

Girard observes that the *old* scapegoating mechanism is no longer very effective. The required unanimity is no longer possible; someone is sure to recognize that the accused is innocent and cry "scapegoat," thus exposing what needs to remain hidden. "The knowledge we have acquired about our violence, thanks to our religious tradition, does not put an end to scapegoating but weakens it enough to reduce its effectiveness more and more. . . . We haven't given up having scapegoats, but our belief

---

2. Girard, *One by Whom Scandal Comes*, 68. Emphasis added. A fuller version of this quote is in excursus 1.

3. Girard, *Evolution and Conversion*, 62; *Reading the Bible*, 48.

4. Girard, *I See Satan Fall*, 158.

in them is 90 percent spoiled."[5] As Mark Heim comments, in the modern world "it is increasingly difficult to be unconscious of scapegoats."[6]

This is why Girard says that the gospel revelation can be destabilizing. Heim observes that "the gospel of the cross is a disruptive element that makes it more difficult to assemble a unanimous mob on the old terms."[7] Girard emphasizes this with a particularly striking metaphor: "The Cross is the revelation of a destabilizing truth . . . the spiritual equivalent of nuclear power."[8] Girard contends that "the modern world [is] essentially deprived of sacrificial protection . . . [and thus] more and more exposed to violence."[9] With this loss of sacrificial protection, we now experience "mimetic rivalry on a planetary scale."[10] Social media in particular acts as an "algorithmic-mediated tribalism,"[11] precisely designed to magnify our inherent mimetic rivalry. *Going viral* is today's version of mimetic contagion.

The potential for mimetic rivalry and violence has to some degree been attenuated by our capitalist and consumer culture. "The modern Western economy is the first civilization that has learned to use mimetic rivalry positively," in the form of economic competition. But turning "mimetic desire and its possible crisis into a positive instrument of economic growth . . . has a side-effect: when more and more of the same objects are offered, they become less and less mimetically desired."[12] In other words, there are limits to the capacity of consumerism to provide an effective check on our mimetic rivalries.

One disconcerting aspect of Girard's insights is that, especially in his later works, he makes no effort to downplay the apocalyptic warnings in the Gospels (Matt 24:15–31; Mark 13:14–31). He views them not as predictions of God's wrath but as warnings about the possible destructive escalation of *human* violence that follows our loss of sacrificial protection. Girard's biographer observes that in the modern world, "scapegoating can no longer serve as a brake on violence, but escalates it instead. . . . The victim pool is enlarged with more and more accusations

---

5. Girard, *I See Satan Fall*, 184, 157.
6. Heim, *Saved from Sacrifice*, 210.
7. Heim, *Saved from Sacrifice*, 220.
8. Girard: *One by Whom Scandal Comes*, 63; *When These Things Begin*, 74.
9. Girard, *Evolution and Conversion*, 158.
10. Girard, *Evolution and Conversion*, 170.
11. Foster, *Theology of Consent*, 52.
12. Girard, *Evolution and Conversion*, 170, 173, 58.

and more scapegoats, in a process that becomes self-devouring."[13] Girard comments:

> One has to see this process from the mimetic perspective and in Christian apocalyptic terms, in the sense that the more there is an opening in a world where [sacrificial] ritual is dead, the more dangerous the world becomes. It has both positive effects, in the sense that there is less sacrifice, and negative effects, in that there is an unleashing of mimetic rivalry. . . . We live in a world where we take care of victims in a way no society or historical time ever did, but we are also in a world that kills more people than ever, so we have a feeling that both the "good" and the "bad" are increasing all the time.[14]

Girard's vision of the future comes across as quite pessimistic; a sympathetic interpreter says that "the trajectory of mimetic theory is, in a word, bleak."[15] Girard sees humankind now facing a stark choice, much like the choice we saw in the book of Revelation: we can follow the beast to Armageddon; or we can follow the Lamb to the new Jerusalem. The outcome is not predetermined; the choice is ours. Commenting on the question that is put to Saul on the road to Damascus ("Saul, Saul, why do you persecute me?"), Girard writes:

> This is the fundamental question. Christian conversion is our discovery that we are persecutors without knowing it. All participation in the scapegoat phenomenon is the same [as Saul's] sin of the persecution of Christ. And all human beings commit this sin.
>
> [Jesus's] revelation of the scapegoat mechanism . . . deprives us more and more of sacrificial protection, therefore forcing us to abstain from violence if we want to survive. In order to reach the Kingdom, man has to renounce violence.[16]

A closely related topic for mimetic theory is the term "sacrifice." In Girard's early work, he consistently identified sacrifice with the ritual sacrifice of archaic religion, and thus "sacrifice" invariably has a negative connotation. Rebecca Adams says that in effect Girard "scapegoats"

---

13. Haven, *Evolution of Desire*, 235.
14. Girard, *Evolution and Conversion*, 182.
15. Foster, *Theology of Consent*, 183.
16. Girard, *Evolution and Conversion*, 142, 148.

sacrifice as well as mimetic desire, by identifying them as solely negative.[17] Girard himself came to recognize this: "I have changed my mind. . . . I was mistaken, not once but twice."[18] He concedes that in his earlier work he neglected the positive aspect of sacrifice ("the sacrifice of Christ"). At the same time, he also reevaluates mimetic desire in more positive terms: "It isn't bad in itself, in fact it is very good. . . . People can no more give it up than they can give up food or sleep."[19]

The crux of the problem is the ambiguous meaning of "sacrifice," which obscures two different and almost opposite meanings. Girard identifies these as "archaic sacrifice" and "the sacrifice of Christ."[20] Richard Crocks helpfully describes the first as "something done to you," while the second is something the individual chooses of his or her own accord, a kind of renunciation. Greek has two different words for the two kinds of sacrifice (*thyein* for the first sense, *askesis* for the second), but in English we have only one word, "sacrifice."[21] Jonathan Foster makes much the same point, by grammatically distinguishing *nonreflexive sacrifice*, something that one experiences but does not initiate, something done to the individual, from *reflexive sacrifice*, something one both initiates and experiences, something one *chooses*.[22]

Girard says that this distinction crystallized for him through pondering "the inexhaustible text" of the judgment of Solomon (1 Kgs 3:16–28). The story is usually cited as an example of Solomon's wisdom, but the real hero is not Solomon but the unnamed "good prostitute." In the story, two prostitutes lived together in the same house, and both gave birth around the same time. One woman's baby died during the night "because she lay on him" (perhaps the earliest known report of sudden infant death syndrome). While the second woman slept with her baby, the first secretly traded the body of her dead infant for the second woman's living child. Upon awakening, the second woman instinctively knew the dead infant was not hers and accused the first of exchanging the dead for the living infant. The first prostitute denied this and continued to claim that the living infant was in fact hers.

17. Adams, "Loving Mimesis." See above, ch. 21.
18. Girard: *Evolution and Conversion*, 155; *One by Whom Scandal Comes*, 43.
19. Girard, *When These Things Begin*, 43; see also Adams and Girard, "Violence, Difference, Sacrifice," 25–26.
20. Girard, *One by Whom Scandal Comes*, 40–41.
21. Cocks, "Two Kinds of Sacrifice."
22. Foster, *Theology of Consent*, 137–40.

Their conflict quickly escalated, and they took their dispute to King Solomon. He listened to their competing stories, called for his sword, and proposed a bloody solution: "Divide the living boy in two; then give half to the one and half to the other." At this point, the real mother, "because compassion for her son burned within her," relinquishes her claim: "Give her the living boy; do not kill him." King Solomon recognized that only the true mother of the living infant would renounce her claim for the sake of the child's life and thereupon granted the living infant to his real mother.

Girard says that this story perfectly illustrates the two types of sacrifice. Solomon (with the agreement of the first prostitute) proposes resolving the dispute by what amounts to a blood sacrifice of an innocent child. But the good prostitute, *out of compassion*, renounces what is most dear to any mother, her claim to her own child. "The good prostitute *sacrificed* rivalry for the sake of her child, whereas the bad prostitute agreed to *sacrifice* the child for the sake of the rivalry."[23] The difference between the two types of sacrifice is crucial: "on the one hand, sacrifice as murder; on the other hand, sacrifice as the readiness to die in order not to participate in sacrifice as murder.... The moral history of humanity is shifting from the first to the second meaning."[24] The first is the sacrifice *of* others; the second the sacrifice *for the sake of* others. In this, the good prostitute prefigures Christ's sacrifice.[25]

Mark Heim has expressed the dilemma or double bind that faces those who begin to recognize the distinction between the two types of sacrifice, those who begin to see through the scapegoat mechanism to the innocence of the victim, given that everything we do is based on imitation. Under normal circumstances,

> The only models we have are to imitate the persecutors, or imitate their victims. Passive acceptance [by victims] merely reinforces the violent process. Direct resistance fosters more conflict and violence, which in turn heightens the appetite for sacrifice.... Christ opens a way out of this dilemma. His path to the cross eschews all violence, yet it exposes the evil of scapegoating at every step. The resurrection vindicates the victim and condemns the persecutors, but without turning to vengeance.[26]

---

23. Girard, *One by Whom Scandal Comes*, 43. Emphasis in original.
24. Girard, *Evolution and Conversion*, 155.
25. Haven, *Evolution of Desire*, 275.
26. Heim, *Saved from Sacrifice*, 221.

In agreement with this, Girard says, "Christ died because he refused to submit to the law of violence."[27] Elsewhere, his interlocutor in *Evolution and Conversion* offers that "this is why the victim is at the core of the Bible: *God himself becomes the victim who ends the unjust usage of victims.*" Girard responds: "The God of Christianity isn't the violent God of archaic religion, but the non-violent God who willingly becomes a victim in order to free us from our violence."[28]

This discussion of the nuances of *sacrifice* brings us now to the significance of *victims*. Here we tread carefully: we must not say anything that would further disempower those who have been victimized or in any way minimize the reality of their suffering. The gospel must, above all, be a gospel of liberation. I endorse what Jonathan Foster has said: "White, straight, rich (relatively speaking) Christian males, who have been afforded the opportunity to sit and think about such things, should go out of their way to say that imitating Christ *always includes liberation.*"[29]

Everything we have said about Girard's mimetic theory emphasizes the innocence of the scapegoated victim—not absolute innocence (as if that were even possible) but innocence of the crimes of which they have been accused by the mob. They are *involuntary* victims, caught up in a system of violence. But some may voluntarily *choose* to become a victim of violence *rather than to participate in the system of violence*. This requires near superhuman (divine?) strength, but those who, like Jesus, chose this course became "like a kind of rock that jammed up the machinery of scapegoating."[30] Foster expresses this exactly: "Jesus is a stand-in for all those victimized by the world's scapegoating structures. The revelation subverts our violent mythic machinery by declaring the way forward isn't unanimity *against* the victim; it's solidarity *with* the victim."[31]

Girard identifies what he calls "the modern concern for victims" as an important aspect—perhaps the single most important aspect—of our globalized civilization. It is "unifying the world for the first time in history."[32] It is our absolute value, "the one rubric that gathers everything

---

27. Girard, *When These Things Begin*, 91.
28. Girard, *Evolution and Conversion*, 151–52. Emphasis added.
29. Foster, *Theology of Consent*, 200. Emphasis in original.
30. Foster, *Theology of Consent*, 41.
31. Foster, *Theology of Consent*, 36. Emphasis in original.
32. Girard, *I See Satan Fall*, 166. Chapter 13 (161–69) is called "The Modern Concern for Victims."

together. . . . The most effective power of transformation is not revolutionary violence, but the modern concern for victims."[33]

All human groups of course exhibit some degree of compassion towards their own, but Girard contends our modern universalizing concern for victims has its origins in the Judeo-Christian Scriptures. The Hebrew Scriptures advocate for care of the "alien who resides with you" (Lev 19:33–34); the New Testament has the parables of the sheep and the goats (Matt 25:31–46) and the good Samaritan (Luke 10:25–37), as well as the command to love even your enemies (Matt 5:44).

This universalizing of compassion begins to flourish in the charitable institutions of the Middle Ages, like l'Hotel-Dieu, the "House of God" hospital in Paris, that took in all in need. The impulse to universal charity gained momentum with the humanism of the European Enlightenment, although as Girard points out, "humanism and humanitarianism develop first on Christian soil."[34] All this was greatly accelerated in the aftermath of World War II and the Holocaust, with treaties like the *Universal Declaration of Human Rights* (1948) and the Geneva Conventions (1949). Girard observes that this emphasis on codifying human rights "is an indirect acknowledgement that every individual or every group of individuals can become the 'scapegoat' of their own communities. . . . Emphasis on human rights amounts to a formerly unthinkable effort to control uncontrollable processes of mimetic snowballing."[35]

Our concern for victims, Girard says, is "the secular mask of Christian love. . . . Our world did not invent compassion, it is true, but it has universalized it."[36] Understandably, as we have become more and more concerned with the plight of victims, we have also become more self-critical about our failures. Girard notes the paradox:

> It is often said that our [twentieth] century is the worst because it has made more victims than all others put together. That is

---

33. Girard, *I See Satan Fall*, 166, 168.

34. Girard, *I See Satan Fall*, 163. Girard can be criticized here for an excessively "Eurocentric" view of the Enlightenment. For a different view, which documents the influence of the "indigenous critique" of European culture by North American Indians from New France, some of whom traveled in Europe, see Graeber and Wengrow, *Dawn of Everything*, 27–77. It is their contention that much of eighteenth-century Enlightenment thought can be traced to the dialogue between indigenous North American statesmen and Jesuit missionaries, who documented the indigenous attitudes of "reasoned debate, personal freedoms, and the refusal of arbitrary power" (44).

35. Girard, *I See Satan Fall*, 167–68.

36. Girard, *I See Satan Fall*, 165, 169.

certainly true . . . [but] it is also true that our world protects more victims than any other. These two things are true at once. There is more good *and* more evil than ever before.[37]

As is so often the case with mimetic theory, Girard goes on to identify a dark underside to our otherwise admirable concern for victims. Our concern can be traced back to the realization that we cope with mimetic rivalry by scapegoating innocent victims, but now "the concern for victims has become a paradoxical competition of mimetic rivalries, of opponents continually trying to outbid one another."[38] Nothing could better illustrate the pervasive nature of mimetic rivalry than this transformation of our modern concern for victims into yet another vehicle for mimetic competition. We compete to determine who is the more genuine and deserving victim, which in turn has given rise to "the virtually universal feeling of being victimized . . . [with] each person vehemently insisting that he is the victim."[39]

Any number of examples could be cited, in politics, international relations, and daily life, but let me mention one rather obvious one: in our hyper-partisan politics, the left sees itself as the champion of historically oppressed groups (i.e., victims), while the right increasingly proclaims that *they* are the true victims. All issues get reduced to who is the "real" victim, which is never resolved (e.g., the Israeli-Palestinian conflict; how far back do you go to determine who the "real" victim is?). As Jonathan Foster remarks, "When will we arrive at a place unanimated by past hurts? I think, maybe, never."[40]

This competition in the end gives us only a caricature, whereby the concern for victims perversely gives rise to new persecutions—and new victims. In words that seem to capture the current state of our politics, Girard remarks, "One can persecute today only in the name of being against persecution. One can only persecute persecutors. You have to prove that your opponent is a persecutor in order to justify your own desire to persecute."[41] Girard summarizes:

---

37. Girard, *When These Things Begin*, 9. Emphasis added. See also Girard, *I See Satan Fall*, 165.
38. Girard, *I See Satan Fall*, 164.
39. Girard, *One by Whom Scandal Comes*, 73.
40. Foster, *Theology of Consent*, 53.
41. Girard, *Evolution and Conversion*, 184.

> The concern for victims seems to me to be both a positive and a negative phenomenon. The error arises from ideology—the idea that everything is either [all] good or [all] bad. The revelation of the innocence of the victim is the true Christian insight. It flourishes today, but over the course of the last century it managed to become the motive force for new ways of manufacturing victims. Its effect has therefor been equivocal.[42]

Have we, with our modern concern for victims, painted ourselves into a corner? If so, how to escape? Even as we seek to right past wrongs, we would do well to heed Girard's warning that we not engage in our own version of scapegoating, of persecuting the persecutors. The only way out, according to African American womanist theologian Karen Baker-Fletcher, is to recognize that although degrees of involvement will vary, we are all *both* "sinners and the sinned against, victimizers and victims, oppressors and oppressed . . . all caught up in a common heritage" of hatred and violence.[43] Each of us, in our own way, can no doubt identify with Jesus as victim, but each of us must also recognize the ways in which we have been complicit with those who crucify. Girard elaborates:

> If you asked everyone today: "Do the people around you take out their frustrations on scapegoats?" everyone would answer in the affirmative; but if you then asked the same people: "And do *you* have scapegoats?" everyone would answer in the negative. To become Christian is, fundamentally, to perceive that it isn't just others who have scapegoats.[44]

Clearly, some have been more sinned against than others, but in this "world of crucifixion and unnecessary violence,"[45] we have a shared responsibility to break the cycle of violence. And we cannot break the cycle of violence through more violence but only through some form of forgiveness. Jonathan Foster reminds us that "the sins of previous generations never really leave us. . . . [Despite] the oft-repeated adage 'forgive and forget,' if one could truly forget, forgiveness would not be necessary. It's our inability to forget that invites us to forgive, again and again."[46]

---

42. Girard, *One by Whom Scandal Comes*, 73.
43. Baker-Fletcher, *Dancing with God*, 92.
44. Girard, *When These Things Begin*, 2. Emphasis in original.
45. Baker-Fletcher, *Dancing with God*, 37, 39, 48.
46. Foster, *Theology of Consent*, 53.

If we are all *both* "sinners and sinned against, victim and victimizer," then forgiveness will need to be mutual; all will need to both seek and grant forgiveness. But forgiveness by itself is not sufficient; sinners and sinned against must join hands in the overcoming of evil. Even in our mutual forgiveness, we need to be clear: it is not the *suffering* of victims that is redemptive but *overcoming evil*—including especially the evil of violence.[47]

These are not new insights. They are certainly congruent with George Fox discerning the "nature of Cain, Esau and Judas" in himself. Jesus counseled us to attend to the speck in our own eye before criticizing the log in our neighbor's. In the twentieth century, Soviet dissident Aleksandr Solzhenitsyn, a man well acquainted with evil, gave classic expression to the insight: "The line separating good and evil passes not between states, nor between classes, nor between political parties, but right through every human heart, and through all human hearts."[48]

Perhaps Jean-Paul Sartre expressed it most succinctly: in the end, each of us is "half-victim, half-accomplice—like everyone else."[49]

---

47. Baker-Fletcher, *Dancing with God*, 134. See also discussion of Baker-Fletcher in Weaver, *Nonviolent Atonement*, locs. 2524–2571 of 5050.

48. Aleksandr Solzhenitsyn, *The Gulag Archipelago*, vol. 1, quoted in Foster, *Theology of Consent*, 174.

49. Jean-Paul Sartre, from his 1948 play *Dirty Hands*, quoted in Lewis, "Progressives Who Flunked," para. 9.

28

"Conversion of the Heart" for Friends Today

> We are in danger of spiritual starvation, not because there is no bread, but because we have persuaded ourselves that we are not hungry.
>
> —Simone Weil[1]

WE HAVE BEEN EXAMINING the idea of *conversion of the heart*: the sense that, for early Friends, convincement was "the beginning, not the end" of their spiritual journey. Howard Brinton, in his *How They Became Friends*, reiterates the point we made earlier: "In the main Friends considered *conversion* a gradual process, often life-long, subsequent to the *convincement* of the truth of Quaker principles."[2]

We started by exploring a New Testament perspective through the lens of mimetic theory (chs. 19–22). We then turned to some of the language and metaphors early Friends used to describe this process: the seed (and the enmity between "the two seeds"), the daily cross, the refiner's fire, truth, the Lamb's war (chs. 23–26). The sense we get is that this process of "continuing conversion" resulted from an inward struggle

---

1. Weil, *Waiting for God*, xxxi.
2. Brinton, *How They Became Friends*, 7. Emphasis added.

that involved "turning within" or "going deep." Sometimes this occurred in an individual's solitariness, but often it occurred in the company of other Friends, in small and mostly silent meetings. Some of the magic of early Friends seems to have involved the interplay of the individual Friends inward process with the presence and support of a meeting of like-minded individuals engaged in the same journey.

We turn now to the question of the relevance of all this for Friends today. As we saw in the introductory chapter, the world today is very different from seventeenth-century England. In addition to all the profound scientific, technological, and economic changes, we now live in cultural milieu of profound secularization. Questions of religious truth and authority are no longer the burning questions they were in the 1650s. Twenty-nine percent of US adults now describe themselves as religiously unaffiliated "nones"—a larger share of the population than Evangelicals (24 percent), Roman Catholics (21 percent), or mainline Protestants (16 percent). Some of these "nones" are atheist or agnostic, but the largest number describe themselves as simply "nothing in particular."[3]

Quakers of all stripes account for barely one-fiftieth of 1 percent of the United States population (about 76,000)—compared to over 20 percent of the European population of North America in 1700.[4] We live in a rapidly secularizing society, which to all appearances has waning interest in religious matters in general and Quakers in particular.[5] In the words of Simone Weil above, we seem to have "persuaded ourselves that we are not hungry."

In this setting, what can contemporary Friends say about the need for conversion of the heart—and how have they been going about it?

I have been associated with the Religious Society of Friends now for over fifty years, since I was eighteen. In 1971, Quakers were understandably consumed by political activism, focused on opposition to the Vietnam war. But my sense is that over the last several decades, we have seen a shift. Thankfully, we still have our political activists, but simultaneously there has been a noticeable upsurge of interest among Quakers in what we might call "nourishing the spiritual life,"[6] and this upsurge has

3. Pew Research Center, "About Three-in-Ten U.S. Adults."
4. Unger, "Quakers," para. 14.
5. Some have argued that the "spiritual but not religious" contingent of the nones might find that Quakers have much to offer them, with our decentralized, egalitarian, experiential, and non-credal approach to religion.
6. The title of a pamphlet by Paul Lacey. Birkel speaks similarly of "nurturing the

been in response to a perceived need on the part of many Friends. Even among many self-identified activists, there is a deep yearning, a hunger for spiritual nourishment, what Thomas Kelly called "a passionate quest for the real whole-wheat Bread of Life."[7] In the midst of the wider culture's increasing secularization, this is an important and hopeful sign for the future of the Religious Society of Friends.

In response to this perceived need, there has been a myriad of new programs and initiatives—a sometimes confusing abundance of opportunities. What follows is by no means a systematic study but a sampling of those programs of which I have personal knowledge.

Perhaps the place to start is with the Spiritual Formation Program, which began in the 1980s in Baltimore Yearly Meeting. The initial impetus came in part from their realization that a fund intended to support traveling ministers was no longer being used. By design, the Spiritual Formation Program was intended to be accessible for busy modern Friends: a September weekend opening retreat, local groups of eight to twelve that met monthly to discuss spiritual readings, smaller Friendship Groups of three to five that also met monthly for companionship and mutual support, and a closing weekend retreat in May. Participants were also encouraged to engage in some type of individual daily spiritual practice or discipline.[8]

In early 1999, a group interested in bringing the Spiritual Formation Program to Philadelphia Yearly Meeting (PYM) began to meet, and the initial cohort of the PYM version of spiritual formation held its opening retreat in October 1999. I had been somewhat involved in the initial discussions, and, wanting to participate myself, I was able to recruit eleven others from my own meeting to enroll, so that we accounted for about a third of that initial cohort.

The Spiritual Formation Program lived up to our expectations. Our local group continued to meet after the formal program ended, and the following year several more from our meeting enrolled in the second PYM cohort. Eventually, those Lancaster Friends who had been through the PYM program organized a modified Spiritual Formation Program for our monthly meeting. Our aim was to make the program even more accessible to local Friends, largely by replacing opening and closing

---

inward life," the title of ch. 4 in his *Silence and Witness*.

7. Kelly, *Testament of Devotion*, 28.
8. Meyer, *Baltimore Yearly Meeting*.

weekend retreats at a distant retreat center with all-day Saturday sessions at our meetinghouse. This came to fruition in 2004–5, with about forty-five Friends participating on some level—representing about half of our active members. In the experience of my meeting, Friends proved hungry for this nourishment of the spiritual life.

My experience in spiritual formation led me to enroll in the School of the Spirit's program "On Becoming a Spiritual Nurturer" in early 2002. The School of the Spirit had begun in 1991 under the auspices of Philadelphia Yearly Meeting, with Frances Taber, Kathryn Damiano, and Sandra Cronk as core teachers. The first two iterations were yearlong programs, but in 1995 the program expanded to two years, with a series of six long-weekend retreats in the Philadelphia area, interspersed with reading, writing, and spiritual practice.[9]

The last cohort of "On Becoming a Spiritual Nurturer" was in 2018–19, but the School of the Spirit has sponsored other programs over the years. I participated in "The Way of Ministry" program in 2008–9, with four Pendle Hill retreats over nine months. Currently the School of the Spirit's focus is on "Participating in God's Power," a program of similar design, with five long-weekend retreats over the course of a year. The second iteration of this program started in early 2024.

The School of the Spirit and spiritual formation use a similar design, with a series of three- or four-day retreats, a limited time duration of nine to eighteen months, and a combination of reading, small group support, and individual spiritual practice. Both these programs seek to foster some sense of community among the participants—but in the end this is an artificial community that ends when the program ends. In my experience, it is uncommon for participants to stay in communication afterwards, and virtually unheard of for the community to reassemble after the formal end of the program. My own sense is that spiritual formation or similar programs that occur at the monthly meeting level will have a longer-lasting impact on the spiritual nurture of individual Friends, if for no other reason than that the community that is fostered will be the local meeting.

A somewhat different approach is represented by "faithfulness groups," which involve groups of four to six participants, meeting monthly for mutual support, spiritual discernment, and accountability. Faithfulness groups have the advantage of not requiring any time away at retreats (and so no financial cost) and no special leadership training.

---

9. For a brief history of the origins of the spiritual nurturer program, see School of the Spirit, "History."

With no fixed duration, they can potentially play an ongoing role in the life of participants.

Faithfulness groups represent the latest iteration of a group process that has its roots in the Shalem Institute's peer support groups for spiritual directors. In one such group of Quakers in the Philadelphia area, the focus gradually evolved to include not just spiritual directors but anyone seeking to be faithful to various kinds of leadings and ministry. I participated in a variation of this during "The Way of Ministry," which at that time was called a "spiritual accountability group." Since 2017, these groups have been known as "faithfulness groups." Marcelle Martin has been the guiding influence for their evolution and growth, and her book *A Guide to Faithfulness Groups* details the history as well as giving useful guidance for the conduct of such groups.[10]

After participating in the "Nurturing Faithfulness" program of New England Yearly Meeting in 2022–23, led by Marcelle Martin, I became somewhat of a champion of faithfulness groups within my own meeting. Although not for everyone, I found there was significant interest within my meeting, and it was reasonably easy to get new groups to form. Currently, our meeting has four ongoing faithfulness groups, with about twenty Friends participating. The group in which I participate started as my support group for my participation in "The Way of Ministry," evolved into a mutual accountability group, and has now been meeting regularly for over twelve years. My experience is that local faithfulness groups have significant potential to contribute to this *conversion of the heart*; perhaps ongoing "faithfulness" can be considered simply as an alternative expression for this continuing conversion.

For ten years (from approximately 2000 to 2010), I served on the steering committee of Philadelphia Yearly Meeting's program on "Deepening and Strengthening Our Meeting Communities." Here, the unit of intervention was not individual Friends but the local meeting. The program was born out of the observation (by our yearly meeting's then clerk, Arlene Kelly) that by the time a local meeting was in crisis, it was difficult for the yearly meeting to render meaningful assistance. The program was meant to work preventively to strengthen local meetings, before there was a crisis. Sometimes the program worked with single meetings; at other times with a cohort of three meetings or with several monthly meetings within a quarterly meeting. Participating meetings typically felt they very

---

10. Martin, *Guide to Faithfulness Groups*. An appendix also gives a helpful description of other examples of "other kinds of sacred and healing circles."

much benefitted from the program; a recurrent theme was that Friends in their local meetings were hungering for spiritual nurture—and not always finding it.

This is a sampling of some of the ways that the Religious Society of Friends has responded *corporately* to the perceived need for nourishing the spiritual life. Undoubtably there are similar examples within the programmed, evangelical, and conservative branches of Friends.

But my sense is that, whether within one of these formal programs or separately, the real work of conversion of the heart must take place within the individual. Often enough, the beginning steps take place (sometimes simply by osmosis) in the context of a supportive meeting community but eventually will require some degree of intentionality, self-examination, and spiritual practice on the part of the individual.

Many voices deserve to be heard; I will lift up just three, to illustrate the kind of process that might be involved. As we will see, even if the process is necessarily centered on the individual, the meeting can play a crucial role. Often enough, the process involves a reimmersion in the beliefs and language from the Quaker tradition, taking inspiration from those who came before.

Let us start with Ben Pink Dandelion, whose important 2014 Swarthmore Lecture *Open for Transformation* we cited in chapter 18. There we explored how "transformation" was perhaps a modern equivalent to "convincement." But keeping in mind that Friends have always viewed convincement as only the initial step in a process of ongoing conversion, perhaps transformation can also be thought of as a modern equivalent of "conversion." In his lecture, Dandelion states unequivocally that "the Quaker way is a way of transformation":[11]

> We are transformed in our spiritual experience to act collectively as co-agents with God in the transformation of the world. We are transformed in order to transform.
>
> We cannot encounter the Divine and not be changed by the experience.... Transformation is still the heart of Quakerism. We are personally and collectively transformed and in turn seek to transform.... If as Quakers we are not open to transformation, or do not understand that Quakerism is centered on that kind of experience, we misunderstand Quakerism.[12]

---

11. B. Dandelion, *Open for Transformation*, 3.
12. B. Dandelion, *Open for Transformation*, 3, 18–19. A shorter version of this quote

Having made the case that the Quaker way is a way of transformation, Dandelion next turns his keen sociologist's eye to the corrosive effects of secularization on the Society of Friends over the last 150 years, a process perhaps more advanced in his Britain Yearly Meeting than in the United States, but nevertheless resonating with much of what I said above. "It looks and feels as if we have taken the secularization of wider society into the very heart of the way we approach our faith and practice . . . [constantly moving] us further towards a secularized individualism."[13] "The way we in which we relate to the secular world and are influenced by it seems to me to be the biggest challenge to our future as a religious society."[14] In our ever-increasing tolerance of theological and behavioral diversity, "we have been misled by our desire to please everyone."[15] We have lost our ability to articulate what it is to be a Quaker, at times forgetting our "primal language" that fosters meaningful communication with one another on matters of belief.[16] We have emphasized *seeking* to the exclusion of *finding*; belief is not only more pluralistic but also more marginal. All truth is said to be "partial, personal, and provisional," what Dandelion calls "the absolute perhaps."[17] We have "become allergic to public expressions of explicit faith . . . a place where God is reduced to a concept to be placed within inverted commas rather than experienced at the heart of our being." He concludes by wryly noting, "It is a challenging time to be a Quaker."[18]

Despite this analysis, Dandelion (in his ch. 3) ends on a note of hopeful optimism, with what amounts to a manifesto for our renewal. He sees many signs of this renewal, starting with his own small meeting in the north of England. "We are called to renew our sense of covenant, to renew our understanding of the universal ministry . . . renew our understanding of meeting for worship and meeting for worship for church affairs, renew joy, renew community, renew our sense of, and openness to, personal and collective transformation."[19] For this renewal to occur, we will "need to nurture personal transformation and affirm *convincement*

---

appeared in ch. 18.

13. B. Dandelion, *Open for Transformation*, 65.
14. B. Dandelion, *Open for Transformation*, 68.
15. B. Dandelion, *Open for Transformation*, 64.
16. B. Dandelion, *Open for Transformation*, 62.
17. B. Dandelion, *Open for Transformation*, 40, 41.
18. B. Dandelion, *Open for Transformation*, 65. See 25–68 for fuller discussion.
19. B. Dandelion, *Open for Transformation*, 92.

in its traditional meaning . . . to again feel God's transforming role in our lives and in turn act as agents together of transformation . . . to see the whole of our lives as about being Quaker."[20] This will require that we "get beyond the paralyzing limits of individualism . . . [because] the Quaker way is, ultimately, not about the individual but the meeting community."[21] "We will need to be clear and assertive about who we are, careful not to 'dumb down' our message. . . . We are a worshipping community."[22]

Ben Pink Dandelion combines an analysis of the corrosive effects of secular individualism with an impassioned plea for the central role that personal transformation must play in the renewal Friends corporate witness. He calls for a rededication to our tradition—but we are left wanting more specifics.

From the other end of the Quaker spectrum, conservative Friend Lloyd Lee Wilson has spoken explicitly about the expectation and need for an ongoing "conversion of manners" as being "integral to Quaker spirituality, [allowing] us time to start slowly, time to listen for guidance in relatively small matters, time to become familiar with the true Divine Voice."[23] Elaborating on the unique Quaker understanding of being "born again," he comments that "in my experience and in the writings of Friends, this birth event . . . was only the beginning of a new life. What counts is not when or where one was reborn, but how one lives the subsequent life."[24]

Lloyd Lee Wilson gives some very practical instruction on how we might assist this "growth into holiness."[25] He describes two complementary modes of discernment. First, we can learn to heed "the promptings of love and truth in the heart," becoming "familiar with the Divine call by following leadings in small things—lots of small things," and then carefully reflect on our experience. In this way, one gradually "comes to know the true Divine Voice, and to be able to discern that voice in larger matters."[26] Recall from excursus 1 that in process theology, there is in

---

20. B. Dandelion, *Open for Transformation*, 90, 91, 90. Emphasis added.
21. B. Dandelion, *Open for Transformation*, 74.
22. B. Dandelion, *Open for Transformation*, 75. See 71–91 for fuller discussion.
23. L. Wilson, *Holy Surrender*, 12. See also L. Wilson, *Essays*, 37.
24. L. Wilson, *Wrestling with Our Faith*, 20.
25. L. Wilson, *Wrestling with Our Faith*, 20.
26. L. Wilson, *Holy Surrender*, 12. The memorable phrase from "Advice and Queries": "Take heed, dear Friends, to the promptings of love and truth in your hearts. Trust these as the leadings of God whose Light shows us our darkness and brings us to new

every moment a "call forward": a lure, a beckoning, an invitation into a future of individual and communal flourishing, grounded in God's love for the world. Learning to heed these promptings of love and truth in the heart can become a daily discipline. Early Friends were fond of turning the prophet Zechariah's query into an advice: "Do not despise the day of small things" (Zech 4:10 KJV).

The second mode of discernment, equally important, is to be intentional about what Lloyd Lee Wilson calls "the spirituality of subtraction," by asking ourselves what is "not of God" and removing that from our lives. "As one adds at one end and subtracts at the other, what develops in the middle is a particular, unique personal life in God that has been God's desire for that person always."[27] This strikes me as eminently sound and practical advice for making real progress on the road to conversion of the heart: becoming more attentive to seeking and heeding Divine guidance in even small ways, while at the same time cultivating a willingness to let go of those things that separate us from God.

Like Ben Pink Dandelion, Lloyd Lee Wilson emphasizes the importance of the meeting community in nurturing spiritual growth and, in particular, the role of the meeting in recognizing and naming the spiritual gifts of its members—and of individuals in claiming, nurturing, and exercising these gifts.[28] "Individuals become stewards of those gifts, but they are essentially the community's gifts. [There is] mutual accountability of the individual and meeting for the proper development and use of spiritual gifts.... *If we are serious about spiritual growth*, we will welcome the oversight and guidance of others."[29]

The third contemporary Friend I would like to lift up is Sandra Cronk, who has been described as "one of the most quietly influential Friends in the unprogrammed branch of Friends during the last decades of the twentieth century."[30] Before her untimely death in 2000 at age fifty-eight, Sandra spent eleven years on the faculty of Pendle Hill, followed by a decade as one of the founders and teachers in the School of the Spirit.

Sandra Cronk's ministry focused mainly on teaching and spiritual nurture, but her *Dark Night Journey* (1991), written largely out of her

---

life" (in Britain Yearly Meeting, *Quaker Faith and Practice* 1.02).

27. L. Wilson, *Holy Surrender*, 12–13.
28. L. Wilson, *Essays*, 91–114, "Community Stewardship of our Spiritual Gifts."
29. L. Wilson, *Wrestling with our Faith*, 46–47. Emphasis added.
30. From the preface to Cronk, *Lasting Gift*, xii. The introduction to this volume gives a valuable summary of her life and ministry, xvii–lii.

own life experience, endures as a major work of Christian and Quaker spirituality. There she describes the long tradition of "the apophatic path to God," a path that emphasizes silence, emptiness, absence, darkness, and the limits of language.[31] Spiritual traditions often involve an intertwining of the apophatic with the cataphatic paths, but certainly Quakerism has a stronger affinity than most traditions with the apophatic path (though it is not, she emphasizes, exclusively apophatic).[32] The apophatic path is sometimes chosen, but more commonly is thrust upon one, when the "pillars of the autonomous self" crumble, perhaps through illness, death of a loved one, divorce, job loss, or even loss of comfortable and familiar images of God. In this place of darkness, there is a "stripping away" of aspects of the old self, followed by (in the words of her subtitle) an "inward re-patterning toward a life centered in God."

This repatterning of the old self can be experienced as a kind of death. "Our understanding of our 'self' changes radically during a time of darkness and stripping. . . . [However,] the term 'death of self' does not mean the extinguishing of our personhood. Rather it speaks of the extinguishing of our previous way of defining and experiencing ourselves in the world."[33] She explicitly links this experience to "our participation in Christ's crucifixion and resurrection," echoing what we have heard from early Friends (as well as the apostle Paul).[34]

This repatterning also involves "a shift to a new way of knowing," especially of knowing God—a kind of "unknowing."[35] Instead of knowing *about* God as an object, now "the primary knower is God. . . . We now know ourselves as God knows us, as loved by God. . . . Love is the most common word to describe the relationship with God found in this new way of knowing."[36]

In this repatterned self, our "false sense of self-sufficiency" is stripped away—but also any sense of inadequacy or lack of worth (echoing the sins of "inordinate self-will" and "inordinate self-loss" from ch. 14). From our center in God, we can now see our "self" as a gift from God, not something we "possess" as an achievement.[37] And from this

---

31. Cronk, *Dark Night Journey*, 21–43.
32. Cronk, *Dark Night Journey*, 34–35.
33. Cronk, *Dark Night Journey*, 65.
34. Cronk, *Dark Night Journey*, 71.
35. Cronk, *Dark Night Journey*, 52.
36. Cronk, *Dark Night Journey*, 53.
37. Cronk, *Dark Night Journey*, 78.

new center, we can also see other selves as a gift of God, freeing us from any need for rivalry or competition.

If transformation (Dandelion's word), growth into holiness (Wilson's words), or inward repatterning (Cronk's term)—what we have been calling the "conversion of the heart"—are essential to Quaker spirituality, and (in the opinion of all three) the local meeting community has a role to play in nurturing this conversion, are local meetings in fact rising to meet that responsibility?

In a previous publication, I have argued that "the dynamics of membership in Quaker Meeting" involve a number of stages that we can picture as a series of concentric circles, and that the Quaker journey can be thought of as moving over time from the periphery to the center. However, there is always "a danger of mistaking this first and preliminary stage for the whole meaning of membership, of confusing the periphery for the center."[38] Beyond meeting as a place of acceptance and belonging (the outermost circle), a Quaker meeting should aspire to be "a place of transformation." Transformation can come in a variety of ways: through deep engagement with the testimonies, through daily spiritual practice and discipline, or through the process of following a significant leading. It may also come through the repatterning experience of the dark night journey. The meeting can assist this dynamic of transformation, perhaps by providing structured programs for spiritual practice, perhaps by offering a clearness committee or faithfulness group to assist in the discernment of leadings. "The meeting's most important contributions at this stage are an attitude of expectation and the capacity to respond authentically to requests for help. . . . A meeting will foster transformation to the extent that it lifts up the expectation that individuals will have leadings, has a mechanism for responding to individual requests for clearness, and can confidently assist in the discernment process."[39]

Behind this dynamic view of membership, leading to "meeting as a place of transformation," there is an important theological point. John the Evangelist writes that "we love because [God] first loved us" (1 John 4:19). Love is not an external command, an obligation imposed from without, but a free and grateful response to the experience of the grace of God's love toward us. But how do we experience God's love in our lives?

---

38. Gates, *Members One of Another*, 13.
39. Gates, *Members One of Another*, 24.

It seems to me that there are two different but complementary facets of God's love as we experience it. The first is the experience of unconditional acceptance: grace, the unwarranted but unconditional love of God that does not depend on anything we do. By analogy with human love, this is a parent's love of a newborn infant: adoring love that is unconditional, not dependent on any particular action or trait on the part of the child but simply rejoicing in the child's existence.

As a child grows and develops, this unconditional love continues, but eventually another facet of parental love enters, not in opposition to the first but complementing it. This is love that by its constancy, firmness, and patience can transform a self-centered toddler into a social being capable of sharing toys, using a fork, and speaking in sentences. There is a facet of God's love that is like that: never quite satisfied with the way we are but always inviting, encouraging, and leading us to become who we are meant to be. Beyond here-and-now acceptance, it is a leading toward future possibilities, a love that challenges and transforms us:

> This goes to the very heart of why we gather in community in the first place. We all need to belong to a group in which we can feel acceptance and support, and that is a very valid reason why we choose to be together. But there is another reason that God calls us into community: we are people in need of transformation, and community is that place of transformation.
>
> God calls us into community because it is only in community that we can learn God's transforming lessons of love, service, compassion, and forgiveness.[40]

Clearly, transformation still happens for individual Friends, but it is not at all clear to me how well the average Quaker meeting does in lifting up the expectation and providing opportunities for transformation. Perhaps we can say that for contemporary Friends who are committed to *the conversion of the heart*, there is a plethora of opportunities, formal programs as well as individual guidance from seasoned Friends. But if we truly believe that "transformation is still the heart of Quakerism," we may need to be more intentional in our expectations and practice. To paraphrase Simone Weil, there is in fact bread for our nourishment, if only we can persuade ourselves that we are hungry.

---

40. Gates, *Members One of Another*, 27, 28. See 25–28 for fuller discussion.

Epilogue
An Easter Reckoning

> To be a Christian is to join a community of argument. The one thing that has united Christians over the centuries is the debate about what it means to be Christian. Christianity is a millennia-long conversation about the significance of the Jesus story.
>
> —Mark Russ, *Quaker Shaped Christianity*[1]

WHAT BEGAN WITH AN intention to persuade Friends (and others) of the religious significance of René Girard's mimetic theory has gradually enlarged to become my personal explication of a "Quaker shaped Christianity." Indeed, looking over what I have written in these pages, I am somewhat surprised by how *Christian* it sounds.

Partly that is unavoidable, when grappling with Girard's mimetic theory; it is also unavoidable when we take early Friends seriously. In these pages, we have fully entered into that long conversation about the significance of the Jesus story, a conversation that for us has included as conversation partners René Girard and also early Friends. But it is now time for me to seriously engage with a personal and critical evaluation

---

1. Russ, *Quaker Shaped Christianity*, 16.

of where this leaves me, and us, as the Religious Society of Friends. So in that sense, this epilogue represents for me a kind of "Easter reckoning."[2]

Like so many of my generation, I grew up in a thoroughly Christian milieu, on a farm in rural upstate New York, descended on both sides from generations of dairy farmers. My family were regular (but by no means weekly) attenders at a "federated church," formed in the post–World War II years when the struggling Congregational, Methodist, and American Baptist churches in our town of a thousand souls took the radical step of choosing to survive by joining together. There were some other scattered religious influences: my paternal grandfather, having been healed of a serious disease as a young man, was a lifelong Christian Scientist; and my maternal great-grandmother, who died in childbirth when my grandmother was born in 1888, came from a long line of Quakers.

The Federated Church of West Winfield was not particularly evangelical, and certainly not fundamentalist, but it was Bible-centric, what today would probably be called mainline Protestant. After my mother died when I was ten years old, I was left (along with the expected psychological and social dislocation) with lots of "big questions." Why do people, even good people, die? What happens when we die? Why do people *live*? With life so fragile, what can we say about the purpose of our lives? And where is God (and Jesus) in all this? Even at a tender age, these questions came to me with some urgency.

At fourteen, while home alone watching a televised Billy Graham crusade, I had a kind of conversion experience. I say "kind of" because it was an entirely private affair. I am quite certain that friends and family would not have noticed any outward change; I was already a "good kid" and remained so. But I did start seriously reading my Good News Bible, became more regular in attending church, was baptized by immersion (my family belonging to the Baptist faction), and joined the Federated Church.

Inevitably, my initial enthusiasm waned over the next few years, partly with the realization that the church was not speaking to the social turmoil of the late 1960s. When I turned eighteen, and after considerable soul-searching, I registered for the Selective Service as a conscientious objector. The essay I wrote for my draft board was based almost entirely on my reading of the New Testament (with a bit of Thoreau added in). With

---

2. *An Easter-Reckoning* is the title of an obscure 1653 pamphlet by Quakers Richard Farnworth and Thomas Aldam, cited in Guiton, *Early Quakers*, 463. The pamphlet is mostly a polemic against "hireling priests"; it is not about Easter nor about a "reckoning" in the modern sense.

little from my own tradition to support this position, I began to read and was immediately drawn to Quakers, both by what I read and by the family connection through my grandmother's memory of her Quaker relatives.

When I went off to college a few months later, I was probably a setup for a typical "loss of faith" experience so common among young people then (and now). But instead, responding to a notice on a bulletin board, I began attending Quaker meeting with a small group of students, carpooling (and occasionally hitchhiking) to a meeting twenty miles away. With my very first meeting, I instinctively knew I had found my spiritual home. "Quaker shaped Christianity" allowed me to remain a Christian while still taking my questions seriously. These Quakers not only accommodated my restless seeking; they also pointed me to some answers.[3] Through the subsequent fifty years, I have continued to consider myself as both Christian and Quaker—not necessarily a given among liberal Quakers, which for that reason has sometimes seemed an uneasy home.

In my late twenties, my book-loving mother-in-law gave me an antique copy of Robert Barclay's *An Apology for the True Christian Divinity* (only later did I discover Dean Freiday's *Barclay's Apology in Modern English*). I had the insight that Barclay's *Apology* was really a book about how to read the Bible; Quakerism, in Barclay's reading, was all there. Within a few years, I was offering workshops on Barclay's *Apology* at New England Yearly Meeting and Friends General Conference. Barclay was a bit of a revelation for me; it profoundly shaped my emerging "Quaker shaped Christianity."

For me, the only comparable "book" experience has been the process of exploring Christianity through the lens of Girard's mimetic theory, now extending well over twenty years. Girard has immeasurably deepened and strengthened my grounding in and understanding of the Christian way. I now read the Bible (and in particular "all that violence") as a dual revelation, of one people's gradually unfolding insight that the true God has nothing to do with violence, and the parallel revelation of humanity as rooted in rivalry, idolatry, and "sacred violence." I also gained a more mature understanding of how it is that we can say that "the Easter event" is salvific for us. Following Jesus means being saved from our own violence, and includes a clear-eyed rejection of our culture's propensity to create ever more victims. It is my sincere hope that in some small measure I have been able to convey something of this deeper understanding.

3. It helped that in that small meeting in Bennington, Vermont, there were *four* men who had been conscientious objectors to military service during World War II.

But having said that, I must also admit that I am enough of a Quaker universalist to have some reservations about Girard, and specifically his tendency toward *Christian exclusivism*. In his explication of the deep meaning of the gospel revelation, Girard repeatedly emphasizes the gospel's unique role—what he calls "the singularity of Christianity."[4] But where does that leave our non-Christian brothers and sisters? In this time of religious pluralism, we are obligated to examine our own history and question whether Christian exclusivism has had pernicious (even if unintended) consequences.

In Girard's defense, his views on this can be quite nuanced. He does point out the ways in which the Easter event changed the dynamics of history, even for non-Christians; e.g., in the modern concern for victims. He also makes the claim that modern secularism is an entirely foreseeable outgrowth of Christianity. He contends that Christianity is "the destroyer of *all* religions. . . . The disappearance of religion is a Christian phenomenon *par excellence*."[5] This resonates with George Fox's claim that he was to "bring people off" from the "world's religions" and "will-worship" that was man's invention, and back to the worship "in spirit and in truth."[6]

Especially later in his career, Girard came to acknowledge a positive role for non-Christian religions.[7] He admits that archaic religions, far from being demonic, "were legitimate in their time and place," as a necessary stage in the slow maturation of humanity.[8] In a 2003 monograph, Girard recognizes that "the Vedic tradition [of India] can also lead to a revelation that discredits sacrifice . . . [that] violent institution that is nevertheless fundamental for the development of humanity."[9] He finds in the Vedic Brahmanas a full description of the mimetic nature of desire, the rivalry that results, its resolution in the scapegoat mechanism, and the institutionalizing of this in ritual sacrifice. However, Girard concludes that the biblical revelation is more definitive: "There is on both sides [the same critique of sacrifice], but in India it is expressed in an ironic and satirical fashion."[10]

---

4. Girard, *Sacrifice*, loc. 473 of 679.
5. Girard, *Evolution and Conversion*, 183, 184. Emphasis in original.
6. See, e.g., G. Fox, *Journal*, 35.
7. Girard, *Evolution and Conversion*, 152–56.
8. Girard, *One by Whom Scandal Comes*, 55.
9. Girard, *Sacrifice*, loc. 27 of 679.
10. Girard, *Sacrifice*, loc. 614 of 679. The whole monograph is in the end a defense of "the singularity of Christianity," but it does demonstrate Girard's willingness to take

Perhaps the Quaker understanding of the Inward Light of Christ might help Girard out of his exclusivist predicament. In classic Quaker understanding, the Light "enlightens everyone coming into the world" (John 1:9 NRSV, alternate reading); the Light, which is Christ, is universally present. This Light gives saving knowledge to those who attend to it, even to those who are unaware of the history of Jesus as the Christ. This Light that enlightens everyone "is the universal evangelical principle. In it and by it the salvation of Christ is shown to every man, whether Jew or Gentile, Scythian or Barbarian, of whatever country or kindred."[11]

Might the crucial revelation, which for Girard comes *only* through the historical drama of the Easter event, alternatively come through "the inward work of Christ," *by whatever name it is known?* Could not "the intelligence of the victim" be given through other victims, quite apart from the historical events of Easter? From this Quaker perspective, we can grant Girard's main point—that the historical drama of the Easter event makes that revelation especially compelling—while still allowing for the possibility of other paths to the same understanding. As Girard himself admits, in a late interview, "Many of the things that are in the Gospels can be reached by other means."[12]

Although Girard was never very explicit about any universalist implications of his mimetic theory, his collaborator Paul Gifford has been quite explicit, speaking here specifically to those engaged in the work of reconciliation:

> This conversion operating in reconcilers does not mean that the Christian praxis is inconceivable, inimitable, or otherwise disqualified outside of the original faith-matrix of Christian orthodoxy. The example of the good Samaritan is there to remind us of this. Conversion can proceed from the created goodness of a natural heart; in which case, justification in the sight of God follows from it. . . . If this were not so, could the light that (according to John's prologue) "lightens every man" actually "shine on in the darkness"? There is a capacity for positive mimesis in everyone and the potential in everyone to switch mimetic polarities from negative to positive.

---

other traditions seriously.

11. Barclay, *Apology*, 123.

12. "From Animal to Human," a conversation with René Girard, in Gifford, *Towards Reconciliation*, 131.

Girard's [mimetic] theory is comprehensible to, and appeals to, people of all faiths and none.[13]

A second major reservation I have is Girard's *anthropocentrism*, exclusively centered as he is on the drama of human salvation, while virtually silent about the rest of the natural world. This is hardly surprising, given Girard's description of his project as anthropology—the study of *anthropos*, man. But in an era when the dangers of human-caused climate change have begun to rival and even exceed those of human violence, this seems like a major shortcoming.

We have spoken much in these pages about the crucial role of the victim: the presumed guilt of the victim that drives the scapegoat mechanism; the dawning realization of the victim's innocence, which gradually subverts scapegoating; and the importance of "turning toward the victim," giving us "the intelligence of the victim" that is the essence of conversion. Following Girard, we have spoken exclusively about *human* victims, but is there not a profound sense in which the living Earth is now the primary *victim* of our modern technological culture? And can we recognize that human violence directed toward our planet, in a kind of "Gaia's revenge," is now in turn creating tens of millions of new *human* victims, through human-caused climate change?[14]

If, with Rebecca Adams, we can say that "the essence of the scapegoating process is that *someone or something* is turned into an *object*" (ch. 21), have we not *objectified* and thereby scapegoated the natural world, by reducing it to an object to be exploited for human profit? With this objectification, we have lost sight of the intrinsic value of the nonhuman world—with tragic consequences that unfold daily.

Granted, our centuries-long exploitation of the natural world does not fit the usual scapegoat scenario, but is there not a sense in which this exploitation arises out of the same "disordered desires" when we mimetically desire what others desire, simply because they desire it? And are not these disordered desires identical with the *covetousness* that the tenth commandment prohibits, and the *lusts* in the New Testament that lead to disputes, conflicts, and wars among us? (Jas 4:1–2).

---

13. Gifford, *Towards Reconciliation*, 96, 101.
14. Lovelock, *Revenge of Gaia*. Obviously, "revenge" is used here as a metaphor, to express the fact that our disruption of natural cycles and systems has predictable consequences.

Here, perhaps process theology can help free Girard from his anthropocentrism.[15] Starting at least with Galileo and Descartes, the predominant strand of Western thought has led to the "bifurcation of nature,"[16] attributing to humans (and only to humans) the capacity for freedom, moral agency, and subjective experience, while the rest of the universe is only inert stuff, lacking in these capacities *and therefore lacking intrinsic value*. But in process thought, "there is no gulf separating humans from the rest of the universe." Specifically, experience is simply "participation in reality" and does not presuppose consciousness.[17]

Experience is an attribute of all life, not just human life. For process thought, all life consists of *experiencing subjects*; *experience goes all the way down*. This is not to say that worms or bacteria or electrons are *conscious*, but it is to say that they have some degree of agency, however small, and thus some degree of what can properly be called subjectivity. Thus, Thomas Berry's aphorism (quoted in excursus 1): "The universe is not a collection of objects, but a community of subjects."[18]

As Naomi Klein once wrote, "This changes everything" and leads directly to a radically ecological worldview.[19] We are no longer free to exploit the nonhuman natural world without considering the status of all creatures as experiencing subjects, with intrinsic value. It will always be the case that our lives, and all life, depends on the death of other life for its continued existence. But, in George Fox's words, we need not "make ourselves wanton with the creatures, devouring them upon [our] own lusts," the creatures "being in their own covenant" with the Creator.[20]

A second line of thought may be helpful in augmenting Girard's analysis: a deeper understanding of the Christian doctrine of incarnation—a subject that Girard never really explores. A fundamental belief among Christians is that "God is with us"—*Emmanuel*. In the Western Church, the emphasis has been on God's unique incarnation in Jesus of

15. As discussed in excursus 1, both Foster in *Theology of Consent* and Rabe in *Processing Mimetic Reality* have found value in synthesizing Girard's mimetic theory with Whitehead's process thought.

16. Whitehead, *Process and Reality*, 289, subsequently picked up by many of Whitehead's interpreters.

17. Hosinki, *Stubborn Fact*, 19. See 18–19 for fuller discussion. Consciousness in this view is a particularly intense form of experience, which seems to require a complex central nervous system. But *unconscious* experience pervades all life.

18. Swimme and Berry, *Universe Story*, 243.

19. Klein, *This Changes Everything*.

20. G. Fox, *Journal*, 2. Thanks to Brian Drayton for bringing this passage to my attention.

Nazareth as the Son of God, even to the extent of de-emphasizing other aspects of God's incarnation in all humans and indeed in the living Earth.

But there have always been other strands in the church—the Franciscans, Celtic spirituality, much of the Eastern Church, the medieval mystics, certainly Quakers—that have stressed a much broader view of the incarnation. This "minority opinion," while not denying the importance of God's incarnation in Jesus, has affirmed that God is always and everywhere present throughout God's creation. This is not so much an either/or proposition as a matter of emphasis: both sides affirm the unique incarnation of God in Jesus of Nazareth, and both sides affirm God's incarnation throughout God's creation.

As we saw in excursus 1, process theology is part of the tradition that interprets incarnation broadly, seeing the presence of God in every "drop of experience." God, "in whom we live and move and have our being" (Acts 17:28), is present as the incarnate Logos, the animating "initial aim," in every "actual occasion," inviting, beckoning, wooing us into a future of mutual flourishing. For process thought, "the world lives by its incarnation of God in itself."[21]

Process theologian Anna Case-Winters, in her *God Will Be All in All: Theology Through the Lens of Incarnation,* explores how taking incarnation seriously will necessarily change much of how we think about God, what it is to be human, and how we think about the Christ event. She specifically asks, "When we say 'God is with us,' what do we mean by '*us*'?"[22]

Do we mean that God is only with "us Christians"? Case-Winters urges us to "understand the incarnation [in Jesus of Nazareth] as a decisive *exemplification* of God's ordinary and ongoing presence and action in the world—rather than an *exception* to it—[so that] we may be *delivered from exclusivist claims.*" She goes on to say that "it becomes possible to affirm God's presence, self-revelation, and action in Jesus the Christ with the full wealth of conviction, without presuming that this is the *only* locus of divine presence, self-revelation, and action."[23]

Case-Winters next asks, "Does God with 'us' mean only 'us humans?' Is incarnation irreducibly anthropocentric?"[24] She affirms that with a broad view of incarnation, "bodies matter and matter matters."[25]

---

21. Whitehead, *Religion in the Making*, 149.
22. Case-Winters, *God Will Be All*, 135. See 135–78 for fuller discussion.
23. Case-Winters, *God Will Be All*, 136. Emphasis added.
24. Case-Winters, *God Will Be All*, 144.
25. Case-Winters, *God Will Be All*, 145.

She criticizes the view of "the incarnation as all and only about human beings . . . an emergency measure made necessary by human sinfulness." Instead, she affirms "incarnation as embracing the whole of creation"—a position with considerable scriptural support.[26] "God is making *all things new*" (2 Cor 5:17; Rev 21:5). She concludes that "'God with us' includes the whole of the natural world and not just humans," and that the full realization of this must include *a conversion to the Earth*.[27] "Seeing God present in all things leads to a resacralization of the natural world that changes how we relate to the natural world. The ecological consequences are significant."[28]

Recalling Rebecca Adams's view that *objectification* is the essence of scapegoating, Case-Winters goes on to critique our "objectification of nature":

> It is this habit of objectifying nature that leads us to see the human being as over and above the natural world and even separate from it—anthropocentrism and separatism. The objectification of the natural world has made exploitation and abuse more thinkable. This is a world of mere *objects*—not subjects. . . . Human beings are cast as the only *subjects* in a world of objects.
>
> *Nature becomes a permissible victim.*[29]

Commenting on this objectification of nature, Girard interpreter Robin Collins observes that too often "nature has been considered our *rival*," as if nature is keeping something from us that is rightfully ours. Nature then becomes "an object of acquisitive desire." If instead we can view ourselves as part of and a participant in nature's web of interbeing, then nature can instead become "a source of non-acquisitive desire"[30] or, in Rebecca Adam's terminology, "loving mimesis."

Anna Case-Winters goes on to ask one more question, perhaps a bit removed from the theme of this book, but nevertheless illustrative of her broad view of incarnation. If God is with us, is it "only us Earthlings"?[31]

According to NASA, since the first exoplanet (i.e., a planet outside of our solar system) was discovered in 1992, more than five thousand

26. Case-Winters, *God Will Be All*, 147.
27. Case-Winters, *God Will Be All*, 144.
28. Case-Winters, *God Will Be All*, 151.
29. Case-Winters, *God Will Be All*, 152, 155. Emphasis added.
30. Collins, "Nature as a Source," 308. Emphasis added.
31. Case-Winters, *God Will Be All*, 163.

exoplanets have been confirmed. Most astronomers now accept that there are ultimately millions, tens of millions, even hundreds of millions of planets in the universe. Some proportion of these will, like Earth, be rocky planets located in "the habitable zone" with liquid water and an atmosphere, and thus are candidates for the emergence of life and perhaps intelligent life. Which raises a *theological* question: "How do we think about incarnation in relation to other life-forms in other worlds? Is God with them too?"[32] At this point, the question is entirely theoretical—but just asking the question helps us to sharpen our thinking about incarnation.

Some theologians who have pondered this question believe that "the one incarnation on Earth [is] sufficient for the whole cosmos," even though the logistics of this view are hard to fathom. Or alternatively, perhaps Christ goes from planet to planet, "incarnating" on an "as-needed" basis, responding to wherever a "fall" on the part of any intelligent life that exists elsewhere. Case-Winters advocates for an alternative view: "*Wherever God is, Christ is already present.*"[33] She cautions us about "working with a meaning of incarnation that is too small" and criticizes the "planet-hopping-Christ scenario" as mistakenly assuming that

> God shows up here and there, now and then; underneath that assumption is the unintended acceptance of the ordinary absence of God. Divine incarnation is being treated as an exception to God's ordinary way of being. What if [instead] it is the chief exemplification of God's way of being and God is really, already with us—all of us? [Incarnation] is not an exception to God's ordinary presence and activity in the world process but a place where we can see that God is already present in the whole creation—active everywhere and always.[34]

From process theology (as well as other parts of the tradition), this broad view of incarnation seems to me to provide a helpful and necessary corrective to Girard's tendency toward exclusivism and anthropocentrism. It places mimetic theory in a much broader context.

But, with those reservations in mind, it is worth closing with an appreciation of what Girard *does* contribute. As one reviewer advises us, "Before we point out where Girard has gone wrong, we should first grasp

---

32. Case-Winters, *God Will Be All*, 162.
33. Case-Winters, *God Will Be All*, 172. Emphasis added.
34. Case-Winter, *God Will Be All*, 173.

how right he is."[35] His contributions are considerable, and for me they very much resonate with my Quakerism and "Quaker shaped Christianity."

Girard's mimetic theory gives a convincing account of what is otherwise an anthropological mystery: how and why archaic religion emerged. "The function of religion, at least in pre-state societies where a justice system does not exist, is precisely to contain and control the violence that would otherwise engulf and destroy a community."[36] In this view, religion was not the *cause* of violence, but its *remedy*. "Humans were violent before they were religious."[37]

I find Girard's reading of the Bible, culminating in his interpretation of the Easter event, compelling. Girard helps me, in Fox's words, to "read the Scriptures in the spirit by which they were given forth."[38] By centering the issue of violence, and specifically sacred violence, he is able to trace a gradually emerging overall trajectory to the biblical revelation: that the true God has nothing to do with violence. Girard convincingly shows that religion has evolved beyond its archaic (and bloody) origins.

Girard gives us a solid "gospel anthropology," an understanding of human nature as inherently mimetic; we are intrinsically social and interdependent. "We desire according to the desire of the other," which leads to rivalry and ultimately to violence. Our tendency toward violence, however, arises out of our mimetic nature, and not out of any genetic determinism that would leave us without escape. His view takes sin seriously: "The original sin is the bad use of mimesis . . . and all human beings commit this sin."[39]

Girard, and more fully some of his followers, shows how the mimetic nature that leads to violence can also be our salvation. Accepting the mimetic nature of our desire leaves us free to choose whom or what we imitate. Conversion "means choosing Christ or a Christlike individual as a model for our desires. . . . Conversion is the discovery that we have always, without being aware of it, been imitating the wrong kind of models who lead us into the vicious circle of scandals" and more violence.[40] Furthermore, because there is no rivalry and no violence in God or in

---

35. Bratton, Review of *Towards Reconciliation*, 372.
36. Michael Kirwan, in Girard, *Evolution and Conversion*, viii.
37. Rabe, *Processing Mimetic Reality*, 133.
38. G. Fox, *Journal*, 24 (and elsewhere).
39. Girard, *Evolution and Conversion*, 142.
40. Girard, *Evolution and Conversion*, 123, 160.

Christ, imitating Christ means "thwarting all rivalry.... To imitate Christ is to do everything to avoid being imitated."[41]

Finally, and of special interest to Friends, is the significance of Girard's mimetic theory for our task of peacemaking and reconciliation. This begins with his uncompromising insight that Christianity, as he understands it, represents the denunciation and renunciation of the scapegoat mechanism: the end of scapegoating.[42] "The Cross has destroyed once and for all the cathartic power of the scapegoat mechanism.... In order to reach the Kingdom man has to renounce violence."[43]

Girard himself sometimes conveyed pessimism about the future prospects for peace, warning of the very real danger of apocalyptic (but human, not divine) violence. However, some of his followers see mimetic theory as contributing a useful and practical framework for peace and reconciliation work. Girard collaborator Paul Gifford offers that "at the most immediate level, that of practical peacemaking and peacebuilding, Girard's understanding of violence and the sacred can offer a model for analyzing specific human situations so as to identify and transform their dynamic of malignancy." He cites as an example the Northern Ireland peace process, culminating in the Belfast/Good Friday Agreement of April 1998. "It may not be known widely that the principal input of theory, and a substantial inspiration to creativity in the Northern Ireland peace process, is acknowledged by leading actors . . . to have been Girardian."[44] Beginning in 1979, the Corrymeela Community used Girard's ideas to lay the groundwork for eventual reconciliation. According to Derick Wilson, its former director:

> The mimetic hypothesis became, from then on, central to the practice of residential education programs and to the theological, political, and educational understandings of violence, scapegoating, healing, and reconciliation that the community promoted, involving children, young people, and adults from all areas of political and civic life. "Mimetic" understandings were developed and applied to politics, faith, civil society groups, education, and community work practice.... Participants and

---

41. Girard, *Battling to the End*, 122–23.
42. Girard, *Evolution and Conversion*, 61–62. See also Heim, "The End of Scapegoating."
43. Girard, *Evolution and Conversion*, 169, 148.
44. Gifford, *Towards Reconciliation*, 107.

facilitators alike began to see ways they can, in beneficent emulation, promote "good mimesis" and dissolve "bad mimesis."[45]

Paul Gifford writes that "violence and the sacred [i.e., "sacred violence"] is everybody's problem . . . . The problem is *with* us because it is *in* us; to that extent, we are all 'problematic.'"[46] Gifford asks, what does Girard contribute to our understanding of this? "What difference does he make? The simplest way of expressing this is perhaps to say that he takes us directly to the heart of the human problem."[47] It is Girard's contention that we cannot overcome our violence until we first understand it and recognize the "archaic-sacral man latent still in each one of us," all too prone to revert to its former ways.[48] To emphasize again: there is no genetic (and therefore insurmountable) disposition to human violence. Our violence is mimetic, and "what is mimetically induced can be mimetically reversed: by foregrounding our relation to the victim, by changing the structural dynamics of desire, and by offering newly collaborative models of peace-and-prosperity building."[49]

Quakers have been persistent over generations in their efforts to work for peace and reconciliation, but our results have not always matched our good intentions. Sometimes, as in our involvement with the Indian boarding schools in the nineteenth century, our good intentions have been disastrous to the very people we intended to help. We have been accused of basing our work on a naive appeal to "that of God in everyone," while disregarding "that of something else" that is also present in everyone. Perhaps grounding our peace work in the realism of mimetic theory, as in Northern Ireland, might bring us closer to our shared goal.

I conclude this "Easter reckoning" by quoting Girard's final words in *Evolution and Conversion*—with the hope and prayer that someday Christianity, and Quakerism, might live into this vision:

> Because of our inability to live without scapegoats, Christianity is a source of disruption in our world. Christianity constantly suggests that our scapegoats are nothing but innocent victims. Christianity shows that the guilty ones are the murderers of scapegoats, and those who approve of their murders. Let me

---

45. Derek Wilson, "Communities of Contrast," 196, 199. See also Gifford, *Towards Reconciliation*, 107–11.

46. Gifford, *Towards Reconciliation*, 105. Emphasis added.

47. Gifford, *Towards Reconciliation*, 97.

48. Gifford, *Towards Reconciliation*, 92.

49. Gifford, *Towards Reconciliation*, 98.

conclude by saying what I have already said: this compassion for the victim is the deeper meaning of Christianity. We will always be mimetic, but we do not have to engage automatically in mimetic rivalries. We do not have to accuse our neighbor; we can learn to forgive him instead.[50]

---

50. Girard, *Evolution and Conversion*, 187.

Bibliography

Abbot, Margery Post, et al. *The A to Z of the Friends (Quakers)*. Lanham, MD: Scarecrow, 2006.

Adams, Rebecca. "Loving Mimesis and Girard's 'Scapegoating of the Text': A Creative Reassessment of Mimetic Desire." In *Violence Renounced: René Girard, Biblical Studies, and Peacemaking*, edited by Willard M. Swartley, 277–307. Telford, PA: Pandora, 2000.

Adams, Rebecca, and René Girard. "Violence, Difference, Sacrifice: A Conversation with René Girard." *Religion and Literature* 25 (1993) 9–33.

Alison, James. *Broken Hearts and New Creations: Intimations of a Great Reversal*. London: Continuum, 2010.

———. *Jesus the Forgiving Victim: Listening for the Unheard Voice*. Glenview, IL: Doers, 2013. Kindle.

———. *The Joy of Being Wrong: Original Sin Through Easter Eyes*. New York: Crossroad, 1998.

———. *Knowing Jesus*. 2nd ed. London: SPCK Classics, 1998.

———. *Raising Abel: The Recovery of the Eschatological Imagination*. New York: Crossroad, 1996.

———. *Undergoing God: Dispatches from the Scene of a Break-in*. London: Continuum, 2006.

Ambler, Rex. "Darkness and Light." In *Good and Evil: Quaker Perspectives*, edited by Jackie Leach Scully and Pink Dandelion, 193–206. London: Routledge, 2016.

———. *Light to Live By: An Exploration in Quaker Spirituality*. London: Quaker, 2002.

———. *The Light Within: Then and Now*. Pendle Hill Pamphlet 425. Wallingford, PA: Pendle Hill, 2013.

———. *The Quaker Way: A Rediscovery*. Alresford, UK: Christian Alternative, 2013. Kindle.

———. "Talks on the Experiment with Light." Unpublished manuscript, last modified July 2004. Microsoft Word file.

Angell, Stephen W., and Pink Dandelion, eds. *The Oxford Handbook of Quaker Studies*. Oxford Handbooks in Religion and Theology. Oxford: Oxford University Press, 2013.

Antonello, Pierpaolo, and João Cezar de Castro Rocha. "Introduction." In *Evolution and Conversion: Dialogues on the Origins of Culture*, by René Girard, 1–12. Bloomsbury Revelations. New York: Bloomsbury, 2008.

Antonello, Pierpaolo, and Paul Gifford, eds. *Can We Survive Our Origins: Readings in René Girard's Theory of Violence and the Sacred*. Studies in Violence, Mimesis & Culture. East Lansing: Michigan State University Press, 2015.

———, eds. *How We Became Human: Mimetic Theory and the Science of Evolutionary Origins*. Studies in Violence, Mimesis & Culture. East Lansing: Michigan State University Press, 2015.

Armstrong, Karen. *St. Paul: The Apostle We Love to Hate*. Icon. New York: Houghton Mifflin Harcourt, 2015. Kindle.

Ashworth, Timothy. *Paul's Necessary Sin: The Experience of Liberation*. Burlington, VT: Ashgate, 2006.

Bailie, Gil. *Violence Unveiled: Humanity at the Crossroads*. New York: Crossroad, 1995.

Baker-Fletcher, Karen. *Dancing with God: The Trinity from a Womanist Perspective*. St. Louis: Chalice, 2006.

Barbour, Hugh. *The Quakers in Puritan England*. Richmond, IN: Friends United Meeting, 1964.

Barbour, Hugh, and Arthur O. Roberts, eds. *Early Quaker Writings, 1650–1700*. Grand Rapids: Eerdmans, 1973.

Barclay, Robert. *Barclay's "Apology" in Modern English*. Edited by Dean Freiday. Philadelphia: Friends, 1967.

Bartlett, Anthony. *Signs of Change: The Bible's Evolution of Divine Nonviolence*. Eugene, OR: Cascade, 2022.

Bashaw, Jennifer Garcia. *Scapegoats: The Gospel Through the Eyes of Victims*. Minneapolis: Fortress, 2022.

Bass, Diana Butler. "Mary the Tower." Diana Butler Bass: The Cottage, July 22, 2022. https://dianabutlerbass.substack.com/p/mary-the-tower?utm_source=publication-search.

Beals, Corey. "Evil: The Presence of Absence." In *Good and Evil: Quaker Perspectives*, edited by Jackie Leach Scully and Pink Dandelion, 141–51. London: Routledge, 2016.

Benson, Lewis. *Catholic Quakerism: A Vision for All Men*. Philadelphia: Philadelphia Yearly Meeting, 1968.

Biddle, Mark E. *Missing the Mark: Sin and Its Consequences in Biblical Theology*. Nashville: Abingdon, 2005.

Birkel, Michael L. *Silence and Witness: The Quaker Tradition*. Traditions of Christian Spirituality. Maryknoll, NY: Orbis, 2004.

Blaugdone, Barbara. "An Account of the Travels, Sufferings, and Persecutions of Barbara Blaugdone." In *Hidden in Plain Sight: Quaker Women's Writings, 1650–1700*, edited by Mary Garman et al., 274–84. Wallingford, PA: Pendle Hill, 1996.

Borg, Marcus. *The Heart of Christianity: Rediscovering a Life of Faith*. San Francisco: HarperSanFrancisco, 2003.

Borg, Marcus, and John Dominic Crossan. *The First Paul: Reclaiming the Radical Visionary Behind the Church's Conservative Icon*. New York: HarperCollins, 2009.

———. *The Last Week: The Day-by-Day Account of Jesus's Final Week in Jerusalem.* New York: HarperCollins, 2006. Kindle.
Bowles, Samuel. "Conflict: Altruism's Midwife." *Nature* 456 (2008) 326–27.
Braithwaite, William C. *The Beginnings of Quakerism.* 2nd ed. Cambridge: Cambridge University Press, 1955.
———*The Second Period of Quakerism.* Introduction by Rufus M. Jones. London: Macmillan, 1919.
———*The Second Period of Quakerism.* 2nd ed. Cambridge: Cambridge University Press, 1961.
Bratton, Mark. Review of *Towards Reconciliation: Understanding Violence and the Sacred After René Girard*, by Paul Gifford. *Journal of Contemporary Religion* 37 (2022) 370–72.
Brinton, Howard H. *How They Became Friends.* Pendle Hill Pamphlet 114. Wallingford, PA: Pendle Hill, 1961.
———. *Quaker Journals: Varieties of Religious Experience Among Friends.* Wallingford, PA: Pendle Hill, 1972.
———. "Stages in Spiritual Development as Recorded in Quaker Journals." In *Children of Light: In Honor of Rufus M. Jones*, edited by Howard H. Brinton, 383–406. New York: Macmillan, 1938.
Britain Yearly Meeting. *Quaker Faith and Practice: The Book of Christian Discipline of the Yearly Meeting of Friends in Britain.* 2nd ed. London: Britain Yearly Meeting, 1999.
Brooks, David. *The Road to Character.* New York: Random House, 2015. Kindle.
Buckley, Paul. *Quaker Testimony: What We Witness to the World.* Pendle Hill Pamphlet 481. Wallingford, PA: Pendle Hill, 2023.
Burgis, Luke. *Wanting: The Power of Mimetic Desire in Everyday Life.* New York: St. Martins, 2021. Kindle.
Caldwell, Samuel D. *The Inward Light: How Quakerism Unites Universalism and Christianity.* Philadelphia: Philadelphia Yearly Meeting, 2010.
Campbell, Douglas A, and Jon DePue. *Beyond Justification: Liberating Paul's Gospel.* Eugene, OR: Cascade, 2024.
Case-Winters, Anna. *God Will Be All in All: Theology Through the Lens of Incarnation.* Louisville: John Knox, 2021. Kindle.
Cayley, David, ed. *The Ideas of René Girard: An Anthropology of Violence and Religion.* N.p.: N.p., 2019. Kindle.
Center for Christogenesis. "What Thomas Merton Would Say Today with Fr. Dan Horan (Part 1)." Christogenesis, Apr. 15, 2024. https://christogenesis.org/podcast/what-thomas-merton-would-say-today-with-fr-dan-horan-part-1/.
Clayton, Phillip, and Arthur Peacock, eds. *In Whom We Live and Move and Have Our Being: Pantheistic Reflections of God's Presence in a Scientific World.* Grand Rapids: Eerdmans, 2004.
Cobb, John B., Jr. *Christ in a Pluralistic Age.* Philadelphia: Westminster, 1975.
———. *Jesus' Abba: The God Who Has Not Failed.* Minneapolis: Fortress, 2015. Kindle.
Cobb, John B., Jr., and David Ray Griffin. *Process Theology: An Introductory Exposition.* Philadelphia: Westminster, 1976.
Cocks, Richard. "Two Kinds of Sacrifice: René Girard's Analysis of Scapegoating." Voegelin View, Apr. 9, 2020. https://voegelinview.com/two-kinds-of-sacrifice-rene-girards-analysis-of-scapegoating/.

Collins, Robin. "Girard and Atonement: An Incarnational Theory of Mimetic Participation." In *Violence Renounced: René Girard, Biblical Studies, and Peacemaking*, edited by Willard M. Swartley, 132–53. Telford, PA: Pandora, 2000.

———. "Nature as a Source of Non-Conflictual Desire." In *René Girard and Creative Mimesis*, edited by Vern Neufeld Redekop and Thomas Ryba, 289–312. Lanham, MD: Lexington, 2014.

Cone, James H. *The Cross and the Lynching Tree*. Maryknoll, NY: Orbis, 2011.

———. *God of the Oppressed*. Rev. ed. Maryknoll, NY: Orbis, 1997.

Cooper, Wilmer. "The Influence of Rufus Jones on the Quaker View of Sin and Evil." *Quaker Religious Thought* 22 (1987) 30–36.

Cowdell, Scott. *René Girard and the Nonviolent God*. Notre Dame, IN: University of Notre Dame Press, 2018.

Cronk, Sandra. *Dark Night Journey: Inward Re-Patterning Toward a Life Centered in God*. Wallingford, PA: Pendle Hill, 1991.

———. *A Lasting Gift: The Journal and Selected Writings of Sandra L. Cronk*. Edited by Martha Paxson Grundy. Philadelphia: Quaker, 2009.

Crossan, John Dominic, and Sarah Sexton Crossan. *Resurrecting Easter: How the West Lost and the East Kept the Original Easter Vision*. New York: HarperOne, 2018.

Damrosch, Leo. *The Sorrows of the Quaker Jesus: James Nayler and the Puritan Crackdown on the Free Spirit*. Cambridge, MA: Harvard University Press, 1996.

Dandelion, Ben Pink. *Convinced Quakerism*. 2003 Annual Walton Lecture. Melbourne, FL: Southeast Yearly Meeting, 2003.

———. *Open for Transformation: Being Quaker*. 2014 Swarthmore Lecture. London: Quaker, 2014.

Dandelion, Ben Pink, et al. *Heaven on Earth: Quakers and the Second Coming*. Birmingham, UK: Woodbrooke College, 1998.

Dandelion, Pink. *An Introduction to Quakerism*. Introduction to Religion. Cambridge: Cambridge University Press, 2007.

Daniels, C. Wess. *Resisting Empire: The Book of Revelation*. Newberg, OR: Barclay, 2019.

Dewsbury, William. *The Discovery of the Great Enmity of the Serpent Against the Seed of the Woman*. London: Calvert, 1655.

De Young, Stephen. *The Religion of the Apostles: Orthodox Christianity in the First Century*. Chesterton, IN: Ancient Faith, 2021.

Drayton, Brian, and William Taber. *A Language of the Inward Landscape: Spiritual Wisdom from the Quaker Movement*. Philadelphia: Tract Association of Friends, 2015.

DuVernay, Ava, dir. *Origin*. Los Angeles: ARRAY, 2024.

Ehrman, Bart. *How Jesus Became God: The Exaltation of a Jewish Preacher from Galilee*. New York: HarperCollins, 2014. Kindle.

Eisenbaum, Pamela. *Paul Was Not a Christian: The Original Message of a Misunderstood Apostle*. New York: HarperCollins, 2009. Kindle.

Ekblad, E. Robert. "God Is Not to Blame: The Servant's Atoning Sacrifice According to the LXX of Isaiah 53." In *Stricken By God? Nonviolent Identification and the Victory of Christ*, edited by Brad Jersak and Michael Hardin, 180–204. Grand Rapids: Eerdmans, 2007.

Enns, Peter. "'God Lets His Children Tell the Story': An Angle on God's Violence in the Old Testament." Bible for Normal People, July 24, 2010. https://

thebiblefornormalpeople.com/god-lets-his-children-tell-the-story-an-angle-on-gods-violence-in-the-old-testament/.
Equal Justice Initiative. *Lynching in America: Confronting the Legacy of Racial Terror.* 3rd ed. Montgomery, Equal Justice Initiative, 2017. https://eji.org/wp-content/uploads/2005/11/lynching-in-america-3d-ed-110121.pdf.
———. *Reconstruction in America: Racial Violence After the Civil War, 1865–1876.* Equal Justice Initiative, 2020. https://eji.org/report/reconstruction-in-america/2020.
Fell, Margaret. *A Call unto the Seed of Israel, . . .* London: Wilson, 1668.
———. "Epistle to Friends (1654)." In *Hidden in Plain Sight*, edited by Mary Garman et al., 457–59. Wallingford, PA: Pendle Hill, 1996.
Fell, Margaret. *See also* Margaret Askew Fell Fox.
Fodor, Jim. "Christian Discipleship as Participative Imitation: Theological Reflections on Girardian Themes." In *Violence Renounced: René Girard, Biblical Studies, and Peacemaking*, edited by Willard M. Swartley, 246–76. Telford, PA: Pandora, 2000.
Foster, Jonathan. *Theology of Consent: Mimetic Theory in an Open and Relational Universe.* Grassmere, ID: SacraSage, 2022.
Fox, George. *The Journal of George Fox.* Edited by John L. Nickalls. Philadelphia: Religious Society of Friends, 1985.
———. *The Power of the Lord Was Over All: The Pastoral Letters of George Fox.* Edited by T. Canby Jones. Richmond, IN: Friends United Meeting, 1989.
———. *Truth of the Heart: An Anthology of George Fox, 1624–1691.* Edited by Rex Ambler. London: Quaker, 2001.
———. *The Works of George Fox.* 8 vols. Repr., New York: AMS, 1975.
Fox, George, and James Nayler. "Saul's Errand to Damascus." In *Early Quaker Writings, 1650–1700*, edited by Hugh Barbour and Arthur O. Roberts, 251–62. Grand Rapids: Eerdmans, 1973.
Fox, Margaret Askew Fell. *The Life of Margaret Fox, Wife of George Fox.* Philadelphia: Book Association of Friends, 1885.
Fox, Margaret Askew Fell. *See also* Margaret Fell.
Friedman, Richard Elliott. *Who Wrote the Bible?* New York: Summit, 1987.
Garman, Mary, et al., eds. *Hidden in Plain Sight: Quaker Women Writings, 1650–1700.* Wallingford, PA: Pendle Hill, 1996.
Garrels, Scott. "Convergence Between Mimetic Theory and Imitation Research." In *How We Became Human: Mimetic Theory and the Science of Evolutionary Origins*, edited by Pierpaolo Antonello and Paul Gifford, 79–100. Studies in Violence, Mimesis & Culture. East Lansing: Michigan State University Press, 2015.
Gates, Thomas. "George Fox and the Bible: A Dual Legacy." *Friends Journal* 70 (2024) 22–24, 52.
———. *Members One of Another: The Dynamics of Membership in Quaker Meeting.* Pendle Hill Pamphlet 371. Wallingford, PA: Pendle Hill, 2004.
———. "New Light on Atonement: No More Scapegoats." *Friends Journal* 68 (2022) 17–20.
———. *Opening the Scriptures: Bible Lessons from the 2005 Annual Gathering of Friends.* Philadelphia: Quaker, 2006.
———. *Reclaiming the Transcendent: God in Process.* Pendle Hill Pamphlet 422. Wallingford, PA: Pendle Hill, 2013.
Gifford, Paul. "*Homo Religiosus* in Mimetic Perspective." In *How We Became Human: Mimetic Theory and the Science of Evolutionary Origins*, edited by Pierpaolo

Antonello and Paul Gifford, 307–37. Studies in Violence, Mimesis & Culture. East Lansing: Michigan State University Press, 2015.

———. *Towards Reconciliation: Understanding Violence and the Sacred After René Girard*. Cambridge, UK: Clarke, 2020.

Gifford, Paul, and Pierpaolo Antonello. "Rethinking the Neolithic Revolution: Symbolism and Sacrifice at Göbleki Tepe." In *How We Became Human: Mimetic Theory and the Science of Evolutionary Origins*, edited by Pierpaolo Antonello and Paul Gifford, 261–88. Studies in Violence, Mimesis & Culture. East Lansing: Michigan State University Press, 2015.

Girard, René. *Battling to the End: Conversations with Benoît Chantre*. Translated by Mary Baker. East Lansing: Michigan State Press, 2010.

———. *Deceit, Desire, and the Novel: Self and Other in Literary Structure*. Translated by Yvonne Freccero. Baltimore: Johns Hopkins University Press, 1966.

———. *Evolution and Conversion: Dialogues on the Origins of Culture*. With Pierpaolo Antonello and Joao Cezar de Castro Rocha. Bloomsbury Revelations. New York: Bloomsbury, 2008.

———. *I See Satan Fall Like Lightening*. Translated by James G. Williams. Maryknoll, NY: Orbis, 2001.

———. *Job: The Victim of His People*. Translated by Yvonne Freccero. London: Atholone, 1987.

———. *The One by Whom Scandal Comes*. Translated by M. B. DeBevoise. East Lansing: Michigan State University Press, 2014.

———. *Reading the Bible with René Girard*. Edited by Michael Hardin. Lancaster, PA: JDL, 2015. Kindle.

———. *Sacrifice*. Translated by Matthew Pattillo and David Dawson. East Lansing: Michigan University Press, 2011. Kindle.

———. *The Scapegoat*. Translated by Yvonne Freccero. Baltimore: Johns Hopkins University Press, 1986.

———. *Things Hidden Since the Foundation of the World*. Translated by Stephen Bann and Michael Metteer. Stanford, CA: Stanford University Press, 1987.

———. *Violence and the Sacred*. Translated by Patrick Gregory. Baltimore: Johns Hopkins University Press, 1977.

———. *When These Things Begin: Conversations with Michel Treguer*. Translated by Trevor Cribben Merrill. East Lansing: Michigan State University Press, 2014.

Gorman, Michael J. *Reading Revelation Responsibly: Uncivil Worship and Witness, Following the Lamb into the New Creation*. Eugene, OR: Cascade, 2011. Kindle.

Gottlieb, Dan. "Tell Me Your Story." Awakin, n.d. https://www.awakin.org/v2/read/view.php?tid=571.

Grace, Eden. *Good News to the Oppressed: Friends Witness in the 21st Century*. 2019 Michener Lecture. Melbourne, FL: Southeastern Yearly Meeting, 2019.

Graeber, David, and David Wengrow. *The Dawn of Everything: A New History of Humanity*. New York: Farrar, Straus and Giroux, 2021.

Graves, Michael P. *Preaching the Inward Light: Early Quaker Rhetoric*. Studies in Rhetoric & Religion. Waco: Baylor University Press, 2009.

Green, Joel B., and Mark D. Baker. *Recovering the Scandal of the Cross: Atonement in New Testament & Contemporary Contexts*. Downers Grove, IL: IVP Academic, 2000.

Griffin, David Ray. "Panentheism: A Postmodern Revelation." In *In Whom We Live and Move and Have Our Being: Panentheistic Reflections of God's Presence in a Scientific World*, edited by Philip Clayton and Arthur Peacocke, 36–47. Grand Rapids: Eerdmans, 2004.

Griswold, Robert. "The Friends of Truth: A Case for Reclaiming Our Earlier Name." *Friends Journal* 53 (2007) 21–22.

Guiton, Gerard. *The Early Quakers and "The Kingdom of God": Peace, Testimony and Revolution*. San Francisco: Inner Light, 2012.

Gutiérrez, Gustavo. *On Job: God-Talk and the Suffering of the Innocent*. Translated by Matthew J. O'Connell. Maryknoll, NY: Orbis, 1987.

Gwyn, Douglas. *The Apocalypse of the Word: The Life and Message of George Fox*. Richmond, IN: Friends United Meeting, 1986.

———. *The Covenant Crucified: Quakers and the Rise of Capitalism*. Wallingford, PA: Pendle Hill, 1995.

———. *Seekers Found: Atonement in Early Quaker Experience*. Wallingford, PA: Pendle Hill, 2000.

———. *A Sustainable Life: Quaker Faith and Practice in the Renewal of Creation*. Philadelphia: Quaker, 2014.

Halvorsen, Maren Elizabeth. "The Day of Small Things: The Quaker Understanding of Conversion and the Inner Light in the Writings of Isaac Penington." PhD diss., University of Washington, 2002.

Hammerton-Kelly, Robert G. *Sacred Violence: Paul's Hermeneutic of the Cross*. Minneapolis: Fortress, 1992.

Hardin, Michael. *The Jesus Driven Life: Reconnecting Humanity with Jesus*. 2nd ed. Lancaster, PA: JDL, 2013.

———. *Mimetic Theory and Biblical Interpretation: Reclaiming the Good News of the Gospel*. Cascade Companions. Eugene, OR: Cascade, 2017. Kindle.

Hartley, L. P. *The Go-Between*. London: Hamilton, 1953.

Haven, Cynthia L. *The Evolution of Desire: A Life of René Girard*. Studies in Violence, Mimesis & Culture. East Lansing: Michigan State University Press, 2018.

Heim, S. Mark. "The End of Scapegoating." Institute for Faith and Learning at Baylor University, 2016. https://ifl.web.baylor.edu/sites/g/files/ecbvkj771/files/2024-02/PatternsofViolenceArticleHeim.pdf.

———. *Saved from Sacrifice: A Theology of the Cross*. Grand Rapids: Eerdmans, 2006. Kindle.

Hewitson, Gerald. *Journey into Life: Inheriting the Story of Early Friends*. 2013 Swarthmore Lecture. London: Quaker, 2013.

Hidden Brain Staff. "Healing 2.0: Change Your Story, Change Your Life." Hidden Brain, Oct. 30, 2023. https://hiddenbrain.org/podcast/healing-2-0-change-your-story-change-your-life/.

Hochschild, Adam. *King Leopold's Ghost*. Boston: Houghton Mifflin Harcourt, 1998.

Hoover, Nadine Clare. *Walking in the World as a Friend: Essential Quaker Practices*. Alfred, NY: Creative Commons, 2020. https://quakerrecollaborative.org/wp-content/uploads/2023/04/Walking-in-World-as-a-Friend.pdf.

Hosinki, Thomas E. *Stubborn Fact and Creative Advance: An Introduction to the Metaphysics of Alfred North Whitehead*. Lanham, MD: Rowman and Littlefield, 1993.

Howard-Brook, Wes, and Anthony Gwyther. *Unveiling Empire: Reading Revelation Then and Now*. Bible & Liberation. Maryknoll, NY: Orbis, 1999.

Howgill, Francis. "The Inheritance of Jacob Discovered, After His Return Out of Egypt." In *Early Quaker Writings, 1650–1700*, edited by Hugh Barbour and Arthur O. Roberts, 167–79. Grand Rapids: Eerdmans, 1973.

Hubbard, Geoffrey. *Quaker by Convincement*. Baltimore: Penguin, 1974.

James, William. *The Varieties of Religious Experience*. New York: Collier, 1961.

Jersak, Bradley. *A More Christlike Word: Reading Scripture the Emmaus Way*. Kensington, PA: Whitaker, 2021. Kindle.

Jersak, Bradley, and Michael Hardin, eds. *Stricken By God? Nonviolent Identification and the Victory of Christ*. Grand Rapids: Eerdmans, 2007.

Johnson, Elizabeth A. *Creation and the Cross: The Mercy of God for a Planet in Peril*. Maryknoll, NY: Orbis, 2018.

Jones, Rufus. *The Double Search: Studies in Atonement and Prayer*. Repr., Richmond, IN: Friends United, n.d.

Jones, T. Canby. "The Nature and Functions of the Light in the Thought of George Fox." *Quaker Religious Thought* 39 (1974) 53–71.

Keeler, Janaki Spickard. *Abraham, Sarah, Hagar, and Us*. Pendle Hill Pamphlet 478. Wallingford, PA: Pendle Hill, 2022.

Kelly, Thomas. *A Testament of Devotion*. San Francisco: HarperSanFrancisco, 1992.

Klein, Naomi. *This Changes Everything: Capitalism vs. the Climate*. New York: Simon and Schuster, 2014.

Knox, John S. "Sacro-Egoism and the Shifting Paradigm of Religiosity." PhD diss., University of Birmingham, 2009.

Kolp, Alan. "Fox Loved the Apostle Paul." *Quaker Religious Thought* 25 (1991) 7–26.

———. *Fresh Winds of the Spirit*. Richmond, IN: Friends United Meeting, 1991.

Konner, Melvin. "Violent Origins: Mimetic Rivalry in Darwinian Evolution." In *How We Became Human: Mimetic Theory and the Science of Evolutionary Origins*, edited by Pierpaolo Antonello and Paul Gifford, 137–60. East Lansing: Michigan State University Press, 2015.

Lacey, Paul. *Leading and Being Led*. Pendle Hill Pamphlet 264. Wallingford, PA: Pendle Hill, 1985.

———. *Nourishing the Spiritual Life*. London: Quaker Home Service, 1999.

LaHaye, Tim, and Jerry B. Jenkins. *Left Behind*. 16 vols. Carol Stream, IL: Tyndale, 1995–2007.

Lewis, Helen. "The Progressives Who Flunked the Hamas Test." *Atlantic*, Oct. 13, 2023. https://www.theatlantic.com/ideas/archive/2023/10/hamas-pop-intersectionality-leftism-israel/675625/.

Lindsey, Hal. *The Late Great Planet Earth*. With C. C. Carlson. Grand Rapids: Zondervan, 1970.

Lovelock, James. *The Revenge of Gaia: Earth's Climate Crisis & The Fate of Humanity*. London: Penguin, 2006.

Martin, Marcelle. *A Guide to Faithfulness Groups*. San Francisco: Inner Light, 2019.

———. *Our Life Is Love: The Quaker Spiritual Journey*. San Francisco: Inner Light, 2016.

May, Gerald. *Addiction and Grace: Love and Spirituality in the Healing of Addictions*. San Francisco: HarperSanFrancisco, 1988.

McAdams, Dan P. "The Psychology of Life Stories." *Review of General Psychology* 5 (2001) 100–122.

McFague, Sallie. *Models of God: Theology for an Ecological, Nuclear Age*. Philadelphia: Fortress, 1987.

Mercadante, Linda. *Victims and Sinners: The Spiritual Roots of Addiction and Recovery*. Louisville: Westminster John Knox, 1996.

Merrill, Noah. "The Invitation." New England Yearly Meeting, Aug. 2, 2020. https://neym.org/news/2020/08/invitation.

Meyer, Elizabeth. *The Baltimore Yearly Meeting Spiritual Formation Program: Deepening the Spiritual Experience of Modern Friends*. Baltimore: Baltimore Yearly Meeting, 2004.

Miller, Ann. "Comments." *Quaker Religious Thought* 22 (1987) 42–45.

Miller, Marlin. "Girardian Perspectives and Christian Atonement." In *Violence Renounced: René Girard, Biblical Studies, and Peacemaking*, edited by Willard M. Swartley, 31–48. Telford, PA: Pandora, 2000.

Moore, Rosemary. *The Light in Their Consciences: The Early Quakers in Britain, 1646–1666*. University Park: Pennsylvania State University Press, 2000.

Myers, Ched. *Binding the Strong Man: A Political Reading of Mark's Story of Jesus*. Maryknoll, NY: Orbis, 1988.

Nayler, James. "A Door Opened to the Imprisoned Seed in the World." In *The Works of James Nayler (1618–1660)*, edited by Licia Kuenning, 4:183–230. Farmington, ME: Quaker Heritage, 2003.

———. *The Lamb's War Against the Man of Sin*. In *Early Quaker Writings, 1650–1700*, edited by Hugh Barbour and Arthur O. Roberts, 102–16. Grand Rapids: Eerdmans, 1973.

———. "Saul's Errand to Damascus." In *The Works of James Nayler (1618–1660)*, edited by Licia Kuenning, 1:1–40. Farmington, ME: Quaker Heritage, 2003.

Nelson, Susan Dunfee. "The Sin of Hiding." *Soundings* 65 (1982) 316–27.

New Scientist. *Human Origins: 7 Million Years and Counting*. Boston: Brealey, 2018.

Oord, Thomas Jay. *God Can't: How to Believe in God and Love After Tragedy, Abuse, and Other Tragedies*. Grassmere, ID: SacraSage, 2019. Kindle.

———. *Open and Relational Theology: An Introduction to Life-Changing Ideas*. Grassmere, ID: SacraSage, 2021.

———. *Pluriform Love: An Open and Relational Theology of Well-Being*. Grassmere, ID: SacraSage, 2022. Kindle.

———. *The Uncontrolling Love of God: An Open and Relational Account of Providence* Downers Grove, IL: IVP Academic, 2015. Kindle.

Penington, Isaac. *Knowing the Mystery of the Life Within: Selected Writings of Isaac Penington in their Historical and Theological Context*. Edited by R. Melvin Keiser and Rosemary Moore. London: Quaker, 2005.

———. *The Works of Isaac Penington*. Edited by Licia Kuenning. 4 vols. Glenside, PA: Quaker Heritage, 1995.

Penn, William. *No Cross, No Crown*. Edited by Ronald Selleck. Modern English ed. Richmond, IN: Friends United Meeting, 1981.

———. "Spirit of Truth Vindicated." In *Collection of the Works of William Penn*, 2:91–151. London: Sowle, 1726.

Penney, Norman, ed. *The First Publishers of Truth: Being Early Records (Now First Printed) of the Introduction of Quakerism into the Counties of England and Wales*. London: Headley Brothers, 1907.

Perry, Bruce, and Oprah Winfrey. *What Happened to You: Conversations of Trauma, Resilience, and Healing*. New York: Flatiron, 2021.

Peterson, Eugene H. *Reversed Thunder: The Revelation of John & the Praying Imagination*. San Francisco: Harper and Row, 1988.

Pew Research Center. "About Three-in-Ten U.S. Adults Are Now Religiously Unaffiliated." Pew Research Center, Dec. 14, 2021. https://www.pewresearch.org/religion/2021/12/14/about-three-in-ten-u-s-adults-are-now-religiously-unaffiliated/.

Pickvance, Joseph. "Conviction and Convincement." *New Foundation Papers* 1 (1980) 8–10.

———. *A Reader's Companion to George Fox's Journal*. London: Quaker Home Service, 1989.

Pinker, Steven. *The Better Angels of our Nature: Why Violence Has Declined*. New York: Penguin, 2012. Kindle.

———. *Enlightenment Now: The Case for Reason, Science, Humanism, and Progress*. New York: Penguin, 2018. Kindle.

Punshon, John. *Portrait in Grey: A Short History of the Quakers*. London: Quaker Home Service, 1984.

———. *Reasons for Hope*. Richmond, IN: Friends United Meeting, 2001.

———. *Testimony and Tradition: Some Aspects of Quaker Spirituality*. 1990 Swarthmore Lecture. London: Quaker Home Service, 1990.

Rabe, Andre. *Processing Mimetic Reality: Harmonizing Alfred North Whitehead and René Girard*. Grassmere, ID: SacraSage, 2023.

Redekop, Vern Neufeld, and Thomas Ryba, eds. *René Girard and Creative Mimesis*. Lanham, MD: Lexington, 2014.

Reeve, Zoey. "Mechanisms of Internal Cohesion: Scapegoating and Parochial Altruism." In *How We Became Human: Mimetic Theory and the Science of Evolutionary Origins*, edited by Pierpaolo Antonello and Paul Gifford, 161–85. Studies in Violence, Mimesis & Culture. East Lansing: Michigan State University Press, 2015.

Robinson, John A. T. *The Priority of John*. London: Meyer-Stone, 1985.

Rohr, Richard. *The Universal Christ: How a Forgotten Reality Can Change Everything We See, Hope For, and Believe*. New York: Convergent, 2019.

Rosen, Matt. "Awakening the Witness, with Matt Rosen—First Monday Lecture November 2023." YouTube, Nov. 6, 2023. https://www.youtube.com/watch?v=ygHpj5IFCME.

———. "The Light Will Be Shining at the End of It All." *Friends Journal* 70 (2024) 10–11, 48.

Russ, Mark. *Quaker Shaped Christianity*. Winchester, UK: Christian Alternative, 2022.

Sacks, Jonathan. *Not in God's Name: Confronting Religious Violence*. New York: Schocken, 2015.

Sanders, E. P. *Paul and Palestinian Judaism*. Philadelphia: Fortress, 1977.

School of the Spirit. "History." School of the Spirit, n.d. https://www.schoolofthespirit.org/about/history/.

Schüssler Fiorenza, Elisabeth. *Revelation: Vision of a Just World*. Edited by Gerhard Krodel. Proclamation Commentaries. Minneapolis: Fortress, 1991.

Schwager, Raymund. *Jesus in the Drama of Salvation: Toward a Biblical Doctrine of Redemption*. New York: Crossroad, 1999.

———. *Must There Be Scapegoats? Violence and Redemption in the Bible*. San Francisco: Harper and Row, 1987.

Scott, Job. *Journal of the Life and Travels of Job Scott*. Vol. 1 of *The Works of That Eminent Minister of the Gospel, Job Scott*. Philadelphia: Comly, 1831.

Scully, Jackie Leach, and Pink Dandelion, eds. *Good and Evil: Quaker Perspectives*. London: Routledge, 2016.

Smith, James K. A. *You Are What You Love: The Spiritual Power of Habit*. Grand Rapids: Brazos, 2016.

Spencer, Carole. "Quakers in Theological Context." In *The Oxford Handbook of Quaker Studies*, edited by Stephen W. Angell and Pink Dandelion, 141–57. Oxford Handbooks in Religion and Theology. Oxford: Oxford University Press, 2013.

Steinmair-Posel, Petra. "Original Sin, Grace, and Positive Mimesis." In *René Girard and Creative Mimesis*, edited by Vern Neufeld Redekop and Thomas Ryba, 221–31. Lanham, MD: Lexington, 2014.

Stendahl, Krister. *Paul Among Jews and Gentiles*. Philadelphia: Fortress, 1976.

Suchocki, Marjorie Hewitt. *The Fall to Violence: Original Sin in Relational Theology*. New York: Continuum, 1994.

———. *God, Christ, Church: A Practical Guide to Process Theology*. Rev. ed. New York: Crossroad, 1989.

———. *In God's Presence: Theological Reflections on Prayer*. St. Louis: Chalice, 1996.

Swartley, Willard. "Discipleship and Imitation of Jesus/Suffering Servant: The Mimesis of New Creation." In *Violence Renounced: René Girard, Biblical Studies, and Peacemaking*, edited by Willard M. Swartley, 218–45. Telford, PA: Pandora, 2000.

Swimme, Brian, and Thomas Berry. *The Universe Story: From the Primordial Flaring Forth to the Ecozoic Era—a Celebration of the Cosmos*. San Francisco: HarperSanFrancisco, 1992.

Taber, William. "What Is Quaker Spirituality?" In *Companions Along the Way: Spiritual Formation Within the Quaker Tradition*, edited by Florence Ruth Kline, 27–29. Philadelphia: Philadelphia Yearly Meeting, 2000.

Teilhard de Chardin, Pierre. "Trust in the Slow Work of God." Santa Clara University, n.d. https://www.scu.edu/media/offices/jesuit-community/pdfs/Trust-in-the-Slow-Work-of-God.pdf.

Thurman, Howard. *Jesus and the Disinherited*. New York: Abingdon-Cokesbury, 1949.

Tousley, Nikki Coffey. "Sin, Convincement, Purity, and Perfection." In *The Oxford Handbook of Quaker Studies*, edited by Stephen W. Angell and Pink Dandelion, 172–86. Oxford Handbooks in Religion and Theology. Oxford: Oxford University Press, 2013.

Trible, Phyliss. *Texts of Terror: Literary-Feminist Readings of Biblical Narratives*. Overtures to Biblical Theology. Philadelphia: Fortress, 1984.

Trueblood, D. Elton. *Robert Barclay*. New York: Harper and Row, 1968.

Unger, Stephen H. "Quakers: Earliest Activists for Peace, Freedom, Women's Rights, and the Environment." Columbia University Computer Science Department, Mar. 19, 2018. https://www.cs.columbia.edu/~unger/articles/quakers.html.

Van der Kolk, Bessel. *The Body Keeps the Score: Brain, Mind, and Body in the Healing of Trauma*. New York: Penguin, 2015.

Vining, Elizabeth Gray. *Friend of Life: The Biography of Rufus Jones.* New York: Lipincott, 1958.
Wallis, Jim. *America's Original Sin: A Study Guide on White Racism.* Washington, DC: Sojourners, 1995.
Warren, James. *Compassion or Apocalypse: A Comprehensible Guide to the Thought of René Girard.* Winchester, UK: Christian Alternative, 2013. Kindle.
Weaver, J. Denny. *The Nonviolent Atonement.* 2nd ed. Grand Rapids: Eerdmans, 2011. Kindle.
Weil, Simone. *Waiting for God.* New York: Harper Perennial Modern Classics, 2009.
Whitehead, Alfred North. "First Lecture: September 1924." *Process Studies* 48 (2019) 159–81.
———. *Process and Reality: An Essay in Cosmology.* Edited by David Ray Griffin and Donald W. Sherburne. Corrected ed. New York: Free, 1978.
———. *Religion in the Making.* New York: World, 1960.
Whitehead, John. "The Enmity Between the Two Seeds." In *The Written Gospel Labours of That Ancient and Faithful Servant of Jesus Christ, John Whitehead,* 3–42. London: Sowle, 1704.
Wikipedia. "Charles Lynch (Judge)." Wikipedia, last edited Jan. 27, 2025. https://en.wikipedia.org/wiki/Charles_Lynch_(judge).
———. "Dunbar's Number." Wikipedia, last edited Mar. 25, 2025. https://en.wikipedia.org/wiki/Dunbar%27s_number.
———. "The Great Disappointment." Wikipedia, last edited Dec. 9, 2024. https://en.wikipedia.org/wiki/Great_Disappointment.
———. "Lynching." Wikipedia, last edited Mar. 27, 2025. https://en.wikipedia.org/wiki/Lynching.
———. "What Would Jesus Do?" Wikipedia, last edited Dec. 27, 2024. https://en.wikipedia.org/wiki/What_would_Jesus_do%3F.
Wilken, Robert Louis. *The Spirit of Early Christian Thought: Seeking the Face of God.* New Haven, CT: Yale University Press, 2003.
Wilkerson, Isabel. *Caste: The Origins of Our Discontent.* New York: Random House, 2020.
Williams, James G. *The Bible, Violence, and the Sacred: Liberation from the Myth of Sanctioned Violence.* Valley Forge, PA: Trinity, 1991.
Wilson, David Sloan. *Darwin's Cathedral: Evolution, Religion, and the Nature of Society.* Chicago: University of Chicago Press, 2002.
Wilson, Derek. "Communities of Contrast: Modeling Reconciliation in Northern Ireland." In *Can We Survive Our Origins: Readings in René Girard's Theory of Violence and the Sacred,* edited by Pierpaolo Antonello and Paul Gifford, 191–213. Studies in Violence, Mimesis & Culture. East Lansing: Michigan State University Press, 2015.
Wilson, Lloyd Lee. *Essays on the Quaker Vision of Gospel Order.* Burnsville, NC: Celo Valley, 1993.
———. *Holy Surrender.* 2006 New England Yearly Meeting Keynote Address. Worcester, MA: New England Yearly Meeting, 2006.
———*Memoir of the Life and Religious Labors of Lloyd Lee Wilson.* San Francisco: Inner Light, 2021.
———. *Wrestling with Our Faith Tradition: Collected Public Witness, 1995–2004.* Philadelphia: Quaker, 2005.

Wink, Walter. *The Human Being: Jesus and the Enigma of the Son of Man*. Minneapolis: Fortress, 2002.

———. *The Powers That Be: Theology for a New Millennium*. New York: Doubleday, 1998.

Zahnd, Brian. *Radical Forgiveness: God's Call to Unconditional Love*. Lake Mary, FL: Charisma, 2013. Kindle.

———. *Sinners in the Hands of a Loving God: The Scandalous Truth of the Very Good News*. New York: Waterbrook, 2017. Kindle.

www.ingramcontent.com/pod-product-compliance
Lightning Source LLC
Chambersburg PA
CBHW070231230426
43664CB00014B/2268